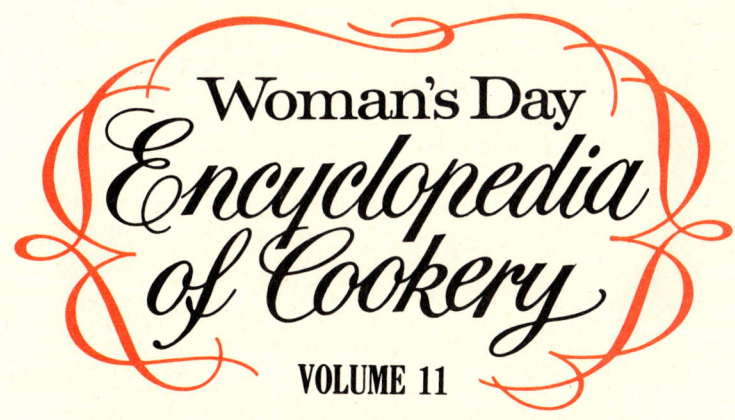

Woman's Day
Encyclopedia of Cookery
VOLUME 11

*in 12 volumes—over 2,000 pages—
with more than 1,500 illustrations in color,
1,000 entries and 8,500 recipes
1,200 menus, 50 specialty cook books
and a host of delightful features by distinguished food writers.*

Prepared and edited by the Editors of Woman's Day
Editor: EILEEN TIGHE
Managing Editor: EVELYN GRANT   *Food Editor:* GLENNA MCGINNIS
Art Consultant: HAROLD SITTERLE   *Photographic Editor:* BEN CALVO
Associates: OLIVIA RISBERG, CHARLOTTE SCRIPTURE,
CAROLYN STORM, JOHANNA BAFARO

SPECIAL PROJECT STAFF
Editor: NIKA STANDEN HAZELTON   *Art Director:* LEONARD A. ROMAGNA
Associates: L. GERALDINE MARSTELLER, HELEN FEINGOLD,
SUSAN J. KNOX, INEZ M. KRECH

FAWCETT PUBLICATIONS, INC.   NEW YORK

SIXTH PRINTING

No part of this book may be reproduced in any form without permission in writing from the publisher, except by a reviewer who wishes to quote brief passages in connection with a review written for inclusion in a magazine, newspaper or broadcast.

Direct all correspondence regarding recipes, sale of replacement volumes or complete gift sets to:

Woman's Day Encyclopedia of Cookery
Fawcett Publications, Inc.
One Astor Plaza
New York, New York 10036
(212) 869-3000

Printed in U.S.A. by
FAWCETT PRINTING CORPORATION
Rockville, Maryland

Copyright © 1966 by Fawcett Publications, Inc.,
Publishers of Woman's Day. All Rights Reserved.

VOLUME 11

SOUFFLÉ TO TONGUE

Definitions and 770 Recipes
How to buy, store, prepare, cook, and serve •
Nutritive Food Values • Caloric Values

HOW TO COOK SUPERBLY: SOUFFLÉS 1685	STRAWBERRY 1776
SOUP COOK BOOK 1689	STRUDEL 1779
SOUR-CREAM COOK BOOK 1697	STUFFING 1780
SOUTH AMERICAN COOKERY 1702	STURGEON 1782
	SUCCOTASH 1783
SOUTHEAST ASIAN COOKERY 1710	SWEDISH COOKERY 1785
SOUTHERN COOKERY 1719	SWEETBREAD 1794
SOUTHWESTERN COOKERY 1726	SWEET-POTATO COOK BOOK 1795
SOYBEAN 1733	SWISS COOKERY 1799
SPAGHETTI 1735	SWORDFISH 1806
SPANISH COOKERY 1740	SYRUP 1807
SPARERIBS 1747	TANGERINE 1809
SPICE 1749	TARTS 1811
SPICE CHART 1750	THE PLEASURES OF TEA DRINKING 1816
SPINACH 1754	TETRAZZINI 1819
SPONGECAKE 1756	THANKSGIVING 1820
SQUAB 1758	TIMBALE 1824
SQUASH 1758	TOAST COOK BOOK 1825
STEAKS, CHARCOAL-BROILED 1764	TOMATO COOK BOOK 1831
STEW 1773	TONGUE TWISTERS 1837
STOCK 1774	100 MENUS 1840
	To help you plan more varied meals with the recipes in this volume

GENERAL INFORMATION 1844
COMPLETE RECIPE INDEX 1845

Foreword

To the best of our knowledge, no work of this magnitude ever has been undertaken by any author, editor, or publisher in America. The editors of Woman's Day, with a special staff of experts, present to you this Encyclopedia of Cookery, a comprehensive and colorful library on all culinary matters. The twelve-volume encyclopedia contains in its 2,000 pages over 8,500 recipes from all over the world, 1,500 food illustrations in color, 1,200 menus, 50 special cook books and over 1,000 food definitions. In addition, there are full details about all foods, their nutritive and caloric values, how to buy, serve, prepare, and cook them. There is a history of food and cooking, articles on nutrition, diet, entertaining, menu planning, herbs and spices. Every topic of culinary interest is covered. Five years of intensive work have gone into its preparation, backed by twenty-five years of food and cookery experience in the publication of Woman's Day.

We think you will find this Encyclopedia of Cookery the most complete and authoritative work ever published on the subject. It is a library for everyone who cares about good food and the fine art of preparing it.

The Editors

SOUFFLÉ—A savory or sweet dish usually made of a basic ingredient in the form of any one of many chopped or puréed foods, a thick sauce, and eggs, and baked until puffed. Savory soufflés are served as hors-d'oeuvre and entrées, sweet soufflés as desserts.

How to Cook Superbly: Soufflés

by Helen Evans Brown

To achieve a perfect soufflé, light as a cloud and high as the sky, is not as tricky as you've heard tell. True, old wives had tales of fallen soufflés and fallen pride, but that was in the days before regulated and insulated ovens. And, except for some dessert soufflés using high-priced liqueurs, they are not expensive. Many can be made from leftovers, plus no more eggs than you'd scramble for breakfast. So read the basic recipe carefully, then try your first one on the family. Soon you'll be making them as casually as you used to whip up a tunafish casserole. How proud the family will be, and how impressed the guests!

EQUIPMENT

Chances are that you can get along with the equipment you already have, although it is nice to have a special soufflé dish. These are usually made of fairly thin white china, but glass or silver ones are also used. The classic French one has straight fluted sides with a ⅜-inch rim. It comes in sizes ranging from 1 to 8 cups and is, of course, ovenproof. An earthenware cassoulet or glass ovenproof casserole, preferably with straight sides, can also be used. If either is too shallow, a 2- or 3-inch collar of buttered paper can be fastened around the rim to increase its height. Fold paper two or three times to make it stiff, butter, and fasten, buttered side in, around the outside of the casserole, securing with a pin, paper clip, or string. Oiled foil can be substituted for the paper.

Some French cooks claim you need an unlined copper bowl and balloon whip for beating the egg whites properly, but I believe that any large bowl will do except one made of aluminum, which sometimes turns the egg whites gray in color. Certainly a balloon whip, which is a bundle of large wire loops bound together into a handle, is nice, but a smaller whip as used for omelets or crêpes, or even an egg beater or electric mixer will do (see directions for beating egg whites). You will also need standard measuring spoons and cups; a food mill, strainer, or electric blender; a saucepan; and a flexible spatula or rubber scraper; but you probably have all these on hand in your kitchen already.

HERE'S WHY

Soufflés are usually a combination of a thick sauce, a flavoring material most often in the form of finely chopped or puréed foods, and eggs. The yolks are added to the sauce (although sometimes they are omitted), and the whites are beaten in a manner to incorporate as much air as possible, before folding carefully into the other mixture. It is this imprisoned air expanding from the heat of the oven that makes the soufflé rise. When the cooked soufflé is taken from the oven, it should be taken to the table and served at once. It is a rule of the kitchen that a soufflé should be served immediately. If there is any waiting to be done, let it be by the guests.

There are two basic kinds of soufflé, a savory one made with fish, meat, vegetables, or cheese, and a dessert one made with sweetened puréed fruit, or with a liqueur. The average soufflé (1½ to 2 quarts) serves from 4 to 6 persons. If you plan to serve more, it is better to make 2 soufflés than to cook the doubled recipe in an extra-large dish. Before you start the preparation of a soufflé, read the recipe for Basic Savory Soufflé so you'll know what you are about. You will note that these recipes call for more egg whites than yolks. This isn't necessary, but is a sure way to guarantee extra lightness, and you'll have extra yolks for hollandaise and custards, and for thickening soups and sauces.

BASIC SAVORY SOUFFLÉ (FOR 4)

4 whole eggs plus 1 egg white
Butter
Bread crumbs or grated cheese
1 cup very finely chopped cooked meat, fish, or shellfish, or
¾ cup grated cheese
Salt, pepper, and/or other appropriate seasoning
3 tablespoons butter
3 tablespoons all-purpose flour
1 cup milk

■ **Separating Eggs**—Eggs are most easily separated when cold, but the whites can be beaten to greater volume when at room temperature. Therefore, remove eggs from refrigerator, separate, and let stand for at least 1 hour before beginning the soufflé. When separating eggs, make sure that the whites go into a perfectly clean dry bowl. The tiniest bit of grease, moisture, or egg yolk will keep the whites from beating properly. If any yolk should get into the white, scoop it out with a piece of eggshell. When ready to proceed with the soufflé, preheat oven to moderate (375°F.). Savory soufflés can be baked at lower temperatures and sweet soufflés at higher ones, but it is good practice to use 375°F. for all, until you've gained experience.

■ **Preparing Soufflé Dish**—Spread sides and bottom of 6-cup dish with butter, then add about ¼ cup dry bread crumbs or grated cheese, and turn and tilt so that the sides and bottom are completely covered; shake out surplus crumbs.

■ **Preparing Meat, Fish, or Vegetable**—If the main ingredient of your soufflé is meat, fish, or shellfish, it should be cooked, then chopped or ground very fine. If it's a vegetable such as peas or

SOUFFLÉ

spinach, it should be cooked, then forced through a food mill or strainer, or whirled smooth in an electric blender. It should then be further cooked until all excess moisture has evaporated, then measured. Corn is best when scraped from the uncooked cob, then simmered until thick. Cheese should be a firm or dry type, like Cheddar, Parmesan, or Gruyère. The seasonings should be quite definite, as they will be diluted by the sauce and the egg whites. Start with 1 teaspoon salt and 2 or 3 turns of the pepper mill, then taste and add more salt if necessary. Of course, in the case of ham or other salty ingredients, you should start with less salt, say ½ teaspoon. You may also want other seasonings such as herbs and spices. With corn soufflé, try basil; with cheese, mustard or hot pepper sauce; with chicken, tarragon or chives or both; with fish, thyme, or play your own tune. Another way to add flavor to bland ingredients is with 2 or 3 chopped shallots or green onions which have been sautéed in 1 tablespoon butter. In this case, use only 2 tablespoons butter for the *roux,* adding it to the shallot mixture and proceeding with the *roux* (see below).

■ **Making Sauce**—Now make a *roux* with the butter and the flour. In other words, melt the butter, stir in the flour, and cook, stirring, over low heat for 2 or 3 minutes. Add milk, stir until smooth and thick, reduce heat, and cook for at least 5 minutes to remove the raw taste of the flour. Remove from the heat and, using a wire whisk, beat in 1 egg yolk at a time, beating vigorously after each addition. Or, if you prefer, beat egg yolks slightly, then stir into the mixture. Add prepared meat, vegetables, or cheese and return to low heat; cook, stirring, for a minute or two. Careful here, you don't want scrambled eggs! Let cool slightly. At this point you can refrigerate the mixture until just before you want to finish the soufflé. If you do this, however, be sure to reheat it as the mixture will be too cold and stiff to incorporate easily into the whites.

■ **Beating Egg Whites**—The most important part of soufflé making is the beating of the egg whites. They should have as much air as possible incorporated into them, which is easiest with a balloon whip, or with the type of kitchen mixer that has a large wire whip attachment. If you have neither, use an ordinary whisk, lifting it high as you beat: down, along, up, and over is the action. A rotary egg beater or electric hand beater should be lifted in and out of the mixture while beating. With an ordinary electric mixer use a rubber scraper, lifting the whites

Basic Savory Cheese Soufflé

around the edges and back into the whirlpool as it turns. This is the way to incorporate as much air as possible. The whites, when properly beaten, should have increased greatly in volume and be shiny and stiff enough to hold a good peak when lifted on the beater. Do not beat after this has been attained or they will become dry and bumpy-looking, and your soufflé won't be so light.

■ **Combining Whites with Sauce**—Now you are ready for the final step. Your oven is hot, your sauce warm (not hot, not cold), your soufflé dish prepared, your egg whites beaten. Add from ¼ to ⅓ of the egg whites to the sauce mixture and, using a rubber scraper, carefully and thoroughly mix together, using an up-and-over motion. This lightens the sauce so that it can be combined easily with the remaining egg whites. Now add the remaining whites to the mixture and gently fold or cut them in, again using a rubber scraper. To do this, cut down through the mixture to the bottom, then along the bottom, and up and over and down again. Do this quickly, gently, and casually. Don't try to mix too thoroughly, it's quite all right to have wisps and blobs of white showing. Now, still working quickly, scrape into the soufflé dish, smooth top or not as you wish (I wish!), then run your thumb or finger around the inside of the dish to a depth of about ½ inch if you are using the classic French soufflé dish.

■ **Baking the Soufflé**—At this point, if it's absolutely necessary, the soufflé can be put in a draftproof place (such as in a cupboard or under a box) for 30 minutes or longer before baking. However, if everything else is ready, the final beating and incorporating of egg whites is so quick and easy that this is rarely necessary. Put the soufflé in the middle of the oven and on the bottom shelf. (Some chefs even start soufflés on the bottom of the oven itself, later moving them to the shelf.) Close the door and forget it for at least 20 minutes. Nothing will happen to it, so why take a chance on having a cold draft collapse it because you peeked before it achieved its full height? How long to bake a soufflé is a matter of controversy. The French bake a 6-cup one from 20 to 30 minutes. They like the inside very soft, almost runny, so that it will sauce the firmer part of the soufflé. Many Americans prefer their soufflés cooked evenly throughout. You might try both ways, say 25 and 35 minutes, then take a family vote. But please don't bake it too long, or your soufflé will be tough and dry. After you've gained experience you can tell when it is right for you by shaking it. If it wobbles all over, it's not done; if it just shakes in the middle, it's done French style; and if it is as firm as a cake, it's done to most Americans' liking. It must be admitted, however, that the firmer soufflé will not collapse as quickly as the one *à la français*. Put it on a heated tray or plate or wrap a napkin around the dish, and serve at once, to 4 persons if it is to be the main dish; to 8 if it takes the place of a vegetable.

VARIATIONS OF BASIC SAVORY SOUFFLÉ

■ **Soufflé Laurette**—Make a cheese soufflé as above. Put half the mixture in the soufflé dish, break 4 eggs on top, fill dish with remaining soufflé, and bake as directed. The eggs will cook right in the soufflé. If you like your eggs well done, poach them before layering in the soufflé.

■ **Other Savory Soufflés**—You can make them by combining 2 or more ingredients. Spinach and ham, ham and cheese, chicken livers and onions, corn and tomato, mushrooms and chicken, liver and bacon, and lots of others. Think up your own and be a creative cook!

■ **Cassolettes**—These are individual soufflés, made in 1- to 1½-cup dishes. Any mixture can be used, but cheese ones are particularly good as a first course or luncheon dish. Make soufflé as above, divide among 6 small dishes, and bake in preheated hot oven (400°F.) for 8 to 12 minutes.

■ **Tomato Soufflés**—Scoop out large tomatoes and turn upside down to drain. Do not chill. Fill with cheese soufflé mixture and bake in preheated moderate oven (375°F.) for 15 to 20 minutes. A fine first course!

SWEET SOUFFLÉS

These are made in exactly the same way as the savory soufflés except that the soufflé dish is lined with sugar rather than with crumbs or cheese, and sugar is added to the sauce. Sometimes only the egg whites are used, but that is another story! The flavoring may be chocolate, vanilla, a liqueur, puréed fruits or jams, glacéed fruits, nuts, or combinations of several of these flavors.

LIQUEUR SOUFFLÉ

4 egg yolks
5 egg whites
Butter
½ cup sugar
4 tablespoons flour
1 cup milk
Pinch of salt
Grated rind of 1 orange
Grated rind of 1 lemon
2 tablespoons fresh lemon juice
⅓ cup Curaçao, Cointreau, or Grand Marnier

Remove eggs from refrigerator and separate. Let stand at room temperature. Prepare a 6-cup soufflé dish by buttering, then rolling ¼ cup sugar around sides and bottom; shake out excess. Make a *roux* with 3 tablespoons butter and flour; add milk, remaining sugar, and salt and cook, stirring, until thick. Remove from heat and beat in 1 egg yolk at a time. Add grated rinds and lemon juice and return to low heat. Cook for another minute or two, or until very thick and smooth. Cool slightly, then beat in liqueur. Beat egg whites and combine mixtures exactly as in Basic Savory Soufflé recipe. Pour into prepared mold, smooth top, and run finger around edge. Bake in preheated moderate oven (375°F.) for 25 to 35 minutes, depending upon how you like your soufflé. Makes 4 servings.

VARIATIONS OF SWEET SOUFFLÉS

■ **Orange Soufflé**—In recipe for Liqueur Soufflé, substitute 1¼ cups fresh orange juice for the milk and the liqueur. Proceed as directed in recipe.

■ **Vanilla Soufflé**—In recipe for Liqueur Soufflé, omit liqueur, rinds, and juice and substitute ½ cup heavy cream and 2 teaspoons vanilla extract. Proceed as in recipe.

■ **Soufflé Rothschild**—To Vanilla Soufflé add ⅓ cup finely chopped candied fruit. If desired, 1 tablespoon kirsch may be substituted for the vanilla.

■ **Burnt-Almond Soufflé**—In recipe for Liqueur Soufflé, substitute 2 tablespoons brandy for the liqueur, omit rinds and lemon juice, and add 1 teaspoon almond extract and ¾ cup very finely ground burnt almonds before folding in whites. To prepare almonds, blanch, remove skins, toast in preheated moderate oven (350°F.) until very brown, then put through special nut grater, or chop with knife and crush between sheets of wax paper with rolling pin.

■ **Chocolate Soufflé**—Melt 2 ounces (2 squares) unsweetened chocolate in top part of a double boiler. Make a *roux* with 3 tablespoons butter and 3 tablespoons flour. Add 1 cup milk and ¾ cup sugar. Cook until thick and smooth. Add a pinch of salt and 4 egg yolks, one at a time. Add melted chocolate, return to low heat, and cook for a minute or two, stirring constantly. Remove from heat, add 1 teaspoon vanilla extract, and cool slightly. Beat 5 egg whites, as above, fold into chocolate mixture, and pour into a buttered and sugared soufflé dish. Bake in preheated moderate oven (375°F.) for 20 to 30 minutes. Serve with whipped cream if desired.

■ **Other Sweet Soufflés**—A layer of sugared puréed or finely cut fruit may be put in the bottom of the soufflé dish, and a Liqueur, Orange, or Vanilla Soufflé poured over it. Bake as usual.

SOUP COOK BOOK

*A soup for every occasion:
delicate appetizer soups; cool, jellied soups;
wholesome main-dish soups;
bisques, chowders; plus
garnishes for flavor and appearance.*

SOUP COOK BOOK

SOUP—Basically the liquid in which any solid food is cooked: meat, poultry, cereal, vegetables, or fruits. Soups may be clear or thick, hot or cold. There is no limit to the number and kinds of soup, but all can be classified generally into three groups: 1) *Thin, clear soups* based on bouillon, consommé, or broth; 2) *Thin, light, delicate soups* such as bisques, thin cream soups, vegetable broth; 3) *Heavy, thick soups* which include beef or other meat soups, vegetable soups such as minestrone, poultry soups such as mulligatawny, fish soups, chowders, and thick cream soups. A chilled or jellied soup may fall into any of these three main types.

Bouillon comes from the French word *bouillir*, meaning "to boil." A bouillon is a broth made by simmering meat, fish, or vegetables in water to extract their flavors. The terms bouillon and broth are often used interchangeably. When a clear broth is desired, the bouillon must be clarified, and a clarified broth is called consommé.

A *bisque* is a rich cream soup, nowadays usually made with fish or shellfish. Originally a bisque was a soup made with boiled meats, poultry, or game and garnished with bread crumbs.

A thin and light soup can be the first course of a dinner, or when a hearty sandwich or salad is added, it can be part of the main course for a luncheon or supper. In warmer weather, substitute chilled or jellied soup. Hearty soups are heavy enough to be served as the main course for dinner.

HOT APPETIZER, LUNCH, AND SUPPER SOUPS

AVOCADO-CHICKEN SOUP

To 3 cups cooled chicken broth, add the pulp of 1 ripe avocado mashed smooth, salt and pepper to taste, and ¼ teaspoon red pepper. Heat. At the last moment add 1 cup light cream. Heat, but do not boil. Add a few cubes of avocado and serve at once. Makes about 5 cups.

PALE-PINK TOMATO SOUP
- 8 medium tomatoes
- 5 cups chicken bouillon
- ¼ teaspoon sugar
- Salt and pepper

Peel tomatoes. Add to chicken bouillon with sugar and simmer gently for 1 hour. Break tomatoes up with a fork and strain soup, being careful not to force any tomato pulp through strainer. Season with salt and pepper to taste. If the color is not a delicate yellowish pink, add a drop or two of red food coloring. Chill and freeze. Serve hot with Garlic Toast, Italian Style (page 1826). Makes about 1½ quarts.

BELGIAN BUTTERMILK SOUP
- 2 tablespoons all-purpose flour
- 3 cups milk
- 1 quart buttermilk
- 2 egg yolks, beaten
- Brown sugar to taste

Mix flour with 1 cup of the milk to a smooth paste. Bring remaining milk to a boil. Stir in flour mixture. Cook, stirring constantly, until thickened and smooth. Gradually stir in buttermilk. Bring to a boil. Remove from heat. Place egg yolks in soup tureen. Gradually stir soup into the egg yolks. Serve hot, with brown sugar on the side. Makes about 2 quarts.

CHIVE AND CRESS SOUP
- 3 tablespoons butter or margarine
- ½ cup minced chives
- 1 cup chopped watercress
- 3 tablespoons flour
- 4 cups milk
- Salt and pepper to taste
- Dash of cayenne

Melt butter over low heat in heavy pot. Add chives and cress and cook for 5 minutes. Add flour and stir; add milk slowly and cook, stirring, until thickened. Season. Makes 1 quart.

DANISH BROWNED CABBAGE SOUP

Shred 2 pounds cabbage, discarding core, and put in a heavy pan with ½ cup butter and 1 tablespoon sugar. Cook over low heat, stirring occasionally, until browned. This will take 35 to 45 minutes. Add 6 cups beef stock or canned bouillon, and salt and pepper to taste. Cover and simmer for 40 minutes. Makes about 2 quarts.

CANADIAN PARSLEY SOUP
- 5 cups chicken bouillon or water
- 1 cup chopped parsley
- 1 medium head romaine lettuce, chopped
- 4 medium potatoes, diced
- ½ teaspoon salt
- ⅛ teaspoon pepper
- 2 tablespoons butter
- Minced parsley

Bring bouillon to a boil. Add parsley, lettuce, and potatoes. Season with salt and pepper. Simmer, covered, over low heat for 1 hour. Strain through sieve or food mill, or whirl in blender. Stir in butter. Serve hot, garnished with additional parsley. Makes about 2 quarts.

SAVORY POTATO-CHEESE SOUP
- 2 cups diced peeled potatoes
- 1 cup chopped onion
- ½ cup diced celery
- 2½ cups boiling water
- 2½ teaspoons salt
- ¼ cup butter or margarine
- ¼ cup all-purpose flour
- ¼ teaspoon pepper
- ½ teaspoon powdered mustard
- 1½ teaspoons steak sauce
- 2 cups milk
- 8 ounces sharp Cheddar cheese, grated
- 1 teaspoon minced parsley
- 1 cup canned stewed tomatoes
- Pinch of dillweed

Put first 4 ingredients and 1 teaspoon of the salt in Dutch oven or heavy kettle. Bring to boil, cover, and simmer for about 15 minutes. In a saucepan, melt butter and blend in flour. Add remaining salt, the pepper, mustard, steak sauce, and milk. Cook, stirring constantly, until smooth and thickened. Add remaining ingredients and potato mixture. Simmer for a few minutes. Makes about 1½ quarts.

ITALIAN ONION SOUP
- 2 large onions, sliced
- 2 tablespoons butter or margarine
- 2 tablespoons all-purpose flour
- 6 cups rich bouillon
- 4 egg yolks, beaten slightly
- ½ cup grated Parmesan cheese
- Chopped parsley

Sauté onions slowly in butter until brown. Add flour, stir, and add a little bouillon. Blend, and add the remaining bouillon; simmer for 30 minutes. Mix egg yolks, cheese, and parsley. Add a little hot liquid, then add egg mixture to rest of soup, stir, and serve. Makes about 1½ quarts.

QUICK FRENCH POTATO SOUP
- 8 medium potatoes, peeled and diced
- Fresh chervil, minced
- 3 cups water or chicken bouillon
- 3 cups milk
- Salt and pepper
- 3 tablespoons butter

Cook potatoes and ⅓ cup chervil in water and milk until tender. Strain through a sieve or a food mill, or whirl in a blender. Return to heat and heat through thoroughly. Season with salt and pepper to taste. Stir in butter. Sprinkle with 1 tablespoon chervil and serve very hot, with toasted French bread. Makes about 2 quarts.

NEAR-EAST WHITE-BEAN SOUP
- 2 cups dried white beans, washed
- 6 cups water

1 onion, chopped
1 garlic clove, minced
2 tablespoons olive oil
1 canned tomato, chopped
½ teaspoon crumbled dried thyme
1 tablespoon wine vinegar
Salt and pepper to taste

Cover beans with water, bring to boil, and boil for 2 minutes. Cover and let stand for 1 hour. Cook onion and garlic in oil for 5 minutes. Add to beans with remaining ingredients except vinegar and salt and pepper. Cook, covered, until beans are tender. Mash beans slightly, add vinegar, and season. Makes about 1½ quarts.

BACON, BEAN, AND ONION CHOWDER
4 slices of bacon, diced
2 cups minced onions
2 cups (one 1-pound can) Boston-style baked beans
2 cups diced potatoes
½ teaspoon crumbled dried thyme
2 cups water
1 can (14½ ounces) undiluted evaporated milk
Salt and pepper to taste
Chopped parsley

Cook bacon until crisp and remove from saucepan. Add onions and cook for 5 minutes. Add beans, potatoes, thyme, and water. Simmer for about 15 minutes. Add milk and seasonings; heat. Sprinkle with bacon and parsley. Makes about 2 quarts.

SAVORY BLACK-BEAN SOUP
3 cups dried black beans
1 ham bone
3 quarts water
2 ounces salt pork, minced
1 garlic clove, minced
1 bay leaf
Pinch of ground thyme
2 onions, chopped
1 carrot, diced
Salt and pepper
Sherry
Lemon slices and hard-cooked egg slices

Soak beans and bone in the water overnight. Cook in same water with next 4 ingredients for 2 hours. Add onions and carrot; simmer for 1 hour longer; remove bone. Put mixture, a small amount at a time, in blender; whirl until smooth. Return to kettle; heat, and add seasonings and sherry to taste. Serve with garnish of lemon and egg. Makes about 2 quarts.

PORTUGUESE EGG SOUP
1 cup sliced onions
1 garlic clove, minced
1 tablespoon olive oil
6 cups water
6 beef bouillon cubes
½ teaspoon crumbled dried thyme
1 teaspoon celery salt
¼ teaspoon pepper
French bread
4 eggs
Minced parsley

In large saucepan cook onions and garlic in olive oil until golden. Add water, bouillon cubes, and seasonings. Bring to boil and simmer for 5 minutes. Break French bread into bits and toast lightly in preheated moderate oven (350°F.). Drop eggs, one at a time, into simmering broth, and poach for 5 minutes, or until just cooked. Remove, putting one egg in each of 4 hot bowls. Add some bread, and fill bowls with broth. Garnish with parsley. Makes about 1½ quarts.

MINESTRONE
1 cup dried pea beans
2 quarts water
¼ cup olive oil
1 cup diced celery
1 onion, minced
2⅓ cups (one 1-pound, 3-ounce can) tomatoes
2 cups shredded cabbage
1 garlic clove, minced
Few parsley sprigs
1 tablespoon salt
½ cup elbow macaroni
½ teaspoon each of crumbled dried basil and oregano
¼ teaspoon pepper
Grated Parmesan cheese

Cover washed beans with water, bring to boil, and boil for 2 minutes. Heat oil in kettle, add vegetables, and sauté lightly. Add beans with water and remaining ingredients except cheese. Cook, covered, for 2 to 3 hours. Serve with cheese. Makes 2 quarts.

MULLIGATAWNY SHORBA
6 to 8 pounds chicken backs and necks
4 cups water
½ cup sliced carrot
2 tablespoons instant minced onion
½ cup chopped celery
2 tablespoons parsley flakes
½ cup chopped mushroom stems
¼ cup instant minced onion
¼ cup water
2 tablespoons butter or margarine
4 teaspoons flour
1 tablespoon curry powder
4 teaspoons salt
½ cup heavy cream
¾ cup cooked rice

Combine first 7 ingredients, cover, and cook until chicken is tender. Remove chicken, reserving broth. Soften the ¼ cup onion in the ¼ cup water. Brown in the butter. Stir in flour, curry powder, and salt. Gradually add chicken broth and cook for 7 to 8 minutes. Rub through a fine sieve. Stir in heavy cream. Heat thoroughly. Do not boil. Serve with 2 tablespoons rice in each bowl. If desired, pick a little of the chicken from the bones and add a few pieces to each serving. Makes about 2 quarts.

VERA CRUZ GARLIC SOUP
6 garlic cloves
3 tablespoons olive oil
2 quarts bouillon, preferably beef
Salt and pepper to taste
Thick slices of crusty bread, toasted
Poached or fried eggs
Parsley

Brown garlic in oil in heavy pan. Add bouillon and seasoning and heat to boiling. Boil for 5 minutes. Add bread cut into 4 squares and simmer for 1 minute. Put 1 square of bread in each soup plate, add 1 egg to each plate, and cover with soup after removing garlic. Garnish with a sprinkling of parsley. Makes 2 quarts.

EGG-PETAL SOUP WITH CUCUMBERS
¼ pound lean pork
1½ teaspoons sherry
1½ teaspoons soy sauce
1½ teaspoons cornstarch
2 tablespoons cooking oil
6 cups chicken bouillon
1 green onion, sliced
1 cucumber, sliced
¼ teaspoon monosodium glutamate
Salt and pepper
1 egg, slightly beaten

Cut pork into shreds. Combine sherry, soy sauce, and cornstarch and mix thoroughly with pork. Heat oil in a deep kettle and quickly brown pork. Add bouillon and simmer for 10 minutes. Add onion, cucumber, and monosodium glutamate. Season to taste with salt and pepper and simmer for 5 minutes more. Bring to a fast boil and slowly add beaten egg, stirring constantly. To make sure that egg will cook in shreds or "petals," turn off the heat the moment you add it. Makes about 1½ quarts.

JUICE-INTO-SOUP
4 cups tomato juice
3 beef bouillon cubes dissolved in 2 cups hot water
2 whole cloves
1 small onion, sliced
1 bay leaf
4 peppercorns, bruised
Celery tops
¼ teaspoon ground basil
½ teaspoon sugar
Croutons or popcorn

Combine all ingredients except croutons in a saucepan. Cover. Bring to a boil, lower heat, and simmer for 15 minutes. Strain. Garnish with croutons. Makes about 1½ quarts.

SOUP COOK BOOK

CHILLED AND JELLIED SOUPS

CRÈME MONGOLE
- 1 can each (10½ ounces) of tomato soup and green-pea soup
- ¾ cup water
- 1 cup light cream
- 2 teaspoons Worcestershire
- ¼ cup sherry

Mix all ingredients except sherry. Heat slowly, stirring frequently. Remove from heat and add sherry. Makes about 1 quart.

FRENCH TARRAGON SOUP
- 5 cups clear chicken bouillon
- 4 teaspoons chopped fresh tarragon or 2 teaspoons crumbled dried tarragon
- 1 envelope unflavored gelatin
- Lime or lemon slices and chopped parsley or chives

Simmer chicken bouillon for about 5 minutes, then add tarragon. Dissolve gelatin in ¼ cup cold water and add to chicken bouillon. Chill for a good 4 hours. Serve in individual cups topped with a lime slice and chopped parsley. Makes 5 cups.

CHILLED CLAM BISQUE
- 1 can (8 ounces) tomato sauce
- 1 can condensed pea soup
- 1 can (10½ ounces) minced clams, undrained
- 2 cups milk

Mix all ingredients and chill thoroughly. Makes about 1½ quarts.

BLACK-BEAN CHILLER
- 1 can (10½ ounces) black-bean soup
- 1 soup can cold water
- 3 tablespoons dry sherry
- ¼ teaspoon ground oregano
- Freshly ground pepper to taste
- Slices of lemon and hard-cooked egg

Heat bean soup and water as directed on can. Add sherry, oregano, and pepper. Chill for about 4 hours. Top each serving with a slice each of lemon and egg. Makes 2½ cups.

BOMBAY REFRESHER
- 1 can (10½ ounces) cream-of-chicken soup
- 1 soup can milk
- 1 tablespoon curry powder
- 3 tablespoons fresh lemon juice
- Chutney, sliced green apples, pistachio nuts, and coconut

Mix first 4 ingredients. Chill until icy cold. Makes 2½ cups. When serving, add chutney, tart sliced apples, and pistachio nuts to taste. You can crush the nuts if you prefer, but serving them whole seems to add to the texture. Top with coconut. Makes 2½ cups.

CHILLED LENTIL SOUP, SYRIAN STYLE
- 1½ cups dried lentils
- 2½ pounds Swiss chard

Bombay Refresher

French Tarragon Soup

WOMAN'S DAY

ENCYCLOPEDIA OF COOKERY

SOUP COOK BOOK

½ cup olive oil
¾ cup chopped onions
3 or 4 garlic cloves to taste
1 teaspoon salt
1 celery stalk, chopped
¾ cup fresh lemon juice
1 teaspoon all-purpose flour
Chopped chives

Wash and pick over the lentils. Cover with cold water and cook, covered, until tender. Wash Swiss chard leaves and chop them. Add these and 1 cup water to the lentils. Continue cooking until Swiss chard is done, adding more water if necessary. Heat olive oil in a skillet and add onions. Crush garlic cloves with salt and add these and the celery to onions. Continue cooking until onions, garlic, and celery are tender and blended. Add these to lentil mixture. Mix lemon juice with flour and stir it into the soup. Cook gently, stirring occasionally, until soup is rather thick. Chill. Garnish with chives. Makes about 2 quarts.

SUNSET SOUP

1 can condensed tomato soup
1 soup can fresh orange juice
Cracked pepper
Sliced quartered oranges (optional)

Combine soup and juice; stir until smooth. Season to taste with pepper. Chill thoroughly. Serve in individual bowls topped with an orange slice, if desired. Makes 2½ cups.

Note: This soup, which has the rosy-orange hue of a summer sunset, is delicious before a fish dinner.

APPLE AND ONION SOUP

¼ cup butter or margarine
1 large Bermuda onion, sliced thin
2 large green apples, sliced paper-thin
3 cans (10½ ounces each) beef consommé
½ teaspoon curry powder
1 cup light cream
Watercress (optional)

Melt butter in top part of double boiler over direct heat. Add onion and cook gently for 5 minutes, or until onion is transparent. Add apple slices. Continue cooking, stirring constantly, for about 5 minutes. Add the consommé and curry. Simmer for about 25 minutes, stirring occasionally. With a wooden spoon, rub mixture through a fine sieve, or purée in an electric blender. Place mixture over boiling water and add cream. Continue cooking and stirring until heated through, no longer. Remove from heat and cool, stirring occasionally. When completely cool, refrigerate until well chilled. Stir just before serving in individual chilled bowls. Garnish with watercress, if desired. Makes 6½ cups.

TOMATO QUICKIE

1 can condensed tomato soup, chilled
½ cup heavy cream
½ cup milk
½ cup peeled, seeded, and chopped tomatoes
Salt and pepper to taste
Chopped fresh dill
Tomato wedges (optional)

Combine the first 6 ingredients and 2 tablespoons chopped dill and chill for about 1 hour. Garnish with additional dill and tomato wedges, if desired. Makes about 2 cups.

CHILLED SCANDINAVIAN FRUIT SOUP

½ cup each of dried prunes and apricots
½ cup seedless raisins
1 cinnamon stick
2 cooking apples, peeled
2 fresh pears
2 cups (one 1-pound can) unsweetened sour red cherries
1 box (3 ounces) cherry-flavored gelatin
1 cup boiling water
Lemon slices

In large kettle, soak prunes, apricots, and raisins in 3 cups cold water for 1 hour. Add cinnamon stick, sliced apples, and pears. Simmer, covered for 15 minutes, or until fruit is tender. Add undrained cherries and bring to boil. Dissolve gelatin in boiling water; stir gently into fruit. Chill overnight. Serve with lemon. Makes 8 servings.

HOT HEARTY MAIN-DISH SOUPS

VEAL-VEGETABLE SOUP

Leftover bones
Water
1 onion
1 garlic clove
1 bay leaf
1 celery top
1 parsley sprig
Salt
1 to 2 cups cubed cooked veal or beef
2 onions, sliced
2 celery stalks, sliced
3 carrots, sliced
½ small cabbage, cut into chunks
2 cups (one 1-pound can) tomatoes
2 cups (one 1-pound can) shoestring beets
1 teaspoon sugar
2 tablespoons fresh lemon juice
Pepper
Dairy sour cream
Meat Pastries (page 1696)

Cover bones with water. Add onion, garlic, bay leaf, celery top, parsley, and ¼ teaspoon salt. Simmer, covered, for about 2 hours. Strain; there should be about 2 quarts stock. Add veal, sliced onions, celery, and carrots, the cabbage and tomatoes, and liquid from beets. Cover and simmer for about 1 hour. Add sugar, lemon juice, and salt and pepper to taste. Add drained beets and simmer for about 15 minutes. Top each serving with a tablespoon of sour cream and serve with Meat Pastries. Makes about 3 quarts.

PHILADELPHIA PEPPER POT SOUP

2 veal shins
5 quarts water
Salt
2 pounds boneless veal
1 pound fresh tripe, finely cut
4 cups all-purpose flour
4 cans (10½ ounces each) consommé
4 cans (10½ ounces each) tomato soup
Red pepper
Ground allspice
4 hard-cooked eggs, cut into chunks
Butter Balls

Simmer veal shins with 4 quarts of the water and 2 tablespoons salt for 2 hours. Strain, and add veal and tripe to broth. Simmer for 2 hours, or until meats are tender. Cut veal into pieces, and return to mixture. Cook flour until golden brown in skillet. Blend in remaining water, and stir into veal broth. Add consommé and tomato soup. Simmer for 1 hour. Season with salt, red pepper, and allspice. Add eggs and Butter Balls, and simmer for ½ hour. Makes 10 to 12 servings.

Butter Balls

Mix well 2 cups all-purpose flour, 3 teaspoons baking powder, and ¾ cup melted butter or margarine. Shape into tiny balls about the size of a dime. Press firmly, and chill for several hours.

BEEF AND VEGETABLE SOUP

1 beef soup bone
1 pound soup beef, cubed
Salt
½ teaspoon peppercorns
1 bay leaf
1 medium onion, sliced
1 large carrot, diced
3 celery stalks, sliced
1 cup each of cut green beans, corn, green peas, and diced potatoes
2⅓ cups (one 1-pound, 3-ounce can) tomatoes
1 medium green pepper, diced
Pepper

Put bone, meat, 1 tablespoon salt, peppercorns, bay leaf, and 2 quarts water in large kettle; or use a large electric fryer. Bring to boil; simmer, covered, for 1 hour. Add vegetables; bring to boil. Simmer, covered, for 1 hour longer, or until meat is tender. Remove meat from bone and put meat back in soup. Season with

salt and pepper to taste. Makes about 2½ quarts.

Note: Other vegetables, such as diced yellow turnip, cauliflower, Lima beans, chopped cabbage, etc., can be substituted for those listed above.

BEEF SOUP À LA PAYSANNE
- 2 pounds beef short ribs
- 2 quarts water
- Salt
- 1 large onion, sliced
- 2 tablespoons uncooked fine barley
- ¼ cup green split peas
- ¼ cup uncooked brown rice
- ½ cup broken spaghetti
- ½ green pepper, chopped
- ½ cup chopped parsley
- 1 cup sliced celery
- 2 cups sliced carrots
- 1 cup canned tomatoes
- Pepper

Have meat cut into pieces; put in large soup kettle with water, 1 tablespoon salt, the onion, barley, peas, and rice. Simmer, covered, for 1 hour. Add spaghetti and green pepper; simmer, covered, for 1 hour longer. Add remaining ingredients except pepper. Simmer for 30 minutes, adding more water if necessary. Season with salt and pepper to taste. Remove bones, and cut meat into small pieces. Skim fat from soup and add meat. Makes about 2 quarts.

LAMB AND BARLEY SOUP
- 2 lamb shanks (about 3 pounds)
- 3 quarts water
- ½ teaspoon peppercorns
- 1 cup green split peas
- ½ cup uncooked barley
- 3 cups chopped carrots
- 1½ cups each of chopped onions and celery
- ¼ cup chopped parsley
- Salt and pepper

Have bones of lamb shanks cracked. Wash shanks and cut off fat. Simmer shanks in water with peppercorns, peas, and barley for 2 hours. Add vegetables and simmer for 1 hour longer. Remove shanks; cut meat into small pieces and return to soup. Cool, and skim off fat. Reheat, and season with salt and pepper to taste. Makes 3 quarts.

UJHAZY CHICKEN SOUP
- 1 ½-ounce package dried mushrooms or ¼ pound fresh mushrooms
- 1 stewing chicken (about 4 pounds), cut into pieces
- 6 cups water
- 1 bouquet garni (3 parsley sprigs, 1 onion, 8 peppercorns, and ½ teaspoon ground ginger)
- 2 teaspoons salt
- 2 celery stalks, sliced
- 1 large carrot, sliced
- 1 parsnip, sliced
- Noodles

Wash dried mushrooms. Soak in cold water to cover for 30 minutes. Drain; reserve liquid. Cut mushrooms into strips; reserve. Or slice fresh mushrooms. Wash fowl and place in soup kettle. Add water and bring to a boil. Remove scum carefully as it rises. Add *bouquet garni* and salt. Simmer, covered, for 2 hours, or until almost done. Remove chicken pieces from broth and reserve broth. Cut meat from bones and into strips. Return meat to broth. Add vegetables and mushroom liquid. Simmer, covered, for 40 minutes, or until meat and vegetables are tender. Remove *bouquet garni*. While soup is simmering, cook 1 cup very fine egg noodles according to package directions. Add to soup at serving time. Makes about 2 quarts.

TURKEY SOUP, PARMENTIER
- 1 large onion, minced
- 3 cups sliced raw potatoes
- 3 cups turkey broth
- 1 package (10 ounces) frozen peas and carrots
- 2 tablespoons butter or margarine
- 1½ cups each of light cream and milk
- ⅛ teaspoon each of ground sage and thyme
- Salt and pepper
- 2 cups finely diced cooked turkey
- Paprika, chopped parsley, and croutons

Cook onion and potatoes in broth for about 20 minutes; add peas and carrots and cook for 10 minutes longer. Add butter, liquids, herbs, and salt and pepper to taste. Add turkey, and heat. Serve with a sprinkling of paprika and parsley, and with croutons. Makes about 2 quarts.

ITALIAN CHOWDER
- ¼ pound salami, chopped
- 2 tablespoons olive oil
- 1 onion, chopped
- 6 cups water
- 2 carrots, sliced
- 2 cups coarsely shredded cabbage
- ½ cup chopped celery and leaves
- 1½ teaspoons salt
- Dash of cayenne
- About 2¼ cups (one 1-pound, 3-ounce can) chick-peas, drained
- ½ cup uncooked macaroni
- 1 garlic clove, minced
- 2 tablespoons minced parsley
- Grated Romano cheese (about ½ cup)
- ½ cup light cream
- Few escarole leaves, chopped

Brown salami in olive oil in kettle. Add onion and brown lightly. Add next 6 ingredients. Simmer, covered, for 1 hour. Add chick-peas and simmer for 30 minutes. Add macaroni and simmer for 20 minutes longer. Just before serving stir in garlic, parsley, ¼ cup cheese, cream, and escarole. Serve with additional cheese if desired. Makes about 2½ quarts.

CORN-FRANKFURTER SOUP
- 1 onion, minced
- ⅓ cup diced celery
- 1 bay leaf
- ½ teaspoon crumbled dried basil
- 2 tablespoons shortening
- 1 cup boiling water
- 2 cups cream-style corn
- 1½ cups milk
- 1 cup canned tomatoes
- 1 pound frankfurters, sliced
- 2 teaspoons salt
- ⅛ teaspoon pepper
- ½ cup shredded process American cheese
- Chopped parsley

Cook onion, celery, bay leaf, and basil in shortening for 5 minutes. Add water and corn; cook, covered, for a few minutes longer. Remove bay leaf. Add remaining ingredients except parsley; heat until cheese melts, stirring constantly. Garnish with parsley. Makes about 2 quarts.

OVEN FISH CHOWDER
- 2 pounds cod or haddock fillets
- 4 potatoes, sliced
- Few celery leaves, chopped
- 1 bay leaf
- 2½ teaspoons salt
- 4 whole cloves
- 1 garlic clove
- 3 onions, sliced
- ½ cup butter or margarine
- ¼ teaspoon dillseed
- ¼ teaspoon white pepper
- ½ cup dry white wine
- 2 cups boiling water
- 2 cups light cream
- Chopped parsley

Put all ingredients except cream and parsley in 3-quart casserole. Cover and bake in preheated moderate oven (375° F.) for 1 hour. Heat light cream to scalding. Add to chowder. Serve with garnish of chopped parsley. Makes about 2½ quarts.

SCALLOP CREAM SOUP
- 3 cups milk
- 1 cup heavy cream
- 2 tablespoons butter or margarine
- 2 teaspoons sugar
- 1 teaspoon Worcestershire
- 1½ teaspoons salt
- ¼ teaspoon pepper
- 1 pound sea scallops
- Paprika and chopped parsley

In top part of a large double boiler, over boiling water, heat first 7 ingredients. Mince scallops and add to milk mixture. Cook for 5 minutes. Serve sprinkled with paprika and chopped parsley. Makes about 1½ quarts.

SOUP COOK BOOK

BONITO CHOWDER
- 1 tablespoon butter
- 1 onion, minced
- 1 cup diced potatoes
- ½ cup diced celery
- 1 carrot, diced
- 1 cup boiling water
- 1 can (7 ounces) bonito
- 3 cups milk
- 1 teaspoon salt
- ¼ teaspoon pepper
- Dash of ground thyme
- 2 tablespoons all-purpose flour
- Chopped chives

Melt butter in large saucepan, add onion, and cook until onion is golden. Add vegetables and water; cover. Cook for 15 minutes, or until vegetables are tender. Add bonito, 2¾ cups of the milk, and the seasonings; heat well. Blend remaining ¼ cup milk with flour and add slowly to hot mixture, stirring constantly. Cook until slightly thickened, stirring constantly. Serve with a sprinkling of chives. Makes about 1½ quarts.

CRABMEAT-RICE SOUP
- 3 tablespoons butter or margarine
- ½ cup chopped onion
- ¼ cup chopped green pepper
- ¼ cup diced celery
- 3 cups chicken broth or bouillon
- 1 cup canned tomatoes
- ¼ cup uncooked rice
- 1 tablespoon chopped parsley
- ½ bay leaf
- ½ teaspoon salt
- ⅛ teaspoon pepper
- 1 pound crabmeat, flaked

Melt butter in large saucepan. Add onion, pepper, and celery. Sauté until lightly browned, about 10 minutes. Add rest of ingredients, except crabmeat, and bring to boil. Cover and simmer for 30 minutes, or until rice is tender. Add crabmeat and cook for 3 to 5 minutes longer. (If thinner consistency is desired, add 1 cup tomato juice.) Makes about 1½ quarts.

BASIC RECIPE FOR PEA SOUP
- 1 pound green or yellow split peas
- 2¾ quarts water from cooking smoked pork, tongue, or corned beef
- 3 medium onions, chopped
- 2 carrots, diced
- 2 or 3 small bay leaves
- Few celery tops, chopped
- Few parsley sprigs, chopped
- 4 small chili peppers or dash of cayenne

Wash and drain peas. Put in 6-quart kettle with all ingredients. Bring to a boil; cook hard for 2 minutes. Turn off heat; let stand for 1 hour. Bring to boil, reduce heat, and simmer, covered, for 1 hour, or until peas are soft. Season with salt and pepper. Serve as is, or purée through sieve or food mill, or in an electric blender. For partially smooth soup, mash vegetables with potato masher, or beat with rotary beater or electric mixer. Makes about 2½ quarts.

PEA SOUP VARIATIONS
■ **Flavor Switch**—Use part or all beef, lamb, fresh pork, chicken, or turkey broth.

■ **Make it Meatless**—Instead of broth, use 8 vegetable bouillon cubes and 2½ quarts water (use vegetable cooking water if on hand).

■ **See Some Meat**—Just before serving, add ½ to 1½ cups chopped cooked smoked pork, tongue ends, or any other cooked meat.

■ **Pennies from Frankfurters**—Brown thin slices of frankfurters lightly in butter and add to hot pea soup.

■ **Cold Cuts in Hot Soup**—Sliver or cube salami or other cold cuts and add to hot soup.

■ **Corn'n'Sausage Special**—Heat soup with cooked corn and pieces of cooked pork-sausage links or sausage meat.

■ **Add Cheese and Bacon**—At last minute, top each bowl with a bit of grated sharp cheese and crumbled crisp bacon.

■ **Mongole Soup, Sort of**—Cook together for a few minutes 1 quart pea soup, 1 can (10½ ounces) tomato soup, and 1 soup can water.

■ **Hurry-Curry**—Heat 1 quart pea soup with 1 can (10½ ounces) cream-of-celery soup, 1 soup can milk, and 1 to 2 teaspoons curry powder.

■ **Garlic Croutons on Top**—Let 2 garlic cloves, minced, stand in ½ cup cooking oil for at least 2 days. Fry cubes of bread in oil until golden. Just before serving soup, float bread cubes on bowls of soup.

■ **Sour Cream Afloat**—Top each serving of hot soup with dairy sour cream and chopped chives or green-onion tops.

SEAFOOD-VEGETABLE CHOWDER
- 1 pound small shrimps
- 6 slices of bacon, diced
- 2 medium onions, chopped
- 1 can (6 ounces) minced clams and liquid
- 1 medium potato, diced
- 1 package (10 ounces) frozen succotash
- 2 cans (10¼ ounces each) frozen oyster-stew soup
- 3 cups milk
- 3 tablespoons butter or margarine
- 3 tablespoons all-purpose flour
- 1 can (6 ounces) lobster, cut up
- 1½ cups heavy cream
- ½ cup dry sherry
- Salt and pepper to taste

Cover shrimps with boiling water and cook; drain, reserving liquid. Peel and devein shrimps. In large kettle cook bacon until crisp. Remove bacon, and pour off about half of fat. Cook onions in fat in kettle for 5 minutes. Combine shrimp liquid and liquid drained from clams; add enough water to make 4 cups. Add to onions with potato and succotash. Simmer for about 15 minutes. Add soup, milk, and blended butter and flour. Cook, stirring constantly, until thickened. Add remaining ingredients, including shrimps and drained clams, and heat. Makes about 2½ quarts.

SOUP GARNISHES AND ACCOMPANIMENTS

Vary the flavor and appearance of a simple soup with the addition of one of the following: avocado slices or strips, whipped cream with a little mashed pimiento folded in, paprika, chopped fresh herbs, popcorn, toasted chopped nuts, grated cheese, thin rounds of cooked frankfurter or sausage.

As accompaniments, try some of the new crackers such as those flavored with bacon, onion, or potato; sesame crackers; Swiss and ham flavored crackers; vegetable crackers; shredded wheat wafers; oblong buttery crackers, as well as the old favorites: oyster crackers, saltines, soda crackers, rye wafers, and pilot crackers. Or try the following:

MEAT PASTRIES
- 1 cup finely chopped cooked meat
- ½ cup chopped celery
- 2 teaspoons instant minced onion
- Gravy
- Salt and pepper
- 1 package (3 ounces) cream cheese, softened
- 1 package (10 ounces) piecrust mix

Combine meat, celery, onion, and enough gravy to moisten. Season to taste. Blend cream cheese and piecrust mix; add a little less water than package calls for. Chill. Roll thin; cut into 4-inch rounds. Fill each with a small amount of filling. Fold in half and press edges together with fork. Brush with milk. Bake in preheated hot oven (400°F.) for 15 minutes, or until lightly browned. Makes 12.

ITALIAN BREAD DUMPLINGS
- 2 slices of stale bread
- 1 egg
- ¼ cup grated Romano cheese
- 2 tablespoons chopped parsley
- 1 teaspoon crumbled dried basil

1 garlic clove, minced
1 teaspoon salt

Soak bread in water for 5 minutes; squeeze almost dry. Mix in remaining ingredients. Shape into tiny balls ½ inch in diameter. Drop into boiling chicken or beef bouillon and cook, covered, for 15 minutes. Makes 4 to 6 servings.

DUMPLING FLOATS
1 egg, slightly beaten
½ teaspoon each of salt and paprika
⅛ teaspoon pepper
2 tablespoons water
¾ teaspoon baking powder
¾ cup all-purpose flour
1 teaspoon cooking oil

Blend egg with seasonings and water. Stir in remaining ingredients. Drop by half-teaspoonfuls into boiling soup. Cover and simmer for 15 minutes. Makes 4 servings.

TOASTS FOR SOUP
Celery-Seasoned Toast
2 loaves day-old salty rye or French bread
1 cup butter or margarine
Celery seed

Remove ends from bread. Spread cut end of loaf thinly with butter. Using sharp knife, cut off very thin slice and butter cut end again, continue until loaves are finished. Put slices on cookie sheets. Sprinkle with celery seed and bake in preheated very slow oven (275°F.) for 20 minutes. Edges will curl and toast will be golden and dry. Store in airtight container in refrigerator or cool place and reheat before using.

Croutons
See page 1826

Cheese Croutons
3 cups hot Croutons (page 1826)
1 teaspoon each of salt and paprika
Grated Parmesan cheese
Very finely minced chives or other herb

Drop hot Croutons in bag containing remaining ingredients and shake until croutons are evenly coated.

Garlic Toast, Italian Style
See page 1826

Melba Toast
See page 1826

Twist Toast
Remove crust from fresh bread sliced very thin. Spread with thick coating of butter. Fold diagonally. Then twist bread into a roll and hold together with toothpicks. Toast on all sides; remove toothpicks and serve toast at once.

SOUR CREAM COOK BOOK

SOUR CREAM—In its simplest form, sour cream is unpasteurized heavy sweet cream that has been allowed to stand in a warm place until it has become sour. This method of souring cream results in a product that varies greatly in texture and flavor.

The commercial dairy sour cream that is sold in the dairy counters of our food stores is made from sweet cream chemically treated with lactic-acid bacteria to produce a thick cream with a mild tangy flavor. The cream is pasteurized and homogenized to distribute the fat evenly throughout. The lactic-acid bacteria is then added and the cream is held at the proper temperature for a specific length of time. When the cream is ready, it is chilled to stop the action of the bacteria and then packaged. Commercially made sour cream is uniform at all times.

Just a word of caution when heating dairy sour cream. It reacts to high temperature and may curdle. It may also do this when held for a long period of time at a low temperature. In most cooked dishes it is best to add the dairy sour cream near the last and keep the temperature low. If it does happen to curdle, only the appearance is affected, not the taste.

Availability—Commercial dairy sour cream is widely distributed and available year round, sold in cartons.

Storage—Refrigerate covered and use as soon as possible. Do not freeze.
☐ Refrigerator shelf: 3 to 4 days

Nutritive Food Values—Contains some sodium, calcium, phosphorus, potassium, thiamine, and riboflavin. Good source of vitamin A, with some vitamin D.
☐ 3½ ounces = 180 calories

 DIPS

SOUR-CREAM HAM DIP
1 cup dairy sour cream
½ cup firmly packed ground cooked ham
1¼ teaspoons dry sherry
1¼ teaspoons prepared mustard
¾ teaspoon instant minced onion

Mix all ingredients and chill until ready to serve. Makes about 1½ cups.

BACON DIP
1 package (8 ounces) cream cheese
3 tablespoons finely cut chives
1 cup dairy sour cream
1 teaspoon fresh horseradish
Dash of garlic salt
Cayenne to taste
6 bacon strips, cooked crisp

Soften cheese at room temperature. Blend with next 5 ingredients. Mix with 4 crumbled bacon strips. Top with a sprinkling of the remaining bacon, crumbled. Makes about 3 cups.

 SOUPS

SOUR-CREAM, POTATO, AND MUSHROOM CHOWDER
½ pound mushrooms, coarsely chopped
1 medium onion, chopped
2 tablespoons butter or margarine
1 cup ½-inch dices of raw potato
1 cup boiling water
2 cups milk
2 egg yolks, beaten
¼ cup sherry
2 cups dairy sour cream
Salt and pepper
¼ teaspoon ground thyme
Dash each of ground cloves and mace
Chopped parsley

Cook mushrooms and onion in butter in kettle for 3 or 4 minutes. Add potatoes and water. Bring to boil, cover, and cook for 10 minutes, or until potatoes are tender. Add milk. Mix next 3 ingredients and stir into first mixture. Heat only to the scalding point. Season with salt and pepper to taste, the thyme, cloves, and mace. Serve garnished with parsley. Makes about 1½ quarts, or 6 servings.

CHILLED SOUR-CREAM TOMATO SOUP
4 cups (two 1-pound cans) tomatoes
5 green onions, minced fine
1 teaspoon salt
1 teaspoon sugar
Dash of pepper
¼ teaspoon each of ground marjoram and thyme

SOUR CREAM COOK BOOK

1 teaspoon curry powder
2 teaspoons grated lemon rind
Juice of 1 medium lemon
1 cup dairy sour cream

Force tomatoes with juice through coarse sieve or food mill. Add remaining ingredients except sour cream. Mix well and chill for several hours, or overnight. Strain again through coarse sieve. Beat in sour cream with rotary beater. Serve very cold in bouillon cups, with a garnish of chopped parsley if desired. Makes about 1½ quarts, or 6 servings.

COLD PLUM SOUP

12 to 20 (one 1-pound, 14-ounce can) purple plums
2 tablespoons fresh lemon juice
Dash of salt
Ground cinnamon to taste
1½ cups dairy sour cream
1 lemon, sliced
Whole cloves

Pit plums and push through food sieve. Add lemon juice and enough water to make 4 cups of mixture. Add salt and cinnamon. Beat in sour cream. Chill. Serve with lemon slices studded with cloves. Makes 5 cups.

 ## MAIN DISHES

SLAVIC CASSEROLE

1 small onion, minced
2 tablespoons butter or margarine
1 can (3 ounces) chopped mushrooms, drained
3 cups diced cooked meat such as ham, chicken, beef, or veal (alone or in combination)
1 cup diced cooked potato
1 dill pickle, diced
½ cup chopped olives
Salt and pepper
1½ cups dairy sour cream
2 hard-cooked eggs, chopped
2 tomatoes, peeled and sliced
½ cup grated Cheddar cheese

Cook onion in butter for 2 or 3 minutes. Add mushrooms, and cook for 2 minutes. Add to meats, potato, pickle, and olives; mix well. Season with salt and pepper; stir in sour cream. Put in shallow 2-quart baking dish, and sprinkle with eggs. Put tomato slices around edge, and sprinkle cheese over top. Bake in preheated moderate oven (350°F.) for 25 to 30 minutes. Makes 6 to 8 servings.

SOUR-CREAM CABBAGE ROLLS

1 small head cabbage
½ pound each of lean pork and beef, ground
1 teaspoon instant minced onion
1 cup cooked rice
Dash each of ground nutmeg and pepper
1 teaspoon salt
Dash each of garlic salt and powdered mustard
1 can (8 ounces) tomato sauce
1½ cups dairy sour cream
Chopped chives or dill
Cooked noodles tossed with butter and dillseed

Blanch cabbage in boiling water for 5 minutes. Cool slightly, remove leaves carefully, and cut out coarse veins. Mix meat and next 7 ingredients. Add just enough tomato sauce to moisten. Place 1 heaping tablespoon of filling in center of each leaf, tuck ends over filling, and roll. Place in large shallow baking dish; cover with sour cream. Bake in preheated moderate oven (375°F.) for 1½ hours, covering with lid or foil for first hour. Brown under broiler if not browned enough after baking. Serve with chive garnish and with noodles. Makes about 16 rolls.

VEAL CHOPS SUPREME

Give 4 veal chops (1½ inches thick and boned if possible) a good coating of seasoned all-purpose flour. Brown in hot skillet in 2 tablespoons sweet butter. Place in shallow baking dish. Add hot water to skillet and pour over chops, enough to half cover chops. Bake, covered, in preheated moderate oven (375°F.) for 1 hour. Remove chops; stir 1 cup dairy sour cream into liquid. Serve over chops. Makes 4 servings.

THOUSAND ISLAND EGGS

½ cup dairy sour cream
¼ cup chopped stuffed olives
1 tablespoon chopped chives
¼ cup ketchup
Salt and pepper to taste
Dash each of garlic salt and hot pepper sauce
4 teaspoons butter
4 eggs

Mix all ingredients except butter and eggs. Put 1 teaspoon butter in each of 4 individual casseroles or baking cups. Put in preheated hot oven (400°F.) to melt butter quickly. Remove from oven; break 1 raw egg into each; egg will begin to cook immediately. Pour sour-cream mixture over eggs. Bake for 15 minutes. Makes 4 servings.

CHICKEN IN PAPRIKA SOUR-CREAM SAUCE

1 frying chicken (3 pounds), cut up
¼ cup margarine
1 onion, chopped
1 small green pepper, chopped
1½ tablespoons paprika
1 cup chicken bouillon
3 tablespoons all-purpose flour
1 cup dairy sour cream
Salt and pepper to taste

Wash and dry chicken pieces. Brown on all sides in margarine in skillet. Remove chicken and cook onion and green pepper in drippings remaining in pan for 2 or 3 minutes. Blend in paprika. Add bouillon and put chicken back in skillet. Simmer, covered, for 45 minutes, or until chicken is tender. Remove chicken to a hot platter. Strain liquid in skillet and skim off most of fat. Blend flour and sour cream in skillet and gradually stir in strained liquid. Cook, stirring constantly, until thickened. Season with salt and pepper. Pour over chicken. Makes 4 servings.

SOUR-CREAM VEAL LOAF

1½ pounds veal, ground
2 cups grated raw carrots
1 small onion, minced
1 can (3 ounces) chopped mushrooms, drained
½ cup fine dry bread crumbs
1 teaspoon salt
¼ teaspoon pepper
1 teaspoon steak sauce
1 cup dairy sour cream

Put all ingredients in bowl and work lightly with hands until thoroughly mixed. Press into greased loaf pan (9 x 5 x 3 inches). Bake in preheated moderate oven (375°F.) for about 1½ hours. Remove from oven and let stand in pan for about 10 minutes. Pour off any liquid and turn loaf out on hot platter. Makes 6 to 8 servings.

ROAST LAMB WITH SOUR-CREAM SAUCE

½ leg of lamb (4 pounds)
1 garlic clove, cut
All-purpose flour
Salt
2 tablespoons butter or margarine, melted
3 bay leaves, crumbled
2 onions, chopped
½ cup wine vinegar
¼ teaspoon sugar
1½ cups dairy sour cream
Chopped fresh dill or dillweed
Pepper

Wipe lamb with damp paper towel. Rub on all sides with garlic. Pat a thin coat of flour on lamb, and put meat on rack in roasting pan. Mix ½ teaspoon salt and next 5 ingredients. Use this mixture as a sauce for basting lamb. Roast lamb, uncovered, in preheated very hot oven (450°F.) for 30 minutes, basting once or twice with sauce. Reduce heat to moderate (350°F.) and roast for about 2 hours longer, or until meat thermometer registers 185°F. Remove roast to a hot platter. Rinse pan thoroughly with ½ cup water, scraping up browned bits. Strain into a saucepan. Add sour cream and heat gently. Season to taste with salt, dill, and pepper. Serve with the lamb. Makes 6 servings.

LIVER IN MUSTARD SOUR-CREAM SAUCE

4 slices of bacon
1½ pounds pork liver, sliced
⅓ cup all-purpose flour
Salt, pepper, and paprika to taste
3 onions, sliced
2 teaspoons powdered mustard
1 cup water
½ cup dairy sour cream

Dice bacon and cook in large skillet until browned. Remove bacon. Dredge liver with the flour and brown on all sides in fat remaining in skillet. Season with salt,

SOUR CREAM COOK BOOK

pepper, and paprika. Remove liver and cook onions in skillet for a few minutes. Put liver back in skillet. Blend mustard and water and pour over liver. Bring to boil, cover, and cook for 15 to 20 minutes, or until liver is tender. Add sour cream and heat gently. Top with bacon. Makes 4 to 6 servings.

BEEF IN SOUR CREAM
- 4 slices of bacon, diced
- 2 pounds beef stew meat, cut into 1-inch cubes
- 4 onions, chopped
- 1 garlic clove, minced
- 2 teaspoons salt
- ¼ teaspoon pepper
- ½ teaspoon crumbled dried majoram
- ⅔ cup dry white wine
- 2 cups dairy sour cream
- Chopped parsley and paprika

Cook bacon in kettle until browned. Remove bacon and set aside. Add beef to fat remaining in kettle and brown on all sides. Add onions and garlic and cook for a few minutes. Stir in bacon and next 4 ingredients. Bring to boil, cover, and simmer for 1½ hours, or until meat is tender. Add a little broth or water if mixture becomes dry. Stir in sour cream and heat gently. Sprinkle with parsley and paprika. Makes 4 to 6 servings.

DRIED BEEF IN SOUR-CREAM SAUCE
- ¼ pound dried beef
- ¼ cup butter or margarine
- 2 tablespoons minced onion
- 3 tablespoons all-purpose flour
- 1 cup milk
- 1 cup dairy sour cream
- 1 can (3 ounces) chopped mushrooms, drained
- 1 cup shredded sharp Cheddar cheese
- 2 tablespoons chopped parsley
- Salt and pepper to taste

Cut beef into julienne strips. Add to butter in saucepan. Add onion and cook for 2 or 3 minutes. Blend in flour. Gradually add milk and cook, stirring constantly, until thickened. Add remaining ingredients, and heat. Makes 4 servings.
Note: Serve in popovers, over buttered toast triangles, on toasted English muffins or rice.

 VEGETABLES

HAPSBURG CUCUMBERS
Score 3 peeled medium cucumbers with a fork and slice paper-thin. Slice 1 large mild onion paper-thin. Arrange alternate layers of cucumber and onion in a bowl, sprinkling each layer heavily with salt. Pour on ice water just to cover and refrigerate for several hours. Drain in strainer, wash quickly in running water, and drain again. Cover with equal parts of oil and vinegar and marinate for several hours. Drain; add 1 cup dairy sour cream and some pepper. Top with chopped parsley and paprika. Makes 6 to 8 servings.

Note: You must prepare this Austrian favorite several hours ahead.

FRIED TOMATOES, COUNTRY STYLE
- 6 large beefsteak tomatoes, half ripe if possible
- Salt and pepper
- Garlic salt
- Fine dry bread crumbs
- 2 tablespoons each of butter and bacon fat
- 1 tablespoon all-purpose flour
- ½ teaspoon crumbled dried basil
- ½ teaspoon paprika
- 1½ cups dairy sour cream
- Chopped green onions

Cut tomatoes into ¾-inch slices. Season to taste with salt, pepper, and garlic salt and coat with crumbs. Melt half of butter and fat in large skillet and let it get very hot. Sauté tomatoes quickly on both sides, turning carefully. Remove; add more fat to pan if needed. Add 1 teaspoon salt and next 3 ingredients, stirring constantly. Add sour cream slowly over low heat. Heat just to thicken. Pour over tomatoes and top with green onions. Makes 6 servings.

POLISH BEETS
- About 4 cups (two 1-pound cans) baby beets and liquid
- 3 tablespoons butter or margarine
- 1 tablespoon brown sugar
- Monosodium glutamate
- Salt and pepper to taste
- 1 tablespoon fresh lemon juice
- 2 tablespoons cornstarch
- ½ cup dairy sour cream
- Chopped fresh dill or dill salt

Heat beets in beet liquid. Add consommé to beet juice if necessary to make 1 cup. In another pan make sauce with butter, the hot liquid, sugar, seasonings, lemon juice, and cornstarch blended with a little cold water. Cook until clear. Add sour cream. Heat, stirring constantly, and add hot beets. Top with dill. Makes 6 to 8 servings.

SOUR-CREAM SPINACH SALAD
- 1 pound fresh spinach, washed
- ½ to ¾ teaspoon salt
- Dash of pepper
- 2 hard-cooked eggs, chopped
- ¾ to 1 cup dairy sour cream
- Lettuce or other greens

Chill spinach and chop coarsely. Add salt, pepper, and eggs to ½ cup of the sour cream. Just before serving, fold in spinach. Serve on lettuce and garnish with remaining sour cream. Makes 6 servings.

CUCUMBERS, RADISHES, AND ONIONS IN SOUR CREAM
Put in a bowl 2 sliced peeled cucumbers, 8 sliced radishes, and 2 sliced peeled onions. Mix ¾ cup dairy sour cream, ¼ cup vinegar, and ½ teaspoon steak sauce. Add seasoned salt and pepper to taste and pour over vegetables; toss lightly. Makes 6 servings.

 SAUCES

CREAMY MUSTARD SAUCE
In saucepan mix 1 cup dairy sour cream, ¼ teaspoon salt, and 1 tablespoon each of minced onion, prepared mustard, and steak sauce. Heat gently. Makes about 1 cup.
Note: Serve on cold ham, grilled ham, or luncheon meat.

CUCUMBER SAUCE
Peel and quarter 2 cucumbers; chop fine and drain. Add 1 cup whipped dairy sour cream, pinch of sugar, dash of garlic powder, 3 shakes of hot pepper sauce, and 1½ to 2 tablespoons white-wine vinegar. Blend. Makes 2 cups.
Note: Serve with salmon or any poached fish.

4 SOUR-CREAM SALAD DRESSINGS
■ **Walnut-Ginger Dressing**—Mix ¼ cup finely chopped candied gingerroot, ½ cup minced walnuts, and 1 tablespoon honey. Fold into 2 cups dairy sour cream. Good for fruit salads. Makes 2¾ cups.
■ **Fresh-Mint Dressing**—Mix ¼ cup finely chopped mint and 2 teaspoons sugar; let stand for 5 to 10 minutes. Fold mint, ¼ teaspoon salt, and 2 teaspoons fresh lemon juice into 2 cups dairy sour cream. Chill. Good for fruit salads. Makes 2¼ cups.
■ **French Cream Dressing**—Stir ⅓ cup French dressing and ½ teaspoon salt into 2 cups dairy sour cream. Good for green or vegetable salads. Makes 2⅓ cups.
■ **Olive Dressing**—Mix ¼ cup finely chopped olives, 1 teaspoon white vinegar, and dash of salt. Fold into 2 cups dairy sour cream. Chill. Good for green or meat salads. Makes 2¼ cups.

SOUR-CREAM HOLLANDAISE
In top part of a small double boiler mix 4 egg yolks, 1 cup dairy sour cream, 1 tablespoon fresh lemon juice, dash of hot pepper sauce, and ½ teaspoon salt. Put over simmering water and cook, stirring vigorously, until smooth and thickened. Makes 4 servings.
Note: Serve on hot broccoli, cauliflower, or asparagus.

 **DESSERTS AND CAKES**

POMPUSHKES
- 1 cup cottage cheese
- 2 eggs, beaten
- 1 cup grated peeled tart apples
- ¼ teaspoon each of salt, ground nutmeg, and cinnamon
- 1 teaspoon granulated sugar
- 1 cup sifted all-purpose flour
- 1 teaspoon baking powder

Dairy sour cream
Cooking oil
Confectioners' sugar

With fork beat cheese to break up curds; mix with eggs and apples; beat. Sift all dry ingredients except confectioners' sugar and add alternately to apple mixture with ¼ cup of the sour cream. Beat. In deep heavy skillet heat oil, 1 inch deep (375°F. on a frying thermometer). Drop batter by tablespoons into fat. Brown, turn, take out, and drain on paper towels. Sift confectioners' sugar over hot fritters and serve with sour cream. Makes 4 to 6 servings.

Note: These Slavic fritters can be served with steak or chicken as well as for dessert.

TROPICAL SHERBET

1 can (6 ounces) frozen strawberry-lemon punch
1 cup (one 9-ounce can) crushed pineapple
2 cups dairy sour cream, whipped
2 egg whites
1 tablespoon minced preserved gingerroot
Fresh strawberries

Blend punch and juice drained from pineapple. Mix in sour cream, put in ice-cube trays, and freeze to mush. Have large bowl and beater chilled. Beat egg whites until stiff. Remove sherbet and beat in chilled bowl. Fold in egg whites, pineapple, and gingerroot. Return to trays and freeze. Top each serving with a berry. Makes 6 servings.

DEVONSHIRE PEARS

1 can (1 pound, 13 ounces) pear halves
Juice of 1 orange
Juice of ½ lemon
¼ teaspoon ground ginger
1 cinnamon stick
3 whole cloves
1 cup currant jelly
Red food coloring
1 cup heavy cream
½ cup dairy sour cream
2 tablespoons sugar
1 teaspoon vanilla extract

Drain pears, reserving syrup. In saucepan, mix syrup with orange and lemon juices and spices. Let stand for 1½ hours. Add pears, and simmer until thoroughly heated. Cool; chill. Beat jelly until smooth. Add small amount of red food coloring and 3 tablespoons liquid from chilled pears. Remove pears to serving dish, and cover with the jelly mixture. Whip heavy cream until stiff. Fold in remaining ingredients and spoon in a circle on pears. Makes 8 servings.

SOUR-CREAM GINGERBREAD

⅓ cup soft butter or margarine
½ cup firmly packed light brown sugar
½ cup molasses
2 eggs
½ cup dairy sour cream
1⅔ cups sifted cake flour
1 teaspoon baking soda
¼ teaspoon salt
1 teaspoon ground ginger
Granulated sugar

Cream butter and brown sugar until fluffy. Beat in molasses. Add eggs, one at a time, beating well after each addition. Add sour cream alternately with sifted flour, baking soda, salt, and ginger, beating until smooth. Grease a baking pan (9 x 9 x 2 inches) and sprinkle the inside with granulated sugar. Pour in batter and sprinkle top with granulated sugar. Bake in preheated moderate oven (350°F.) for about 30 minutes. Serve warm or cold. Makes 8 to 10 servings.

SOUR-CREAM RAISIN NUT COOKIES

½ cup soft butter or margarine
1 cup firmly packed brown sugar
1 egg
2 cups sifted cake flour
2 teaspoons baking powder
½ teaspoon each of salt, baking soda, and ground nutmeg
½ cup dairy sour cream
½ cup seedless raisins
¾ cup chopped nuts

Cream butter and sugar until light. Beat in egg. Add sifted dry ingredients alternately with sour cream, beating until smooth. Stir in raisins and nuts. Drop by teaspoons onto lightly greased cookie sheets. Bake in preheated hot oven (400°F.) for 10 to 12 minutes. Makes about 4 dozen.

SOUR-CREAM MOLASSES SQUARES

1 cup butter
½ cup sugar
1 cup light molasses
1 egg
3½ cups sifted cake flour
1 teaspoon baking soda
1 teaspoon each of ground cinnamon and ginger
¾ teaspoon salt
½ cup dairy sour cream
Sour-Cream Frosting
Chopped nuts

Cream butter and sugar until light. Beat in molasses and egg. Add sifted dry ingredients and sour cream and beat until smooth. Spread in greased baking pan (1 x 10 x 15 inches). Bake in preheated moderate oven (350°F.) for about 30 minutes. Cool in pan. Then spread with Sour-Cream Frosting and sprinkle with nuts, pressing down into frosting. Cut into 35 squares.

Sour-Cream Frosting

In heavy saucepan mix 1 cup dairy sour cream, 2 cups sugar, and dash of salt. Put over high heat and cook rapidly, stirring vigorously, for about 10 minutes, or until small amount of mixture forms a soft ball when dropped into very cold water. Remove from heat, add ½ teaspoon vanilla extract, and beat until smooth and creamy. Spread quickly.

CHOCOLATE CAKE WITH SOUR-CREAM FROSTING

2¼ cups sifted cake flour
1½ teaspoons each of baking soda and salt
1⅔ cups sugar
⅓ cup shortening, at room temperature
1 cup buttermilk
1 teaspoon vanilla extract
1 whole egg and 1 egg yolk
3 ounces (3 squares) unsweetened chocolate, melted
½ cup dairy sour cream
Sour-Cream Chocolate Frosting

Measure sifted flour; add baking soda, salt, and sugar. Stir shortening in mixing bowl just to soften. Sift in dry ingredients. Add buttermilk and vanilla; mix until all flour is dampened. Beat for 2 minutes at medium speed of mixer or 300 strokes by hand. Add remaining ingredients except Frosting and beat for 1 minute in mixer or 150 strokes by hand. Pour into 2 round 9-inch layer-cake pans lined on bottom with wax paper. Bake in preheated moderate oven (350°F.) for about 30 minutes. Cool for 10 minutes before turning out on racks. Peel off paper. Cool. Spread Sour-Cream Chocolate Frosting between layers and on top and sides of cake.

Sour-Cream Chocolate Frosting

In top part of a double boiler melt 12 ounces semisweet chocolate pieces. Beat in 1 cup dairy sour cream.

PEACH CREAM CAKE

Season 2 cups fresh peaches with sugar and fresh lemon juice to taste. Chill for several hours. Split 8-inch layer of white cake and place bottom half on heatproof plate. Add a layer of fruit, then top half of cake and more fruit. Spread evenly with 1 cup dairy sour cream, whipped. Sprinkle with cinnamon and ½ cup brown sugar. Put under broiler for about 5 minutes. Makes 6 to 8 servings.

SOUR MILK—Before milk was sold pasteurized, as it is today, milk that stood at room temperature would sour naturally, producing curds and whey. This could be used in making cakes or other pastries. Pasteurized milk will not sour in this way, since many of the natural bacteria have been killed in the pasteurizing process. The milk will only spoil and be unfit to use. When using old recipes calling for sour milk, buttermilk can be substituted. Or, if buttermilk is not available, fresh milk can be soured as follows: For each cup needed, put 1 tablespoon of vinegar in a measuring cup and fill it up with milk; let stand for 5 minutes.

SOUTH AMERICAN COOKERY

Torrijas   Puchero

SOUTH AMERICAN COOKERY by *Jean Gormaz*—What springs to your mind when someone says "South America"? Visions of green, lush, mysterious, tropical countries where deposed dictators hide out from extradition? Or do you think of the rhythms of the samba, the head-hunters of the Amazon, the thousands of tons of coffee that pour yearly out of Brazil; or perhaps of the empty Inca city of Machu Picchu, desolate and mist-shrouded on its mountain peak?

All of those things are true, but they are only tiny sparks thrown off by this many-faceted diamond of a continent.

Tropical? Well, certainly, in some regions. A great part of South America lies around the Equator and the Tropic of Capricorn, but its southernmost tip reaches right down among the ice floes and the dinner-jacketed penguins of the Antarctic, a flora to fauna giant stride from coconuts and that orchid whose fruit is the vanilla bean, to the hardy little Patagonian sheep and a kind of Alaskan king crab called *centolla*. There's steamy heat and tropical fruit in the Guianas, in northern Brazil, in the jungles that border the Amazon River, and in the banana-laden coastal valleys of Ecuador, yet Uruguay and the Argentine have their *pampas,* rolling wheat and cattle prairies like those of the Middle West, and the Chilean lake district resembles the Scottish Highlands with its blue peaks, clear rivers full of salmon trout, and soft drizzling rain.

Another mitigating feature of South America's climate is the long chain of the Andes Mountains, many of them capped with eternal snows, which run down the Pacific side of the continent a hundred to two hundred miles inland. The tropical and subtropical countries that border them built their capitals—strange, cool garden cities—at fantastically high altitudes as a refuge from the debilitating heat. It is probably on account of the ice-cold mountain nights that so many heavy, meat-laden soups, so many dishes spiced with cayenne and chili pepper, are eaten in Quito and Bogotá. La Paz, in Bolivia, is the highest of them all, twelve thousand feet above sea level.

The great metropoli of South America, Caracas, Rio de Janeiro, Montevideo, Buenos Aires, Santiago, and Lima, have each their own special flavor: scenic, urban, and gastronomic.

The taste of Caracas is wealth. The Venezuelan oil wells have made its towering buildings and superhighways, have filled the highways with chrome-glittering American cars, its shops with imported goods, and its magnificent hotels with French chefs. But the wealth is not for all, only for the minority: for the old landed families, the industrialists, and certain of the professional classes. The clerks and the workers are poor; they eat mostly beans and corn and root vegetables, and they live, by our standards, miserably.

The usual Latin-American contrast between the haves and the have-nots is shown in Rio de Janeiro by the sleek luxury of Copacabana beach and the teeming poverty of the *favelas,* the clusters of tar-paper shacks that crowd the hills around the city. How much meat you have in your *feijoada,* Brazil's tasty national dish made with black beans, is a clear index to your income. Yet, in spite of its *favelas,* Rio is a beautiful city, one of the most beautiful in the world. To sail into its harbor is like moving into a dream: against the vivid green rounded hills the white fingers of the skyscrapers stand in a wide watchful circle; the tranquil blue bay is island dotted and the surf rolls gently up onto its pale curving beaches.

Moving down the Atlantic coast of South America from Rio, the next great port is Montevideo in Uruguay, that small, highly organized nation whose wealth is based on wheat and cattle. Montevideo has an oddly Spanish-Mediterranean air, buff-pink buildings, wide squares, and an active bustle everywhere; flowers and parks and modest villas and family hotels on its miles of ocean front, where seafood is a specialty.

Buenos Aires is a real metropolis, gray, solid, full of muscular statuary and elegantly planned perspective; massive, rich, and primarily commercial. Eating habits are not now on quite such a grand scale as formerly—tons of thick tender baby beef, *ollas* full of meat, and vegetable *puchero,* mountainous piles of Italian pasta, dripping juices and tomato sauce. Yet, in spite of recent upsets, perhaps it is still the richest city of South America.

Uruguay, Paraguay, southern Brazil, and Argentina are all on the Gran Chaco, the enormous sea-level plain on the Atlantic side of South America. The people who really live in the plains, in their empty immensities, are like plains people everywhere, a little melancholy needing comfort. Their comfort is Paraguay's curious green tea which is called *maté.* They hold the little carved cups in their hands and sip it boiling hot through a pipelike silver strainer, the *bombilla,* sipping and dreaming under the empty bowl of the southern night sky.

Over on the Pacific side, the towering Andes side, are Santiago and Lima. Santiago, Chile's capital, is famous for its Californian climate, beautiful women, excellent wine that's nearly as cheap as water, and a fantastic variety of seafood only equaled by that of Vigo in Spain and Marseille in France. This gourmet's paradise is the most European of all Latin-American cities and its people are an inextricable mixture of a little Indian, a lot of Spanish, German, Italian, Yugoslav, French, English, and more recently, Arab.

Under a soft gray tropical sky, under an everlasting cloud ceiling through which the sun seldom breaks more than twice a day for a little while, Lima eats the spiciest food in South America: tongue-burning skewered heart, and *seviche,* raw fish pickled in lemon juice and vinegar, spiced with loads of chili pepper; maybe it's to shatter the gentle, climatic monotony. Peru's Lima could still be living the days of the *conquistadores;* here are all the old Spanish-Colonial buildings, and not far away are Cuzco, the Inca capital, and, ten thousand feet above sea level, the fabulous Inca city of Machu Picchu.

There is a Spanish saying: "Tell me whom you know and I'll tell you who you are." It could be neatly misquoted: tell me what you eat and I'll tell you who you are. Oversimplifying anthropology, types of cultures can be divided thus: "maize culture" and "wheat culture." The first, that of the primitive Indian tribes of South America, the second, that of their civilized European conquerors. And one type of culture has not superimposed itself upon the other, but both have intertwined. Maize flour, dried meat, and hot chili pepper are mixed in with beans and rice and oil and fish, those standbys of the Iberian peninsula. Add to these the results of the massive immigrations—Italian, German, Yugoslav, and Arab—and there you have the South American cuisine, as fantastic a variety of splendid food as you could find anywhere.

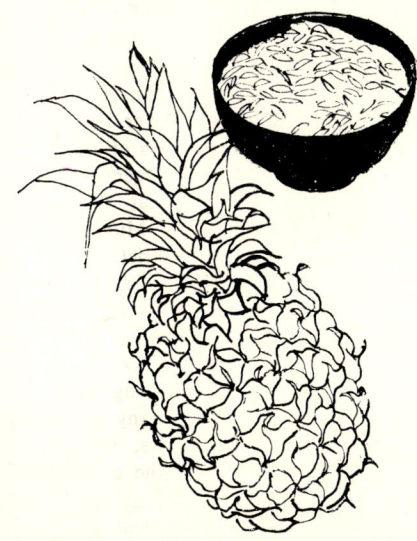

SOUTH AMERICAN COOK BOOK

SOUPS AND STEWS

SOPA A LA LIMEÑA
(From Peru: Soup, Lima Style)

- 1 garlic clove, crushed
- 1 onion, chopped
- 2 tomatoes, peeled and cubed
- 1 teaspoon crumbled dried oregano
- 1 tablespoon salt
- 2 tablespoons cooking oil
- 2 quarts water
- 1 cup uncooked rice
- 1 cup cooked dried chick-peas
- 2 ears of corn, but into 2- or 3-inch lengths
- 4 small potatoes, peeled and halved
- ½ cup milk
- 1 egg, well beaten
- ½ to 1 pound fish, fried and cut into pieces
- ¾ pound cooked shrimps

Sauté garlic, onion, tomatoes, oregano, and salt in oil. Add water, rice, chick-peas, corn, and potatoes. Cook until vegetables are tender. Add milk beaten with egg, the fish, and shrimps. Heat through before serving. Makes 8 to 10 servings.

VATAPÁ
(From Brazil: Fish Stew)

With 4,889 miles of Atlantic coastline and 27,318 miles of navigable waterways is it any wonder Brazilians eat lots of fish? Here is the country's favorite seafood dish.

- 1 onion, sliced
- 1 garlic clove, sliced
- 2 hot chili peppers, seeded and sliced
- 1 bay leaf
- 3 tablespoons palm nut or olive oil
- 2 cups water
- 1 pound fish steaks or chunks with skin and bones
- 1 pound shrimps, shelled and deveined
- ½ cup Brazil nuts, blanched almonds, or peanuts, roasted and ground
- ½ pound dried shrimps, shelled, toasted, and ground
- 5 cups thin coconut milk
- Salt
- Manioc flour, rice flour, or cornmeal
- 1 cup coconut cream, or evaporated milk
- 2 tablespoons cornstarch

Sauté onion, garlic, peppers, and bay leaf in 1 tablespoon oil. Add the water, fish, and shrimps. Simmer for 15 minutes, or until done. Remove skin and bones, break up fish and shrimps, and strain broth. Simmer ground nuts and dried shrimps in coconut milk for 15 minutes. Strain. Add the fish broth and salt to taste. Bring to boil, and add manioc to make a fairly thick mush. Cook for 30

SOUTH AMERICAN COOK BOOK

minutes, stirring frequently. Add fish, shrimps, and 2 tablespoons oil. Serve hot with a slice of cold pudding made by thickening the coconut cream with cornstarch, adding more salt to taste, and putting aside to cool. Makes 6 or more servings.

Note: Dried shrimps may be bought at Chinese as well as Spanish food stores. *Vatapá* can also be made with mussels and other shellfish. Unsweetened grated coconut, which is needed to make coconut cream and milk, is now available frozen in some large food stores.

CALLALU
(From British Guiana: a main-course soup)
- 2 onions, minced
- 3 celery stalks, chopped
- 3 tablespoons butter or margarine
- 1½ quarts water
- 1 cup sliced okra
- 2 cups chopped fresh spinach
- 1½ teaspoons salt
- ½ teaspoon crumbled dried thyme
- Dash of dried chili pepper
- ½ pound fresh shrimps, cooked
- ½ pound ham, diced
- ½ pound crabmeat

Cook onions and celery in butter for 2 or 3 minutes. Add water, okra, spinach, and seasonings. Cover, bring to boil, and simmer for 10 minutes. Meanwhile, peel and devein shrimps. Add ham and shrimps to soup. Simmer for 10 more minutes. Pick over crabmeat and add to soup. Serve hot. Makes 4 servings.

SOPA DE CALABAZA MARACAY
(From Venezuela: Pumpkin Soup Maracay)
- 2 tablespoons butter or margarine
- 2 tablespoons all-purpose flour
- 2½ cups milk
- ¼ teaspoon each of ground cinnamon and nutmeg
- 1 teaspoon salt
- ¼ cup firmly packed brown sugar
- 2 cups canned pumpkin
- ½ cup beef consommé
- 2 egg yolks, beaten

Melt butter in large saucepan. Blend in flour. Add milk, a little at a time. Stir until mixture is a smooth sauce. Combine seasonings, brown sugar, and pumpkin. Mix well. Add to sauce. Add consommé. Simmer for a few minutes. Pour a little hot liquid into beaten eggs. Mix well and return to saucepan. Simmer for 2 minutes. Makes 6 to 8 servings.

SOPA DE MONDONGO
(From Nicaragua: Tripe Soup)
- 1 pound tripe
- 3 quarts water
- 2 tablespoons vinegar
- 1 garlic clove
- 2 onions, chopped
- 2 green peppers, chopped
- 1 cup cubed squash
- 1 cup drained kernel corn
- 1 cup cubed white potatoes
- 1 cup cubed sweet potatoes
- 1 cup shredded green cabbage
- ½ cup uncooked rice
- Salt and pepper to taste

Soak tripe in 1 quart water and the vinegar for 1 hour. Drain and rinse. Cook in remaining water for about 3 hours, or until tender. Chop fine. Strain the liquid and add garlic, onions, green peppers, squash, corn, potatoes, cabbage, rice, and salt and pepper. Cook until vegetables are tender. Add more water if necessary. Remove garlic clove. Add tripe, and serve. Makes about 2 quarts.

ZOO-TOSOPY
(From Paraguay: Ground-Meat Stew)
- 1 pound ground beef
- 6 cups cold water
- 2 large onions, chopped
- 2 large tomatoes, chopped
- 2 firm green bananas, cut into 1-inch chunks
- 2 tablespoons fat or cooking oil
- ¼ cup uncooked rice
- Salt and pepper

Mix beef and cold water in kettle and stir until blended. Bring to boil, cover, and simmer for about 10 minutes. Sauté onions, tomatoes, and bananas in the fat for about 5 minutes. Add to beef mixture with the rice. Season to taste. Cover and simmer for about 30 minutes. Makes about 1½ quarts, or 4 servings.

FEIJOADA
(From Brazil: Black Bean Stew)
The most popular dish in Brazil, Feijoada *always contains black beans, pork, and dried beef. It is served with plain rice and sprinkled with* farinha *(manioc flour) or* Farofa, *a popular dish made from manioc. A* Feijoada Completa *may also include a dish of greens such as collards or kale, and oranges cut into bite-size chunks sprinkled with vanilla sugar, which help to balance the richness of the meat and beans.*

- 3 cups dried black beans
- 6 cups water
- 1 pound dried beef in 1 piece
- ½ pound smoked sausage (Spanish garlic type)
- ½ pound smoked pork (cut from chops or loin)
- ½ pound smoked tongue
- ¼ pound slab bacon, cubed
- 1 pig's foot
- 2 pig's ears
- 1 onion, chopped
- 2 garlic cloves, minced
- 2 hot chili peppers, seeded and chopped
- 2 tablespoons cooking oil or lard
- Salt and pepper
- Farofa, page 1709

Wash the beans, bring to boil in the water and boil for 2 minutes. Remove from heat and soak for 1 hour. Soak dried beef overnight; drain. Bring to boil in fresh water, boil for 5 minutes, drain again, and cut into small chunks. Add beef to beans and simmer for 1 hour. Add all other meats to beans and cook until everything is tender and beans are easy to mash. In separate pan, sauté onion, garlic, and peppers in the oil (Brazilians would use *dendê* or palm nut oil). Add half the cooked beans and stir until well mashed. Add this mixture to meats and remaining beans, and cook for a few minutes more. The result should be soupy rather than a thick stew. Add salt and pepper if needed (the salt in the meats may be enough). Remove meats and slice any requiring it. Moisten meats with soupy beans and sprinkle with farinha or *Farofa*. Serve with boiled rice covered with beans and sauce. Makes 6 or more servings.

Note: Manioc flour, Spanish sausage, and dried beef may be bought at Spanish food stores.

FISH AND SHELLFISH

CAMARÕES A BAHIA
(From Brazil: Shrimps, Bahia Style)
- 2 pounds large shrimps
- 3 cups boiling water
- 1 onion, sliced
- Few celery leaves
- 2 sprigs of parsley
- 1 tablespoon salt
- 2 cups sliced okra
- 2 tablespoons coconut cream
- ½ cup farinha, toasted for 10 minutes in 500°F. oven

Wash shrimps and cover with the boiling water. Add onion, celery, parsley, and salt; simmer for 5 minutes. Remove shrimps, celery, and parsley. Add okra to water and cook until tender. Shell shrimps and return to water together with coconut cream. Keeping below boiling point, thicken with toasted farinha. Makes 6 servings.

Note: A good variation is to use less liquid and substitute canned hearts of palm (Brazilian Palmito) for the okra. It will need only heating through, not cooking. Serve with rice.

SEVICHE
(From Peru: Pickled Fish)
- 1 pound fillet of flounder
- 3 hot green chili peppers
- 3 hot red chili peppers
- 3 medium onions, sliced paper-thin
- 6 lemons, juiced
- Salt and pepper
- Parsley

Slice raw fish into thin strips. Split peppers. Remove seeds and discard. Cut crosswise into thin strips. Combine remaining ingredients with fish and peppers. Chill overnight. Season to taste. Serve sprinkled with parsley. Makes 4 servings.

ESCABECHE DE MARISCOS
(From Ecuador: Seafood in Pickled Sauce)
- 3 pounds filleted fish or shrimps or 3 large lobsters
- Salt
- All-purpose flour
- ¼ cup cooking oil

WOMAN'S DAY

SOUTH AMERICAN COOK BOOK

2 large red onions, peeled and cut
   into small slices
   Juice of 2 lemons
1½ cups of olive oil
1½ cups white vinegar
   Salt and pepper to taste
1 tablespoon Worcestershire
½ tablespoon chili sauce
1 tablespoon prepared mustard
5 mustard pickles, minced, with 1
   tablespoon sauce

Cut seafood into medium-size pieces. Sprinkle with salt; roll in flour. Fry in oil. Set aside to cool. Marinate onions in lemon juice 30 minutes. Blend well olive oil, vinegar, salt, and pepper. Add Worcestershire, chili sauce, and mustard. Pour juice from onions. Mix onions with mustard pickles and sauce. Add to oil-vinegar sauce. Add seafood. Let stand for several hours before serving. If shrimps or lobster are used, boil and add to sauce without frying. Makes 4 to 6 servings, depending on use.

PESCADO AL HORNO
(From Bolivia: Baked Fish)

6 tablespoons butter
2 onions, chopped
1 cup bread crumbs
2 egg yolks, lightly beaten
2 tablespoons heavy cream
7 tablespoons fresh lemon juice
   Salt and pepper to taste
¼ teaspoon ground nutmeg
6 to 8 fish fillets, about 2 pounds
   (sole or any similar fish)

Melt ¼ cup butter and sauté onion until tender; add bread crumbs. Sauté, stirring constantly, until golden. Remove from heat. Add egg yolks; mix well. Stir in cream. Add 5 tablespoons lemon juice, salt, pepper, and nutmeg. Mix well. Spread bread-crumb mixture evenly over fish fillets. Roll up each one and fasten with toothpicks. Melt remaining butter with remaining lemon juice; pour into a baking dish. Add stuffed fillets. Bake in preheated hot oven (400°F.) for 30 minutes, basting frequently. Makes 4 to 6 servings.

MAIN DISHES

CARNE ASADA
(From Argentina: Broiled Beef)

This is a way of broiling beef for the asado (cookout).

5 pounds beef ribs
   Salt and pepper to taste
1 large onion, chopped
1 tomato, chopped
1 green pepper, diced
2 garlic cloves, crushed
1 tablespoon minced parsley
2 tablespoons olive oil
2 tablespoons vinegar

Season meat with salt and pepper. Put over prepared hot coals. Broil, turning on each of 4 sides, until of desired doneness, from 1¼ to 1¾ hours, depending on thickness of roast. Mix remaining ingredients together; cook until mixture is a thick sauce. Cover meat with sauce before serving. Makes 4 to 6 servings.

BIFE SAUTÉ A LA MINUTA CON ARROZ
(From Venezuela: Fried Beef with Rice)

3 pounds flank or round steak
5 tablespoons olive oil
1 onion, minced
1 garlic clove, crushed
2 bay leaves, crumbled
2 teaspoons salt
½ teaspoon pepper
   Hot cooked rice

Slice steaks into thin strips ¼ inch wide and 3 inches long. Heat olive oil in skillet. Add steak strips. Stir with a fork. Add onion, garlic, and seasonings. Cook until beef is browned. Serve with rice. Makes 6 servings.

PASTEL DE CARNE
(From Uruguay: Meat Pie)

Dough:

½ cup butter, melted
2 tablespoons each of milk and water
⅛ teaspoon salt
   Dash of vinegar
1 to 1½ cups all-purpose flour

Filling:

1 small onion, chopped
2 tablespoons butter or shortening
1 pound ground beef
1 large tomato, chopped
   Salt and pepper to taste
½ cup raisins
1 egg, beaten

Combine melted butter, milk, and water. Add salt and vinegar. Add enough flour to make of consistency of a biscuit dough. Do not work too much. Roll out, reserving enough dough for a top crust. Line a deep dish or casserole with dough, letting some overlap the sides of the dish.

Sauté onion in butter until tender. Add meat; brown. Add tomato, salt and pepper, and raisins. Cook for 5 minutes. Fill casserole with meat mixture. Cover with top crust, pressing edges of dough to seal. Brush top with beaten egg. Bake in preheated hot oven (400°F.) for 45 minutes. Makes 4 or 5 servings.

PASTEL DE PAPAS O CHOCLOS
(From Chile: Potato or Sweet-Corn Pie)

Topping:

10 medium to large potatoes, cooked,
   mashed until fluffy, and seasoned
   to taste (5 cups mashed) or
12 ears of corn, grated, or cut off cob
   and minced, then precooked slowly in
   2 tablespoons shortening or lard
   and seasoned with a little salt

Filling:

4 large onions, finely chopped
¼ cup cooking oil
1 pound beef, finely chopped or
   ground, preferably chopped
1 teaspoon salt
4 teaspoons sugar
¼ cup seedless raisins, soaked
4 hard-cooked eggs, quartered
12 ripe black olives, cut into pieces

Prepare topping and set aside. Cook chopped onions in oil until soft. Add meat and sauté until browned. Add salt and 1 teaspoon sugar. Arrange this mixture in a 2-quart baking dish or casserole that is not too shallow. Dot with raisins, eggs, and olives. Cover with Topping. Sprinkle with remaining sugar, and brown for 15 to 20 minutes in preheated moderate oven (375°F.). Makes 6 to 8 servings.

ALBÓNDIGAS
(From Paraguay: Meatballs)

3 onions, minced
1 garlic clove, minced
2 tablespoons cooking oil or shortening
2 pounds ground beef
1 cup soft bread crumbs
1 hard-cooked egg, cut into wedges
2 cups tomato juice
2 whole tomatoes, chopped
   Salt to taste

Cook 2 onions and the garlic in oil. Mix with beef and bread crumbs. Form into balls, placing a piece of hard-cooked egg in the center of each. Brown in a skillet. Meanwhile, simmer tomato juice, remaining onion, and tomatoes until thickened into a sauce. Season with salt. Add meatballs. Continue cooking for about 45 minutes, stirring occasionally. Makes 8 servings.

ESTOFADO
(From Argentina: Stew)

There are several versions of this dish. It is sometimes called a soup, but it is served as a main dish.

Estofado I

1 onion, chopped
1 green pepper, chopped
2 tomatoes, chopped
2 tablespoons olive oil
1 teaspoon salt
¼ teaspoon pepper
1 teaspoon sugar
2 cups bouillon
   Corn cut from 12 ears
1 small pumpkin, peeled, seeded,
   and cut into cubes

Sauté onion, pepper, and tomatoes in oil. Add salt, pepper, sugar, bouillon, and corn. Simmer, covered, for about 30 minutes, or until corn is tender. Add pumpkin pieces and cook until tender, adding more bouillon if necessary. It should be a thick and juicy stew. Makes 6 to 8 servings.

Estofado II

Corn cut from 3 ears
1 pound stew meat, cubed
1 teaspoon sugar
3 small summer squash
4 white potatoes, peeled
4 sweet potatoes, peeled
4 carrots, scraped
1 onion, chopped
1 green pepper, chopped
   Dash of paprika
1 tablespoon minced parsley
2 tablespoons cooking oil

Cook corn in salted boiling water for a

SOUTH AMERICAN COOK BOOK

few minutes. Sprinkle meat with sugar and add to corn. Simmer for 30 minutes. Add squash, white potatoes, sweet potatoes, and carrots. Cook over low heat until thick, about 2 hours. Sauté onion, green pepper, paprika, and parsley in oil in a skillet. Add to stew. Makes 4 to 6 servings.

PUCHERO
(From Argentina: Meat and Vegetable Stew)

- 3 pounds beef brisket
- 2 pounds beef short ribs
- ½ pound highly seasoned sausage
- ¼ pound salt pork, sliced
- 2 parsley sprigs
- 1 celery stalk
- 2 leeks
- 1 teaspoon salt
- ½ teaspoon pepper
- Water
- ½ pound chick-peas, soaked overnight and partially cooked
- 4 carrots, scraped
- 4 sweet potatoes, peeled
- 1 pound pumpkin, cut into large pieces
- 3 ears of corn, cut into 2-inch pieces
- 2 onions

Put meats, sausage, salt pork, parsley, celery, leeks, and salt and pepper with enough water to cover in a large pot. Bring to boil. Skim. Add chick-peas and simmer until meat is cooked. Add vegetables and cook slowly until tender. Skim while cooking. Correct seasoning. Serve with cooked rice and horseradish sauce or mustard. Makes 12 to 16 servings.

HALLACAS
(From Venezuela: Meat Pies)
The national dish

Dough:

- 4 cups beef bouillon
- 2 tablespoons sugar
- 2 tablespoons paprika
- ½ cup butter
- 3 cups white cornmeal
- 2 small eggs, slightly beaten

Combine bouillon, sugar, and paprika. Bring to boil. Add butter. When melted, stir in cornmeal. Cook, stirring constantly, until mixture is smooth and quite thick. Remove from heat, stir in eggs, and set aside.

Filling:

- 3 tablespoons olive oil
- 2 garlic cloves, crushed
- 1 onion, chopped
- 1 pound ground beef
- About ½ cup (one 6-ounce can) chicken
- 6 green onions, chopped
- 2 tablespoons capers
- 2 tablespoons sugar
- 1 teaspoon salt
- 1 chili pepper, minced
- ¼ cup chopped mustard pickles
- ¼ cup vinegar
- 4 tomatoes, peeled and chopped
- ⅓ cup bread crumbs
- ¼ cup minced parsley
- ½ cup sherry

Heat oil in large skillet. Add garlic, onion, and beef. Cook until redness in meat is gone. Pour off any fat. Add chicken, green onions, capers, sugar, salt, chili pepper, pickles, and vinegar. Simmer for 10 minutes. Add remaining ingredients. Simmer for 5 minutes. Remove from heat. Makes about 5 cups filling.

Garnishes:

- 2 hard-cooked eggs, sliced, and each slice halved
- Pitted ripe olives, sliced
- Stuffed green olives, sliced
- Seedless raisins

Place strip of aluminum foil 8 inches square on a flat surface. Pinch off some *hallaca* dough and flatten on foil to make a strip 5 inches long, 2½ inches wide, and ¼ inch thick. Top with about 2 tablespoons of filling. Flatten it out. Top with a little of each garnish. Pinch off enough dough to top *hallaca*. Flatten out. Pinch edges together to seal in filling. Pull up foil on long sides over dough, pulling tightly over *hallaca*. Roll down until foil fits snugly. Twist long ends firmly. Pull under *hallaca* to seal tightly. Drop wrapped *hallaca* into boiling water and cook for 1 hour. Unwrap and serve. Makes 14 to 16 *hallacas*, 6 to 8 servings.

PUERCO ASADO
(From Colombia: Roast Leg of Pork)

- 10-pound leg of pork
- 3 medium onions, chopped
- 2 garlic cloves, crushed
- 1 cup wine vinegar
- ½ bottle Worcestershire
- 1 cup ketchup
- 2 whole allspice
- Salt and pepper to taste

Puncture leg of pork with fork or sharp-pointed knife. Combine remaining ingredients to blend well. Pour over pork and marinate for 3 days, turning once or twice each day. Cook in preheated slow oven (300°F.), allowing 30 minutes per pound. Baste with sweet red wine while cooking if desired. Makes 6 to 10 servings.

CARIMAÑOLAS
(From Panama: Fritters)

- ¼ pound pork
- ½ small tomato
- ½ small onion
- 1½ teaspoons cooking oil
- ⅛ teaspoon ground oregano
- ¼ teaspoon salt
- ⅛ teaspoon pepper
- ¼ teaspoon crushed red pepper
- 1 teaspoon chopped parsley
- 1 hard-cooked egg, chopped
- 1 egg, beaten
- 2 pounds sweet potatoes, steamed and mashed
- Fat for deep frying

Grind pork, tomato, and onion. Cook in oil for about 15 minutes, or until pork loses its redness. Add seasonings, parsley, and chopped egg. Stir gently to mix. Add beaten egg to potatoes. Knead to make a dough. On floured board, pat or roll flat about 3 tablespoons of potato dough. Fill dough with 1 heaping teaspoon of meat mixture. Bring dough up, over, and around meat, similar to shape of a football. Repeat for all dough and filling. Fry in deep hot fat (375°F. on a frying thermometer) for 4 or 5 minutes, until golden. Serve hot. Makes 6 servings (16 to 18 fritters).

POLLO CON SALSA
(From Honduras: Chicken in Sauce)

- 1 frying chicken (about 3½ pounds), whole
- ¼ cup cooking oil
- ⅛ to ½ teaspoon hot chili powder
- ¼ cup ground sesame seeds
- 3 whole cloves
- 1 cinnamon stick
- 1 teaspoon brown sugar
- ¼ teaspoon fenugreek seed
- ½ teaspoon salt
- ¼ teaspoon pepper
- 2 cups boiling water
- 2 tomatoes, chopped
- 1 green pepper, chopped
- 1 onion, chopped

Brown chicken in oil on all sides; remove from pot. Add chili powder, sesame seeds, cloves, cinnamon, brown sugar, fenugreek, and salt and pepper; brown in oil. Add boiling water, tomatoes, green pepper, and onion. Simmer until tender. Add chicken and cook until tender, turning occasionally. Add more water if necessary. Makes 4 to 6 servings.

Note: Peanuts can also be included in the sauce. Pork, instead of chicken, may be used.

ENCHILADAS DE GALLINA
(From Costa Rica: Chicken Enchiladas)

- ½ cup chopped cooked chicken
- ½ cup chopped olives
- ½ cup raisins, scalded
- ½ cup chopped almonds
- 12 tortillas
- 2 eggs, lightly beaten
- ½ cup lard
- 6 large tomatoes, peeled and minced
- 1 onion, chopped
- 2 hot green peppers, minced
- Salt to taste
- Cooking oil
- Chopped lettuce, sliced radishes, onion slices

Combine chicken, olives, raisins, and almonds. Dip tortillas into eggs. Place a little chicken mixture on each; roll up and fry in hot lard. Combine tomatoes with onion, peppers, and salt. Fry in oil until of a sauce consistency. Spoon over fried tortillas. Garnish with chopped lettuce, sliced radishes, and onion slices. Makes 6 servings.

Note: Canned tortillas may be too stiff to roll up. To soften, place tortillas on rack over hot water and steam until pliable.

PAVO A LA NICARAGÜENSE
(From Nicaragua: Stuffed Turkey)

- 1 turkey (12 to 15 pounds)
- Fresh lemon juice
- 4 tomatoes, chopped
- 1 cup plus 2 tablespoons butter
- ½ teaspoon Worcestershire
- ½ teaspoon salt

SOUTH AMERICAN COOK BOOK

10 cups stale-bread cubes
2 quarts milk
1 pound pork, ground
½ cup tomato juice
2 tablespoons sugar
1¼ cups raisins
⅓ cup chopped sour pickles
⅓ cup green olives, pitted and chopped
½ pound prunes, pitted
3 cups water
   Juice of 1 lemon

Wash and clean turkey. Rub inside and out with lemon juice. Prepare a sauce by simmering half of tomatoes with ½ cup butter, the Worcestershire, and salt. Cool. Prepare the stuffing: Soak bread in milk. Set aside. Fry pork in 2 tablespoons of the butter; add tomato juice and sugar. When partially cooked, add bread which has been soaking in milk, and remaining butter. Cook over low heat for 1 hour. Add raisins, remaining tomatoes, pickles, olives, and prunes. Mix well. Spoon into cavity; truss turkey. Put turkey on a rack in a roasting pan. Brush turkey with tomato sauce. Pour water and lemon juice into roasting pan. Roast in preheated moderate oven (350°F.) for about 3½ hours, or until tender. Baste about every 15 minutes with pan drippings. Makes 15 to 18 servings.

HUEVOS CON SALSA DE CHILES
(From Honduras: Eggs Poached in Chili Sauce)

1 can (4 ounces) hot green chili peppers
1 to 2 teaspoons all-purpose flour
¼ teaspoon salt
4 eggs

Sieve chili peppers and their liquid into 7- or 8-inch skillet. Stir in flour and salt. Bring to boil and simmer for a few minutes, until slightly thickened, stirring constantly. Space 4 eggs on top of chili sauce, cover, and simmer over low heat until poached to desired doneness. Serve with chili sauce from pan. Makes 2 servings.

EMPANADAS DE QUESO
(From Bolivia: Cheese Turnovers)

1 cup thin white sauce made with 2 tablespoons each of shortening and all-purpose flour and 1 cup milk
½ pound sharp cheese, diced
2½ cups sifted all-purpose flour
¼ cup melted shortening
1 teaspoon salt
   About 1 cup lukewarm water
   Fat for deep frying

Make white sauce; add cheese. Cook in top part of a double boiler until well blended. Set aside to cool. Mix flour, shortening, salt, and enough water to make a soft dough. Roll out very thin. Cut into 4-inch rounds. Place 1 tablespoon cheese mixture on each round of dough. Fold over; press edges together to seal. Fry in deep hot fat (375°F. on a frying thermometer) until tender. Makes about 2½ dozen turnovers.

VEGETABLES

BUÑUELOS DE ESPINACA
(From Uruguay: Spinach Fritters)

1 package (10 ounces) frozen chopped spinach, thawed and drained
1 tomato, diced
1 onion, diced
1 green pepper, diced
2 tablespoons cooking oil
   Salt and pepper
2 tablespoons grated Parmesan cheese
2 cups all-purpose flour
2 teaspoons baking powder
1 egg, beaten
1 cup milk
   Fat for deep frying

Sauté spinach, tomato, onion, and green pepper in oil until tender. Add salt and pepper to taste and the cheese. Mix well. Let cool. Combine flour, ½ teaspoon salt, baking powder, egg, and milk. Mix in spinach mixture. Drop by spoonfuls into deep hot fat (360°F. on a frying thermometer) for 2 or 3 minutes, or until golden. Makes 3 dozen fritters.

TORREJAS DE COLIFLOR
(From Peru: Cauliflower Fritters)

2- pound cauliflower
1 onion, chopped
½ teaspoon salt
⅛ teaspoon pepper
1 cup sifted all-purpose flour
1 cup water
3 eggs, well beaten
   Fat for deep frying

Cook cauliflower until tender but not soft. Cool. Cut into pieces. Mix with onion, salt, and pepper. Mix flour and water. Add beaten eggs. Combine with cauliflower mixture. Drop by tablespoonfuls into deep hot fat (360°F. on a frying thermometer). Fry until golden. Makes 6 servings.

PAPAS CON SALSA HUANCAINA FRÍA
(From Peru: Potatoes with Cold Huancayo Sauce)

6 yellow chili peppers
   Salt
1 cup creamed cottage cheese
4 hard-cooked egg yolks, mashed
   Olive oil (1 to 2 tablespoons)
   Undiluted evaporated milk (1 to 2 tablespoons)
6 medium potatoes, peeled and cooked

Remove seeds from chilies and let peppers stand in cold salted water for 2 to 3 hours. Drain and chop fine or grind. Force cheese through a sieve or food mill. Put in a bowl with the chilies and egg yolks. While beating with a wooden spoon, slowly add oil and evaporated milk alternately until a smooth paste is formed. Add salt to taste and pour over potatoes. Makes 6 servings.

FRIJOLES NEGROS BATIDOS
(From Ecuador: Mashed Black Beans)

1 pound dried black beans
6 cups water
1 onion, chopped
4 garlic cloves, minced
4 slices of bacon, diced
2 tablespoons lard
½ fresh hot chili, cut into thin strips
¼ teaspoon chili powder
   Salt and pepper

Wash beans and cover with the water. Bring to boil and boil for 2 minutes. Cover and let stand for 1 hour. Then simmer until tender. Drain, and force beans through a food mill or coarse sieve. Cook onion, garlic, and bacon in the lard until lightly browned. Add bean purée and cook, stirring, until thoroughly heated and blended. Add chili, chili powder, salt and pepper to taste. Makes 6 servings.

KIVEVE
(From Paraguay: Creamed Squash)

1 pound winter squash, peeled and cut into small pieces
   Salt
   Water
2 tablespoons butter or margarine
½ to ¾ cup yellow cornmeal
2 to 3 tablespoons sugar
¼ pound mild Cheddar cheese, diced

Cook squash in salted water until tender. Drain; mash. Add butter, cornmeal, and sugar. Cook in top part of a double boiler over boiling water for about 5 minutes, stirring often. Lower heat; cook, covered, for about 30 minutes. Add cheese. Mix well. Serve hot. Makes 4 to 6 servings.

EMPANADAS DE PLÁTANOS
(From Guatemala: Banana Fritters)

2 pounds green bananas*
½ teaspoon salt
   Dash of pepper
   About 1 cup all-purpose flour
1 package (3 ounces) cream cheese or ½ cup mashed black beans
   Fat for deep frying

Cut bananas without peeling into 2-inch pieces. Boil in skins until tender. Peel; mash pulp with a silver fork. Add salt, pepper, and enough flour to make a paste which can be handled. On floured board flatten out paste into 16 small cakes. Divide cheese into 16 pieces. Put 1 piece in the middle of each cake. Fold over cakes. Fry in deep hot fat (375°F. on a frying thermometer) for 2 or 3 minutes until golden. Makes 16 fritters.
* Plantains are used in Guatemala.

LLAPINGACHOS
(From Ecuador: Potato and Cheese Patties)

2 pounds potatoes
   Salt and pepper to taste
3 tablespoons minced onions
   Butter (about ⅓ cup)
¼ pound soft cheese
   Eggs
   Peanut Sauce

Boil and mash potatoes. Season with salt and pepper. Sauté onion in butter. Add cheese. Form the potatoes into small patties, placing some of the cheese and onion mixture in the center of each. Fry

SOUTH AMERICAN COOK BOOK

in butter until golden-brown on both sides. Serve with a fried egg on top of each patty. Spoon some Peanut Sauce over each egg. Makes 8 to 10 patties, or 6 servings.

Peanut Sauce
- 3 tablespoons minced onion
- 3 tablespoons butter
- 1 tablespoon green pepper
- 1 tomato, peeled and chopped
- ½ cup ground or finely chopped peanuts
- 3 to 4 tablespoons water
- Salt and pepper to taste

Sauté onion in butter. Add green pepper and tomato and sauté until mushy. Add peanuts and mix well. Slowly add enough water to make mixture of sauce consistency. Season with salt and pepper.

ARROZ CON COCO Y PASAS
(From Colombia: Rice with Coconut and Raisins)
- 1 coconut
- 5 cups boiling water
- ½ pound raisins
- 1 cup sugar
- 1 teaspoon salt
- 2 cups uncooked rice

Grate coconut. Put it with boiling water and all of coconut milk in saucepan. Simmer for 20 minutes and then strain, squeezing out all excess moisture. Add to this liquid the raisins, sugar, and salt. Boil for 5 minutes. Add rice. Cook over low heat for 30 to 40 minutes, or until rice is tender, adding more water if necessary. Makes 8 to 10 servings.

FAROFA
(From Brazil)

Starch in the Brazilian diet commonly comes from the root called manioc, cassava, or yucca, whose flour is called farinha. If you can't get it from a Spanish food store, substitute our farina. The following dish is the most popular way of preparing this flour as an accompaniment to other food or as an inexpensive meal.

- 1 small onion, chopped
- 1 cup butter or margarine
- 1 pound manioc flour
- Salt

Sauté onion in the butter until golden. Add the flour and salt to taste; stir until flour is golden-brown. It should be crumbly, with small lumps. To make a fancier *Farofa*, in the manner of fried rice, you may add other ingredients such as chopped sausage, hard-cooked eggs, bits of leftover meat and vegetables, at the time you sauté the onion. Makes 6 or more servings.

ENSALADA DE AGUACATE
(From Colombia: Avocado Salad)
- 1 head lettuce
- 2 avocados, peeled and sliced
- 3 hard-cooked eggs, peeled and sliced
- 1 teaspoon fresh lemon juice
- 1 teaspoon grated onion
- ½ teaspoon salt
- Dash of cayenne
- Dash of ground thyme
- ¾ cup olive oil
- ¼ teaspoon powdered mustard

Arrange lettuce leaves, avocados, and egg slices on salad plates. Combine remaining ingredients. Beat with a fork. Pour over salad ingredients. Makes 6 to 8 servings.

DESSERTS

MADUROS EN GLORIA
(From Nicaragua: Heavenly Bananas)
- 6 medium bananas, peeled and sliced lengthwise
- 3 tablespoons butter
- ¼ cup firmly packed dark brown sugar
- 1 cup cottage cheese
- Ground cinnamon (optional)
- ½ to 1 cup light cream or milk

Fry bananas in butter over medium heat until brown on all sides. Arrange in a buttered baking dish. Mix sugar with cheese and season with cinnamon, if desired. Sprinkle over bananas. Add cream until bananas are almost covered. Bake in preheated moderate oven (350°F.) until tender, 30 to 40 minutes. Cream should not be absorbed. Makes 6 servings.

TORRIJAS
(From Honduras: Ladyfingers in Syrup)
- 1 cup firmly packed light brown sugar
- 1 cup water
- 2 cinnamon sticks
- 12 ladyfingers

Boil sugar, water, and cinnamon together for about 10 minutes. Arrange ladyfingers in shallow dish. Pour syrup over and let stand for at least 5 minutes before serving. Serve hot. Makes 4 to 6 servings.

Note: This is the traditional Christmas and Easter dessert.

BAVAROISE FRUITILLAS
(From Chile: Berry Snow)
- 2 envelopes unflavored gelatin
- ⅓ cup cold water
- ⅓ cup boiling water
- 2 cups strawberries or raspberries, crushed, or 2 packages (10 ounces each) frozen berries (Reserve several for garnish)
- ¾ cup sugar
- 2 tablespoons water
- 4 egg whites, beaten until stiff but not dry

Soak gelatin in ⅓ cup cold water, then dissolve in boiling water. Add crushed strawberries. Chill until mixture begins to jell. Cook sugar and 2 tablespoons water in a small heavy saucepan until a few drops form a soft ball in cold water. Remove from heat and gradually add to egg whites, beating constantly. Continue beating gently until cool. Combine egg-white mixture and strawberry mixture and turn into a 1½-quart mold. Chill until set. To serve, unmold on a platter and surround with a garnish of strawberries. Makes 8 servings.

BANANADA COM QUEIJO
(From Brazil: Banana Paste with Cheese)
- 2¼ cups granulated sugar
- ½ cup water
- 3 medium bananas, peeled and sliced
- ¼ cup fresh lemon juice
- Confectioners' sugar
- 1 pound Muenster or cream cheese

Mix granulated sugar and water; cook for 5 minutes, or to a thick syrup. Add bananas and cook until glossy. Remove bananas and mash. Continue cooking syrup until it spins a thread. Return mashed bananas to syrup and cook, stirring, for about 10 minutes longer, or until thick. Add lemon juice and cook for another 3 minutes. Pour into a serving dish and dust with confectioners' sugar. Serve with slices of cheese followed by strong demitasse (Brazilian *cafézinho*). Makes 6 to 8 servings.

Note: A similar paste is made with guavas and other fruits.

PONCHE DE PIÑA
(From Honduras: Hot Pineapple Punch)
- 3 pineapples
- 3 cups water
- 3 cinnamon sticks
- 2 teaspoons whole cloves
- 2 teaspoons whole allspice
- ¾ cup sugar
- 1 cup coconut milk
- 1 quart light rum

Peel pineapples; chop or shred. Add water and let stand overnight. Put in large saucepan with spices, sugar, and coconut milk. Boil for 5 minutes. Strain liquid into large pitcher. Add rum and serve hot. Makes 8 to 12 servings.

Note: If fresh coconut milk is not available, pour sweet milk over shredded coconut. Let stand for several hours. Squeeze through a cloth.

MACEDOINE DE FRUTAS EXOTICAS
(From El Salvador: Tropical Fruits in Liqueur)
- ¼ cup brandy
- ¼ cup Cointreau or Curaçao
- ¼ cup blanched almonds, halved lengthwise
- 2 cups diced fresh pineapple
- 1 sweet apple, diced
- 1¼ cups sliced firm bananas
- 1 cup fresh strawberries, hulled
- ½ cup pitted sweet cherries
- 1 small orange, peeled and sliced
- Sugar

Combine brandy and liqueur. Add next 7 ingredients and mix lightly. Add sugar to taste. Chill. Makes 6 servings.

AGUACATES BATIDOS
(From Panama: Whipped Avocado)
- 3 ripe avocados
- ½ cup confectioners' sugar
- Juice of 1 lime

Cut avocados into halves. Remove pulp, keeping skins intact. Whip pulp to a smooth velvety cream with the sugar and lime juice. Pile lightly into skins and serve. Makes 6 servings.

SOUTHEAST ASIAN COOKERY

by William Clifford

From Burma's border with Pakistan, India, and China to Indonesia's border with the Australian half of New Guinea, the lands of southeast Asia stretch across some 4,000 miles. Each country is highly distinctive, and the grouping of seven of them, containing two or three times that many separate cultures, should not suggest that their cuisines all feature the same garlic and fish sauce.

As a matter of fact, they all do use a lot of garlic, which is the best bactericide in the human diet. It helps keep the intestines healthy in tropical lands where harmful bacteria grow quickly in the food. The peoples of southeast Asia do also use salty dried fish or shrimp pastes and sauces, but with many qualities, in various ways, obtaining different results. Shrimp paste, incidentally, is almost pure protein.

Chinese influence is everywhere. Burma, Laos, and Vietnam have common borders with China, and many unassimilated Chinese live in each of the other four countries, Thailand, Cambodia, Malaysia, and Indonesia. Vietnam, being the closest to China by sea, has had the heaviest exposure, including 1,070 years of Chinese occupation. It was probably Chinese sailors from the coastal province of Fukien who introduced fish sauce here. Chinese soy sauce appears in every country. So do monosodium glutamate, bean curd, bean or pea sprouts, and noodles. As in China there are not just noodles, but egg noodles, plain wheat noodles, rice-flour noodles, pea-starch noodles (the translucent ones called "long rice"), and noodles made from fish. Although chopsticks never penetrated most of the area, the Thais adopted the Chinese practice of placing common dishes in the middle of the table, each person having his own rice bowl and helping himself to bites of everything else with fork and spoon or fingers. Thailand cooks, it is said, with Chinese technique, Indian spices, and local ingredients.

The second most important foreign influence in the area is Indian. Numbers of Indians have until recently maintained separate communities in the two former British colonies, Malaysia and Burma. Indians carried their culture throughout the area in centuries past, notably to Cambodia and Indonesia. The two Moslem countries, Malaysia and Indonesia, tend to borrow certain Indian culinary practices more than the other five, which are Buddhist. But of course Burma shows evidence of living next door to such a big neighbor, and the Thais enjoy very hot peppers in their food, like many Indians.

European influence is slight. Urban Vietnamese may enjoy fine French cuisine, but it does not influence the way they prepare their own food. Indonesia's mark on both the restaurant and home cooking of Holland is certainly greater than the Dutch gastronomic legacy in Indonesia. Except among Europeans and foreign-educated Burmese and Malays, there is hardly a trace of British cookery left.

Everyone in southeast Asia who can afford it eats rice two or three times a day. Poor people are glad just to have enough rice of any kind. Rich people seek out exceptionally fine rice, long grained (one kind is called "fox fangs" in Vietnam), especially tasty. Glutinous or sticky rice is a favorite, not only for sweets as in China and Japan, but steamed for dinner, cold for breakfast, fried in chunks for a snack. It is colored and molded into animal and geometric shapes. Indonesians have a sticky rice that is naturally purple.

Other refinements are legion. People don't eat just bean sprouts (which are one of the two favorite vegetables of Vietnam, the other being morning-glory vines), but tiny pea sprouts, ordinary bean sprouts, and soybean sprouts. Swallows' nests, sharks' fins, and abalone are great delicacies to the Vietnamese, as they are to the Chinese. Seaweed jelly and lotus-seed marmalade are very highly regarded. The Burmese favor seedlings and young shoots for spicing, rather than fully developed seeds, leaves, and roots, with a resultant delicacy and subtlety. Thais flavor their cakes with the smoke of perfumed candles. They also enjoy giving fanciful names to dishes, such as Rama Bathing (see recipes), Vishnu in a Sea of Milk, Galloping Horses, and Three Chums.

Imagination and delicacy appear again in the predilection for salads. In the land of golden pagodas, Burmese happily make a meal of rice, soup, and a bowl of green shoots and tender leaves, with fish sauce to dip them into. Thais eat young leaves of the mango and rose apple, flowers of squash, pumpkins, and gourds, and rose petals (see recipes). Their elaborate salads of many meats and vegetables are dressed with fish sauce, hot peppers, garlic, tamarind, and other indigenous seasonings, blended as skillfully as a French chef makes a good vinaigrette. At the same time the common man is content to go on eating his morning glories and nasturtiums, banana stalks and cucumbers, dipped into plain fish sauce.

Because most southeast Asians have access to the sea, fish is a staple in the diet second only to rice. Fresh-water fish and shrimps flourish in the flooded rice fields and ponds; such species as carp and catfish abound. From the ocean come cuttlefish, crabs, and shrimps; eels, including small ones of golden hue; and all kinds of fat and lean fish. Among the most popular are pomfret, red snappers and their cousins of different colors, gray and red mullet, groupers, garpikes, and whiting. Also shad, anchovies, and other herring; mackerel of several sorts, including horse mackerel or tuna; and scabbard fish, whose bodies can be as much as five feet long but no more than three-fourths inch thick. Barracuda are thought to become poisonous at times, while sharks and rays are considered edible only when small and young. People smoke, dry, or salt many kinds of fish. Families of fortunate fishermen enjoy both roe and milt.

Rather than looking further at the area in a general way, we can perhaps get to the roots more effectively by focusing specifically on one land. From a culinary

SOUTHEAST ASIAN COOKERY

point of view Indonesia is probably the leading country of southeast Asia, having a cuisine that ranks with the other great ones of Asia—Chinese, Japanese, and Indian—in variety and distinction. Indonesia has received many foreign visitors. Following early Hindu and Buddhist influence from India, Arabs and Indian Moslems carried Islamic culture to Indonesia in the 15th century, and today Indonesians are mostly Moslem. In the next century came a brief period of Portuguese influence. It was followed by 350 years of Dutch colonial rule. Large numbers of Chinese began settling in Indonesia in the 18th century, bringing still another culture and cuisine. Yet despite the many outside pressures, the food of the islands has remained distinctively Indonesian.

The largest of Indonesia's 3,000 islands are: Java, where three fourths of the 105,000,000 Indonesians live, Sumatra, Kalimantan (Borneo), Sulawesi (Celebes), and West Irian (New Guinea). Smaller but important are the Moluccas (the fabled Spice Islands) and Bali, which lies just east of Java. A prime tourist attraction, Bali is the only important seat of Hindu culture outside of India.

Indonesia straddles the equator, where seasons are only a matter of more or less rain and there is greater temperature variation between night and day than between summer and winter. Farmers in central Java and some other parts of the islands grow three crops a year, and you can see rice fields in all stages of growth at the same time. Other starches in the poor man's diet include corn, sweet potatoes, tapioca, and the pith of the sago palm.

As in all hot countries, it is the usual practice to begin work early in the morning and stop by noon, have a main midday meal, and sleep until the heat of the afternoon has passed its peak. Then work until sundown and another meal, light or heavy according to taste and resources, after dark. At night people enjoy eating at open-air stands, whereas the midday meal is usually taken at home. A visitor may sample real Indonesian food more readily at these stands than in restaurants, which tend to be Chinese. The open-air stalls are provided with tables and chairs and surrounded by all the colorful, overwhelming life of the tropics.

One of the street stalls' specialties is *sate* (pronounced saté or suh-tay), a small skewer of charcoal-broiled meat that the Indonesians have certainly carried to the greatest heights of any nation that cooks meat on skewers. The skewer itself may be either a simple toothpick of bamboo or a split bamboo that grips the meat on both sides rather than running through it. It is small and charming, like most of the people who prepare it and eat it. What goes on or between the bamboo is bite-size morsels of chicken, beef, lamb, goat, buffalo, pork, ham, liver, kidney, heart, tongue, meatballs, any of these meats curried, shrimps, oysters, mussels, fish—the list is seemingly endless. One Jakarta chef, when asked to list his repertory of *sate,* quickly named thirty-four kinds. Moreover, the ways of seasoning each kind of *sate* are as varied as are the species and herbs and other resources, including imagination, of a richly endowed land.

The ways of seasoning and preparing everything, in fact, vary greatly from place to place. In eastern Java people cook with a shrimp *glace* or jelly, in place of shrimp paste or sauce. In central Java everything is sweet. In west Java much food is baked in banana leaves, and raw salads are especially popular. The city of Padang in Sumatra is thought to have the hottest food, because of "Arab" influence, and this has affected the Malay cooking of Singapore. The city of Menado in Sulawesi also has hot food, but the people here are Christian, which doesn't explain the peppers but does explain the prominence of pork in their diet. Food in Sumatra is predominantly yellow from turmeric; in Sulawesi, red from peppers; and in Java, in between.

The strangest of all Indonesian cooking is probably the indigenous cooking of Bali. The sensible Balinese have not generally adopted the many dietary restrictions of the Indian Hindus, leaving such self-denial to the priests. Consequently a Balinese Hindu may enjoy a bowl of pig's blood soup with bits of fried buffalo skin, followed by a tasty curry of bat. To be sure, foreign visitors are not always offered such delicacies. You may in fact be nourished entirely on Dutch-Javanese food during the few days tourists normally take to see the island, which is a mere ninety miles long.

Balinese foods are most attractively displayed at the temples, where women place tiered offerings of fruits and sticky rice and other edibles including *sate* and whole roast chickens. These intricate structures, woven of split palm leaves and often five or six feet high, look like something in between stands of funeral flowers and the pastry sculptures of Carême.

Balinese women weave palm-leaf baskets to hold flowers as well as food, and they use fresh flowers daily, especially the bright-red hibiscus, for temple decoration. Flower and fruit decorations adorn the dinner table too, and there is a strong decorative sense in the presentation of foods such as Balinese chicken baked in whole coconuts. Chicken is a favorite meat in Bali for everyone who can afford it. Cockfighting, incidentally, is a favorite pastime or sport.

Some of the best food I ate on a visit to Bali in 1952 was prepared by a beautiful Balinese named Pollok, the wife of a resident Belgian painter. Pollok's elaborate lunch, served at a long palm-shaded table on the beach, included turtle-meat *sate,* suckling pig, chicken cooked with coconut milk, beef in two styles, and cold marinated fish (see recipes). Everything was authentic, but the menu had been planned to avoid the more startling Balinese fare. I tasted odder dishes at the modest court of Chokorda (Prince) Agung at Ubud, where numerous foreigners have been intelligently introduced to Balinese life as the Chokorda's paying guests.

What I remember above all other food at Ubud is a breakfast plate, really a deep soup plate, heaped with tropical fruit salad. The fruits were chosen from among the many kinds of bananas, pineapples, papayas, mangoes, custard apples, red prickly rambutans, beige-colored dukus, salaks with skin like a snake, and mangosteens, the heavenly fruit for which Queen Victoria offered a prize of 100 pounds sterling to anyone who could bring it home unspoiled from the East Indies. There was also the melon-shape prickly durian, with creamy fermented-tasting flesh and an odor compared by one authority to rotten garlic. Cut into generous chunks, several of these were mixed, sweetened with palm sugar, and covered with freshly shredded coconut.

The only other food I needed was a generous cup of *kopi susu,* the strong Javanese coffee brewed the Arab way with fine grounds in the cup, sweetened, and blended with hot milk. Java has been synonymous with coffee for a long time; witness our slang use of the word. Of excellent quality, it is usually drunk black. High-quality tea also grows in Java, where black tea is drunk in the afternoon or any time with snacks, while both black and green teas are exported.

Fruit drinks and soda waters are popular throughout Indonesia. Coconut milk appears in many drinks, which may contain crushed ice and be called *es. Es* also means ice cream, which is made in many exotic fruit flavors such as avocado. Coconut milk is also sweetened with palm sugar and combined with tapioca noodles, to come out looking like iced coffee with green strings in it. The name to use in asking for this is *tjendol*. Soft coconut from a dying tree is made into another special drink called *kopior*.

SOUTHEAST ASIAN COOKERY

Bali has a popular sweet wine called *brim,* made from glutinous rice, colored either red or white and very light in alcohol. Stronger Indonesian alcoholic drinks include *tuak,* a salty sour palm wine, and *arak,* in this case a bittersweet palm brandy. At sophisticated parties you may see the men drinking beer, but not the women.

With steamed rice accompanying the meat dishes, Pollok's seaside banquet equaled what a Dutchman would have called a *rijsttafel* or rice table. Dutch colonials liked to display and taste as many dishes as possible, sometimes twenty or thirty of them. Served on separate platters by separate "boys," each one was spooned generously onto a small mountain of rice in front of each guest, who helped himself to additional *sambals* (hot spicy pastes—most of the dishes had been made with these to begin with), *atjars* (sour pickles), and *petjilis* (sweet spicy chutneys), while munching countless *krupuks* (crisp puffy shrimp wafers), and lubricating the whole operation by the happy quaffing of Heinekens.

Most dishes at a Dutch *rijsttafel* were truly Indonesian; some were Chinese; however, the service was different. Indonesians serve a small-scale rice table called *nasi rames,* where several contrasting foods are artistically arranged around white rice. They also cook *nasi goreng* or fried rice, with part of the meats and vegetables mixed through the rice and part on top. But for everyday they just steam some rice and eat it with a soup and one or two dishes of seasoned meats and vegetables. They may add a *sate,* broiled very slowly over charcoal and generally served with a separate sauce. They strive for strong contrast of taste, texture, and appearance, for which four or five foods are enough. They have a very wide range of dishes from which to choose.

Consider, for example, the variety of available soups. Like the French who call a soup *consommé, crème, potage,* or *soupe* according to its nature and importance, so Indonesia has *piendang, sajur, soto,* and *sop. Piendang* is chowder. *Sajur* is a substantial dish of broth and vegetables, like French *potage. Soto* is a pungent broth tasting of meat, garlic, and lemongrass, traditionally sprinkled with raw scallions and celery and deep-fried shallots. *Sop* may mean either a consommé with garniture of the European sort, or a cold fruit soup. As to their ingestion, the Indonesian practice follows the Indian, small cups of soup being served along with everything else.

Preparation of Indonesian meat and vegetable dishes begins with grinding and pounding a spice mixture called a *sambal,* which is comparable to Indian curry paste. It normally contains crushed red pepper, garlic, and shrimp paste fried in a little oil, plus tamarind if a sour taste is desired. Most of the spices and herbs we know find their way into it, one time or another. So do several leaves, roots, and nuts not familiar to us. Some coconut milk is often added to the *sambal goreng* or fried *sambal* with the main ingredient of the dish, meat or vegetable.

Indonesia's cooking fats are coconut oil, beef and mutton suet, peanut oil, and for the Christians and Balinese, lard. The most familiar meats are lamb and mutton, goat, buffalo, and chicken. Shrimps are the leading seafood, but every edible fresh-water and salt-water fish and shellfish is eaten. So is turtle, perhaps more than in any other culture. Indonesian vegetables, in tropical profusion and variety, find their way into salads, soups, and *sambals.* They also get crisply stir-fried in the exemplary Chinese manner. Slices and shreds of green fruits are often cooked as vegetables.

Indonesian curries differ from those of India by their inclusion of coconut milk, lemongrass, and laos root. Salty Chinese soy sauce is used extensively; so is an Indonesian version called *ketjap,* which is sweetened with molasses. Crisp wafers are made from rice or tapioca flours with peanuts (see recipes), shrimps, or tiny dried fish. The fact that variety is important helps to account for so many borrowings—in cooking, and in other realms of life. The Balinese are always taking up a new style of painting, inventing a new dance, adopting and giving their own expression to something foreign that comes along.

In trying to understand why the foods of Indonesia and the rest of southeast Asia came to be so richly and generously seasoned, it's worth remembering that these are the lands where all the spices grow. Where cinnamon and ginger, nutmegs and cloves, seeds and roots and pungent grasses come easily to hand. It's only natural for seasonings to have a subtlety and fresh intensity that must be tasted to be believed.

Sources and Substitutions for Ingredients

The best source for ingredients not widely available are the Chinese food stores in all large American cities. Every southeast Asian country uses ordinary salty soy sauce, a Japanese variety of which is available in large food stores. Indonesian sweet soy sauce, *ketjap,* is made of soybeans, molasses, and laos root. Molasses is our best substitute for the unrefined palm sugar of southeast Asia; brown sugar, the next best.

Some of the names for southeast Asia's shrimp or fish pastes and sauces are *ngapi* and *nampyaye* in Burma, *kapi* and *nam pla* in Thailand, *nuớc nam* in Vietnam, *trassi udang* in Indonesia. These are prepared by salting shrimps or small fish such as anchovies and allowing them to ferment in the sun. The liquid that drips off is the sauce; what's left is the paste. Some pastes have been fried or baked; some sauces are stronger than others; all are very salty and fishy. The easiest to find of the sauces, which look like cider vinegar, is the one that comes from the Philippines, *patis.* Because of the frequent use of fish sauce and paste it is worth the trouble to get at least one. If you must substitute, perhaps anchovy paste and a little vinegar come closest.

Shallots are the local member of the onion family in greatest favor, and the best substitution is scallions, but you can also use ordinary onions. Green gingerroot can be bought at oriental, Mexican, and Puerto Rican food stores; ground ginger is a poor substitute. Fresh coriander leaves, which look like big-leaved Italian parsley, are found at Chinese and Mexican stores; ground coriander seed gives only a hint of the taste and none of the aroma, while parsley is a substitute only in appearance.

Tamarind's sour taste is hard to duplicate, the closest approach being perhaps through lime juice with dried prune. Fresh hot green peppers appear in Italian as well as Mexican and oriental markets. They also come bottled (Italian, medium hot) and canned (Mexican, pure fire). For the taste of lemongrass, which is related to the plant that gives us citronella, grated lemon rind is a better substitute than juice. Apply at your closest Chinese food store for glutinous rice and rice flour, pea-starch noodles (also called bean-thread, cellophane, glass, or transparent noodles), egg-roll wrappers, bean curd, and sesame oil.

Although coconuts are freely available, they are troublesome to open and scrape. Packaged coconut makes good milk and cream, but it must be unsweetened if the liquid is to be used in meat dishes. The sweetened coconut commonly found in our food stores is fine for desserts. A possible substitute for coconut cream is evaporated milk flavored with ground almonds.

1713 SOUTHEAST ASIAN COOKERY

Nasi Goreng　　　Panggang Golek　　　Yam of Roses

ENCYCLOPEDIA OF COOKERY

SOUTHEAST ASIAN COOKERY

INDONESIA

ES ADVOKAT
(Iced Avocado Drink)

- 1 large avocado, mashed
- 1 cup double-strength brewed coffee, espresso if possible
- 2 tablespoons sugar
- 4 cups milk

Combine all ingredients and mix with electric blender, egg beater, or wire whisk until smooth. Pour into tall glasses half filled with crushed ice. Makes 6 servings.

REMPEJEK KATJANG
(Crisp Peanut Fritters)

- ¾ cup rice flour
- ¼ cup all-purpose flour
- 1 teaspoon minced onion
- ½ small garlic clove, crushed
- ½ teaspoon caraway seed
- ¼ teaspoon ground coriander
- ¾ cup warm coconut milk
- 1 egg, beaten
- 1 cup salted peanuts
- Cooking oil
- Salt

Mix together flours, onion, garlic, caraway seed, and coriander. Blend in coconut milk and egg, adding more milk if necessary to make a thin smooth batter. Stir in nuts. Pour cooking oil into large skillet to depth of one half inch; heat to 360°F. on a frying thermometer. Drop batter by tablespoonfuls into hot oil and cook for 5 minutes, or until lightly browned on both sides, turning occasionally. Drain; season to taste with salt. Makes about 20 fritters, or 5 to 10 servings.

IKAN GORENG ATJAR
(Cold Pickled Fish)

This is the fried, then pickled or marinated fish that was served cold at Pollok's table on the beach in Bali.

- 2 to 3 pounds sea bass or porgies, cut into 2-inch sections
- ¼ cup tamarind juice or fresh lime juice
- Salt
- 2 cups cooking oil
- 6 garlic cloves, sliced (or less to taste*)
- 1 onion, sliced
- 1 teaspoon minced gingerroot
- 1 teaspoon ground turmeric
- 1 tablespoon brown sugar
- 1 cup vinegar

Rub pieces of fish with tamarind juice and salt. Fry in hot oil (375°F. on a frying thermometer) for 5 minutes on each side. Drain. Pour off most of oil from pan, leaving 2 tablespoons. Fry garlic, onion, and gingerroot for 2 minutes. Add turmeric, sugar, and vinegar; bring to boil, add fish, and simmer for 5 minutes. Chill. Keep for a day or two before serving. Makes 6 to 8 servings.

*You may want to experiment with the quantity of garlic you use.

SATE AJAM
(Broiled Chicken on Skewers)

Sate is the famous Indonesian skewer of broiled meat, and this recipe works equally well with small cubes of chicken, beef, lamb, pork, or shrimps. The skewers are sometimes steamed before being grilled, and sometimes the meats are tenderized by many sharp cuts across the skewered cubes. But more important for both tenderness and flavor is marinating. The marinade may be plain or fancy, reflecting the taste of the cook or the customs of a particular region.

- 1 frying chicken (2 to 3 pounds)
- ½ cup coconut milk (prepared from unsweetened coconut)
- ¼ cup soy sauce
- 1 tablespoon brown sugar
- 6 kemiri nuts, ground (substitute 6 macadamia nuts or 3 Brazil nuts)
- ½ teaspoon crushed red pepper
- ½ teaspoon trassi udang (shrimp paste), optional*
- 1 teaspoon ground turmeric
- 1 teaspoon ground coriander
- ½ teaspoon ground caraway seed
- ½ teaspoon ground ginger
- 2 garlic cloves, crushed
- 1 onion, minced

Remove raw chicken from bones and cut into small bites. Combine all other ingredients and marinate chicken in them for at least 1 hour, preferably overnight. Thread chicken on bamboo skewers and broil over charcoal, turning skewers frequently and dipping into marinade each time they are turned until chicken is tender. Makes 6 servings.

Note: A sauce based either on peanuts or soy sauce normally accompanies *sate*. A simple way to make one is to take the leftover marinade, add ¼ cup peanut butter, and simmer for 10 minutes. Add another ½ cup coconut milk if necessary.

Trassi udang adds a strong fish flavor. You may experiment with the quantity.

BABI KETJAP
(Braised Pork in Soy Sauce)

Indonesia's many Christians and Chinese enjoy this pork dish. For Moslems the same recipe may be followed using lamb (kambing ketjap) or beef.

- 1½ pounds pork, cut into small cubes
- 2 tablespoons cooking oil
- 1 large onion, chopped
- 2 scallions, chopped
- 2 garlic cloves, minced
- 1 teaspoon ground ginger
- ¼ cup soy sauce
- 1 tablespoon brown sugar
- ½ cup water

Fry the meat in very hot oil until lightly browned. Add onion, scallions, garlic, and ginger; reduce heat and sauté for 5 minutes. Add soy sauce, sugar, and water, and simmer for 40 minutes. Makes 6 servings.

KERIE KAMBING
(Indonesian Lamb Curry)

Curry, or kerie, is made in Indonesia with coconut milk and lemongrass, in addition to curry powder or such traditional curry spices as ground coriander and cuminseed. Gulai is similar to kerie, but it tends to contain the sweeter spices as well, such as cloves, nutmeg, cinnamon, and cardamom.

- 1½ pounds boneless lamb, cut into 1½-inch cubes
- ¼ cup cooking oil
- 1 onion, sliced
- 1 tablespoon curry powder
- 2 teaspoons ground coriander
- 2 cups coconut milk
- 2 garlic cloves, minced
- 2 strands lemongrass or grated rind of 1 lemon
- Salt and pepper

Fry meat in hot oil for 5 minutes. Add onion, curry powder, and coriander, and fry for 5 minutes more. Add coconut milk, garlic, and lemongrass; reduce heat, cover, and cook for 1 hour, or until meat is just tender. Season to taste. Makes 4 servings.

TELUR MASAK BALI
(Balinese Spiced Eggs)

- 6 hard-cooked eggs, shelled
- ¼ cup cooking oil
- ¼ garlic clove, minced
- 1 small onion, minced
- 1 teaspoon trassi udang (shrimp paste) or anchovy paste*
- 1 tablespoon tamarind juice
- 2 tablespoons soy sauce
- 1 teaspoon brown sugar
- 1 teaspoon minced gingerroot
- 1 cup water

Fry eggs in oil until golden, rolling around to prevent burning. Drain, and pour off all but 2 tablespoons oil. Fry garlic and onion for 2 minutes. Add eggs and all other ingredients, cover, and simmer for 20 minutes. Cut each egg into halves and serve with sauce. Makes 6 servings.

*The anchovy paste produces a flavor more familiar to the Western palate.

NASI GORENG
(Fried Rice)

Indonesian fried rice may contain shredded chicken, minced beef, ham, bacon or pork, shrimps, (fresh and dried), crab, or lobster. It may be garnished with thin omelets or fried eggs, raw vegetables, and pickles to suit your fancy. The rice must be steamed or boiled early enough to get completely cold and dry before being fried. Indonesians cook it the day before.

- 3 onions, chopped
- 3 garlic cloves, minced
- ¼ cup cooking oil
- 4 cups cooked rice
- 1 cup shredded cooked chicken
- 1 cup diced ham, preferably Smithfield
- ½ pound small shrimps, peeled and deveined

½ teaspoon crushed red pepper
2 teaspoons trassi udang (shrimp paste) or anchovy paste
1 tablespoon paprika
1 tablespoon laos (Java root powder), optional
1 teaspoon ground coriander
1 teaspoon ground cuminseed

Cook onions and garlic in oil until golden. Add rice and cook until brown, stirring constantly. Add all other ingredients, mix well, and cook until shrimps turn fully pink. Garnish as desired, including fresh coriander leaves if available. Makes 6 servings.

GADO GADO
(Vegetables with Peanut Sauce)

The vegetables for this dish, some raw, some lightly cooked but still crisp, are arranged on a platter and served with a bowl of spicy peanut sauce. The sauce is medium-hot, but the dish can be kept bland if you limit the use of it. Cooked without fat, this makes a good contrast to fried dishes.

Vegetables:

- 2 cucumbers, sliced
- 1 bunch of red radishes, halved
- 1 large sweet green pepper, slivered
- 2 cups (one 1-pound can) bean sprouts, heated and drained
- 4 potatoes, boiled and quartered
- 1 cup cooked green beans
- 1 cup cooked shredded cabbage
- 1 cup cooked leaf spinach, drained

Sauce:

- 6 tablespoons peanut butter
- 1 teaspoon crushed red pepper
- 1 teaspoon trassi udang (shrimp paste) or anchovy paste
- 2 tablespoons tamarind juice
- 1 teaspoon brown sugar
- 1 garlic clove, minced
- 2 strands lemongrass or grated rind of 1 lemon

Arrange vegetables on platter. Heat the sauce ingredients in 1 cup water, stirring until peanut butter dissolves. Simmer for 30 minutes and serve warm. The vegetables may be eaten hot, lukewarm, or cold. Makes 8 or more servings.

GORENG BAJEM
(Fried Spinach Leaves)

- 2 cups rice flour
- 1 teaspoon salt
- 1 cup water
- 1 pound fresh large-leaved spinach, washed and dried
  Cooking oil for deep frying

Mix flour, salt, and water to make thin batter. Dip spinach leaves into batter and fry one at a time, very quickly, in hot oil (390°F. on a frying thermometer). Makes 6 to 8 servings.

MALAYSIA

PANGGANG GOLEK
(Roast Duck Varnished with Coconut)

Here is a recipe from the Royal Household of Kelantan, a state of Malaysia. The proper spit for roasting the duck is described in the original directions as "a long stick, about the size of a toe."

- 1 duckling (4 to 5 pounds)
  Water
- 1 tablespoon salt
- 1 teaspoon ground coriander
- ¾ teaspoon ground fenugreek seed
- 1 teaspoon ground cinnamon
- ¼ teaspoon ground cloves
- 1 teaspoon ground ginger
- 3 red onions, minced
- 1 teaspoon ground turmeric
- 3 strands lemongrass or grated rind of 1 large lemon
- 2 small dried red peppers, seeded and crushed
- 1 teaspoon brown sugar
- 1 teaspoon tamarind fruit
- 1 cup coconut cream, or evaporated milk

Cover the duck with water, add salt, and cook over low heat until just tender, about 1 hour. Do not overcook, and handle carefully so that it does not come apart. Drain, rub inside and out with mixture of all ingredients from coriander through red peppers. Place on spit and turn slowly over charcoal. Combine sugar and tamarind with coconut cream, mix, and strain off tamarind pulp. Drip liquid gradually on body of duck as it turns until it is well varnished. Makes 4 servings.

MASAK NADI
(Spiced Meat Stew)

In this Kelantan recipe, which could be an Indonesian gulai, evaporated milk is suggested as the best substitute for coconut cream. The dish can be made equally well with lamb, beef, or veal, so long as all tough membrane is removed when the meat is cut.

- 1½ pounds lamb, well trimmed and cut into ½-inch cubes
- 1 teaspoon monosodium glutamate
- ¼ cup cooking oil
- 20 almonds, peeled and ground
- ½ teaspoon coarsely ground pepper
- ½ teaspoon ground cuminseed
- ½ teaspoon ground nutmeg
- 1 garlic clove, minced
- 2 teaspoons minced gingerroot
- 2 tablespoons tomato paste
- ½ cup undiluted evaporated milk

Sprinkle meat with monosodium glutamate and fry quickly in very hot oil. Remove from pan when brown on all sides and just tender. Place all other ingredients except tomato paste and evaporated milk in oil that remains in pan. Fry for 2 minutes. Add tomato paste and milk, bring to boil, add meat, and cook for only 1 minute, just long enough to blend all ingredients. Makes 6 to 8 servings.

SPIKU
Malay Layer Cake

- 12 tablespoons (¾ cup) butter
- 6 tablespoons sugar
- 12 eggs, separated
- ¾ cup sifted all-purpose flour
- 1½ teaspoons grated nutmeg
- 1½ teaspoons ground cinnamon

Cream 6 tablespoons of the butter with the sugar. Add beaten egg yolks. Beat well; then beat in flour and spices. Fold in stiffly beaten egg whites. Divide mixture into halves. Divide half the batter between three 8-inch layer-cake pans, greased and lined on the bottom with wax paper. Bake in preheated hot oven (400° F.) for 8 to 10 minutes. Remove cakes from pans and spread each layer with 1 tablespoon butter. Repeat with other half of batter. Put layers together to make a 6-layer cake.

THAILAND

PHRA RAM LONG SONG
(Rama Bathing)

The emerald water of Rama's bath can be a bed of braised watercress, field greens, or spinach, while a froth of coconut cream suggests the foam of the sea where he sports.

- 2 pounds beef, cut into thin strips
- 2 cups coconut milk
- 1 teaspoon brown sugar
- 1 tablespoon nam pla (Thai fish sauce) or any salty fish or shrimp sauce
- 1 teaspoon crushed red pepper
- 1 onion, minced
- ½ cup ground peanuts
- 6 garlic cloves, minced
- 1 teaspoon ground turmeric
- 1 strand lemongrass or 1 teaspoon grated lemon rind
- 2 tablespoons cooking oil
- ¼ cup all-purpose flour
- 2 tablespoons water
- 1 bunch of watercress
- ¼ cup coconut cream

Simmer beef, covered, in coconut milk, sugar, and *nam pla* until tender. Sauté red pepper, onion, nuts, garlic, turmeric, and lemongrass in oil for 5 minutes. Add beef with its liquid. Thicken with flour mixed with the water, cover, and bring to boil. Simmer for 5 minutes. Cut watercress into 2-inch lengths, place on low heat, and wilt in its own water. Drain and arrange in a ring on a platter. Place meat in the center and cover with coconut cream, beaten to make it frothy. Makes 6 servings.

MI KROB
(Fried Noodles)

Fried noodles, like fried rice, can be made with almost any meat or vegetable and are a favorite dish in every country. A

SOUTHEAST ASIAN COOKERY

tourist pamphlet from Thailand says that mi krob are "good for lunch or with whiskey, especially on rainy nights."

- 8 ounces fine egg noodles
- 1 cup lard or cooking oil
- 1 onion, chopped
- 4 garlic cloves, minced
- ½ pound small shrimps, shelled and deveined
- ½ cup cooked chicken, diced
- ½ cup crabmeat
- ½ cup diced soybean curd
- 1 tablespoon each of soy sauce, nam pla (fish sauce), and fresh lime juice
- 4 eggs
- 2 cups (one 1-pound can) bean sprouts
- 1 tablespoon brown sugar

Cook noodles for 1 minute in boiling water, drain, and spread out to cool and dry. Use ¾ cup of the lard to fry noodles, a portion of the lard and noodles at a time, until crisp, turning only once. In remaining ¼ cup lard fry onion and garlic until golden. Add shrimps, chicken, crabmeat, bean curd, soy sauce, *nam pla*, and lime juice, and fry until shrimps are fully pink. Add 2 eggs and stir to break them up. Add noodles, bean sprouts, and sugar, mix, and heat through. Put half of mixture on hot dish, break remaining 2 eggs in the middle, cover with remaining half of mixture, and garnish as desired, with fresh coriander leaves, chives, peppers, pickled garlic. Add more *nam pla*, soy sauce, or sugar to taste. Makes 6 to 8 servings.

LA TIENG
(Shrimp Nets)

If you like to make filled omelets or crêpes, this lattice-work fantasy belongs in your repertory.

- ½ pound shrimps, shelled, deveined, and diced
- 10 water chestnuts, diced
- 1 hot green chili pepper, seeded and minced
- 1 tablespoon ground coriander
- 1 tablespoon nam pla (fish sauce)
- ½ cup lard or cooking oil
- 4 eggs, well beaten
- Fresh coriander leaves or parsley

Combine shrimps, water chestnuts, chili pepper, coriander, and *nam pla,* and fry in 2 tablespoons of the lard until shrimps turn pink. Cool. Heat remainder of lard in a clean pan, dip your fingers into the beaten eggs, and holding fingers apart, move your hand across the pan, back and forth, up and down, letting the egg drip down to make a net. When firmly cooked, lift out and drain. Place chopped coriander in the center of the net, add 2 tablespoons shrimp mixture, and fold up into squares. The nets should be large enough to allow folding, but thin. Larger ones may take more filling. Makes 4 servings.

YAM OF ROSES

Yam means salad, which in Thailand, as in her neighboring countries, may be made of meats, vegetables (cooked and raw), fruits, salad greens, and flowers—usually dressed not with oil and vinegar, but with fish or soy sauce, garlic, and other herbs. Here is an exotic salad that can be made by anybody who has a rose garden where the roses are unsprayed.

- 1 onion, chopped
- 6 garlic cloves, sliced (or to taste*)
- 2 tablespoons lard or cooking oil
- 2 tablespoons nam pla (fish sauce)
- 3 tablespoons fresh lime juice
- 3 tablespoons brown sugar
- 3 cups diced cooked chicken
- ¾ cup chopped peanuts
- 10 roses

Fry onion and garlic in lard until very brown. Mix fish sauce, lime juice, and sugar, add chicken and peanuts, and let stand for 5 minutes. Remove petals from roses, wash if necessary (they *must* be unsprayed), and mix with chicken. Sprinkle with fried onion and garlic. Makes 4 servings.

*You may want to experiment with less.

KHANOM MO KAENG
(Taro-Coconut-Egg Custard)

One of the popular sweet dishes in Thailand is sankhaya, a coconut-egg custard said to be of Portuguese origin, baked and served in whole coconuts. It's a lot of work to saw open, peel, and scrape coconuts, and here is an equally delicious custard to bake in a dish. If you can't get prepared taro root (Hawaiian poi), use any mashed beans.

- ½ cup taro root or cooked pea beans, well mashed
- 3 eggs
- 1½ cups coconut milk
- ¼ teaspoon salt
- ⅓ cup sugar

Beat all ingredients together well and strain into a greased dish or individual custard cups. Place in pan of hot water and bake in preheated slow oven (300° F.) for 45 minutes to 1 hour, or until set. Makes 4 servings.

FOI TONG
(Shreds of Gold)

- 10 egg yolks
- Half of 1 egg white
- 1½ cups sugar
- 1½ cups water

Strain egg yolks through fine sieve; add egg white and mix well. Boil sugar and water to make a syrup that threads (232° F. on a candy thermometer). Reduce heat, and using a cone or funnel with a small hole, drop threads of egg into hot syrup, making either rectangles or little nests. If the syrup is very hot the shreds will get hard when they cool; if less hot, they can be gathered up and folded when taken out. (Thais eat them both ways.) Makes 6 to 8 servings.

BURMA

HINGHA
(Shrimp and Squash Soup)

- 2 large onions, sliced
- 2 teaspoons ngapi (shrimp paste), optional*
- 2 tablespoons sesame oil
- 2 cups sliced white squash
- ½ pound shrimps, peeled, deveined, and minced
- 4 garlic cloves, mashed
- 3 cups water
- 8 peppercorns, crushed
- Salt

Sauté the onions and *ngapi,* if used, in the oil. Add squash, shrimps and shrimp shells, garlic, and water. Cover and boil until squash is cooked. Remove shrimp shells and stir in peppercorns. Add salt to taste. Makes 6 servings.

■ **Variations**—Use noodles, cabbage, or any other greens in place of squash, and fried or broiled fish instead of shrimps.
*The shrimp paste adds a very strong fish flavor. You may want to experiment with this ingredient.

PAZUNDOK NGAPI GYAW
(Fresh Tomato Balachong)

Balachong is the oily spicy dried shrimp relish the Burmese like to eat with plain rice and many other foods. It can be bottled and kept for weeks. The following version, using fresh shrimps and tomatoes, tastes even better but won't keep. Use it in combination with rice, curries, and vegetables.

- 1 cup finely sliced onions
- ½ cup coarsely sliced garlic (or less to taste*)
- ½ cup sesame oil or any cooking oil
- 1 teaspoon crushed red pepper
- 1 teaspoon ground turmeric
- 1 cup chopped fresh shrimps
- 1 cup peeled sliced tomatoes
- ¼ cup vinegar
- 2 teaspoons ngapi (shrimp paste), or anchovy paste

Fry onions and garlic in oil until golden. Add pepper and turmeric and fry for another 2 minutes. Add shrimps, tomatoes, and vinegar with *ngapi* mixed into it, and fry quickly until shrimps are fully pink. Use warm or cold. Makes 10 or more servings.

HMOH NGA BAUNG
(Fish and Mushroom Soufflé)

- ½ small onion, minced
- ½ garlic clove, minced
- ¼ cup butter or sesame oil
- ½ pound mushrooms, chopped
- Salt
- 1 pound fish fillets
- 1 tablespoon soy sauce
- ½ cup coconut cream, or evaporated milk
- 3 eggs, yolks and whites beaten separately
- Pepper

WOMAN'S DAY

Fry onion and garlic in butter for 2 minutes. Add mushrooms and salt to taste, and fry quickly until soft. Place fish fillets on bottom of greased baking dish, add soy sauce, and cover evenly with mushroom mixture, then with coconut cream. Bake in preheated hot oven (400° F.) for 10 minutes. Season egg yolks to taste with salt and pepper, mix with beaten whites, and spread over fish. Return to oven and bake until brown. Makes 4 servings.

ATHAE CHIN GYAW
(Deviled Liver)

- 2 teaspoons soy sauce
- ½ teaspoon ngapi (shrimp paste), optional
- ½ teaspoon crushed red pepper
- ½ teaspoon ground turmeric
- 1 tablespoon tamarind juice
- 1 pound calf's liver, cubed
- ¼ cup sesame oil or any cooking oil
- 2 onions, sliced

Combine soy sauce, *ngapi*, if used, red pepper, turmeric, and tamarind juice, and rub over liver cubes. Allow to marinate for 15 minutes, then fry cubes quickly in 2 tablespoons oil on high heat. Garnish with onions fried dark brown in remaining oil. Makes 4 servings.

VIETNAM

PHO
(Ginger Beef Soup with Noodles)

- Soup bones with marrow
- 1½ to 2 pounds beef for stew
- 1 tablespoon sliced gingerroot
- 2 onions, sliced
- 2 garlic cloves, sliced
- Water
- ½ pound pea-starch noodles or fine egg noodles
- 2 tablespoons nuoc mam (fish sauce)
- ½ teaspoon pepper

Place the bones, meat, gingerroot, onions, and garlic in 3 to 4 cups water to cover. Cook over low heat until meat is tender, about 1½ hours. (The *nuoc mam* may be put in at the beginning, but many people prefer to minimize the odor by adding it at the end with the pepper.) Cook the pea-starch noodles in boiling water for 30 minutes and let them stand in the same water for another 30 minutes. Drain the noodles and strain the meat broth. Add noodles to broth together with *nuoc mam* and pepper. Chop the meat and marrow and return to broth. Bring to boil, adjust seasonings, and serve. Please note that these noodles are not made mushy by overcooking; they can be cooked for an additional hour without harm. If fine egg noodles are substituted, limit the cooking to 2 minutes in the broth, or just long enough to make them tender. Makes 8 servings.

CHA TOM
(Vietnamese Omelet)

- ½ pound raw shrimps, peeled, deveined, and chopped
- ½ pound cooked pork, diced small
- 12 mussels, chopped
- ½ cup minced mushrooms
- ¼ cup chopped scallions
- ¼ teaspoon crushed red pepper
- 2 tablespoons chopped fresh basil
- 1 tablespoon chopped fresh mint
- 2 tablespoons nuoc mam (fish sauce)
- 8 eggs, beaten
- ¾ cup peanut oil

Combine all ingredients except oil and mix well. Heat 2 tablespoons oil in frying pan, pour in one-sixth of mixture, and cook over low heat until eggs are set. Keep in warming oven while making remaining omelets. Serve with additional *nuoc mam* for dipping bites. Makes 6 servings.

SWEET STICKY RICE

Glutinous or sticky rice is eaten extensively in Vietnam and all her neighboring countries. People like it boiled and fried, hot and cold, sweet and unsweetened, for dinner and for breakfast. Plain boiled leftover sticky rice can be formed into any desired shape, deep fried until golden-brown, sprinkled with salt and pepper, and eaten as a snack.

- 1 cup glutinous rice
- Water
- Salt
- ¼ cup brown sugar
- ½ cup shredded coconut, toasted

Wash rice until water runs clear. Cook in 6 cups boiling water for 30 minutes, or until tender; drain. Add salt to taste. Sprinkle with brown sugar and toss lightly with fork. Sprinkle on coconut. Makes 6 to 8 servings.

LAOS

KAENG PHED
(Fish Stew)

- 1 garlic clove, minced
- 2 onions, sliced
- 1 hot green chili pepper, seeded and minced
- 2 tablespoons peanut oil or lard
- 1 tablespoon paprika
- 1 pound solid fish such as swordfish, cut into 1-inch pieces
- 2 potatoes, sliced and parboiled
- 3 cups coconut milk
- 1 tablespoon fish sauce
- ¼ teaspoon pepper

Fry garlic, onion, and chili pepper in oil until golden. Add paprika and fish; sauté for 2 minutes. Add potatoes and coconut milk, cover, and cook over low heat for 15 minutes. Stir in fish sauce and pepper. Makes 4 to 6 servings.

NHAM
(Salad)

- 1 cup cooked chicken, shredded
- ½ cup bean curd, cubed and fried
- 3 large roasted peppers, shredded
- 2 medium cucumbers, seeded and sliced
- ½ cup chopped fresh mint
- ¼ cup ground peanuts
- ¼ cup minced scallions
- 2 tablespoons fish sauce
- 2 tablespoons fresh lemon juice
- ¼ cup coconut cream or evaporated milk
- 2 teaspoons sugar
- Fresh coriander leaves or parsley

Place chicken, bean curd, peppers, and cucumbers in a salad bowl. Mix together mint, peanuts, scallions, fish sauce, lemon juice, coconut cream, and sugar to make dressing. Pour over ingredients in bowl and toss. Garnish with coriander leaves. Shredded lettuce and tomatoes may be added if desired. Makes 4 servings.

CAMBODIA

MOEUN SNGO
(Chicken Soup)

- 1 frying chicken (2 to 3 pounds), cut through bone into small pieces
- 2 tablespoons raw rice
- 2 garlic cloves, minced
- 2 scallions, chopped
- ½ teaspoon monosodium glutamate
- 1 tablespoon fish sauce
- Water
- 1 teaspoon sugar
- ¼ cup fresh lime juice
- ½ teaspoon pepper
- Salt
- 2 tablespoons chopped fresh coriander leaves or parsley

Place first 6 ingredients in about 6 cups water to cover and simmer until chicken is tender. Lift out any bones and skin that have come loose, and stir in sugar, lime juice, and pepper; add salt to taste. Add coriander just before serving, and provide small cups of additional fish sauce for dipping chicken. Makes 6 servings.

TRAI CAY
(Cambodian Mixed Fruits)

- 1 cup canned litchis, drained and halved
- 1 cup diced fresh pineapple
- ½ cup diced peeled grapefruit sections
- ½ cup diced peeled orange sections
- 1 teaspoon fresh lime juice
- 2 tablespoons syrup from litchis or any sugar syrup

Mix all ingredients and chill for at least 1 hour. Makes 4 servings.

Charlotte Russe

Hoppin' John

Sherried Sweet Potatoes

SOUTHERN COOKERY

Beef-Okra Soup

Shrimps de Jonghe

Southern Cookery

by

Marion W. Flexner

What is meant by "the South?" Strictly speaking, it includes twelve states south of the Mason-Dixon Line: West Virginia, Virginia, Kentucky, Tennessee, North Carolina, South Carolina, Georgia, Alabama, Mississippi, Arkansas, Louisiana, and Florida. Maryland, although considered southern by many Southerners, is listed with the northern states, and Texas, which they would also like to claim, with the western.

Southern cooking is not uniform and never has been. There are about as many different cuisines as there are states. In Colonial Virginia the menus and dishes were almost exact replicas of those served in England because the early settlers were mainly British. Later, due to the influence of Thomas Jefferson, George Washington, and other prominent Virginians, French food and French chefs were imported; but throughout the eighteenth century and early years of the nineteenth, British foods, with perhaps a French accent, predominated. Gradually immigrants from Ireland, Scotland, Germany, Holland, Switzerland, Italy, and Spain drifted into the southern part of the New World and remained to become citizens. Naturally they brought with them their own recipes. They were often altered when certain ingredients were not available and substitutions of local foodstuffs had to be made. Thus new dishes were created which in time came to be associated with a particular region.

SOUTHERN COOKERY

There was another factor which gave distinction to Southern cooking. Until 1860 practically all labor in the South was slave labor and most of the slaves came from Africa. They had their own ideas about seasoning and when they prepared certain dishes in this new land, they added their own flavorings, often producing culinary masterpieces. The Creole cookery of Louisiana is a happy merging of French, Spanish, and African cuisines. Slaves carried benne (sesame) seeds to South Carolina, not only because they liked the taste, but also because they thought they brought good luck. They have remained in favor ever since. In the Florida Keys the cooking is still Spanish with a hint of the West Indies.

All Southerners have a penchant for corn (maize), either fresh, or dried and ground into meal—a heritage from the original Americans, the Indians.

A source of gourmet cooking in antebellum days was to be found on the palatial riverboats, esperially those plying the Mississippi between St. Louis and New Orleans. Here the best the country had to offer was put before the passengers. While merchants and businessmen were supposed to be the chief patrons, many ladies and gentlemen made the journey just for the food. We may be sure the recipes were reproduced in home kitchens when the travelers returned.

In the southern "Black Belt," the soil was so fertile it produced an infinite variety of vegetables and fruits. Southern rivers teemed with fish: succulent catfish, fat perch and bream, black bass (called trout by the natives). From the bayous of Louisiana to Chesapeake Bay, in fact wherever the land touched the sea, came shellfish: oysters, shrimp, crabs, crayfish. The woods were full of game: deer, wild ducks and geese, partridges, doves, and even wild turkey. Wines and other delicacies were imported from Europe, for many wealthy Southerners made annual trips abroad, often returning with foreign cooks. One famous Kentuckian, General William Preston, American Minister to Spain in the 1870's, took his Negro cook to Paris and apprenticed her to an internationally known French chef.

The average person, even today, is apt to think of the South as it was during the peak of its prosperity, roughly speaking from 1820 to 1860. Those were the days when "Cotton was King"; when a small minority of the population, the fabulously rich southern planters and their families, lived in almost feudal luxury in their Georgian or Greek Revival houses on their vast estates. They set such lavish tables, no wonder contemporary writers referred to them as "groaning boards."

Each plantation was, as a rule, a self-sustaining village with life centering around the "big house." Overseers managed the farms and crops. Cattle, sheep, pigs, goats, and fowl were raised and slaughtered for the main table. There was always a dairy where fresh milk, thick cream, sweet butter, and buttermilk were on hand. These were stored in the springhouse along with other perishables before ice boxes were invented.

The mistress of the mansion did no menial labor, but it was no small task for her to plan the meals and direct the household staff. All preserving of fruits and vegetables was done in the home kitchen, usually a brick or stone building, separated from the main dwelling because of fire hazards. Here meat was cured, pickled, and cooked. Sides of beef, mutton, or pig would be skewered and turned on a spit by hand, as they were roasted in the huge open fireplace. Brick ovens, built into the kitchen wall, were used for baking. Bundles of fagots would be burned in the ovens until the bricks were sufficiently heated, then the ashes would be raked out and the dish to be cooked popped in. An iron door would be securely closed. The food remained until the cook, who knew by experience that it was done, removed it. There were no oven regulators then or even in later years when wood-burning iron ranges had been introduced. Cook books suggested that one bake in a quick (hot), moderate, or slow oven.

It took dozens of slaves to run such a menage. Consider what it meant to keep open house the year round for visiting friends and relatives who thought nothing of dropping in for a visit of a week, a month, or even a year. And why not? There was always a ball or a barbecue or a picnic somewhere in the neighborhood, and if nothing had been planned the hostess could always send out invitations to a soirée. This in turn would produce a series of entertainments. Thus it went throughout the year.

After the Civil War, or War Between the States as southerners prefer to call it, "hard times came a'knocking" at many doors. The 1860's and 1870's were lean years, money was scarce, certain foods were costly. A tradition of fine living had been established but was almost impossible to maintain. However, the large majority managed to survive in spite of reverses, due, in a large measure, to the ingenuity of the Southern housewife and her faithful Negro cook. Many an impoverished explanter now sat down to a hearty meal of corn bread and molasses, collard greens or blackeye peas, simmered for hours with a hunk of smoked hog jowl or salt pork, formerly considered fare fit for slaves but not for their masters. This was often washed down with sassafras tea, especially in the spring. Grits were pressed into service, rice, potatoes, yams, peanuts, and all the inexpensive local fruits and vegetables. Watermelon was cheap and delicious and when the luscious pink meat had been eaten, the thick rind was turned into crunchy sweet pickles. Ground or Jerusalem artichokes grew wild along the roadsides. The delicate roots were scraped, boiled, and served with butter, chilled and made into salad with French dressing, or pickled with vinegar, sugar, turmeric, and spices. A large soupbone with enough meat for the family could be bought for a dime and often the butcher threw in a whole calf's liver, gratis, with the meat order. Small farmers hawked their produce through the streets of the sleepy southern towns: eggs, chickens, ducks, cabbage, beans, peas, peaches, etc.

By the turn of the century conditions had improved considerably throughout the South. While menus were shortened and the number of dishes in a single meal reduced, food was still bountiful according to present standards.

Today young homemakers in the South, as in other parts of the United States, depend largely on frozen, canned, packaged, or ready-cooked foods to tide them over. Seldom is a recipe made from scratch. The modern generation is also diet conscious and the taste for highly spiced sauces, rich desserts, and pastries has diminished. Also the lack of domestic help has made entertaining informal. But in the first two decades of the present century this was not yet the case.

In those days breakfast was still a hearty meal, and Sunday breakfast was special. To the usual omelet or scrambled egg and bacon platter would be added, perhaps, boiled spareribs, "crisped" under the flame, accompanied by a sauceboat of savory brown onion gravy and a bowl of snowy grits, doused with melted butter. There might be "fried steak," top round dusted with flour and salt and pepper and pounded thin, then sautéed in bacon drippings or butter, covered with water, and simmered until tender. Again fried chicken or chicken livers would be the *pièce de résistance*. Always the meal would end with waffles or pancakes with molasses or preserves as a topping.

Dinner was served anywhere between two and three in the afternoon depending on the whim of the cook. This was the big meal of the day, and the men came home from work for it. The first course would invariably be soup. Gumbo, vegetable, "carcass soup" made from bones, skin, and scraps of meat and gravy from the roasted chicken or turkey, white and black bean soup, were some of the favorites. Mock turtle or oxtail, well laced with sherry, port, or Madeira might appear for company. Most people knew little and cared less about balanced diets and drew small distinction between green and starchy vegetables. Thus potatoes and rice in some form appeared on every dinner table. But corn was the preferred vegetable and was prepared in numerous ways: boiled in the green shucks, parched, fried, sautéed in butter with bits of minced green pepper, stewed with okra and tomatoes, turned into a sweet custardy pudding, even added to cornmeal muffins. Green beans cooked with bacon or hambone and scraps, fried okra, puréed cymlings with cream and butter, fried or stuffed eggplant, tiny new peas were also well liked. Shellfish was popular. Whenever the hard-shell crabs were on the market, platters of the boiled crustaceans would be put on the table, with a nutcracker and a pitcher of mild vinegar. Lump or backfin crabmeat was mixed with various ingredients and stuffed into the crab shells to be browned under the flame, dumped into a Newburg sauce, or folded into rich Mornay sauce made with mild yellow cheese. Sharp yellow cheese (not Parmesan) was grated over the top and the whole browned in the grill before being brought, bubbling, to the hungry family and guests. Oysters were served in every form: raw on the half shell with cocktail sauce, fried, baked, pickled, or scalloped, the last a constant companion for roast fowl. For distinguished company there might be a roasted turkey, dished up with rich giblet gravy, a roast of beef or leg of lamb. But for home folks ham or roast pork, always escorted to the table with dark orange-colored yams, baked in their jackets and oozing their own honey, was more likely to be served.

A meal wasn't a meal without hot breads and they were numerous: beaten biscuits, the dough given a hundred licks with a flatiron, turned as one would puff paste, beaten until the surface blistered; biscuits made with lard, soda, and buttermilk, or lard, baking powder, and sweet milk; Sally Lunn; southern "light rolls," crusty on the outside, their insides light as milkweed down. Corn breads were relished in the dining room as well as in the kitchen and they were legion: skillet corn bread, baked in the oven until brown and crunchy outside, moist inside; hoecakes; corn pones or dodgers; crackling corn muffins or sticks; corn (pan) cakes; spoon bread. All were made of white cornmeal without sugar. Sugar in corn bread was anathema to Southerners!

Desserts differed with the season and the day of the week. When the weather was cold, orange-lemon wine jelly, prune or date soufflé, rice or bread pudding, baked custard with caramel sauce were likely to appear.

Pies alternated with puddings and soufflés. There might be syrupy wild blackberry with a hint of lemon and cinnamon, topped by a cloud of ground almond meringue; huckleberry made by the same recipe or put between two flaky crusts; custard, sliced or shredded apple, strawberry with latticework across the top, peach, spiced sweet potato, lemon soufflé, chess in a dozen ways; pecan—these were some examples of Southern pies.

On Sunday the accepted dessert was ice cream and cake, both homemade. Fig, peach, blackberry, and strawberry ice cream were served when the weather was warm. Chocolate, caramel, vanilla, French bisque, and tutti-frutti (chopped crystallized fruits and rinds, soaked overnight in rum or brandy, then added to the bisque mixture before freezing) appeared when winter winds blew.

Cake making was an art indulged in by all female members of the Southern household. Blackberry-jam cake with caramel icing; rich chocolate cake with real fudge as frosting; 1-2-3-4 cake with numerous variations of which marble and layered jelly cakes are perhaps best known; gold cake; Lane cake; spice cake with butterscotch frosting; spongecake, angel food flavored with rosewater or vanilla; coconut cake with boiled white icing; poundcake; hickory nut and pecan cakes; fruitcake; white cake with dozens of fillings and frostings—these were only a few in a large repertoire.

"The South," some one remarked recently, "is not really a particular grouping of states, but a state of mind." That may be true, but Southern cooking is real enough, as those who were brought up on it can testify.

Southern Cook Book

SOUPS

BEEF-OKRA SOUP

- 2 pounds lean raw chuck beef, diced
- ¼ pound butter or margarine
- 4 cups (two 1-pound cans) tomatoes
- 1½ pounds fresh or frozen okra, cut into thin slices, crosswise
- Boiling water
- 2 cups cooked Lima beans
- 2 cups diced cooked chicken
- Salt and pepper to taste

In deep kettle, brown meat in butter. Add tomatoes and okra. Cover with boiling water and simmer, covered, over medium heat for 1 hour. Then add 4 cups boiling water. Bring to boiling point. Lower heat and simmer, covered, stirring frequently. Skim soup as it boils. Cook until okra and tomatoes are soft. Add the cooked Lima beans and diced chicken. Season with salt and pepper. Makes 8 to 10 servings.

FRIAR'S CHICKEN SOUP OR STEW

- 2 pounds veal knuckles with at least ½ pound of meat on bones
- 1 teaspoon white pepper
- 1 tablespoon salt
- 1 chicken or rabbit (about 2½ pounds), cut into pieces
- 2 tablespoons chopped parsley
- 2 eggs, well beaten
- Extra white pepper, salt, and ground mace
- Cooked rice

Break up the knuckles of veal; season with white pepper and salt. Put knuckles in deep kettle and add enough cold water to cover bones. Simmer, covered, for about 1½ hours. Drop chicken pieces into kettle, add parsley, and bring again to boil. Simmer slowly until meat and chicken are very tender and almost falling from bones. Remove meat and chicken and take meat from bones of both. Cube meat and return meat to kettle. Stir beaten eggs into the soup and remove immediately from heat or the eggs will curdle. Season with pepper, salt, and mace. Serve in soup plates over cooked rice. Makes 8 to 10 servings.

MAIN DISHES

CRAB CAKES

- ¼ cup butter or margarine
- ¼ cup all-purpose flour
- 1 cup plus 1 tablespoon milk

½ teaspoon powdered mustard
2 teaspoons water
1 pound (3 cups) crabmeat
1¼ teaspoons salt, or salt to taste
1 teaspoon fresh lemon juice
½ teaspoon finely chopped onion
⅛ teaspoon pepper
   Fine dry bread crumbs
1 large egg, beaten
   Fat or oil for deep frying

Melt butter in small saucepan; stir in flour. Cook until mixture bubbles around the sides of pan. Remove from heat and add 1 cup milk gradually. Cook, stirring constantly, over low heat until smooth and thick. Set aside. Mix mustard with water and let stand for flavor to develop while preparing remaining ingredients. Break up crabmeat with tips of fingers or chop fine with knife. Add to sauce along with mustard, salt, lemon juice, onion, and pepper. Mix well. Shape into 8 patties ½ inch thick and 3 inches in diameter. Roll in bread crumbs, then in egg beaten with 1 tablespoon milk, and then in crumbs again. Let patties stand for a few minutes to set crumbs. Fry in deep hot fat (375°F. on a frying thermometer), or brown in shallow hot fat in heavy skillet. Drain on paper towels. Serve hot. Makes 4 servings.

SHRIMPS DE JONGHE

2 pounds shrimps, cooked, peeled, and deveined
¾ cup white wine
½ teaspoon pepper
4 tablespoons butter
1 cup dry bread crumbs
2 garlic cloves, crushed
½ teaspoon salt
   Finely chopped parsley

Spread the shrimps evenly over the bottom of greased baking pan. Add wine and pepper. Dot with 1 tablespoon butter. Combine bread crumbs, garlic, and salt with remaining butter which has been melted. Sprinkle evenly over shrimps. Sprinkle with parsley. Bake in preheated moderate oven (350°F.) for 20 minutes. Serve immediately. Makes 6 servings.

LOBSTER-MUFFIN SANDWICHES

1½ cups lobster meat, canned or fresh
1 teaspoon Worcestershire
   Dash of hot pepper sauce
   White Sauce
6 English muffins, split into halves and buttered
12 thin squares of Swiss cheese
   Buttered bread crumbs
   Parmesan cheese

Flake the lobster meat. Stir in seasonings. Add enough White Sauce to make a stiff mixture. Spread muffin halves lightly with butter. Toast until slightly browned. Cover with lobster mixture. Lay on each muffin a square of cheese; sprinkle with bread crumbs and Parmesan cheese. Put into preheated hot oven (400°F.) for 10 to 15 minutes, or until cheese has melted and crumbs are golden-brown. Serve hot. Makes 6 servings.

White Sauce

3 tablespoons butter
3 tablespoons all-purpose flour
1½ cups milk
½ teaspoon salt
   Pepper to taste

Melt butter in small saucepan; stir in flour to make a smooth *roux*. Slowly add milk and stir until thick. Season with salt and pepper. Makes about 1½ cups.

BARBECUED BEEF

5 to 6 pounds of any cut of beef roast
1 tablespoon pepper
2 cups dry red wine
1 teaspoon salt
½ teaspoon monosodium glutamate
2 cups beef bouillon or consommé
1 to 1½ cups barbecue sauce

Rub the roast well with pepper. Marinate meat in wine for 12 hours, turning frequently. Drain meat; reserve wine. Heat a heavy roasting pan with cover and sear the meat until it is browned on all sides. Sprinkle with salt and monosodium glutamate. In another saucepan heat together the reserved wine and bouillon. Pour over the meat. Cover pan and roast in preheated slow oven (300°F.) for 4 hours. Pour off excess fat. Remove roast from pan and chop meat into bite-size pieces. Add barbecue sauce to pan drippings. Pour enough of pan mixture into chopped beef to make it moist. Reserve sauce. Serve on split toasted hamburger buns or serve in a bowl with French garlic bread. Serve remaining sauce separately. Makes 6 to 8 servings.

BAKED COUNTRY CURED HAM, NORTH-CAROLINA STYLE

Wash an uncooked 10- to 12-pound country-cured ham thoroughly. If ham has been cured in a great deal of salt, soak overnight in cold water to cover. Wipe dry. Remove skin and trim off excess fat, leaving ½-inch layer over the top.

Mix 1 cup brown sugar with 1 tablespoon powdered mustard and rub over the surface of ham. Mix all-purpose flour with enough water to make a dough of drop-biscuit consistency, using about one-half to two-thirds as much water as flour. Spread this dough over the ham, completely covering it.

Place ham on a rack in a large shallow baking pan, fat side up. Bake in preheated slow oven (325°F.) for 25 to 30 minutes per pound. Remove blanket of dough. Score ham fat and stud with cloves. Dribble with molasses, honey, light corn syrup, melted apple or currant jelly, or the juice from spiced peaches or pears. Bake for 30 minutes longer, or until browned and glazed. Makes 24 servings.

Note: Do not try this method of baking ham on one that has been precooked. The dough will not adhere to the ham.

BAKED STUFFED HAM STEAKS WITH SWEET POTATO-SAUSAGE STUFFING

1 cup mashed cooked sweet potatoes
3 cups toasted bread cubes
⅓ cup finely chopped celery
¼ cup finely chopped onion
4 sausage links
¾ teaspoon salt
¾ teaspoon poultry seasoning
1½ tablespoons butter or margarine, melted
2 center cut fully cooked ham steaks, each ½ inch thick

Combine sweet potatoes, bread cubes, celery, and onion. Cut sausage links into ½-inch pieces, brown and add to the mixture, discarding the fat. Blend in salt, poultry seasoning, and butter. Slash fat around ham steaks to prevent curling and place 1 steak in a greased baking dish. Spread with the stuffing. Top with remaining steak. Cover and bake in preheated slow oven (325°F.) for 30 minutes. Remove cover and bake for 30 minutes longer. Makes 6 servings.

BRUNSWICK STEW FOR A CROWD

4- pound stewing chicken
2- pound beef shank
1- pound veal shank
1- pound pork shank or spareribs
2½ quarts cold water
2 tablespoons salt
½ teaspoon whole black peppercorns
3 whole pods red pepper, each 2 inches long
2 cups diced onion
1 cup diced raw potatoes
1 cup green beans, cut into 1-inch pieces
1 cup diced celery
2 cups butter beans or Lima beans
2 cups corn, cut off the cob (fresh, canned whole kernel, or frozen)
3 quarts diced fresh tomatoes or 10½ cups (three 1-pound, 13-ounce cans) tomatoes
1 teaspoon ground black pepper
¼ cup butter or margarine

Wash and cut chicken into quarters. Place in an 8- to 10-quart kettle with remaining meat, the water, salt, peppercorns, and red peppers. Cover and cook slowly for 3 hours, or until the meat falls off the bones. Remove and discard bones. Cut chicken and meat into cubes and return to stock. Add vegetables. Cover and cook gently for 1 hour, stirring frequently to prevent scorching. Stir in ground black pepper and butter. Serve hot as the main dish or with barbecued meat. Makes approximately 1½ gallons, or 12 servings.

Note: Both Brunswick, Georgia, and Brunswick, Virginia, claim to have originated Brunswick stew. This version of Brunswick stew is popular in the states in the deep South. It resembles Kentucky Burgoo, both of which are said to have been made with squirrel in addition to the meats in the recipe above. Because so many ingredients go into this stew, it is difficult to make it in a small quantity. Fortunately it freezes very well.

SOUTHERN FRIED CHICKEN

1 frying chicken (2 to 2½ pounds)
½ teaspoon pepper
2½ teaspoons salt
¾ cup all-purpose flour
Fat for frying
Cream Gravy
Hot cooked rice

Wash chicken and cut into serving pieces (2 drumsticks, 2 thighs, 2 wings, 2 sides, 2 breast pieces, wishbone, back, neck, gizzard, and liver). Combine pepper, salt, and flour in a medium-size paper bag. Add a few pieces of chicken at a time. Shake the bag to coat the chicken well. Fry chicken over moderate heat in ¼ to 1 inch of hot fat in a heavy skillet, turning chicken as it browns on the underneath side, adding more fat if needed. Cooking time is 40 to 50 minutes. Drain chicken on paper towels if chicken is greasy. Serve with Cream Gravy and rice. Makes 4 to 6 servings.

Cream Gravy

Pour off fat left in skillet. Return ¼ cup to the skillet. Add ¼ cup of the seasoned flour left in the bag used for coating if enough is left. If not, add additional ¼ cup all-purpose flour and blend with the fat, scraping the brown bits left in the bottom of skillet. Brown lightly. Stir in 2½ cups milk or 1 cup light cream and 1½ cups milk or water. Stir and cook until mixture is of medium thickness. Serve over the rice, never over the chicken. Makes 6 servings.

VARIATIONS IN PREPARING SOUTHERN FRIED CHICKEN

There are many versions of Southern Fried Chicken. Here are a few:
■ Fry chicken in a small amount of fat.
■ Fry chicken in 1 to 2 inches of fat.
■ Fry chicken in enough fat to cover.
■ Fry chicken in deep fat.
■ Some cooks fry chicken in half lard and half butter, or half vegetable shortening and half butter, or all vegetable shortening.
■ Some cooks dredge chicken with cornmeal rather than flour or use half flour and half cornmeal; others dredge chicken with flour seasoned with salt and pepper.

Still others prefer to add the seasoning to the chicken and let it stand overnight for seasoning to penetrate the chicken.
■ Some cooks wipe chicken dry before dredging while some prefer to dredge wet chicken with flour. Many cooks specify dipping chicken into buttermilk before dredging, or even soaking chicken in milk for 1 hour before rolling in flour.
■ Many specify keeping the cover on while cooking, removing it 5 to 10 minutes before cooking time is up to crisp the skin. Some even cook the chicken in a little water after the chicken has browned. This is not necessary if a young tender chicken is being fried.

MISSISSIPPI "SHUSHED" EGGS

Allow 2 eggs and ½ teaspoon butter for each serving. Brown butter lightly in a heavy skillet. Break eggs into a bowl, add salt and pepper to taste, and beat only until yolks and whites are barely mixed. Pour into the skillet with the browned butter. Stir and cook only until eggs are set. Serve with panfried ham, sausage cakes, or bacon, and hot biscuits, waffles, or pancakes.

VEGETABLES

MUSTARD GREENS WITH IRISH POTATOES

White potatoes are known as Irish potatoes in the South. When just potatoes are mentioned, Southerners assume that sweet potatoes are meant.

2 ounces salt pork
1 inch of boiling water
12 small or 6 medium-size new potatoes
2 pounds fresh tender mustard greens
1½ teaspoons salt
½ teaspoon sugar
¼ teaspoon pepper

Cut pork into thin slices and simmer, covered, in 1 inch of boiling water for 40 to 50 minutes, or until pork is tender. Wash and scrape potatoes. Add to pork; cook small potatoes for 5 minutes, medium potatoes for 10 minutes, adding more boiling water if necessary. Wash mustard greens thoroughly. Cut into 2- to 3-inch lengths and add to pork and potatoes. Add salt and sugar. Cover and cook for 15 minutes, or until mustard greens are tender. Do not overcook. Add pepper. Toss lightly and serve hot with corn bread or corn sticks. Makes 6 servings.

HOPPIN JOHN

1 cup dried blackeye peas (field peas)
3 cups water
1 teaspoon salt
1 medium-size onion, diced
1 ham hock or 2 ounces salt pork, diced
¼ teaspoon pepper
Dash of cayenne
1 cup uncooked long-grain rice
1 tablespoon butter or margarine

Pick over and wash peas. Soak overnight in the 3 cups water. The next day, drain, measuring the water, and adding enough to make 3 cups. Add this to the soaked peas along with salt, onion, and ham hock. Cover, bring to boiling point, and simmer for about 1¼ hours, or until peas are tender and only a small amount of the liquid is left. Pick meat from the ham hock if one is used. Discard ham bone and add meat to the peas along with pepper and cayenne. Cook rice according to package directions. Add butter and mix lightly with the peas. Cook for 2 or 3 minutes for flavors to blend. Serve hot with corn bread. Makes 8 servings.

SOUTHERN STYLE GREEN BEANS

We know that nutritionists don't approve of this method of cooking beans, but Southerners like them this way.

1½ pounds green beans
¼ pound salt pork*
1 teaspoon salt
½ teaspoon sugar
Boiling water

Remove tips from beans and break them into pieces 1 to 1½ inches long. Wash and turn beans into 2-quart saucepan. Wash and score salt pork and add to beans along with salt, sugar, and boiling water to cover. Cook beans slowly, covered, for 2 to 3 hours or until all the water has evaporated. When beans are done, there should be very little or no water left in the saucepan. Serve hot with corn bread. Makes 6 to 8 servings.

* A ham bone may be substituted for the salt pork.

FRIED OKRA

1½ pounds fresh young okra
½ teaspoon salt
¼ teaspoon pepper
½ cup yellow cornmeal
1 tablespoon all-purpose flour
About 3 tablespoons bacon drippings or shortening

Wash okra and cut off tips and stem ends. Cut pods into crosswise slices ¼ inch thick. Sprinkle with salt and pepper. Roll in cornmeal mixed with flour. Sauté in hot bacon drippings until okra is golden-brown. Serve hot. Makes 6 servings.

STEWED CORN

This is the most popular method of preparing corn in the South. In some sections this dish is called fried corn which is a misnomer.

SOUTHERN COOK BOOK

4 ears of corn
½ cup boiling water
⅓ cup milk
2 tablespoons bacon drippings
1½ teaspoons salt
½ teaspoon sugar
⅛ teaspoon pepper
1 tablespoon all-purpose flour
2 tablespoons water
1 teaspoon butter or margarine

Select full tender ears of corn. Remove shucks and silks. Cut corn from the cob with a sharp knife. Then scrape the cob with the bowl of a tablespoon to remove all milk and pulp from the cob. (The use of a tablespoon prevents the corn from splattering.)

Turn corn into a saucepan with water, milk, bacon drippings, salt, sugar, and pepper. Slowly bring to boiling point. Cook, covered, for 10 minutes, or until corn is tender, stirring occasionally. Blend flour with water until smooth and add to the corn. Stir and cook for about 1 minute or until thickened. Add butter. Serve hot as a vegetable. Makes 4 servings.

BRANDIED SWEET POTATOES

4 cups hot mashed sweet potatoes
5 tablespoons butter or margarine
¼ cup sugar
¼ teaspoon each of ground mace and ginger
½ teaspoon salt
¼ cup brandy
2 tablespoons milk or light cream
2 tablespoons grated orange rind

Combine sweet potatoes, ¼ cup butter, sugar, spices, and salt. Mix well. Stir in brandy and milk. Turn into a buttered 1-quart casserole. Brush top with remaining butter, melted, and sprinkle with orange rind. Bake in preheated moderate oven (375°F.) for 30 to 40 minutes, or until browned. Serve hot for company dinner. Makes 6 servings.

Sherried Sweet Potatoes

In the recipe above replace brandy with sherry. If desired, put potatoes on 6 pineapple slices in baking dish. Top each with a marshmallow and brown under broiler.

VIRGINIA FRIED APPLES

2 pounds cooking apples (Winesap, McIntosh, Jonathan, Rome Beauty)
3 tablespoons bacon drippings or butter or margarine
About 2 tablespoons white or brown sugar

Wash apples and core, but do not peel. Cut into slices ¼ inch thick. Heat bacon drippings in a heavy 10-inch skillet. Sprinkle with sugar to taste. Cook apples for about 20 minutes, or until brown on both sides, adding more bacon drippings if necessary to prevent sticking. Serve hot for breakfast or supper with eggs and bacon, ham, or sausage. Makes 4 servings.

BREADS AND STUFFINGS

SPOON BREAD

1 cup white cornmeal
1 teaspoon salt
2½ cups milk
2 teaspoons baking powder
2 large eggs, separated
1 tablespoon butter or margarine

Combine cornmeal, salt, and 1 cup of the milk in 1½-quart saucepan. Heat remaining milk and add. Stir and cook over direct medium-low heat until mixture is smooth and thick. Stir in baking powder. Beat egg yolks and egg whites separately. Gradually stir in egg yolks. Fold in egg whites. Melt butter in 1½-quart casserole or baking pan (9 x 9 x 2 inches). Pour the cornmeal mixture into the casserole and bake in preheated moderate oven (375°F.) for 40 minutes, or until well-puffed and brown on top. Serve at once with butter or margarine. Makes 6 servings.

BEATEN BISCUITS

2 cups sifted all-purpose flour
½ teaspoon salt
⅓ cup shortening
½ cup cold water

Sift flour and salt together. Add shortening and cut it in until mixture resembles coarse meal. Stir in water. Knead dough for half minute on lightly floured pastry board. Put dough through food chopper 8 times, using medium blade. Roll dough ¼ inch thick. Shape with a 1½-inch biscuit cutter. Put on ungreased cookie sheets. Prick tops 2 or 3 times with tines of a fork. Bake in preheated moderate oven (350°F.) for 25 to 35 minutes. Makes 2½ dozen biscuits.

Note: It is not necessary to beat beaten biscuit dough if it is put through food chopper.

Beaten Biscuits with Ham Filling

Beaten biscuits filled with spicy ham filling make a delicious teatime savory or cocktail accompaniment. To use for this purpose, follow directions below:

After dough has been put through food chopper, roll it ¼ inch thick, fold over, and roll again to ¼-inch thickness. Shape as in directions above. Do not prick tops. Biscuits will puff and centers will be hollow. Fill with a spicy Smithfield ham filling* made by mixing 1 cup ground Smithfield ham, 2 tablespoons finely chopped onion, ¼ cup dairy sour cream, ¼ teaspoon powdered mustard, and dash of pepper. (Use medium blade for grinding ham.) Makes 1 cup filling.

*Deviled ham may be used in place of Smithfield Ham Filling.

SOUTH CAROLINA BENNE-SEED BISCUITS

2 cups sifted all-purpose flour
1 tablespoon baking powder
¾ teaspoon salt
½ cup toasted benne seeds (sesame seeds)
¼ cup shortening
About ⅓ cup milk
1 tablespoon untoasted benne seeds

Sift together flour, baking powder, and salt. Blend in toasted benne seeds. (Toast benne seeds in a skillet over medium heat, stirring frequently while browning.) Add shortening and cut it in until the mixture resembles coarse crumbs. Stir in only enough milk to form a soft dough. Turn onto a lightly floured pastry board and knead dough for about 20 seconds. Roll dough ¼ to ½ inch thick. Shape with 1½-inch biscuit cutter dipped into flour. Sprinkle biscuit tops with untoasted benne seeds, patting them lightly into the dough. Place biscuits on ungreased cookie sheets. Bake in preheated very hot oven (450°F.) for 12 to 15 minutes. Serve hot. Makes 16 biscuits.

DESSERTS

LEMON SWEET-POTATO PUDDING

2 cups grated raw sweet potatoes
⅔ cup light corn syrup
1 teaspoon grated lemon rind
1½ teaspoons ground ginger
½ teaspoon ground nutmeg
¼ teaspoon salt
1½ teaspoons baking powder
2 tablespoons butter or margarine
2 large eggs, beaten
Heavy cream, whipped

Combine all ingredients except cream. Pour into a buttered 1-quart casserole. Bake in preheated moderate oven (350°F.) for 50 minutes, or until pudding is firm in center and brown on top. Serve warm with whipped cream. Makes 4 to 6 servings.

Note: Cane syrup or maple syrup can be substituted for corn syrup. The pudding will be just as delicious. In Tennessee this pudding is often topped with damson preserves.

ANGEL PARFAIT

1⅓ cups sugar
⅔ cup water
⅛ teaspoon salt
4 large egg whites
2 cups heavy cream, whipped
2 teaspoons vanilla extract

Mix sugar and water in a 1-quart saucepan. Stir and cook until syrup begins to boil. Continue to cook, without stirring, until the syrup spins a thread when dropped from the tip of a spoon. Add salt to egg whites and beat until they stand in soft stiff peaks. Gradually beat in the syrup. Fold in whipped cream and vanilla extract. Turn into 2 ice-cube trays and freeze until firm and ready to serve. Or make Angel Parfait in the old-fashioned crank ice-cream freezer. Serve in tall parfait or sherbet glasses. Makes 12 servings.

TENNESSEE BOILED CUSTARD

Chilled boiled custard served in glasses, with fresh coconut cake, is a traditional Christmas dessert in Tennessee.

- 3 large eggs, beaten lightly, or
- 6 large egg yolks
- 6 tablespoons sugar
- Dash of salt
- ¼ cup cold milk
- 2¾ cups milk, scalded
- 1 teaspoon vanilla extract, or flavor to taste with whiskey, rum, or sherry

Combine eggs, sugar, salt, and cold milk in top part of a double boiler. Gradually stir in hot milk. Stir and cook over hot, not boiling, water until custard coats a metal spoon. Remove from heat, strain, and cool. Add flavoring (vanilla, whiskey, rum, or sherry). Chill. Makes 3 cups, 4 to 6 servings.

WILD BLACKBERRY COBBLER

- 5 cups fresh wild blackberries
- ¾ cup sugar
- 2 tablespoons all-purpose flour
- ⅛ teaspoon salt
- 2 tablespoons butter or margarine
- Unbaked pastry using 1 cup all-purpose flour

Wash berries and turn into baking dish (10 x 6 x 2 inches). Combine sugar, flour, and salt and sprinkle over berries. Dot with butter. Roll pastry ⅛ inch thick to a rectangle 11 x 7 inches. Arrange over berries; turn under edges, press down firmly, and flute with tines of a fork. Cut a vent in the crust to allow for escape of steam. Bake in preheated hot oven (425° F.) for 30 minutes, or until crust is brown. Makes 6 servings.

Huckleberry Cobbler

Replace blackberries in Wild Blackberry Cobbler with wild huckleberries. Add 1 tablespoon fresh lemon juice.

Peach Cobbler

Replace blackberries in Wild Blackberry Cobbler with 6 cups sliced fresh peaches. Increase sugar to 1 cup.

Apple Cobbler

Replace peaches in Peach Cobbler with sliced apples.

CAKES AND PIES

SOUTHERN CHARLOTTE RUSSE

- About 12 ladyfingers, split
- 2 envelopes unflavored gelatin
- ½ cup cold water
- 4 large egg yolks
- ¾ cup sugar
- ¼ teaspoon salt
- 2 cups milk
- 2 teaspoons vanilla extract or ¼ cup bourbon, rum, or sherry
- 2 cups heavy cream, whipped

Line the bottom and sides of an oiled 2½-quart mold or a 7-inch springform pan with split ladyfingers and set aside. Soften gelatin in cold water and set aside. Combine egg yolks, sugar, salt, and ¼ cup of the milk in top part of a double boiler. Heat remaining milk and gradually add to egg-yolk mixture. Stir and cook over hot water (do not boil) until the custard coats a metal spoon. Remove from heat and stir in softened gelatin. Add vanilla. Cool over ice water until the mixture begins to thicken. Fold in whipped cream. Pour mixture into prepared mold. Chill until firm and ready to serve. Unmold on a pretty silver or crystal serving plate. Garnish as desired with additional whipped cream put through a pastry tube, and glacé cherries or fresh berries or other soft fruit in season. Or serve with apricots or peaches canned in heavy syrup. Makes approximately 10 servings.

LEMON-CHEESE CAKE

- 2 cups sifted all-purpose flour
- ½ teaspoon salt
- 2½ teaspoons baking powder
- 2 teaspoons vanilla extract
- ½ cup softened butter or margarine
- 1½ cups sugar
- 4 large egg whites
- ¾ cup milk
- Lemon-Cheese Filling

Sift flour with salt and baking powder and set aside. Add vanilla extract to softened butter and mix well. Gradually blend in sugar. Beat in egg whites, one at a time. Add flour mixture alternately with milk. Beat batter for half minute. Turn batter into 2 well-greased, lightly floured 9-inch round cake pans. Bake in preheated moderate oven (375°F.) for 25 to 30 minutes, or until a toothpick inserted in the center comes out clean. Cool cakes in pan for 10 minutes. Turn out onto wire racks to finish cooling. When cake is cold, spread Lemon-Cheese Filling between layers and over top layer.

Lemon-Cheese Filling

- 1 cup sugar
- ¼ teaspoon salt
- 2 teaspoons cornstarch
- 4 large egg yolks
- ⅓ cup fresh lemon juice (2 to 3 lemons)
- ¼ cup butter
- ¼ teaspoon vanilla extract
- 2 teaspoons grated lemon rind

Combine sugar, salt, and cornstarch in top part of a 1-quart double boiler. Add egg yolks and mix well. Stir in lemon juice. Cover and cook over simmering water for 20 minutes, or until mixture has thickened, stirring frequently to prevent lumping. Remove from heat and stir in butter, vanilla, and lemon rind. Chill over ice water until firm enough to spread. Makes 1¼ cups, or enough to spread over tops of two 9-inch cake layers.

Lemon-Cheese Tarts

Fill 1½-inch baked tart shells with Lemon-Cheese Filling and top with whipped cream. These are bite-size and are often served at afternoon teas. In some sections, damson preserves are spread over the filling and topped with a little whipped cream.

FRIED FRUIT PIES

- 12-ounce package dehydrated apples, apricots, or peaches
- ⅓ cup sugar or sugar to taste
- 2 tablespoons butter or margarine
- ⅛ teaspoon salt
- Rich Biscuit Dough

Cook dehydrated fruit as directed on package. Remove from heat and mash to a pulp. Add sugar, butter, and salt. Mix well. Cool. Makes about 2¼ cups filling. Divide Rich Biscuit Dough into 10 balls of equal size. Roll each into a circle ¹⁄₁₆ to ⅛ inch thick. Using a saucer as a pattern, cut dough into circles. Place ¼ cup mashed dried fruit on one side of each circle of dough. Moisten edges of dough with water. Fold over, press edges together, and crimp with tines of a fork. Prick tops to allow for escape of steam. Fry in hot shortening in heavy skillet or on a griddle, turning to brown both sides and adding additional shortening as needed. These pies are sometimes fried in deep hot fat or oil (350°F. on a frying thermometer).

Rich Biscuit Dough

- 1½ cups sifted all-purpose flour
- ¾ teaspoon salt
- 1½ teaspoons baking powder
- ¼ cup shortening
- About ½ cup milk

Sift flour with salt and baking powder. Add shortening and cut it into coarse crumb consistency. Stir in enough milk to make a soft dough. Knead on a lightly floured pastry board for about 20 seconds. Makes pastry for 10 Fried Fruit Pies.

SOUTHWESTERN COOKERY

by Sylvia Vaughn Thompson

The Spaniards who settled in what is now our Southwest settled a spectacular arid country of dazzling colors, wind-swept arroyos, and sun-drenched wilderness. If the cuisine of today's Southwest owes much to Spain, it is the geography which made it possible.

The Spaniards found in the Southwest Indians who had been living there for thousands of years—cultivated Pueblos, peaceful Hopis and Zuñis, a proud host of agrarian tribes, as well as fearless hostile Comanches and Kiowas, and raiding nomadic Apaches and Navahos—growing corn, beans, and squashes on acres of irrigated land. Maize, which the Spaniards called corn, although once strange, had become familiar to them. In their colonies to the south, the Mayan government had planted corn and beans along the roadways so that a hungry traveler might simply pluck his supper from the stalk and vine. All shapes and sizes and colors of corn that we know today and some which are no more—seven hundred varieties—were grown in New Spain at the time of Columbus. Fossilized grains of corn pollen have been found in Mexico at a geological level 80,000 years old.

The Spanish *conquistadores* had learned about more than all sorts of corn and beans from the Aztecs and Mayans of New Spain. Sweet potatoes, peanuts, cocoa beans, papayas, avocados, tomatoes, and many sweet and hot members of the pepper family were then raised in what today is Mexico. More than four hundred years ago, the Aztecs were serving flat cakes of corn called *tortillas;* chocolate *(xocoatl)* iced with snow brought down from the mountains and spiced with the seeds from the pod of wild orchids which the Spaniards renamed *vainilla;* an appetizer called *guacamole*—puréed avocado seasoned with hot red peppers; *tamallis* of cornmeal covering chopped meat, wrapped in husks of corn; and a sauce for venison made of peppers, herbs, and chocolate like the *mole* sauce today. When Cortes fled Montezuma's vengeance, he was careful to take back to Spain turkey chicks and brood hens, *cacao* beans, *vainilla* pods, seeds of the *tomatl,* and several sorts of peppers, because neither the turkey nor one plant that the Spaniards found in the New World had ever been known to Europeans.

Within half a century, these fruits and vegetables were among the best gifts the Spaniards had to bestow upon the Indians of their new colony, in what today is our great Southwest. Of their own, the Spanish added some of the foods Columbus had brought from the Old World to the New—oranges, lemons, bananas (from Columbus's stop at the Canary Islands), limes, and melons (most especially well received were the cantaloupes, so called because the Pope had developed the melon at his country place, the castle of Cantalupo). The Spaniards also brought along the first domesticated cattle, sheep, goats, hogs, and chickens the Indians had seen (imagine all those years without the egg of our familiar chicken!).

The Spanish colonists with these presents by no means meant to encourage commerce. And so the Indians of the Southwest passed another two hundred years rather as they had the previous twenty thousand. Then, independence from Spain, annexation of the Southwestern territories, cries of "gold!" in the West, and suddenly there was a rush of people across the land. Some stopped and settled in the golden Southwest instead of fighting their way to doubtful wealth on the coast. These were mostly Anglos, what native Southwesterners affectionately call people of English descent, and they brought with them a whole new color and context of tastes. They wanted to eat oats, wheat, cabbage, and potatoes. They didn't. They wanted to raise cattle and sheep with a vengeance; that they did, with the help of a new breed of man, the cowboy. Cowboys needed to eat on the move, and so the chuck wagon was invented. They liked food that stuck inside them on long cold nights, and found that the beef with chili peppers the Indians ate—add some beans to keep them going—served very well: *chile con carne*. And jerky—pieces of beef hung up to dry much as Indians hung strands of peppers in the sun—kept all winter long in a saddlebag if need be and still gave a man fuel to ride on.

As the railroad was built across the West, it brought more Anglos to build it and more cowboys to drive cattle to it from the territory. When the railroad finally crisscrossed the Southwest itself by 1895, it had the effect on the land of a key in a long-locked door. The mood of expansion and development the railroad excited spread to dam projects and reclamation projects, and suddenly, after thousands of patient years, the door swung open.

But it still is all so new. Arizona and New Mexico didn't become states of the Union, after all, until 1912. And water, if not the source of all good things at least the essential catalyst, is still scarce. Yet from her deficiencies, the Southwest's glories spring. Here, the land, not man, dominates. Its rugged history is so deeply etched in the earth and her people, and so much a part of the everyday, that even though the atomic age was born in the Southwest, descendants of ancient civilizations living within sight of space-age research communities continue very largely in ancient ways. Southwesterners regard the land as their life; they live out of doors a good deal more than in. They eat out of doors—barbecuing, cookouts, picnics, backpacking—as their native predecessors have done. And they dine on a unique combination of culinary traditions—a zesty mixture of Indian, Spanish, Mexican, Southwestern cowboy, Anglo, and of course, 20th-century American.

Southwesterners never seem to feel the press of time or change—a legacy of their imperturbable forebears. What they most enjoy, most often set on their tables, has, somewhere at its heart, a flavor of the past about it.

SOUPS

CHILI PUMPKIN SOUP

Pumpkin is one of the very first crops in our hemisphere. The Indians told of the Great Spirit who came to earth in the shape of a woman. Fatigued by her long journey, she fell asleep. When she arose and walked across the land, pumpkins sprang from the ground by her right hand, beans sprang up by her left, and from her footprints in the earth sprang maize.

Simmer chunks of pared and seeded pumpkin in water until just tender; purée through food mill or in blender. Stir in a little binding of butter and flour and cook gently for 10 minutes. Thin with hot milk, season to taste with salt, pepper, ground cloves, and chili powder.

■ **Variation**—Summer-squash soup is prepared in the same way.

AVOCADO SOUP
For an elegant patio dinner

Place 1 tablespoon grated Swiss cheese in each soup cup. Pour simmering beef consommé onto it, then slip in slices of ripe avocado. Serve at once.

■ **Variation**—Garnish jellied consommé madrilene with avocado and a slice of lemon twisted to make a furl.

SALADS

FRUIT SALADS
The best salads in the Southwest are the simplest

■ Crescents of fresh grapefruit and casaba melon on romaine lettuce, with a light French dressing.

■ Alternate sections of white, pink, and red grapefruit on a background of greens, laced with poppy seeds in French dressing. If red grapefruit is unavailable, soak white segments overnight in raspberry juice.

■ At Christmas, red grapefruit sections alternating with avocado slices are a pretty touch.

■ Rings of oranges and raw onions seasoned, again, with French dressing accompany rare roast beef.

■ Try casaba melons sliced and alternated with grapefruit sections.

■ Ripe tomatoes stuffed with chopped celery, piñons, and the peeled and chopped pulp of the tomatoes; a chili-seasoned French dressing ladled on at the last minute.

■ Grapefruits one more time: they are by far the favorite salad fruit in the Southwest, being both quenching and abundant; emptied of fruit, filled with brilliant colors of jello, chilled, then sliced into quarters and served on greens with a garnish of grapefruit crescents.

BEAN SALADS
The Southwest's potato salad

■ To a drained can of pinto, kidney, or garbanzo beans, add a spicy oil and vinegar dressing, lots of pressed garlic, fresh or dried oregano, and chili powder, and minced onion and celery to taste. Chill overnight before serving.

■ Strips of pimiento, canned green chilies, black olives, rings of green peppers, sliced radishes, any of these are handsome additions to a bean salad.

SEAFOOD

TRUCHA FRITA
(Southwestern Fried Trout)

Mountain streams and man-made lakes are stocked with Southwestern finny delicacies, rainbow trout most especially. If you can't catch it yourself and cook it moments later over a campfire, at least try the Southwestern manner of frying trout.

Clean trout at once. Heat bacon drippings over high heat and fry the fish and a handful of finely chopped onion for each trout until done, turning once. Remove trout to hot serving dish, swirl in 1 tablespoon cider vinegar, a bit of minced parsley, 1 pressed garlic clove, and 1 tablespoon butter. Heat over high heat, scraping and stirring, then pour over fish and onions. Serve at once with a garnish of lemon twist, capers, and parsley.

■ **Variation**—Try boning the fish and skinning it before cooking. Little bluegills, caught back of Southwestern dams, are heavenly cooked this way, especially when fried until this side of crispness.

SEAFOOD IN CHILI

Since early Colonial days, shrimps have been a favorite food of Southwesterners, even though until recent times the shrimps have been dried, from Mexico. But the habit of taste persists, and many favorite Lenten recipes call for dried or powdered shrimps.

Using canned, reconstituted dried, frozen, or fresh shrimps, fresh-flown-in oysters, or King crab from as far away as Alaska, a refreshing hot-weather supper is a cup of seafood sauced either with a favorite chili sauce, or simply best ketchup and a heavy sprinkling of finely chopped canned green chilies. Garnish with lemon and avocado slices. Or serve in an avocado half to begin with. Be sure to use a chili sauce you have made yourself.

SOUTHWESTERN COOKERY

MEAT AND POULTRY

STEAK FRY

Although other cultures may claim the barbecue as their own, it is almost certain the Indians of New Spain initiated the backyard barbecue when they built frames of green wood for smoking their fish. When the Spaniards came with their oversize roasts of meats, they found the barbacoas *ideal, making it easy to handle whole animals at once, and giving the meat an incomparable flavor. In most of West Texas and Arizona, barbecue means just one thing: beef. This is the way steaks taste best.*

Build a rectangle of rocks about 1 x 2 feet and 6 inches high; make a fire inside of hardwood (mesquite, oak, or hickory preferred) an hour ahead of time, so that it may burn down to about 2 inches of glowing embers. Spread the embers evenly. Put a grill on top (an old refrigerator shelf is fine) about 4 inches from the coals. Now put on T-bone steaks 1 inch thick, unseasoned, to "fry." Move steaks as they drip into the fire. When underside is brown and the bone slightly charred, turn. Season well with salt and pepper (never before searing). Turn when the downside is brown, and season that side. Serve the steak while still rare and sizzling.

■ **Variations**—Some Southwesterners have to have sop (see Soppin' Sauce, page 1731) on their beef as it barbecues; if you do, first try just plain melted butter before moving on to something stronger.

Short ribs of beef barbecued either this way or in the patio's barbecue or even on a plugged-in electric roaster are the next most popular cuts in beef country; just be sure the meat is *rare*.

BASQUE BARBECUE

In much of the Southwest, Basque Barbecues are lamb barbecues, often whole 30-pound suckling lambs turning on a spit, so called because many of the sheepmen are of Basque descent. Here is an elegant Southwestern dinner-party meat.

- 7- pound leg of lamb, boned
  Pork tenderloin, a strip cut to fit the length of the lamb, and thick enough just to be enclosed by it
  Rosemary leaves
  Garlic powder
  Salt and pepper
  Fresh lemon juice
  Worcestershire

Have the butcher bone the lamb and cut the pork to suitable size; sprinkle inside of lamb with rosemary leaves, garlic powder, and salt and pepper to taste. Lay on pork tenderloin, roll, and tie securely. Rub lamb with lemon juice and Worcestershire all over, then roast over charcoal 4 inches from coals, either on a rack or spit. If on rack, turn occasionally during cooking. It will take about 2 hours, although a meat thermometer is more reliable; thermometer should register 170° F. Serve with roasted onions. Makes 4 to 6 servings.

CARNE ADOBADA
(New Mexican Cured Pork)

Perhaps feeling most strongly the influences of the early Indian-Mexican cuisine, New Mexicans are less enamored of a big thick steak than they are of a dish of meat skillfully seasoned. Lacking the delicacy of summer's cabrito, *kid meat, rural ancestors of the* conquistadores *like to cure winter's fresh pork in this fashion.*

Remove fat from any tender cut of pork desired; cut into strips 3 inches long, 2 inches thick. Prepare Green Chili Sauce (page 1731) with fresh peppers, but do not cook, simply combine all ingredients. Marinate meat in sauce for 24 hours, or in refrigerator for as long as 1 week. When wanted, cut meat into smaller pieces and sauté in hot lard until done; add some of the Green Chili Sauce, cover, and cook slowly until sauce is thick and meat tender.

CHILE CON CARNE VERDE

After the Spanish conquistadores, *came the Spanish padres who established missions for the Indians. Nuns came after the padres, establishing convents and teaching more civilized methods of cooking to the Indian women. It was the nuns who made the first carne con chile, "meat with chili," and whether this recipe is a first or last variation, it's refreshing after so many pots and cans of indifferent red chili with beans.*

- 3 pounds beef chuck or best boiling meat, lean
- ¼ cup drippings or lard
- 2 cups canned green chilies (fresh, of course, may be used)
- 3 garlic cloves, pressed
- 2 cups chopped canned or fresh peeled tomatoes
- 2 cups broth from meat
  Salt

Simmer meat in ample water until tender but not well done. Cut into small cubes and sauté in fat. Add chopped chilies, garlic, tomatoes, and broth. Simmer slowly, covered, until meat is done. Season with salt to taste. This, like all stews, is better the second day. Perfect for a casual big dinner. Makes 6 servings.

■ **Variations**—In place of beef, use venison to make a fine Deer Chili.

Replace the green chilies with 2 cups or more Red Chili Sauce (page 1731), or at least ½ cup chili powder (in which case increase the tomatoes by 1 cupful). This is *Chile con Carne Colorado*.

Add either 1½ pounds dried pinto beans which have been properly soaked, cooked, seasoned, and drained, or 16½ cups (six 1-pound, 4-ounce cans) pinto beans, drained; add to meat with the chilies, garlic, tomatoes, and broth, and simmer as above. This is the most famous of Southwestern chilies.

Note: *Chile con Carne* must never be made of ground meat, nor be caught with a layer of fat.

HOT TAMALE PIE

Here is as good an example as any we have of Indian-Mexican-Anglo-Cowboy cuisines combining to form a Southwestern flavor unique in the world.

Line a baking dish with cornmeal mush made from *masa harina*, carefully following directions on the package. Fill with *Chile con Carne* with or without beans, as you prefer, fresh chopped tomatoes, chopped raw onions, and chopped canned green chilies; these may be in layers or simply willy-nilly. Top with a pattern of pitted whole ripe olives, add a mountain of grated yellow cheese, then heat in preheated moderate oven (350°F.) for about 15 minutes.

■ **Variation**—A good *Last-Minute Tamale Pie* can be put together in no time by breaking frozen or canned tamales into pieces into a baking dish, covering with canned *chili con carne*, then with the tomatoes, raw onions, green chilies, even a handful of raisins, and the finish of olives and cheese. Or use leftover cooked meat in the pie instead of beef in a tin, and simply season drained canned pinto beans with some good chili sauce in place of a proper *chile con carne*.

COWPUNCHER CHILI PIE

Fill an 8-inch square pan (6 x 8 inches), or its equivalent (1½-quart size) with favorite *chile con carne*, with or without beans. Top with Batter and bake in preheated hot oven (400°F.) for 15 minutes. Makes 6 servings.

Batter

- ¾ cup coarse yellow cornmeal
- ½ cup sifted all-purpose flour
- 2 teaspoons baking powder
- 1 tablespoon sugar
  Generous ½ teaspoon salt
- 1 egg, beaten
- 2 tablespoons melted lard
- ½ cup milk

Mix the dry ingredients, then the wet ingredients. Combine and pour over chili pie. Smooth even.

PUEBLO LAMB CHILI

Here is an Indian hominy stew quite similar to the Mexican-Indian pozole, which by now shouldn't surprise anyone at all. Both are made essentially of hominy and meat, with some decorations of green peppers and/or chilies thrown in. As Southwesterners do, mix or match the combinations as the wind and weather move you.

Sopaipillas

Tamales

Chile con Carne Verde

Broiled ham slices with sweet potato-stuffed orange shells

SOUTHWESTERN COOKERY

- 3 pounds lean lamb cut into 1½-inch cubes
- Bacon drippings
- 8 cups cooked hominy, canned or dried and simmered tender
- 4 cups water
- 10 medium green peppers, seeded and quartered (Indians leave seeds in)
- 3 medium onions, chopped
- 2 garlic cloves, pressed
- Chili powder to taste
- Salt to taste
- Dried oregano to taste

Brown lamb in the drippings. Add hominy and water, green peppers, onions, garlic, and seasonings. Simmer, covered, for 1½ to 2 hours, or until tender. Makes 8 to 10 servings.

■ **Variation**—Omit green peppers and substitute garbanzos for hominy. Use dry ones, and simmer the meat and other ingredients with the presoaked beans as long as it takes to cook them. Secret of garbanzo cooking: never, never let the water stop simmering, or all is lost.

HUNTER'S REWARD

The Southwestern mountains, looming large over every desert of the region and resplendent with wild flowers, native shrubs, and songbirds that make Eastern lady sight-seers weak in the knees, hold a wealth of mule deer, white-tailed deer, bear, elk, antelope, bighorn, and peccary to make Eastern hunters dizzy with choice. Here is a campfire stew deliciously typical of the territory.

- 5 pounds stewing game (properly hung if necessary)
- Drippings
- Big handful of potatoes, maybe 2 big handfuls, in chunks
- Same of onions, in chunks
- 1 or 2 red chili peppers, seeded
- Salt to taste
- 2 cups (one 1-pound can) yellow corn, or more
- 2 cups (one 1-pound can) tomatoes, or more
- 2 cups (one 1-pound can) hominy, or more
- 2 cups (one 1-pound can) okra, or fresh summer squashes if available
- ½ pound bacon, cut up

Cut game into 1½-inch chunks. Brown meat in an iron pot over campfire, using just enough drippings to keep meat from sticking. Cover and let mixture simmer in its own juices very slowly until almost tender; if meat is dry by nature, add some water. Add potatoes, onions, chili peppers, and salt. When everything is ready, add the canned vegetables. If using fresh squash, cut into chunks and add to pot 10 minutes before cooked vegetables. Stew gently, covered, while rendering bacon. Add bacon to the pot. When all the hunters are ready, serve. Makes 10 servings.

Note: Be sure to let the stew simmer for a nice long time; maybe, if it can be hidden from snoopy night raiders, it should be let mellow overnight.

■ **Variation**—Rabbits from the food store rather than from behind a bush are also excellent for this stew, as are tender veal and even kid.

GALLINA RELLENA
(Stuffed Turkey, Southwestern Style)

One of the rare specialties of the Southwest is the turkey population of the Salt River Valley in Arizona. They run free under the olive trees grown there, and gobble up all the olives fallen to the ground. Like the field-salted lambs of Normandy who, nourished on grass growing in salty marshland, come to the table salted to perfection, the olive-fed turkeys are a gourmet-giant's step ahead of their feathered brothers raised on dullard's fare. But whether olive-stuffed or stuffed with this superb Southwestern combination of meat, sweets, chocolate, and spices, there is no roast to rival a perfectly roasted young turkey.

- 1 turkey (12 to 15 pounds)
- Salt and monosodium glutamate
- ½ cup sweet butter
- 1 pound cooked beef, ground after cooking
- 2 cups white raisins
- 1 to 2 ounces (1 to 2 squares) unsweetened chocolate, melted
- 1 cup shelled roasted pinons (Italian pignoli may be substituted, but no other nuts)
- 1 cup beef consommé, not too strong
- 1 teaspoon ground cinnamon
- 1 teaspoon ground coriander
- ½ teaspoon ground cloves
- Salt to taste
- ½ cup dry red wine

Clean turkey, rub inside with salt and monosodium glutamate, then rub outside with butter. Wrap in damp cloth and refrigerate on the night before serving. Remove from refrigerator early next morning, and prepare stuffing. Combine all ingredients except wine; simmer, stirring, until thick. Add wine, bring to boil, then set aside to cool. Stuff turkey as usual and roast as usual, breast side down first half of cooking, basting several times with drippings in pan. Makes 12 to 14 servings.

VEGETABLES AND POTATOES

SWEET POTATOES, NEW INDIAN STYLE
A luxurious dish ancient Indians never knew

Mash cooked sweet potatoes and season; whip with an egg or two, fold in a little whipped cream, then top with chopped garlic that has been browned and some crisp diced salt pork.

QUELITES
(Lamb's-Quarters)

Southwesterners so near nature make abundant use of wild greens and herbs in their cooking. Although the tradition of the curandera, *or herb woman, is dying out in villages, fondness for native greens apart from their curative powers endures. Indians prefer* waco, beeweed, *and leaves of wild parsley, but lamb's-quarters is more popular with the Mexicans and Anglos. Beyond the mesas and their wild bounty, substitute spinach, beet, or turnip greens.*

- 2 tablespoons minced onion
- 2 tablespoons drippings
- 2 cups finely chopped steamed greens (about 2 bunches)
- 1 dried red chili, seeds removed
- Salt to taste
- ½ cup or more cooked pinto beans

Brown onion lightly in drippings. Mix in cooked greens, chili, salt, and beans. Makes 4 to 6 servings.

STUFFED TOMATOES, LAS VEGAS

Southern Nevadans have the same feeling for mutton and lamb that Arizonans and West Texans have for beef, even perhaps a little more strongly, since mutton fanciers are generally in the minority. A great pity that most of us never get to savor a flavorsome joint of mutton; few sheepmen can afford to let their lambs go that long. Tomatoes being a Southwestern specialty and combining their sweet-tartness so well with lamb, here is a city-slick version one might find at any barbecue of a warm Las Vegas night.

- 8 large firm tomatoes
- Salt and pepper to taste
- ¼ pound mushrooms, coarsely chopped
- 1 small onion, minced
- 1 cup uncooked wild rice
- ½ cup minced celery
- 2 tablespoons minced parsley
- Pinch of dried mint
- 3 tablespoons butter
- 1½ cups chicken broth, boiling
- 4 slices of bacon (optional)

Slice lids off tomatoes, carefully scoop out pulp, and discard seeds. Season insides with salt and pepper and turn tomato cases upside down to drain. Sauté mushrooms, onion, rice, celery, parsley, and mint in the butter until all are well coated and begin to take on color; add chopped tomato pulp and boiling broth. Cover and simmer for 20 minutes, or until rice is tender. Season to taste. Fill tomato cases with the mixture. Bake in preheated moderate oven (350°F.) just long enough to heat through. Garnish with a sprinkle of crisp bacon if desired. Makes 8 servings.

WOMAN'S DAY

SOUTHWESTERN COOKERY

FRIJOLES, FRIJOLITOS, Y FRIJOLES REFRITOS
(Beans, Mashed Beans, and Beans Refried)

Of the Three Sisters of Indian agriculture, corn, beans, and squash, beans are the darling of the family. Everybody in the Southwest eats beans; the Anglos once or twice a week, the cowboys every day, and the Indians and Spanish-Mexicans twice, maybe three times daily. And there is really only one bean that means frijoles to Southwesterners: the pinto, or painted bean. Here is the rule for beans for "a frijole man," as J. Frank Dobie called himself.

- 1 pound dried pinto beans
- 1½ pounds salt pork, cubed
- 12 chiles pequenos (little wild Mexican red peppers)
- Grated raw onion
- Vinegar

Wash beans thoroughly; soak overnight. Add salt pork and cook beans until tender, from 3 to 6 hours. (If more salt is needed, add during last hour of cooking.) Add about 2 *chiles* to each plate of beans; mash up in plate along with onion; add vinegar. Makes 6 servings.

■ Variations—Mr. Dobie added that a distinct addition to *frijoles* is 2 or 3 tablespoons honey cooked in a pound of beans.

Frijoles Refritos

These are the best of all possible beans. Begin with beans that have simmered until all liquid evaporates. They are then mashed with a potato masher, moistened with melted bacon drippings (not a lot), a little flour, and some salt if necessary. Panfry for 10 to 15 minutes, stirring to keep from scorching. They're even better the next day, with a bit more drippings stirred in and some grated yellow cheese. Heat just enough for cheese to melt.

TAOS TACOS

Of all the cities of the Southwest, probably Taos, an artists' colony set in the mesaland above Santa Fe, is the purest and most practicing example of Southwestern culture. Nearly all the dwellings are adobe, nearly all the people cherish the country and its heritage, nearly everything the eye falls on is glorious.

Prepare a buffet of tacos by frying corn tortillas in deep lard or oil (plan 2 or 3 for each guest); fold in half. Arrange tacos in hot pottery platter and place in center of buffet. Have fillings lined up for guests to concoct their own tacos: hot chopped beef, pork, chicken and/or turkey seasoned with salt, pepper, and dried oregano; cold diced ripe tomatoes; chopped raw green onions; chopped green chilies; a thick blend of *chile con carne* perhaps; and always shredded lettuce, shredded yellow cheese, and a choice of Green or Red Chili Sauce (page 1731) at the end.

TOSTADAS INDIO

Southern Californians at the very Eastern tip of the state are, through a link with common Indian ancestors, included in the Southwest. Geographically the land is desert and very hot. This is a favorite quick lunch in the heat; yes, old hands in the territory insist that hot food makes them more comfortable.

Spread tortillas with butter, toast in very hot oven (450°F.), then pile into a basket. Serve with a bowl of *Frijoles Refritos* (at left), a bowl of grated yellow cheese, and another of shredded lettuce. Everyone then swipes their *tostadas* through the beans and heaps the cheese and lettuce on top.

SAUCES

SOUTHWESTERN CHILI SAUCE

When an Arizonan, New Mexican, or West Texan runs out of chili pepper sauce, he either has to make up a new batch pronto, or he might as well close up the kitchen; chili sauce is as crucial as salt to Southwestern cooking.

- ½ cup chili powder
- Cold water
- 1 teaspoon salt
- 4 cups boiling water
- 3 tablespoons lard
- 1 garlic clove, pressed

Make a paste of chili powder and a little cold water; add to salted boiling water with the fat; stir to blend, then simmer to the consistency of tomato sauce, for 15 to 20 minutes. Add garlic. For thicker sauce, add more chili powder. Makes about 3 cups.

RED CHILI SAUCE

- 2 garlic cloves, pressed
- 1 small onion, minced
- 2 tablespoons melted lard or drippings
- 2 cups canned or fresh peeled tomatoes (no liquid), chopped
- 2 cups Southwestern Chili Sauce (above)
- 1 teaspoon dried oregano
- Salt

Fry garlic and onion in lard until golden. Add tomatoes and simmer gently for 15 minutes. Stir in chili sauce and oregano and simmer for 5 more minutes. Season with salt to taste. For light dishes, sauce should be reduced even longer. Keep tightly covered. Makes about 3½ cups.

GREEN CHILI SAUCE

Found on Mexican tables in the Southwest three times a day

- 3 green chilies (fresh or canned), seeds included, chopped
- 4 green tomatoes, chopped
- 2 medium onions, chopped
- 1 cup boiling water
- 1 garlic clove, pressed
- 1 teaspoon dried oregano
- Salt to taste

If using fresh chilies, cook for 10 minutes in boiling water to cover; drain. Add tomatoes, onions, and 1 cup boiling water and simmer for 20 minutes. Press through sieve or food mill; add garlic, oregano, and enough salt to flavor highly. Should be as thick as tomato paste. Keep tightly covered. Makes about 1¼ cups.

SOPPIN' SAUCE

Sop is what cowboys daub on the meat as it barbecues. They use a paint brush, a rag tied to a stick, or for really big doings, new brooms dunked into great tubs of sop.

- 1 cup tomato ketchup
- 2 cups Worcestershire
- 1 cup mighty strong coffee beverage
- ½ cup real butter
- 2 tablespoons freshly ground black pepper
- 1 tablespoon sugar (dudes need it)
- 1 tablespoon salt, or to taste

Simmer all ingredients slowly for 30 minutes, stirring occasionally. Best on beef or chicken. Makes about 3 cups.

BREADS

SOPAIPILLAS

These are Southwestern "sofa pillows," deep-fried, hollow like popovers. Yankees butter them, natives don't. They can serve as bread at dinner as an alternative to tortillas, or rolled in cinnamon sugar, they become ethereal buns with coffee, chocolate, or a cup of mocha.

- 4 cups sifted all-purpose flour
- 2 teaspoons salt
- 4 teaspoons baking powder
- ¼ cup lard
- Water
- Lard for frying
- Cinnamon sugar, optional

Sift dry ingredients together. Work in lard with fingertips until mixture has the consistency of cornmeal. Add just enough water to hold together. Let rest in refrigerator for 10 minutes. Roll dough to thickness of ⅛ inch and cut into 1½-inch squares. Fry in deep lard until crisp and brown, for 2 or 3 minutes on each side. Drain and serve hot. For a sweet bread, roll in cinnamon sugar after frying. Makes about 6 dozen.

SOUTHWESTERN COOKERY

BURRITOS FROM TAOS

Sopapillas are an historic bread. Here is a contemporary departure.

Cut *Sopapillas* twice usual size and fry. Then split open a pocket and stuff with a taco blend of meat or poultry and grated cheese. Slip under broiler until cheese melts. Delicious cut very small and stuffed as an hors-d'oeuvre for cocktails.

ARIZONA'S BISCUITS

As Southwestern as chile con carne are the oversize biscuits on Arizona's cattle ranches. Probably they were first cut that big to fit the huge hands holding them!

Prepare your lightest biscuit dough, roll at least ½ inch thick, and cut into circles at least 3 inches wide. Serve with butter and mesquite honey.

■ **Variation**—*Calico Biscuits* have finely chopped green and red peppers blended into the flour and shortening, and minced raw onion added to the milk.

CHUCK WAGON PECAN BREAD

This is a recipe very nearly a hundred years old, from a cook who served it to cowhands along the Pecos River.

- 3½ cups sifted all-purpose flour
- 1 cup sugar
- 1 teaspoon salt
- 3 teaspoons baking powder
- 1 cup milk
- 2 cups chopped pecans
- ¼ cup melted lard
- 1 egg

Combine all ingredients and stir well. Pour into greased baking pan (9 x 5 x 3 inches). Bake in preheated moderate oven (350°F.) for 1 hour. Turn out and cool on rack. Keeps well, wrapped up tightly.

DESSERTS

ICED PINEAPPLE

With such a beautiful bounty of fresh fruits to choose from—Salt River Valley honeydews, casabas, and cantaloupes; Texas watermelons; Oak Creek Canyon peaches; apples, dates, grapes, and raisins from all over the area—Southwesterners enjoy a light simple refreshing bit of fruit to finish every meal. Time was when all the fruits were dried fruits; because there was little sugar for canning, fresh crops were set out in baskets to let the sun do the preserving.

A new twist to a Mexican custom: cut a pineapple lengthwise fully into halves. Use a knife to slice out the pulp; cut away core, then chop pineapple fruit coarsely. Return to shells and chill. To serve, cover with alternating slabs of pineapple, lemon, and lime ice. Sprinkle with orange-flavored brandy if desired.

CARAMELA

The lovely bittersweet flavor of caramelized brown sugar is another hallmark of Southwestern cooking. And ice cream, one of the culinary latecomers to the region, naturally was welcomed with open arms. A simple ice cream on a stick finishes many company barbecues, for example, although as with everything else they like best, highly flavored ice creams are more popular with Southwesterners than bland. In Phoenix, one store sells licorice ice cream, but the recipe is a secret, sad to say. Southwesterners have a fondness for airy light creams—Bavarians, the Spanish natillas (Yankees call it Floating Island)—something cool that will float down after a meal of zesty chilies.

- ½ pound light brown sugar
- 4 cups heavy cream
- 4 egg yolks

Follow directions carefully: Melt sugar slowly in large saucepan and cook until it all turns to syrup. With wooden spoon *slowly* stir in the cream, blending each trickle of cream thoroughly before adding more. Remove from heat while you whisk egg yolks lightly in a large bowl. Pour sugar and cream into yolks slowly, whisking madly as you go. Freeze in molds or ice-cube tray. Makes 8 to 10 servings.

Note: This is as delicious but as ephemeral a frozen cream as ever was; it melts quickly, so serve without dallying on the way. A triumph of simplicity.

■ **Variation**—If you can buy *piloncillos*, little pillars of Mexican brown sugar, by all means make the ice cream with them.

"PIEBOX" SPECIAL VINEGAR PIE

"Piebox" is slang for chuck wagon. The range hands called it that with both affection and optimism, hoping there would be a pie in the wagon for their dessert. All the Southwest is pie-eating country; cakes just don't rate as high. In the days when apples hadn't yet been planted in the land, cattlemen loved their Vinegar Pie, its faint but tantalizing smell of apples from the cider vinegar filling the ranch house while the pie baked. Here is a flossy version that would lift a cowboy's eyebrows.

- Pastry for 1-crust 9-inch pie, unbaked
- ¼ cup all-purpose flour
- 1 teaspoon ground cinnamon
- ¼ teaspoon ground cloves
- ½ teaspoon ground nutmeg
- ¼ teaspoon ground coriander
- Dash of salt
- 4 egg yolks
- 2 egg whites
- 1 cup sugar
- 1 cup dairy sour cream
- 2 tablespoons cider vinegar
- ½ cup raisins
- 1½ cups coarsely chopped pecans
- Whipped cream to garnish

Line pie pan with the pastry and freeze the pastry while you prepare filling. Sift dry ingredients together. Whisk egg yolks just to blend; beat egg whites until stiff. Fold sugar into whites thoroughly but not overmuch, and stir with wooden spoon into yolks. Add sifted dry ingredients with a few strokes, then sour cream. Mix all remaining ingredients but whipping cream and fold into filling. Spread in pastry-lined pie pan and smooth top. Bake in preheated very hot oven (450°F.) for 10 minutes. Lower heat to hot (400°F.) and bake for 5 minutes. Then bake at moderate (350° F.) for about 15 minutes more, or until set. Cool on rack, then garnish border with a flourish of unsweetened whipped cream.

ANISEED COOKIES

Cookies, too, outrank cakes in popularity in this part of the country. And aniseeds, from the Mexican influence, are a favorite cookie flavoring.

- ½ cup sweet butter (or half lard, half butter)
- 1½ cups firmly packed brown sugar (white sugar is good too)
- 3 eggs
- Few drops of oil of anise from the drugstore or 1 teaspoon aniseeds
- 3 cups sifted all-purpose flour
- Lots of freshly roasted aniseeds

With your hand, cream butter with the sugar. Add eggs, one at a time. When quite creamy, blend in anise oil, then the flour. Drop from teaspoon onto greased cookie sheet and sprinkle with aniseeds. Bake in preheated moderate oven (350° F.) until bottoms are golden, tops pale, about 12 minutes. Cool. Let ripen in airtight can for a week before eating. Makes 4 dozen.

SOUTHWESTERN MOCHA

If chili, oregano, and garlic light the main course, then cinnamon, chocolate, and mocha spell dessert. Here is a dessert in a cup, all warmth and fragrance, very like the Southwest it represents.

- 4 ounces (4 squares) Mexican chocolate or sweet cooking chocolate
- 4 cups rich milk
- ½ teaspoon ground cinnamon, or more to taste if Mexican chocolate is not used
- 2 eggs
- ½ teaspoon finely grated orange rind
- ½ teaspoon vanilla extract
- ½ cup black coffee

Melt chocolate over boiling water; whisk in milk and cinnamon. Heat in top part of a double boiler over boiling water for 20 minutes. If not sweet enough, add a bit of sugar. Whisk eggs with rind and vanilla and pour hot chocolate onto them in a stream, whisking constantly. Add coffee, and beat, beat, beat to a froth. Serve at once. Makes 4 servings.

WOMAN'S DAY

SOYBEAN

SOYBEAN—This bean, also called soya, soy pea, soja, and soi, is found in the hairy pods of an erect bushy legume, native to Asia. Soybeans contain a large proportion of assimilable protein, have a considerable fat content, and are low in carbohydrates, having no starch at all. They form an important part of the daily diet in China and southeastern Asia where they serve as a meat substitute.

The soybean is one of the world's oldest plants. It has been cultivated in China for over 4,000 years. The Chinese find it so necessary to life that they have made it one of the five sacred grains necessary to civilization; the others are rice, wheat, barley, and millet. There are records as early as 2207 B.C. which give detailed instructions on soil conditions, planting, and uses, showing that the bean was already in wide cultivation by this early date. Chinese folklore tells of three gods of bean curds, who are invoked by bean-curd sellers. One is a great war god said to have been a bean-curd seller in his youth.

In America, too, soybeans are cultivated as a high-protein, low-cost food. Special varieties are grown with a nutty or bland flavor that may be cooked and eaten like navy beans. Soybeans are also grown commercially for making margarine, cooking oils, soaps, emulsifiers, plastics, and many other compound industrial products. Over one third of the edible fats consumed in the United States are made with soybean oil.

Soybean cake is fed to livestock, and soybean oil meal for livestock and poultry is the most important of modern high-protein feeds. In short, even in our land of plenty, the soybean is an essential crop, and an exceedingly important one in states like Michigan, Illinois, Missouri, Iowa, and Minnesota.

The soybean plant resembles ordinary field and navy beans. There are over 1,000 varieties cultivated in Southeastern Asia, varying from less than one foot tall to five or six feet. Nearly all varieties, however, are covered with fine tawny or gray hair. The pods range in color from tan to nearly black. The seeds, or beans, may be yellow, green, brown, black, or a combination of these colors. The seeds vary in size, weighing anywhere from 1,200 to a pound to 3,500 to a pound. Wild beans are even smaller.

Soy sauce is perhaps the best known culinary soybean product. This is prepared from boiled beans, roasted wheat flour, salt, and a ferment. The common extract of soy sauce widely manufactured in the United States (called *ch'au-yau* in Cantonese) is only one of three types of this flavoring. Pearl sauce is a dark thick sauce with a mild flavor; "raw extract" is light brown with a good taste. These special Chinese types are both considerably milder than the commercial soy sauce. Although soy sauce is very "salty," it has a special flavor of its own and should not be substituted for salt.

Although soy sauce is the most widely used soybean product in this country, Far Eastern cooking relies heavily on other soy foods. Bean curd, the fermented milk from the bean, is eaten throughout Southeast Asia as a protein food. It may be eaten as an accompaniment to other foods, or used in various dishes. It is sometimes boiled in syrup and eaten as a candy, or soaked in salted water, roasted, and eaten as a nut. The *dow fu pok* of the Chinese and *aburage* of the Japanese is a deep-fried bean curd. In Chinese groceries Americans will find *fooh jook,* the dried "cream" of boiled soybean milk. It is sold in long narrow beige strips, and often used in soups. *Tiem jook* is the sediment of boiled soybean milk. This is dried into stiff shiny tan sheets, and is used in stewed meatless dishes.

Bean sprouts, widely eaten by the Chinese as a green vegetable, either raw or cooked, are grown from the beans. They are available canned or frozen in this country.

Availability—Fresh soybeans are not generally available. Occasionally they can be bought in the areas where they are grown during the late summer months.

There are almost endless soybean products sold in health-food stores: canned plain; Boston style, with tomato sauce; dried whole and split; soybean flour: full-fat, high-fat, low-fat, and defatted; seeds for sprouting; soybean oil; soybean milk, fluid and powder; sweetened and flavored milk concentrate: liquid and powder. Chinese stores sell soybean curd or *torfu.*

Soy sauce is available in most food stores.

Storage—After opening package of dried soybeans, place unused beans in a clean, covered container and store on kitchen shelf. Soybean flour should be refrigerated. It will keep up to 6 months, covered.
- Dried beans, kitchen shelf: 1 year
- Dried beans, refrigerator shelf, cooked and covered: 1 to 4 days
- Dried beans, refrigerator frozen-food compartment, cooked beans and bean dishes, prepared for freezing: 1 month
- Dried beans, freezer, cooked beans and bean dishes, prepared for freezing: 4 to 6 months

Nutritive Food Values—Soybeans are high in protein, contain some calcium, phosphorus, a high amount of potassium, some iron, small amounts of vitamin A, thiamine, riboflavin, and niacin.
- Soybean flour, 3½ ounces, full-fat = 421 calories
- Soybean flour, 3½ ounces, high-fat = 380 calories
- Soybean flour, 3½ ounces, low-fat = 356 calories
- Soybean flour, 3½ ounces, defatted = 326 calories
- Canned soybeans, 3½ ounces, solids and liquid = 75 calories
- Canned soybeans, 3½ ounces, drained solids = 103 calories
- Dried soybeans, 3½ ounces, cooked = 130 calories
- Soy sauce, 3½ ounces = 68 calories
- Soybean oil, 3½ ounces = 880 calories

Basic Preparation—Packaged dried soybeans are usually sorted and washed before packaging, so need only be rinsed. Beans bought in bulk should be sorted carefully, discarding broken or defective ones, and washed until water is clear. It is necessary to soak beans to replace the water that was lost in drying. In general, 6 cups of water for each 1 pound of beans is the correct amount. Save the nutritious soaking water to use in cooking the beans. There are two methods of soaking:

1. *Quick method:* Measure the soaking water into a large, heavy pot. Add washed beans and bring to a boil. Cover pot and cook for 2 minutes; remove from heat. Let stand for 1 hour, then cook, covered, according to recipe directions, or until tender.

SOYBEAN

2. *Overnight method:* Measure soaking water into a large pot; add washed beans, cover pot, and let stand for 6 to 8 hours. To prevent souring and hard skins, the 2-minute boil is also recommended, even when beans are soaked overnight. Beans may also be refrigerated to prevent souring. Cook, covered, according to recipe directions, or until tender.

FISH IN SWEET-SOUR SAUCE

The fish, served with the Sweet-Sour Sauce which resembles a bed of brightly colored seaweed, is great fun to eat. With your chopsticks, you pick at the fish and fill your plate.

Choose a sea bass, a mullet, or any other fish weighing 2 or 3 pounds complete with head and tail. Remove the fins, and scale and clean the fish.

Prepare a court bouillon for the fish in a kettle with enough water to cover, to which you have added 1 garlic clove, 1 tablespoon salt, 1 tablespoon vinegar, 1-inch piece of gingerroot, and a little orange peel. Bring court bouillon to a boil and cook for 15 minutes. Place fish in the kettle, cover it, and simmer for 15 to 18 minutes. Remove to a hot platter and serve with Sweet-Sour Sauce.

Sweet-Sour Sauce
- 1 tablespoon each of sugar, soy sauce, and Worcestershire
- ¼ cup vinegar
- 3 green onions, finely shredded
- 1 garlic clove, finely chopped
- 1 tablespoon chopped preserved gingerroot
- ½ cup fish stock
- ½ cup Chinese sweet pickles

Heat together all ingredients. Bring to a boil and stir. If it is not thick enough, add a bit of cornstarch mixed with a little water. Serve with the fish.

CHINESE-BEEF CASSEROLE
- 1 beef flank steak (about 1¼ pounds)
- 2 tablespoons all-purpose flour
- ½ teaspoon salt
- Dash of pepper
- 1 garlic clove, minced
- 2 tablespoons cooking oil
- 1 can (10¾ ounces) beef gravy
- 2 teaspoons soy sauce
- 1 teaspoon sugar
- 1 green pepper, sliced
- About 1 cup (one 10-ounce can) tomatoes, drained

Pound steak with edge of saucer or meat hammer; cut diagonally into thin slices. Dredge meat with flour seasoned with salt and pepper. Brown meat and garlic in oil. Add next 3 ingredients; heat and pour into 2-quart casserole. Cover and bake in preheated moderate oven (350°F.) for 1 hour. Add green pepper and tomatoes. Bake, covered, for 1 hour longer. Makes 6 servings.

SOY POT ROAST
- 4 pounds boned chuck or rump pot roast
- ¼ cup vegetable oil
- 1 cup soy sauce
- ½ cup sugar
- 1-inch cinnamon stick, or ½ teaspoon powdered cinnamon
- 2½ cups water
- 1 cup sherry
- 3 tablespoons cornstarch

Brown meat on all sides in hot oil in large heavy kettle or Dutch oven. Mix soy sauce, sugar, cinnamon, and 2 cups water; pour over meat. Cover, bring to boil, and simmer for 3 hours, or until tender. Add sherry after first 2 hours of cooking. When meat is tender, remove to a hot platter. Pour off liquid from pan, reserving 2½ cups. Bring to boil. Stir in cornstarch blended with ½ cup water. Simmer, stirring, until smooth and thickened. Serve with the pot roast. Makes 6 to 8 servings.

SOYBEAN STEW
- 4 slices of bacon
- 4 potatoes, peeled
- 2 large onions, sliced
- 1 green pepper, sliced
- Salt, pepper, and cayenne to taste
- 2½ cups cooked soybeans
- 2 cups (one 1-pound can) tomatoes

Cut bacon into 1-inch pieces and cook in heavy skillet until nearly done. Remove bacon. Add potatoes, onions, and green pepper to fat in skillet. Season with salt, pepper, and cayenne. Add beans and tomatoes. Top with bacon, cover, and simmer for about 1½ hours, adding water if necessary. Makes 4 servings.

COMPANY CASSEROLE
- 2 cups uncooked long-grain rice
- ¼ cup butter or margarine
- 4½ cups hot poultry broth
- 4 cups diced cooked poultry
- 2 cans (4 ounces each) sliced mushrooms, undrained
- ⅓ cup soy sauce
- 1 package (12 ounces) frozen shelled shrimps, cooked and split
- 8 green onions, chopped
- ⅔ cup slivered almonds

Put rice in shallow pan. Brown in preheated hot oven (400°F.) for 10 minutes, shaking pan occasionally to brown evenly. Transfer to a 3-quart covered casserole. Add butter and stir to coat each grain. Add broth; cover and bake in preheated moderate oven (375°F.) for 35 to 40 minutes, or until rice is tender. Mix in poultry, mushrooms, soy sauce, and shrimps. The cooled casserole can be frozen or refrigerated at this point and reheated later. If frozen, let stand at room temperature for several hours before reheating. If refrigerated, heat directly. In either case, stir in green onions; top with almonds. Cover; bake in preheated hot oven (400°F.) for 30 to 40 minutes. If dry, add a little water. Uncover during last 10 minutes. Makes 8 servings.

BAKED SOY CHICKEN
- 1 frying chicken (about 2½ pounds), cut up
- 3 tablespoons soy sauce
- 2 eggs
- 1 teaspoon water
- ¾ cup fine dry bread crumbs

Wash chicken and dry on absorbent paper. Brush chicken with soy sauce so it is completely covered. Beat eggs with water and stir in crumbs. The mixture should be a little thicker than a sauce of pouring consistency. Pat on chicken on all sides to cover. Bake, uncovered, in preheated very slow oven (250°F.) for about 2 hours. Makes 4 servings.

SOYBEAN SHEPHERD'S PIE
- 12 small white onions, peeled
- 4 carrots, halved crosswise
- 2 cups cooked soybeans
- 2 tablespoons all-purpose flour
- 2 tablespoons butter or margarine
- 1 teaspoon salt
- ⅛ teaspoon pepper
- 3 cups seasoned mashed potatoes

Cover onions with water and cook, covered, for 20 minutes. Add carrots, cover, and cook for 10 minutes longer, or until carrots are tender. Drain, reserving liquid. Put onions, carrots, and beans in a 2-quart casserole. Brown flour lightly in the butter. Gradually add 2 cups reserved vegetable liquid and the salt. Cook for 2 minutes. Add pepper and pour liquid over vegetables. Spread potatoes on top. Bake in preheated hot oven (425°F.) for 15 to 20 minutes. Makes 4 servings.

SOY-WHEAT MUFFINS
- ½ cup soybean flour
- 1½ cups whole-wheat flour
- 3 teaspoons baking powder
- 1 teaspoon salt
- 2 tablespoons sugar
- 1 egg, beaten
- 3 tablespoons butter or margarine, melted
- 1 cup milk

Mix dry ingredients. Add remaining ingredients all at once, stirring only enough to moisten dry ingredients. Half-fill muffin-pan sections with the batter. Bake in preheated hot oven (425°F.) for 12 to 15 minutes. Makes 12.

SOYED ALMONDS
- 4 cups blanched almonds (1¼ pounds)
- ¼ cup butter or margarine
- ¼ cup soy sauce

Put almonds in shallow pan (13 x 9 x 2 inches). Roast in preheated hot oven (400°F.) for about 15 minutes, stirring several times. Add butter and soy sauce; stir. Roast for 12 to 15 minutes longer, stirring often, until nuts are coated and fairly dry. Makes 4 cups.

Ham Tetrazzini

SPAGHETTI—One of the most popular members of the pasta family, spaghetti is made from a mixture of semolina, the flour that is milled from durum wheat, and water. The dough is passed through metal discs full of holes to emerge as slender solid rods.

The name spaghetti is Italian, from the plural form of *spaghetto,* "string."

Availability and Purchasing Guide—Spaghetti is widely available in different degrees of thickness. In addition to the standard thickness, there are fusilli, short curly spaghetti, the thickest; spaghettini, thin spaghetti; and vermicelli, angel-hair-thin spaghettini, long and straight, or twisted into a birds' nest, used in soups.

One pound uncooked spaghetti equals 4 to 5 cups. One pound spaghetti weighs 4 pounds after cooking and equals 2½ quarts, or 15 servings of ⅔ cup each.

Storage—Spaghetti in its original or other covered container can be stored at room temperature. Prepared dishes should be refrigerated.
☐ Kitchen shelf: 3 to 6 months
☐ Cooked and in prepared dishes, refrigerator shelf: 4 to 5 days.
☐ Cooked and in prepared dishes, refrigerator frozen-food compartment: 3 to 4 weeks
☐ Cooked and in prepared dishes, freezer: 1 year

Nutritive Food Values—Spaghetti is a fair source of iron and thiamine.
☐ 3½ ounces, cooked *al dente* = 148 calories
☐ 3½ ounces, cooked tender = 111 calories
☐ Spaghetti in tomato sauce with cheese, home recipe, 3½ ounces, cooked = about 100 calories
☐ Spaghetti in tomato sauce with cheese, canned, 3½ ounces = 76 calories

Basic Preparation—Spaghetti should always be freshly cooked in plenty of boiling water salted to taste. To cook 1 pound, it is essential to have a kettle that will hold 6 quarts of water. Add 2 tablespoons salt to 6 quarts water. Bring water to a full rolling boil. Gradually add spaghetti, stirring with a long-handled, two-pronged kitchen fork. The water should keep on boiling hard. As the spaghetti begins to soften, fold it over and over in the water so that it won't stick together. Keep on stirring frequently during the cooking process. Occasionally lift out a strand and taste for doneness. Tasting is essential to get the spaghetti

ENCYCLOPEDIA OF COOKERY

SPAGHETTI

right for one's own taste.

When spaghetti is done,* drain it immediately in a large strainer or colander. Return to pot and add seasonings. Stir to coat all strands. Serve immediately on heated platter and heated plates.

*Spaghetti that is to be cooked further in a casserole should not be more than three-quarters done, or the final product will be mushy.

SPAGHETTI WITH MEATBALLS
- 2 onions, chopped
- 2 garlic cloves, minced
- 2 tablespoons cooking oil
- 3½ cups (one 1-pound, 12-ounce can) tomatoes
- 1 cup water
- 2 leaves fresh or dried basil
- ¼ cup chopped parsley
- ½ teaspoon crumbled thyme
- 2 teaspoons salt
- ¼ teaspoon pepper
- ¼ teaspoon crushed dried red pepper
- 1 can (6 ounces) tomato paste
- Meatballs
- 12 ounces spaghetti, cooked and hot

Sauté onion and garlic until golden in hot oil in large saucepan. Add tomatoes and bring to boil. Simmer, uncovered, for 20 minutes, stirring occasionally. Add remaining sauce ingredients and the browned Meatballs, and simmer, uncovered, for 2 hours longer, stirring occasionally. Add more seasoning, if desired. Serve on hot cooked spaghetti. Makes 6 servings.

Meatballs
- ½ pound ground beef
- ½ pound ground pork
- 2 onions, minced
- 1 garlic clove, minced
- ¼ cup chopped parsley
- ½ cup grated Parmesan cheese
- ½ cup fine dry bread crumbs
- 1 egg
- 2 teaspoons salt
- ½ teaspoon pepper
- 2 tablespoons cooking oil

Mix all ingredients except oil thoroughly. Add a little water if mixture seems dry. Shape into 24 balls and brown slowly in hot oil.

CLAM SPAGHETTI
- ½ cup olive oil
- 1 small garlic clove, minced
- ¼ cup minced onion
- ½ cup minced green pepper or pimiento
- 2 cans (7 ounces each) minced clams, undrained
- ¼ cup minced parsley
- ¼ teaspoon ground thyme
- ½ teaspoon salt
- ¼ teaspoon pepper
- ½ cup tomato juice or white wine
- 1 pound spaghetti

Heat olive oil. Cook garlic and onion in it until soft and golden. Add green pepper and cook for 5 minutes. Add clams and juice, parsley, thyme, salt and pepper, and tomato juice. Simmer for 15 minutes, stirring occasionally. Cook and drain spaghetti. Add sauce and toss well. Makes 6 servings.

TURKEY TETRAZZINI
- Butter or margarine (about ⅔ cup)
- ½ cup all-purpose flour
- 1 cup hot milk
- 1 cup hot chicken bouillon
- ½ teaspoon salt
- ½ teaspoon pepper
- ⅛ teaspoon ground nutmeg
- ¼ cup dry sherry
- ¾ cup heavy cream
- 1 pound thin spaghetti
- ½ pound mushrooms, sliced, or 2 cans (4 ounces each) mushrooms, drained
- 2 to 3 cups diced cooked turkey
- ½ cup grated Parmesan or Romano cheese

Heat ½ cup butter and stir in flour. Combine milk and bouillon and stir into flour mixture. Cook, stirring, until sauce is smooth and thickened. Blend in salt, pepper, nutmeg, and sherry. Stir in cream and remove mixture from heat. Cook and drain spaghetti. Sauté mushrooms in 2 tablespoons butter for 5 minutes. Mix half of sauce with spaghetti and mushrooms. Place in buttered shallow baking dish. Make well in center of spaghetti mixture. Mix remaining sauce with turkey and place in well. Sprinkle with Parmesan cheese. Bake in preheated hot oven (400°F.) for 20 minutes. Makes 6 to 8 servings.

Ham Tetrazzini

Proceed as in Turkey Tetrazzini, but for turkey substitute 2 cups small, thin cooked ham slices. Sauté 1 small green pepper, seeded and cut into rings, with the mushrooms. Mix ham with all of sauce, spaghetti, and mushroom mixture. After putting in baking dish, slice 1 large tomato, and arrange slices on top. Sprinkle with grated Parmesan cheese, and put buttered croutons around edge of baking dish. Bake as directed. Makes 6 to 8 servings.

CHICKEN NORMANDY
- 1 frying chicken (about 3 pounds), cut into serving pieces
- 1¼ teaspoons salt
- ¼ cup butter or margarine
- 1 medium onion, thinly sliced
- 2 tablespoons sliced celery hearts
- 2 tablespoons chopped parsley
- 2½ cups apple slices (one 1-pound, 4-ounce can), drained
- ⅛ teaspoon ground thyme
- ⅛ teaspoon ground nutmeg
- 2 tablespoons heavy cream
- 8 ounces spaghetti

Sprinkle chicken with ¾ teaspoon salt. Melt butter. Add chicken and cook over medium heat until golden-brown on all sides. Remove chicken from skillet. Add onion and celery to drippings in skillet. Cook over medium heat, stirring occasionally, for 5 minutes. Add chicken, parsley, apple slices, thyme, remaining salt, and nutmeg. Cover and cook over low heat, stirring occasionally, for 40 to 45 minutes. Stir in cream just before serving. Meanwhile, cook spaghetti according to directions on package. Drain in colander. Serve chicken mixture over spaghetti. Makes 4 servings.

SPAGHETTI WITH TUNA SAUCE
- 8 ounces spaghetti
- 2 tablespoons butter or margarine
- 1 small onion, chopped
- ¼ cup chopped green pepper
- 2 cans (10½ ounces each) condensed cream-of-mushroom soup
- 1 can (9¼ ounces) tuna, drained and flaked
- ¼ cup heavy cream

Cook spaghetti according to directions on package. Drain and rinse with hot water. Melt butter and sauté onion and green pepper in it until tender. Add soup, tuna, and heavy cream. Heat only until mixture starts to boil. Spoon sauce over hot spaghetti. Makes 4 to 6 servings.

GARLIC LOVER'S SPAGHETTI
- ½ cup olive oil
- ½ cup butter or margarine
- 4 to 6 garlic cloves, minced
- 1 teaspoon salt
- ½ teaspoon pepper
- ½ teaspoon crumbled dried oregano (optional)
- ½ cup chopped parsley
- 1 pound thin spaghetti

Melt together olive oil and butter. The mixture should be warm rather than hot. Lightly sauté garlic in it for 5 minutes. Add salt, pepper, oregano, and parsley; simmer for 5 minutes, stirring constantly. Cook and drain spaghetti. Toss with sauce. Makes 6 to 8 servings.

CARUSO SPAGHETTI
- 2 tablespoons butter or margarine
- 2 medium onions, minced
- 6 fresh tomatoes, peeled, seeded, and chopped
- 1 cup fat-free beef or veal gravy
- ¼ cup olive oil
- 1 can (4 ounces) sliced mushrooms, drained
- 4 canned artichoke bottoms, diced
- 1 cup chopped chicken livers
- 1 teaspoon salt
- ½ teaspoon pepper
- 1 teaspoon grated lemon rind
- 2 tablespoons chopped parsley
- 1 pound spaghetti

Melt butter and cook onions in it until soft and golden. Add tomatoes and gravy. Simmer for 10 minutes. Heat olive oil and in it sauté mushrooms, artichoke bottoms, and chicken livers for about 5 minutes. Add to tomato sauce together with salt, pepper, lemon rind, and parsley. Cover and simmer for 10 to 15 minutes, stirring frequently. Serve on hot cooked spaghetti. Makes 6 servings.

SPAGHETTI AMATRICIANA
- ¼ pound lean bacon, diced
- 1 pound tomatoes, peeled, seeded, and chopped
- 1 teaspoon salt

½ teaspoon pepper
¾ cup dry white wine
1 pound spaghetti or other pasta

Cook bacon until soft and transparent. It must not be crisp. Add tomatoes, salt, pepper, and wine. Simmer for 15 minutes, stirring often. Serve on spaghetti. Makes 6 servings.

TWO-CHEESE FUSILLI

8 ounces fusilli
3 tablespoons butter or margarine
3 tablespoons all-purpose flour
1 cup each of hot milk and light cream
1 teaspoon salt
½ teaspoon pepper
2 cups grated Cheddar cheese
½ pound Swiss cheese, diced
Paprika

Cook and drain fusilli. Melt butter and stir in flour. Stir in combined hot milk and cream. Cook until sauce is smooth and thickened. Stir in salt, pepper, and grated Cheddar. Cook until cheese is melted. In buttered dish arrange a layer of fusilli, diced Swiss cheese, and one third of the cheese sauce. Repeat twice. Sprinkle with paprika. Bake in preheated moderate oven (350°F.) for about 20 minutes. Makes 4 to 6 servings.

Olive Two-Cheese Fusilli

Add ¾ cup chopped pitted black or sliced pimiento-stuffed olives to sauce in above recipe. Proceed as directed.

Pimiento Two-Cheese Fusilli

Add ¾ cup chopped pimientos to sauce in above recipe. Proceed as directed.

Poppy-Seed Two-Cheese Fusilli

Add 1 tablespoon poppy seeds to sauce in above recipe. Proceed as directed.

HOME-FRIED SPAGHETTI

8 ounces spaghetti
4 large eggs
2 teaspoons salt
½ teaspoon pepper
2 teaspoons instant minced onion
¼ cup grated Parmesan cheese
¼ cup butter or margarine

Cook and drain spaghetti. Beat together eggs, salt, pepper, onion, and cheese. Mix thoroughly with spaghetti. Melt butter in skillet. Add spaghetti mixture; fry until brown on both sides. Makes 4 to 6 servings.

SICILIAN SPAGHETTI

3 tablespoons olive oil
1 garlic clove, minced
2 tablespoons minced parsley
1 tablespoon minced fresh basil or 1 teaspoon crumbled dried basil
1 tablespoon minced celery
1 tablespoon capers
12 pitted black olives, minced
4 anchovy fillets, minced
Dash of hot pepper sauce
3 cups plain tomato sauce
1 pound spaghetti

Heat olive oil. Over low heat, stirring constantly, cook all ingredients except tomato sauce and spaghetti in oil for 5 minutes. Add tomato sauce and simmer, covered, over low heat for about 30 minutes. Cook and drain spaghetti. Add sauce and toss well. Makes 6 servings.

SPAGHETTI WITH ZUCCHINI SAUCE

¼ cup butter or margarine
½ cup finely diced onion
¼ cup finely diced green pepper
1 pound zucchini squash, sliced
2 cups diced fresh tomatoes
1 teaspoon salt
⅛ teaspoon pepper
1 can (4 ounces) sliced mushrooms
8 ounces spaghetti

Melt butter over low heat; add onion and sauté for 2 minutes. Add green pepper, squash, tomatoes, salt, pepper, and undrained mushrooms. Cover and cook over low heat for about 40 minutes. Cook spaghetti according to package directions. Drain in colander. Serve hot zucchini sauce over spaghetti. Sprinkle with grated Parmesan cheese if desired. Makes 4 to 6 servings.

SPAGHETTI SAUCES

Few if any dishes are so satisfying as a dish of steaming spaghetti or other pasta dressed with a lovely sauce. Serve your spaghetti with plenty of grated Parmesan or Romano cheese, preferably freshly grated. And here's an Italian spaghetti trick to make the dish even more succulent. When you've poured the sauce over your spaghetti, add a piece of butter (2 to 4 tablespoons for each pound of pasta) and toss it right in. It smooths the flavor no end.

TOMATO SPAGHETTI SAUCE

1 garlic clove, minced
1 green pepper, minced
⅓ cup chopped celery
1 large onion, chopped
3 parsley sprigs
2 medium carrots, diced
2 tablespoons olive oil
2½ cups chopped fresh or canned (one 19-ounce can) tomatoes
2 bay leaves
6 peppercorns
¼ teaspoon thyme
2 teaspoons salt
Dash of cayenne
6 whole cloves
1 tablespoon sugar
1 can (6 ounces) tomato paste
½ pound mushrooms, sliced
1 tablespoon butter or margarine

Put first 7 ingredients in kettle. Cover and cook gently for 15 minutes; do not brown. Stir frequently. Add remaining ingredients except tomato paste, mushrooms, and butter and simmer, covered, for about 45 minutes. Force through a coarse sieve or food mill. Add tomato paste. Sauté mushrooms in the butter for about 5 minutes. Add to sauce, and heat. Makes enough sauce for 12 ounces spaghetti, or 4 generous servings.

TOMATO-MEAT SPAGHETTI SAUCE

1 medium onion, minced
2 garlic cloves, minced
¼ cup olive oil
1 pound ground beef
3½ cups (one 28-ounce can) tomatoes
1 can (6 ounces) tomato paste
2 teaspoons salt
⅛ teaspoon cayenne
1 teaspoon sugar
Pinch of basil
1 bay leaf
2 cups water

Lightly brown onion and garlic in the olive oil in large saucepan. Add meat and brown lightly, breaking up with fork. Add remaining ingredients, bring to boil, and simmer, uncovered, for about 1½ hours. Makes enough sauce for 1 pound spaghetti, cooked, or 6 servings.

MARINARA SAUCE

¼ cup olive oil
2 tablespoons chopped parsley
1 onion, minced
1 garlic clove, minced
6 anchovy fillets
About 3½ cups (one 1-pound, 13-ounce can) Italian tomatoes
Salt, pepper, and crumbled dried oregano
12 ounces spaghetti, cooked
Grated cheese

Heat olive oil. Add parsley, onion, garlic, and anchovy fillets. Brown lightly. Add Italian tomatoes and salt, pepper, and oregano to taste. Simmer, uncovered, for about 20 minutes, stirring occasionally. Serve on spaghetti, sprinkled with grated cheese. Makes 6 servings.

MUSHROOM-OLIVE SAUCE

¼ pound mushrooms, sliced
2 tablespoons butter or margarine
2 garlic cloves, crushed
1 tablespoon powdered mustard
1 tablespoon water
3 tablespoons olive oil
½ teaspoon sugar
2 tablespoons heavy cream
10 diced pitted ripe olives
2 to 3 teaspoons capers
8 ounces spaghetti, cooked
Salt to taste

Sauté mushrooms in butter with garlic for about 5 minutes. Cool. Blend mustard with water. Gradually blend in olive oil. Add sugar, cream, olives, and capers. Add mushrooms, and pour over spaghetti. Toss lightly, and season. Makes 4 servings.

GARBANZO SAUCE

1 onion, chopped
1 garlic clove, minced
½ cup diced celery and tops
3 tablespoons olive oil
About 2¼ cups (one 1-pound, 3-ounce can) garbanzos (chick-peas) with liquid in can
Water
About 2¼ cups (one 1-pound, 3-ounce can) tomatoes
1 can (6 ounces) tomato paste

SPAGHETTI

1 bay leaf
1 teaspoon salt
Dash of cayenne
½ teaspoon crumbled dried oregano
1 pound spaghetti, cooked
Grated Parmesan cheese

Sauté onion, garlic, and celery in olive oil until golden. Drain garbanzos, reserving liquid. Measure liquid; add water to make 2½ cups. Mash garbanzos. Add garbanzos, liquid, tomatoes, tomato paste, bay leaf, salt, cayenne, and oregano to onion mixture. Simmer, uncovered, for 2 hours, stirring occasionally. Serve on spaghetti, with a sprinkling of grated cheese. Makes 8 servings.

TREVISANO SAUCE

¼ pound each of salt pork and lean pork meat, cut into ½-inch cubes
½ pound each of veal and chicken, cut into ½-inch cubes
1 garlic clove, minced
2 onions, chopped
2 green peppers, chopped
4 ripe tomatoes, peeled and diced
1 cup dry white wine
¼ teaspoon pepper
1 bay leaf
1 tablespoon tomato paste
½ teaspoon crumbled dried thyme
Salt to taste
8 ounces spaghetti, cooked

Partially cook salt pork and pour off fat. Add other meats and brown lightly. Add all but last 3 ingredients. Simmer, uncovered, stirring occasionally, for 1 hour, or until thick, adding water as needed. Add last 3 ingredients. Serve, with cheese, on spaghetti. Makes 4 servings.

ANCHOVY SAUCE

1 tablespoon all-purpose flour
¼ cup olive oil
2 tablespoons dry wine
¾ cup water
1 can (6 ounces) tomato paste
1 bay leaf
1 can (2 ounces) flat anchovy fillets, mashed to a paste
Salt and pepper
8 ounces spaghetti, cooked

Brown flour lightly in oil. Add wine, water, tomato paste, and bay leaf. Simmer, uncovered, for 15 minutes. Add anchovies, anchovy oil, and salt and pepper to taste. Simmer for 5 minutes. Serve on spaghetti, with grated cheese. Makes 4 servings.

ROASTED-PEPPER SAUCE

¼ pound salt pork, diced
2 garlic cloves, minced
1 teaspoon crumbled dried oregano
¼ teaspoon fennel seed
1 jar (7½ ounces) roasted peppers, cut into strips
1 can (10½ ounces) tomato purée
2 tablespoons minced parsley
1 can (3 ounces) sliced mushrooms with liquid
Salt and pepper
8 ounces spaghetti, cooked

Brown salt pork and remove from skillet. Pour off all but about 2 tablespoons fat. Add garlic; brown lightly. Add crisp pork, oregano, fennel seed, roasted peppers, tomato purée, parsley, mushrooms with liquid, and salt and pepper to taste. Simmer for a few minutes. Serve on spaghetti. Makes 4 servings.

PARSLEY-OLIVE SAUCE

½ cup butter or margarine
½ cup chopped parsley
1 cup green olives, pitted and chopped
¼ teaspoon pepper
8 ounces spaghetti, cooked
Salt to taste

Melt butter. Add parsley, olives, and pepper. Pour over spaghetti, toss, and add salt to taste. Makes 4 servings.

WHITE TUNA SAUCE

1 onion, chopped
1 garlic clove, chopped
¼ cup olive oil
2 cans (7 ounces each) tuna fish
½ teaspoon pepper
8 ounces spaghetti, cooked
Salt to taste

Sauté onion and garlic in oil until golden-brown. Add tuna, and simmer for 5 minutes. Add pepper. Pour over spaghetti. Toss, and add salt. Makes 4 servings.

QUICK WHITE CLAM SAUCE

2 tablespoons chopped parsley
1 garlic clove, minced
1 medium onion, chopped
2 tablespoons olive oil
½ teaspoon salt
Dash of pepper
1 can (10½ ounces) minced clams
8 ounces spaghetti, cooked

Sauté parsley, garlic, and onion in hot oil for 5 minutes. Add salt, pepper, and minced clams with liquid. Simmer for 5 minutes longer. Serve on spaghetti. Makes 4 servings.

TOMATO PURÉE SAUCE

2 tablespoons chopped parsley
¼ cup butter
1 can (10½ ounces) tomato purée
1 tablespoon water
8 ounces spaghetti, cooked

Sauté parsley in butter for 2 minutes. Add tomato purée and water; heat. Serve on spaghetti. Makes 4 servings.

PARMESAN PARSLEY SAUCE

⅓ cup butter or margarine
1 garlic clove, minced
8 ounces spaghetti, cooked
¾ cup finely chopped parsley
½ cup grated Parmesan cheese

Melt butter in small saucepan; add garlic and simmer until butter is lightly browned. Pour over spaghetti. Add parsley and cheese. Toss well; serve with additional cheese if desired. Makes 4 servings.

BOLOGNESE MEAT SAUCE

¼ pound bacon or Italian prosciutto, minced
1 tablespoon butter
1 medium onion, minced
1 carrot, minced
1 small piece of celery, minced
½ pound lean beef, ground
¼ pound chicken livers, minced
1 tablespoon tomato paste
½ cup dry white wine
1 cup beef bouillon
Salt and pepper
⅛ teaspoon ground nutmeg
1 teaspoon grated lemon rind
2 whole cloves (optional)
1 cup heavy cream

In heavy saucepan cook bacon in butter until soft and golden. Add onion, carrot, and celery. Cook over low heat until browned. Add beef and brown evenly. Add chicken livers and cook for 2 or 3 minutes. Stir in tomato paste and wine and cook for another 2 minutes. Add bouillon, salt and pepper to taste, nutmeg, lemon rind, and cloves, if desired. Simmer, covered, over low heat for 40 minutes. Before serving, heat cream but do not boil. Stir into sauce. Makes enough sauce for 12 ounces spaghetti, cooked, or 4 generous servings.

STRACOTTO SAUCE

This is one of the best of all Italian pasta sauces. It is really an essence of meat flavored with mushrooms and Marsala. The mushrooms should be the imported dried ones, found in practically all food stores, since they are more flavorful than our fresh ones. Stracotto in Italian literally means cooked for a very long time, and the secret of this sauce is just that—long slow cooking.

1 pound beef chuck or round
½ cup butter or margarine
1 medium onion, minced
1 medium carrot, minced
1 celery stalk, minced
½ cup minced parsley
½ cup dry Marsala or Madeira
1 cup beef bouillon
1 ounce dried mushrooms
1 medium tomato, peeled and chopped
Salt and pepper to taste
1 teaspoon grated lemon rind

Cut meat into tiny dice or run through coarse blade of food chopper. It must not be ground as finely as hamburger. Heat butter in heavy saucepan. Add onion, carrot, celery, and parsley and cook over medium heat for 5 minutes, stirring frequently. Add meat, wine, and bouillon. Soften dried mushrooms in water to cover for 5 minutes; chop. Add mushrooms and water to sauce. Add tomato. Season with salt, pepper, and lemon rind. Simmer over lowest possible heat, it should be barely a flicker, for 3 hours, or until meat is almost dissolved. Stir occasionally. Check for moisture; the sauce should be thick. Enough for 1 pound of pasta.

Spaghetti with Meatballs

SPANISH COOKERY

by Marcia Colman Morton

Flamenco, bullfights, dusty olive trees baking in an adobe square, wild-maned girls dressed in polka-dot flounces and with roses in their teeth, spicy food that sets your blood on fire—ah, Spain, that most oversimplified of all European countries.

Spain is no never-never little storybook land, easily grasped in a few phrases. How could it be? For one thing, it's so big—in all Europe, only Russia and France are bigger—and so varied. Its nearly thirty million people live in separate provinces as different as separate countries in their customs, their speech, and their cooking. I, for instance, who am used to the Barcelona dialect, can hardly understand the people of Malaga in the south; while the Catalans in the countryside around Barcelona, and the northern Basques, go far beyond mere dialect shadings—each people has its own ancient distinctive language.

The cooking varies so much that there is even a popular Spanish saying about it: "In the south they fry, in the central regions they roast, and in the north they stew." But whatever they do, the food is seldom really spicy; savory is a more fitting word for what is, after all, European cooking, not Mexican. Just as flamenco is not quite the whole story of Spanish dance. True, the passionate chants and heel stampings of flamenco haunt the gypsy- and Moorish-tinged nights of Andalusia. But other provinces twirl and skip like German or French peasants; while the stately Catalonian *sardana* is measured out to a unique reedy music, more reminiscent of Greek music and dance than of flamenco.

Partly all this variety is a matter of geography, in a country stretching over so many different terrains: the indeed sunny languor of Andalusia, with its white-stucco walls and red-tile roofs; the just-as-authentically Spanish salt-aired Atlantic coast around San Sebastián, with its half-timbered houses so reminiscent of French Normandy; the snowy peaks of the Pyrenees, where Alpine chalets nestle and skiers' cries echo down the slopes; the green fields of Catalonia, where vegetables grow verdant under pleasant rains; the hard-headed businessmen and energetic bustle that make Barcelona "the New York of Spain"; the icy winds of a Madrid winter, and the cosmopolitan chic of that city, with its white skyscrapers and a night life and boulevards and elegant shops to rival Paris itself.

Geography determines the food, too. Spaniards of the central region (fanning out from the center of the center, Madrid) eat roast meats because they have such tender suckling pigs, such delicate young lambs grazing on wild herbs, to work with. And they roast these good things simply, as people do everywhere when the basic ingredients are too delicious to tamper with.

But everywhere in Spain the beef is a tough customer. So the national beef dish is not a roast but a *cocido,* meaning stew. Roughly this is a simmering casserole in which the meats vary according to what is on hand, as do the vegetables. Ingredients and methods change a little from region to region, but always chick-peas are *the* essential ingredient, and always a *cocido* is cooked long and lovingly to make sure the beef is chewable in the end. (The *cocido* recipe given here is as close as you can come to one that most Spaniards would agree to call classic.)

Until quite recently chicken, too, was a matter for casserole cooking and slow coaxing into tenderness. I remember driving for miles to find the occasional farm that raised specially fed pullets and capons for roasting. Then, in the early 1960's, Spain began to import huge quantities of frozen American fowl, and a grateful nation learned the delights of juicy barbecued chicken. Little shops that serve nothing else now dot the Spanish cities the way pizza parlors dot ours.

Just because meats and domestic fowl have been, historically, in short supply, the Spanish cuisine has developed rich substitutes. Toothsome little roasted wild partridge, for instance, appears on the menu of even a rather humble restaurant. And soup—the Spanish are masters at getting a delicious tureen from surprisingly little—a dash of olive oil and a few garlic cloves, or a hambone and some odds and ends of vegetables. Or beans—every tiny village seems to have its own special way of turning this humble staple into a nutritious, rib-sticking meal that costs pennies.

Sweets are the least of Spanish accomplishments; not so surprising in a country where fresh sweet melons, passion fruit, oranges, and bananas make such a stunning final touch to a meal. The cakes are usually of a Byzantine sweetness, running to marzipan and candied fruits, and not very appealing to non-Spanish palates. They are a vestige of the medieval Moorish invasions of Spain, culinary counterparts to the Moorish towers now crumbling along Spain's Mediterranean coasts, or the tiled mosques and palaces of Granada and Córdoba and Seville. The best pastry is borrowed from other European countries, the French or Viennese classic recipes. If there is a national dessert, it is *flan,* which is nothing but a boiled custard, no different from the recipe available in your most basic cook book. And the *churros* sold at street stands—to be eaten at breakfast, teatime, or any other time you want a snack—are merely fried crullers.

I have saved for last the best part of Spanish cooking, the part that has the most to teach Americans. And that, in a word, is fish. The seafood of Spain is a wonder. It is good everywhere, and everywhere it is cooked with love and care and tender appreciation. "In the south they fry . . ." They fry everything from the tiny fresh whitebait to the succulent red mullet; or they grill quickly, with a few drops of olive oil, the sardines fresh from the sea, and wash them down with red wine and hunks of fragrant bread smeared with the pulp of ripe tomatoes.

It's different in the north, where the epicurean Basques live, basking in their reputation as the best cooks in Spain. Appetites atingle from the brisk salt breezes, "in the north they stew" heartily, aromatically. "They" are often the men. All over Spain, sociability is still often exclusively masculine, with the women kept at home in a near-Oriental seclusion. In Madrid the nightclubs entertain mostly male audiences; in Seville the men meet only each other over afternoon coffee, in cafés that have the conviviality of private men's clubs. In San Sebastián, the Basque capital, male sociability takes a gastronomic turn. In that city's famous eating clubs the men meet weekly, to laugh, drink, and vie in cooking for each other. They invent intricate stews, based mostly on the cod and tuna, shellfish and squid that abound in their Atlantic waters.

But however the Spanish cook the sea's bounty, in whatever part of the country—a savoring respect for fish is the Spanish cuisine's most valuable lesson for Americans. We, who have as beautiful a supply of seafood as do the Spanish, but who usually toss it in a skillet and hope for the best, can learn how to prepare fish so that it comes to the table greeted by the smile and the sigh of pleasure it deserves.

APPETIZERS

ALCACHOFAS RELLENOS CON SARDINAS
(Sardine-Stuffed Artichokes)

6 whole raw artichokes
Juice of 1 lemon
½ cup olive oil (about)
Salt
1 raw egg yolk
1 teaspoon prepared mustard
1 teaspoon vinegar
3 large canned sardines, boned
Pepper
Chopped parsley
6 large pitted green olives

Discard tough outer leaves of artichokes. Cut off spiny tips of remaining inner portion of each artichoke and core out center thistles. Sprinkle artichokes with half of lemon juice. Cook with ¼ cup of the olive oil and the remaining lemon juice in salted boiling water to cover until tender, about 20 minutes. Drain thoroughly. Meanwhile, beat together egg yolk, mustard, vinegar, and enough olive oil to make a mayonnaise. Mash the sardines with about 1 tablespoon of this mayonnaise, or enough to make a velvety mixture. Season with salt and pepper to taste. Heap sardine mixture into artichoke centers and top with remaining mayonnaise. Garnish each with chopped parsley and an olive. Makes 6 servings.

SARDINAS CON SALSA DE TOMATES
(Sardines in Tomato Sauce)

Canned whole sardines
Tomato sauce, canned or homemade
Green peppers
Hard-cooked egg white

Dry sardines on paper towels to drain off all the oil. Arrange them on a platter in any attractive pattern desired (a star shape is popular in Spain). Pour the tomato sauce over fish; if sauce is mild, add a little freshly ground black pepper. Split the green peppers into flat pieces, halves or thirds; remove seeds and white portion of pulp. Broil under medium heat until the skin browns and puckers. Skin will peel off easily with a thin-bladed knife. Slice peppers and egg white into thin julienne strips, and sprinkle generously over the tomato sauce. Serve cold, accompanied by crackers or thin toast triangles.

SALMONETES LEVANTINOS
(Red Mullet Levantine)

For this recipe the Spanish use the smallest red mullet, available all along the Mediterranean coastline of Spain; if unavailable here, substitute small butterfish, porgies, or any small but meaty fish; or use larger fish cut into quarters.

12 to 24 small fish or equivalent, about 4 pounds
2 tablespoons olive oil
Salt
2 garlic cloves, minced
½ bay leaf, broken up
1 teaspoon ground saffron
Fennel seed, ground cuminseed, and ground thyme to taste
2 tablespoons chopped parsley
4 tomatoes, peeled, seeded, diced
½ bottle dry white wine
Quartered lemons

Prepare fish for cooking, but do not remove skin or bones. Wash; dry thoroughly. Oil generously a large baking pan. Arrange fish in it so that pieces don't touch. Sprinkle with salt, spices, herbs, and tomatoes. Pour wine over top. Bake in preheated moderate oven (350° F.) for 30 minutes, or until sauce begins to bubble. Continue baking for 10 to 15 minutes longer, or until fish is just done; time depends on size of fish. Let fish cool in sauce. Remove to platter, carefully so as not to break fish. Strain sauce over top. Serve cold, garnished with lemon quarters. Makes 12 servings.

PESCADO A LA VINAGRETA
(Fish Vinaigrette)

½ pound fish (scrod, haddock, flounder, etc.), cooked
2 tablespoons chopped onion
1 garlic clove, minced
1 tablespoon chopped capers
2 tablespoons chopped parsley
1 cucumber, peeled, seeded, and diced
1 hard-cooked egg, chopped
3 tablespoons olive oil
3 tablespoons vinegar
Salt and pepper
1 or 2 firm tomatoes, peeled, seeded, and diced

Use leftover cooked fish; or, if you start with raw fish, simmer it gently until it's thoroughly cooked; when cold, cut into cubes. Arrange cubed fish in shallow bowl. Add onion, garlic, capers, parsley, cucumber, and egg. Sprinkle with oil and vinegar. Season with salt and pepper to taste. Toss gently so as not to break up fish. Cover bowl, and marinate salad in refrigerator for about 2 hours. Gently toss in diced tomato. Makes 4 servings.

Anchoas a la Vinagreta
(Anchovies Vinaigrette)

Substitute anchovies for fish in preceding recipe (two or three 2-ounce cans of flat fillets), and omit salt since the anchovies provide their own saltiness.

SALADS

ENSALADA A LA ANDALUZA
(Andalusian Vinaigrette Salad)

¼ cup olive oil
¼ cup vinegar
¼ teaspoon pepper
2 cucumbers, peeled, seeded, and diced
Salt to taste

SPANISH COOKERY

6 green peppers
3 tomatoes
½ garlic clove (optional)
2 tablespoons chopped onion

Mix oil, vinegar, and pepper for a dressing; reserve. Heap diced cucumber in a bowl; sprinkle with salt and let stand for 20 minutes, or until water has run out. Drain on paper towels. Remove to small bowl and toss with half of the reserved dressing. Split green peppers into flat pieces, halves or thirds; remove seeds and white portion of pulp; broil under medium heat until the skin browns and puckers; peel off skin with thin-bladed knife; dice. Heap diced peppers in a bowl; sprinkle with salt and let stand for 15 minutes to drain. Remove to small bowl and toss with remaining dressing. Plunge tomatoes into boiling water for a few seconds to loosen skins; dry with paper towels. Peel and quarter the tomatoes and remove seeds; dice; add salt to taste and let stand for 15 minutes. If you like a touch of garlic (I don't, in this salad), rub a salad bowl with a cut garlic clove. Add diced cucumbers and green peppers (which have been marinating for about 30 minutes by now) and their dressing. Add tomato and onion; toss lightly. Chill before serving. Makes 6 to 8 servings.

ENSALADA DE ARROZ A LA VALENCIANA
(Rice Salad Valenciana)

2 quarts water
2 tablespoons salt
⅔ cup uncooked rice
1 tablespoon dry sherry
2 green peppers
2 tomatoes
1 tablespoon powdered mustard
¼ teaspoon pepper
¼ cup olive oil
¼ cup vinegar

Bring water and salt to a boil. Add rice and cook, uncovered, for about 20 minutes, or until rice is cooked but still firm. Drain rice and remove to heatproof casserole. Stir in sherry and let rice cool completely. Prepare green peppers and tomatoes as directed in recipe for Ensalada a la Andaluza, above, but do not add any dressing to them; instead, in large bowl, moisten mustard with a little cold water to make a paste; add pepper, oil, and vinegar; mix for a dressing. Stir in diced green peppers, tomatoes, and finally, the cooled rice. Marinate salad in refrigerator for at least 30 minutes. Makes 6 servings.

SOUPS

GAZPACHO
(Cold Salad-Soup)

½ cup soft bread crumbs
  Water
½ garlic clove, minced
1 teaspoon salt
3 tablespoons olive oil
3 tablespoons vinegar
1 or 2 tablespoons chopped onion (optional)
4 tomatoes, sliced
1 canned pimiento, diced
  Green peppers, tomatoes, and cucumbers
3 slices of toast, diced
3 hard-cooked eggs, chopped

Moisten bread crumbs with ½ cup cold water. Add garlic, salt, oil, vinegar, onion if desired, tomatoes, and pimiento. Marinate in refrigerator for about 30 minutes; then put through fine sieve, food mill, or blender. Blend in up to 2 cups cold water, just enough to make a fairly thick soup. Chill; or use less water, and add a few ice cubes. Serve in large tureen, surrounded by individual small serving bowls containing green peppers, tomatoes, and cucumbers, each prepared separately as in Ensalada a la Andaluza, (page 1741), and each tossed with one-third the dressing specified in that recipe, toast cubes, and chopped hard-cooked egg. Each person is served a plateful of soup to which he adds the accompaniments in any proportion he likes. Makes 6 servings.

SOPA DE AJOS
(Garlic Soup)

8 garlic cloves
½ cup olive oil or more
  Pinch of cayenne
8 slices of stale sliced white bread, cubed
2 quarts boiling water
  Salt and pepper
6 eggs, beaten

In Dutch oven, sauté garlic cloves in hot oil until golden brown; remove and reserve. Stir cayenne into oil. Fry bread cubes in same oil until they're firm and golden, but not charred or crumbly. (Beautiful bread cubes, says a little Spanish peasant cook book I have, "are the grace of this soup.") Carefully pour in the boiling water so as not to damage the bread cubes. Add salt and pepper to taste. Put reserved garlic cloves through a press, or mash them; mix to a paste with a little cold water; add to soup. Simmer, covered, for about 1 hour. Slowly pour in eggs, and continue simmering until egg is just set. Makes 6 to 8 servings.

■ **Variations**—Omit beaten eggs; instead, garnish with cubes of German-style salami or *chorizo* (Spanish sausage).

Omit eggs; instead, garnish with diced red and/or green peppers which have been grilled, peeled, and seeded, or with canned pimiento.

Omit eggs. Pour finished soup into individual broilerproof casseroles, and toast under a medium heat for a few minutes.

SOPA DE ALMENDRAS
(Almond Soup)

2½ cups blanched almonds, ground
1½ quarts cold water
1 bay leaf
  Peel cut from ½ lemon
1 cinnamon stick
5 tablespoons butter
  Salt
8 slices of white bread, crusts removed, diced

In large bowl, soak almonds in the water for 1 hour. Strain through cheesecloth into soup kettle, squeezing hard to extract all the essence. Add bay leaf, lemon peel, cinnamon stick, and butter. Simmer for 10 minutes. Add salt to taste. Toast diced bread in oven until golden; heap into soup tureen. Strain soup over bread carefully, so as not to break up the toast cubes. Serve immediately. Makes 6 servings.

MEAT

The most classically Spanish meat dish is not a roast or grill but a sort of stew, called cocido *or* puchero, *which provides soup and main course both. The same is true of their fish recipes. So although some of them might technically fit into the Soups category, I am dividing them into Meat and Fish.*

COCIDO
(Spanish Boiled Beef)

*1 pound beef (chuck, round, rump, etc.)
*¼ chicken
 2 beef marrowbones and 1 hambone (optional)
 1 tablespoon salt
 2 quarts cold water
 ½ pound dried chick-peas, soaked overnight
 1 onion
 3 leeks, sliced
 2 carrots, sliced
 1 white turnip, sliced
 1 parsley sprig
 1 pound potatoes, peeled and quartered

In soup kettle, combine beef, chicken, and bones; the hambone, if you have one, adds a nice smokiness. Add salt, and enough *cold* water to cover, about 2 quarts. Bring to a boil over high heat, and carefully skim off the scum that rises. Reduce heat and simmer, covered, for 1 hour. (This method, starting the meat in *cold* water and bringing it to a boil, is used for beef soups in much of Europe because it lets the beef richness flow into the soup. Starting the meat in *boiling* water seals in the juices and gives

SPANISH COOKERY

you more succulent beef at the end, but the soup suffers. So take your choice.) While the soup is simmering, drain the presoaked chick-peas. Pour boiling water over them so they'll be hot when you add them to the soup, and drain again; wrap loosely but securely in cheesecloth so they won't fall apart in the soup, and plunge into soup kettle. Taste the soup, and correct for salt sparingly (the vegetable side dish for a *cocido,* see Verduras, at right, adds its own considerable saltiness). Skim soup carefully again. Continue simmering, covered, for about 1 hour longer. Add onion (pretoasted in oven if you want its brownness to enrich the color of the soup, then sliced), leeks, carrots, turnip, and parsley. Simmer for about 1 hour longer. (In Spain the soup is cooked, start to finish, for about 5 hours, because it takes that long for the tough Spanish beef to become tender. But most of our superior American beef will be done with about 3 hours of cooking.) Strain off the soup; save to use for stock or to serve as clear consommé or garnished with rice, noodles, toasted bread cubes, etc. Leave everything else in the kettle and add the potatoes. Simmer for another 30 minutes, or until potatoes are tender; there will be enough liquid left in the kettle, even after straining the soup, to steam the potatoes.

■ **To serve:** Remove cheesecloth package of chick-peas; drain. Heap chick-peas in center of large platter. Slice beef and chicken, and arrange over chick-peas together with slices of Relleno (see below). Garnish with vegetables from soup kettle. In separate bowl, serve Verduras. The Spanish also often accompany a *cocido* with a dish of tomato or other piquant sauce, a serving bowl of one of the bean recipes, and a plate of fried green peppers. Makes 4 to 6 servings.

*This relatively small amount of beef and chicken makes a *cocido* for 6 in Spain, along with all the side dishes. For meat-loving Americans, you may want to increase the quantity.

RELLENO
(Pork Roll for Cocido)

- ¼ pound lean pork, chopped fine
- 1 garlic clove, minced
- 2 tablespoons chopped parsley
- 1 egg, beaten
- Soft bread crumbs
- Salt and pepper
- All-purpose flour
- Olive oil

Mix together chopped pork, garlic, parsley, egg, enough bread crumbs to bind, and salt and pepper to taste. Form mixture into thick roll. Dredge lightly with flour. Sauté in hot oil until golden brown. Drain, slice, and serve as described for Cocido, above. Makes 6 servings.

VERDURAS
(Vegetable Side Dish for Cocido)

- ¼ pound chorizo (Spanish sausage), cubed
- ¼ pound lean ham, diced
- 2 ounces salt pork or bacon, diced
- ¼ pound blood sausage, cubed
- 2 pounds sliced cabbage, green beans, Brussels sprouts, etc. (alone or in combination)

In large saucepan, combine meats and any green vegetable you like. (Personally, I panfry the meats first to get rid of excess fat, but the Spanish use them raw. They like the resulting "richness" in the vegetables.) Cover with just enough cold water to keep from sticking. Simmer until done, about 15 to 20 minutes. Makes 6 servings.

FISH

SOPA DE PESCADO A LA VASCA
(Basque Fish Soup)

- 2 medium onions, diced
- 2 leeks (white part), diced
- 3 garlic cloves, minced
- 2 carrots, diced
- ¼ cup chopped parsley
- ¼ cup olive oil
- 2 pounds mixed fish in large hunks or slices (scrod, haddock, bass, etc.)
- 3 large tomatoes, quartered
- 2 quarts boiling water (about)
- Salt and pepper
- 6 slices of French or white bread, crusts on, cubed

Sauté onions, leeks, garlic, carrots, and parsley in hot oil until cooked but not browned. Add fish, tomatoes, and just enough boiling water to cover. Season with salt and pepper to taste. Simmer, covered, for 30 minutes, or until fish is cooked but still firm. Carefully remove fish; discard skin and bones; cut flesh into bite-size pieces; reserve. Meanwhile, let soup continue simmering for 30 minutes or more, to bring out flavor. Arrange cubed bread in flameproof casserole or Dutch oven. Strain soup over bread; bring to a simmer. Add reserved fish; simmer for about 5 minutes. Serve immediately. Makes 6 servings.

MARMITAKO
(Basque Fresh-Tuna Stew)

- 1 medium onion, chopped
- ¼ cup olive oil
- 1 pound fresh tuna, in large pieces (if unavailable, use swordfish)
- 2 garlic cloves, minced
- ¼ cup chopped parsley
- 2 tomatoes, peeled, seeded, and diced
- 2 large potatoes, peeled and cubed
- ¼ pound peas, shelled
- ½ cup beef bouillon
- 1 red pepper or canned pimiento, diced
- 1 bay leaf
- Pinch of cayenne
- Salt and pepper
- Toast triangles

Sauté onion in hot oil until golden. Add fish and sauté for a few minutes. Add garlic, parsley, and tomatoes; sauté. Add potatoes, peas, bouillon, diced pepper, bay leaf, and cayenne. Simmer, covered, for about 1 hour. Season with salt and pepper to taste. Serve, garnished with toast triangles. Makes 6 servings.

ZARZUELA DE MARISCOS
(Literally, Musical Comedy of Shellfish)

- 1 onion, chopped
- ¼ cup olive oil
- 1 or 2 garlic cloves, minced
- ¼ cup chopped parsley
- 2 tablespoons tomato paste
- 1½ pounds small shrimps, shelled
- 1½ pounds lobster or lobster tail, cut into bite-size pieces
- ½ cup dry white wine
- Salt and pepper
- 20 raw clams
- 1 teaspoon ground saffron

Sauté onion in hot oil until golden. Stir in garlic, parsley, and tomato paste. Add shrimps and lobster. Pour wine over top. Season with salt and pepper to taste. Cover, and simmer for 10 minutes, or until shrimps and lobster are half cooked. Meanwhile, simmer clams in water until they are cooked and open. Remove half shells; add clams, on the half shell, to simmering shrimps and lobster. Sprinkle everything with saffron, and continue cooking until shrimps and lobster are done. Serve hot in soup plates. Makes 6 servings.

BACALAO A LA VIZCAÍNA
(Basque Salt-Cod Casserole)

This dish is even better reheated the next day. It may work with fresh cod, although I've never tried it.

- 2 pounds dried salt cod, best quality (use only the lean side portions, not the fatty center)
- ½ cup olive oil
- Lard
- ¼ pound bacon, diced
- ¼ pound smoked ham, diced
- 4 large mild red onions, chopped
- 2 garlic cloves
- 3 parsley sprigs
- 2 cups boiling water
- 8 to 10 canned pimientos (enough to give the finished dish a rich red color), diced
- 3 tomatoes, peeled, seeded, and cubed
- 2 hard-cooked egg yolks
- ½ cup soft bread crumbs
- Salt and pepper
- Pinch of cayenne
- Sugar (if necessary)

Cut cod into 6 equal servings. To remove salt, soak for about 20 hours in fresh cold water, changing water 4 or 5 times. Several hours before you plan to cook the cod, start the sauce (for which they take over 5 hours in Spain, but you may need less). In large skillet (which can be covered later) or Dutch oven, heat oil, ¼ cup lard, bacon, and ham. When mixture bubbles, add onion, whole garlic cloves, and parsley. Cover, turn down heat as low as possible, and cook for 3

ENCYCLOPEDIA OF COOKERY

SPANISH COOKERY

hours, or until onion is very soft but not at all burned. Add boiling water and continue simmering for 2 hours longer, or until onions are completely fallen apart. Add more boiling water as necessary to keep from sticking. Add pimientos, tomatoes, and egg yolks mashed with bread crumbs and mixed to a fine paste with a little cold water. Simmer for a few minutes longer. Put everything through a sieve, food mill, or blender so you have a smooth sauce. Add salt and pepper to taste, and if you want to be authentic, a pinch of cayenne. Meanwhile, when the cod has soaked for 20 hours, dry it thoroughly with paper towels. Remove any scales, being careful not to damage the skin (which adds a smooth, gelatinous quality to the finished dish's sauce). In large saucepan, combine cod and unsalted cold water to cover; bring to a boil. As soon as water starts to boil, take out the pieces of cod; carefully remove bones. Grease a heatproof casserole with lard or bacon fat. In it, arrange a layer of cod; pour sauce over; repeat until all the cod and sauce are used up. Sauce should just cover the fish, not drown it. Cook slowly until fish is done, about 20 minutes. During cooking, shake the casserole often so the sauce runs down to the bottom. Also, with a wide pancake turner or spatula, loosen the bottom layer of fish often to keep it from sticking, being careful not to break the pieces. Taste from time to time, and add salt and pepper if necessary; or a pinch of sugar if the cod is making the sauce too salty. Finished dish should be savory, neither too salty, too peppery, nor too sweet, and of a good red color. Makes 6 servings.

MERLUZA ASADA AL HORNO
(Baked Fish)

The Spanish usually bake a whole fish this way, but I don't see why this recipe couldn't also be used for sliced fish steaks.

- 1 large striped bass
- ½ cup olive oil
- 2 onions, chopped fine
- 2 garlic cloves, minced
  Salt and pepper to taste
- 2 tablespoons bread crumbs
- ¼ to ½ cup dry white wine
- 2 tablespoons chopped parsley
  Juice of 1 lemon

Clean fish and remove scales, but leave it whole. With small sharp knife, make a few slits crosswise along the top. Pour two-thirds of the oil into a baking dish. Spread an even layer of half the onion and garlic in dish and lay the fish on top. Sprinkle with salt and pepper, the remaining onion, garlic, and oil, the bread crumbs, and wine. Bake in preheated hot oven (400°F.), allowing 12 minutes per pound. Before serving, sprinkle fish with parsley and lemon juice. Makes 6 to 8 servings.

EGGS

HUEVOS A LA FLAMENCA
(Eggs Flamenco)

Omelets of all kinds are very popular in Spain, but not too different from French recipes. This egg dish, however, is ubiquitous throughout the country, and as authentically and exclusively Spanish as its name.

- 1 small onion, chopped fine
- 1 garlic clove, minced
- 3 tablespoons olive oil
- ¼ cup chopped ham
  Pinch of cayenne
- 1 tomato, peeled, seeded, and diced
  Salt and pepper
- 1 teaspoon sugar
- 1 cup beef bouillon
- ¼ pound green beans, Frenched
- ½ pound green peas, shelled
- ¼ pound asparagus tips
- 6 eggs
- ¼ pound chorizo or smoked pork sausage links, browned whole
- 1 pimiento, cut into julienne strips
- ½ pound ham cut into julienne strips
- 1 or 2 tablespoons chopped parsley
- 6 to 12 toast triangles

Sauté onion and garlic in hot oil for 2 or 3 minutes. Add chopped ham and continue to cook until onion is translucent but not golden. Stir in cayenne and turn down heat. Stir in tomato, salt and pepper to taste, and sugar. Add bouillon and vegetables. Cook over low heat until vegetables are just tender; do not overcook. (If asparagus tips are canned, add them only after other vegetables are done.) Transfer everything to a shallow baking dish, arranging vegetables evenly, being careful not to break the asparagus tips. Break eggs onto the bed of vegetables and sauce, spacing eggs out a little. Slice the drained, prebrowned *chorizo*. (In Spain the sausage is cooked along with the vegetables, then removed and sliced, but this procedure makes the sauce too fatty for American taste, so I panfry the sausage separately to remove excess fat.) Garnish each egg with some sliced *chorizo* and a few strips of pimiento and ham. Set baking dish on lower rack of oven; bake until whites of eggs are just set. Sprinkle with chopped parsley, set toast triangles around edge of dish, and serve immediately. (In Spanish restaurants, Eggs Flamenco are usually served in individual little clay baking dishes, 1 or 2 eggs in each. But for most American households, and Spanish, it's easier to serve one large dishful, and it's very attractive, too. Makes 6 servings.

BEANS

Throughout Spain, bean casseroles are a staple, either as a hearty main dish or an accompaniment to simple meat courses. Here are a few recipes using both fresh and dried beans.

JUDIAS VERDES A LA VASCA
(Basque Green Beans)

- 1 pound green beans
  Salt
- ¼ cup olive oil
- 1 onion, chopped
- 2 garlic cloves, minced
- ¼ pound smoked ham, diced
- 2 or 3 canned pimientos, diced
  Pepper
- 2 tablespoons chopped parsley

Cook green beans in lightly salted water until just tender; do not overcook. Drain; reserve cooking water. In hot oil, sauté onion until golden. Add garlic, ham, and pimiento; sauté until cooked. Add drained green beans, salt and pepper to taste, and parsley. Continue cooking, stirring, until beans are hot. If necessary, add a little of the reserved cooking water to keep beans from sticking, but this dish should not be very liquid. Makes 4 to 6 servings.

FABADA A LA ASTURIANA
(Asturian Bean Casserole)

- 1 pound white navy beans, soaked overnight
  Salt
- 1 onion, quartered
- ¼ cup olive oil
- ½ pound chorizo
- ½ pound blood sausage
- ½ pound ham
- ¼ pound bacon
- 1 teaspoon ground saffron

Bring beans and fresh cold water to a rolling boil. Drain, and again bring beans to a boil in fresh *salted* cold water. Add onion and oil. When water is at a rolling boil, add meats, cut into large dice, and saffron. Lower heat and simmer, covered, for 2 to 3 hours, or until beans are tender. Add salt to taste. Makes 8 servings.

Note: Sometimes a few chopped chili peppers or pimientos are added to the beans during the last few minutes of cooking.

JUDIAS BLANCAS A LA LERIDANA
(Lima Beans Lérida)

- 1¼ pounds fresh baby Lima beans, or 2 packages (10 ounces each) frozen
  Salt
- 2 onions, chopped
- 2 tablespoons olive oil
- 1½ pounds potatoes, peeled and cubed
- ½ pound German-style salami
- 1 to 2 cups sliced cabbage
- 2 garlic cloves, minced
- 1 teaspoon ground saffron
  Pepper

WOMAN'S DAY

Paella de la Costa Brava

Combine beans, enough salted water to cover generously, onions, and oil. (In these bean recipes, instead of adding oil and raw onions as the Spanish do, I prefer first to sauté the onions in the oil until translucent but not golden and then to add *that* to the beans and fresh cold water; seems to taste better and less oily.) Simmer, covered, for 15 minutes, or until beans are half cooked. Add potatoes, salami, and cabbage. (Again, the Spanish add the raw cabbage; I prefer to precook it for a few minutes first to remove some of the strong odor and make it more digestible, then add the drained cabbage.) Mash together garlic and saffron; mix to a paste with a little cold water; stir into simmering beans. Continue simmering, covered, for 15 to 20 minutes, or until potatoes are completely tender; add boiling water as necessary to keep from sticking. Season with salt and pepper to taste. Makes 8 servings.

COSTA BRAVA SPECIALTIES

The *Costa Brava,* "Rugged Coast," is a 110-mile strip in the *region* Catalonia, stretching along Spain's southeast corner from, roughly, Barcelona to the Pyrenees, shoreline all the way. Mountains parade spectacularly here beside the Mediterranean under a Riviera sun. Sea meets rock in a twisting, jagged riot of color, pink boulders thrusting out into turquoise grottoes and emerald bays. In the tile-roofed towns, burro-drawn carts still crawl along unpaved roads and automobiles get a second look. The children have yet to catch up with lollipops; they nibble on roses instead.

The women defy their century. They fill their water jugs at the village well, crush garlic with marble mortar and pestle, blend pastry dough with their hands on their marble work tables. Their spice shelves hold only what they've held for centuries: bay leaves, cinnamon, saffron, paprika. But with these and with nuts, olives, and crackers, they simmer marvels on their wood-burning stoves.

When my husband and I rented a house on the Costa Brava one spring, our $18-a-month cook taught me *paella,* of course, but also a gamut of dishes from soup (based on cheese) to nuts (as a steak sauce). Before I went to live in the little Costa town of Bagur, I'd heard the usual horror story about Spain: "They cook everything in rancid olive oil!" Yes, they do, in the very cheap places that use the same oil over and over, from potatoes to fish to veal and back again. But this has nothing to do with the practice in decent restaurants, nor with the fine,

ENCYCLOPEDIA OF COOKERY

SPANISH COOKERY

fresh, golden oil our cook Mela used. As anyone knows who has cooked with olive oil, a good pure grade heats with a beautiful evenness; and it does not intrude its own taste in the robust sort of dishes the Costa loves. Fish, for instance.

The sea, as the defining element, gives the Costa Brava its contour and much of its cuisine; the waters teem with luscious food. By day, the village boys go down roads lined with fig trees and the silvery olive to skim mussels from the shore rocks, or *bogavante* (the local lobster variant), or sea urchins, the little orange shellfish that are eaten fresh with a sprinkle of lemon juice, a morsel of the sea itself. Under starlight the fishing boats sail out for sardines, sole, bass; for *rapé* (a kind of codfish) and for the pink-scaled firm-fleshed red mullet, called "redhead" *(cap rox)* in the Catalan language, as opulent a plateful as you'll get from any ocean.

A Catalan housewife prepares her matchless seafood with the simplicity that is a cook's highest praise for her materials. On a bed of red-hot coals she grills fresh sardines or mullet, dry or with a splash of olive oil, to a crackling smokiness. Sometimes she pops slices of *rapé* or sole into an eggy baking-powder batter. Fried quickly in deep olive oil, the dough puffs out, leaving the fish inside white and meltingly tender. Or she tosses a whole basketful of fruits of the sea into the glory that is a *paella*.

Only she calls it by the more usual Spanish name, *arroz*, rice. The word *paella* is derived from the two-eared skillet in which the dish is cooked and served. The name *arroz* explains the philosophy of the *paella* on its native ground: it is, before everything, rice cooked as deliciously as possible. A Spanish cook will use the cheapest chicken and pork cuts for a *paella* because the meats are not primarily meant to be eaten, but rather to flavor the rice. Mela's *paella* is savory and succulent, and not nearly so difficult to prepare as its splendor leads guests to believe. One thing will help a lot: for this recipe you'll need at least a 12-inch skillet, a couple of inches deep. And you cook a *paella* uncovered, from beginning to end.

PAELLA DE LA COSTA BRAVA

Boil cut-up, small chicken 30 minutes, or until thoroughly cooked. In large skillet lightly greased with olive oil, fry for 15 minutes: boiled chicken, ½ pound sausage links, and ½ pound pork (2 center-cut chops) cut into small pieces. Add sliced green pepper; ½ pound fish (haddock is wonderful); ½ pound shrimps and/or crayfish, rinsed and dried (add shells and all for flavor); ¼ to ½ pound sliced squid, if you like it and it's available. Fry together (with meats in skillet) for 5 minutes, adding more olive oil if it's needed to keep ingredients from sticking. Add 1 cup rice, mix thoroughly with meats. Add 2 dozen mussels or small clams, scrubbed and dried, but with shells. Keep on low heat.

In separate saucepan: Heat ½ cup olive oil; chop in 2 large, ripe tomatoes and 1 onion. Add ¼ teaspoon cinnamon, 1 teaspoon paprika, 1 bay leaf, 1 teaspoon salt, ¼ teaspoon dark-red ground saffron, and 2 cups boiling water. Mix thoroughly. Add 1 pound fresh, or 1 package (10 ounces) frozen, peas; cook for 10 minutes. Add mixture slowly to skillet, reserving 1 teaspoon liquid; add 2 sliced, canned pimientos; cook for 10 minutes more, or until rice is soft. (You needn't stir.)

Meanwhile: Mix 2 crushed garlic cloves with 1 tablespoon chopped parsley; add reserved teaspoon of the liquid to make a paste. Add to skillet; stir in; cook for 5 minutes more, or until all liquid is absorbed by rice, which turns saffron yellow. (By this time, the haddock has probably flaked into the rice, too.) Let stand for 5 minutes. Mussels, peppers, and pimientos act as *Paella's* decorative garnish. Makes 6 servings.

Mela had several chopped-meat extravaganzas up her sleeve. There was, for instance, the dish she called *Guisado de Cosas Rellenas* or "Stew of Stuffed Things," that went the ubiquitous stuffed cabbage one—no, five—better. This was a steaming platter of artichokes, zucchini chunks, onions, potatoes, and green peppers, all scooped out and filled to bursting with diced beef, then steamed together in a big shallow pot. In her *Guisado*, Mela forswore the unfair advantage of *foie gras*. The meat was spiced only with egg, salt, paprika, and a pinch or two of cinnamon. The vegetable jackets were the only flourish needed.

It was not, however, only a hamburger heaven at our house. Mela could do interesting things even to steak intact. Now beefsteak as we know it in the States is as unheard of on the Costa Brava as in most of Europe. They have a so-called *entrecot*, but it's closer to veal than to beef. You have to go to Barcelona and order *carne de toro* (bull meat, and usually a late hero of the arena), and that's more like it! Still, our modest little *entrecot* was dressed with walnut-anchovy sauce that almost made my husband forget the royal American sirloin. And a sirloin given this treatment becomes downright imperial.

STEAK WITH WALNUT-ANCHOVY SAUCE

- 1 garlic clove, crushed
- 3 anchovy fillets
- 5 walnuts, shelled
- ½ teaspoon vinegar
- ⅓ cup olive oil
- 1 pound steak, broiled to desired doneness

With mortar and pestle blend together garlic, anchovies, walnuts, and vinegar. Drop by drop, add olive oil, mixing constantly. Pour lightly over just grilled steak; oven-heat steak for 1 minute. Serve at once. Makes 4 servings.

What an *entrecot* is to a Texas steer, the scrawny Spanish chickens are to our plump capons. To wring succulence from the uninspiring products of the local hen coops, Mela used nuts, crackers, and the perfumed touch of cinnamon, simmering the whole to a peak of gravy-drenched redolence. If she could taste what happens when her recipe has a tender American fowl to work with, she would weep for joy.

POLLO A LA COSTA BRAVA
(Costa Brava Chicken)

- 1 frying chicken (about 3 pounds) cut up
- Salt
- ¼ teaspoon ground cinnamon
- 3 tablespoons olive oil
- 1 garlic clove
- 1 parsley sprig
- 3 graham crackers
- ¼ cup pine nuts
- Cold water
- ¼ cup blanched almonds
- 3 tablespoons chopped onion
- 1 bay leaf
- 1 tomato
- 1 teaspoon all-purpose flour
- 1 tablespoon paprika

Sprinkle chicken with salt and cinnamon. Put in uncovered heavy shallow pot lightly greased with 1 tablespoon of the olive oil and bake in preheated slow oven (325°F.) for 40 minutes. Meanwhile, with mortar and pestle crush together garlic, parsley, graham crackers, and pine nuts. Add 2 tablespoons cold water, or enough to make a paste of nutcracker mixture. Mix in almonds. Put aside. After 40 minutes, remove chicken to platter. Add remaining olive oil to gravy in pot; sauté onion and bay leaf; grate in tomato. Add flour, paprika, 1 teaspoon salt, and 1 cup water. Mix well over low heat. Add nutcracker paste; mix well. Return chicken to pot; cover; cook slowly on top of stove, basting occasionally, for 45 minutes. Makes 4 servings.

Catalan meats may need such cosseting, but Catalan vegetables do not. Abundant and full-flavored, they're so good that it's the custom to eat, say, unadorned string beans as a course in itself. We even had a plain boiled cabbage once that made me regret every slur I'd ever cast on that much maligned leaf. But Mela vied with the rest of the civilized world in glamorizing the sauce-prone eggplant, and her sumptuous Ham-Cheese-Tomato Parlay does equal yeoman service for beans.

HAM-CHEESE-TOMATO PARLAY

Chop 2 large, ripe tomatoes and add to ⅓ cup hot olive oil in saucepan. Add 2 pressed garlic cloves, ½ teaspoon paprika. Cook for 20 minutes on high heat, or until oil and tomato are well blended. Add 1 tablespoon cold water; stir in over heat for 1 minute. Lay vegetable (1 package frozen string beans, boiled, or 1 eggplant, sliced and sautéed) in baking pan; pour sauce over. Sprinkle with 3 tablespoons grated Edam, dot with butter or margarine. Lay slices of boiled ham on top. Bake in preheated hot oven (400° F.) for 15 minutes, or until top is browned and cheese completely melted. Serves 4 as a side dish.

For all these strapping meat and vegetable dishes you would, perhaps, expect to use olive oil, buttressed as it is by zesty onion, tomato, and, above all, garlic. Yet our favorite tureen, *Sopa de Queso* (cheese soup) used olive oil even though it wafted, not a garlic tang, but an almost floral perfume; the secret lay in ¼ teaspoon of cinnamon. Made with the aforementioned Edam-like Cadi cheese, *Sopa de Queso* was so rich, bland, and soothing to the palate that I have adopted it as the perfect luncheon soup for "the girls."

SOPA DE QUESO
(Cheese Soup)

- 2 tablespoons olive oil
- ½ onion, sliced
- ½ tomato, sliced
- ½ bay leaf
- ¼ teaspoon each of paprika and ground cinnamon
- 3 cups boiling water
- ⅓ cup green spinach noodles
- 1 egg
- 1 tablespoon butter
- ¼ cup grated Edam cheese

In olive oil in heavy pot sauté first onion, then tomato with bay leaf. Mix in paprika and cinnamon. Add boiling water; cover and simmer for 1½ hours. Strain, reserving 1 ladleful of clear soup to cool in cup standing in bowl of cold water for 15 minutes. Meantime, put rest of clear soup back over low heat and cook green spinach noodles for 15 minutes, or until done. Beat egg, first with butter softened at room temperature, then with grated Edam until custardy. Add the ladleful of reserved soup (cooled to prevent curdling); blend well. Pour mixture into tureen, then add hot soup with noodles. Blend, season with salt to taste, and serve immediately. Makes 4 servings.

The Spanish stick with olive oil even for pastry. And here I tamper. The crumbly, yolky, miniature doughnuts called *Rosquillas,* delicate even when Mela did them in olive oil, are better with butter.

ROSQUILLAS (Fried Cakes)

- 1 cup all-purpose flour
- ⅓ cup granulated sugar
- 1 egg
- 1 teaspoon baking powder
- ¼ teaspoon vanilla extract
- 2 tablespoons softened butter
- Hot butter or margarine
- Confectioners' sugar

Sift flour into a bowl; add sugar, egg, baking powder, vanilla, and butter softened at room temperature. Mix with wooden spoon until you have a firm dough. Leave in warm room to let dough rise slightly. Shape into circlets or half moons about the diameter of a silver dollar, and as little thicker as you can manage so that they'll cook through. Fry in a small amount of hot butter for about 4 minutes on each side, or long enough so they'll brown but not burn. Sprinkle with confectioners' sugar; serve warm. Makes about 18 cakes.

The fragrant little *Rosquillas* (above) take only minutes of actual working time, yet they give you an impressive homemade, warm pastry dessert. Even quicker is the nameless dainty Mela conjured from an unpromising box of ladyfingers.

MELA'S LADYFINGER DESSERT

- 1 cup milk
- 2 eggs, well beaten
- 3 tablespoons granulated sugar
- 1 tablespoon cornstarch
- 1 teaspoon grated lemon rind
- 24 ladyfingers
- 12 graham crackers, crushed into fine crumbs
- Hot butter or margarine
- Confectioners' sugar

In saucepan combine milk, 1 egg, the granulated sugar mixed with cornstarch, and lemon rind. Stir gently over low heat for 5 minutes, or until mixture thickens. Let cool at room temperature. Split 24 ladyfingers. Fill with cooled custard filling. Dip into remaining beaten egg, then into graham-cracker crumbs. Fry in hot butter for 4 minutes on each side, or until brown but not burned. Sprinkle with confectioners' sugar; serve warm. Makes 24 cakes.

Either of these pastries can be whipped up in batches as large as you care to multiply, so they're nice to keep in mind for entertainments like club teas or television coffee-and-cake. If your hospitality runs more to cocktail parties, though, Mela has something for you there, too: Chick-Pea Fritters. These mealy tidbits, used by the Spanish as a change-off from potatoes, blend beautifully with any meat course I can think of. But I have broadened their scope to include the canapé tray, where they have proven to be irresistible.

FRITURAS DE GARBANZOS
(Chick-Pea Fritters)

- 2 cups cooked chick-peas
- 1 teaspoon chopped parsley
- 1 egg
- ½ garlic clove, mashed
- 2 tablespoons all-purpose flour
- ¼ teaspoon baking powder
- 1 teaspoon salt
- Oil for deep frying

Mash together chick-peas, parsley, egg, garlic, flour, baking powder, and salt. Shape into little balls. Fry in deep hot oil (375°F. on a frying thermometer) until golden-brown and crusted. Drain. Serve warm. Makes about 1½ dozen fritters depending on size.

My Costa Brava recipes have become weekly features at our house. Fun to cook and delicious to eat, they have the added charm of novelty, especially as company dinners. Best of all, they give us and our friends, even those who've never been to Spain, a glimpse of the Costa Brava. Duty-free and good for a lifetime, there's nothing like a recipe for a travel souvenir.

SPARERIBS—A cut of meat consisting of the lower portion of the ribs and breastbone removed from a fresh side of pig or hog. The ribs have only a small amount of meat but the succulence of the meat and fat makes them good eating.

Availability and Purchasing Guide—Year round in food stores. Available fresh. Also sold pickled or cured and smoked. Canned barbecued spareribs are available.

Good quality fresh spareribs are pink in color and have a generous portion of meat between the rib bones and a thin covering of meat over the bones. Because of the amount of bone, it is necessary to allow about 1 pound of spareribs for each serving.

SPARERIBS

Apple-Stuffed Spareribs

Storage—Remove from market paper or loosen wrapper; store unwrapped or loosely wrapped in coldest part of refrigerator.
- Fresh, refrigerator shelf, raw: 3 days
- Fresh, cooked; and canned, opened, refrigerator shelf: 2 to 3 days
- Fresh, refrigerator frozen-food compartment, raw or cooked, prepared for freezing: 2 to 3 weeks
- Fresh, freezer, raw, prepared for freezing: 3 to 4 months
- Fresh, freezer, cooked, prepared for freezing: 2 to 3 months
- Pickled; or cured and smoked, refrigerator shelf: 10 to 20 days
- Pickled; or cured and smoked, refrigerator frozen-food compartment: 3 to 4 weeks
- Pickled; or cured and smoked, freezer: 1 year
- Canned, kitchen shelf: 1 year

Do not refreeze once thawed.

Nutritive Food Values—High in protein, with small amounts of calcium and iron and some phosphorus, thiamine, riboflavin, and niacin.
- 3½ ounces, roasted, meat only cut from ribs = 273 calories
- 3½ ounces, braised, medium fat = 440 calories

Basic Preparation—Spareribs can be braised, roasted, or simmered. They can be broiled, but when this is done, they are usually marinated or precooked first.

- **To Braise**—Brown spareribs (cut into servings, if desired) slowly on all sides in heavy kettle or Dutch oven. Pour off drippings. Season with salt and pepper, and herbs such as marjoram, thyme, or rosemary, if desired. Add 1 cup water, tomato juice, apple juice, bouillon, or other liquid. Cover and simmer for 45 minutes to the pound, or until tender.

- **To Roast**—Put spareribs in a shallow roasting pan. Season with salt and pepper, and herbs, if desired. Roast in preheated moderate oven (350°F.) for 30 to 35 minutes to the pound, or until well browned and done.

- **To Simmer**—Brown spareribs on all sides, if desired, in heavy kettle or Dutch oven. Cover completely with water, bouillon, or other liquid. (Liquid may be hot or cold.) Season with salt and pepper, and herbs, if desired. (Bay leaves, marjoram, rosemary, thyme, parsley, celery, onion, etc., may be added.) Cover and simmer for 30 minutes to the pound, or until tender.

SPICED SPARERIBS
2 pounds spareribs
2 cups beef bouillon

WOMAN'S DAY

1 teaspoon ground allspice
2 teaspoons salt
¼ teaspoon pepper

Cut spareribs into serving pieces and brown slowly on all sides. Add 1 cup of the bouillon and the seasonings. Simmer, covered, for about 1½ hours, adding the remaining bouillon as needed. Makes 4 servings.

APPLE-STUFFED SPARERIBS

Prepare Savory Apple Stuffing. Spread on 1 rack (2 matching sides) of spareribs. Cover with matching rack and tie firmly with string. Put in roasting pan with ½ cup hot water. Season. Cover, and roast in preheated moderate oven (350°F.) for 3 hours, or until done. Remove cover during last hour of roasting. Makes 6 to 8 servings.

Savory Apple Stuffing

Cook ½ cup chopped celery and leaves, 1 chopped onion, and 2 tablespoons chopped parsley in ¼ cup butter or margarine for 5 minutes. Add 4 cups diced peeled tart apples, ¼ cup firmly packed brown sugar, ¾ teaspoon salt, and ¼ teaspoon each of ground sage, marjoram, thyme, and pepper. Cook, stirring, for about 5 minutes. Stir in 2 cups toasted bread crumbs. Makes about 4 cups.

SPICY BARBECUED SPARERIBS

4 pounds spareribs, cut into serving pieces
1 cup vinegar
2 tablespoons Worcestershire
1 tablespoon sugar
⅓ cup ketchup
1 teaspoon each of powdered mustard and salt
½ teaspoon paprika
Dash of hot pepper sauce
1 garlic clove, minced

Put spareribs in shallow roasting pan and roast in preheated moderate oven (350°F.) for 1 hour. Mix remaining ingredients and simmer for 15 minutes. Broil spareribs slowly, brushing frequently with the mixture, for 30 minutes, or until ribs are done. Makes 4 to 6 servings.

CHINESE SWEET-AND-SOUR SPARERIBS

2 cups water
1½ pounds spareribs, cut into 1-inch lengths
¼ cup soy sauce
1 teaspoon salt
1 teaspoon sugar
2 tablespoons sherry

Sauce:
3 tablespoons each of sugar and vinegar
2 tablespoons cornstarch
½ cup water

Heat a heavy pan, add the water, ribs, soy sauce, and salt; when mixture boils, turn down heat and simmer for 1 hour. Add sugar and sherry. Turn heat high and continue to cook until the liquid is all evaporated. Blend sauce ingredients; pour slowly over ribs. Cook for about 2 minutes. Place ribs on a flat dish and top with sauce. Makes 3 or 4 servings.

SPEARMINT (Mentha spicata, var. viridis)—A strong-scented perennial herb, native to the temperate sections of Europe and Asia and widely naturalized in the United States. Of the dozen or so varieties of mint cultivated in the United States, spearmint is the one that is most popularly grown for home culinary use. In fact the words mint and spearmint are often used synonymously, and spearmint can be used in any recipe calling for mint.

Spearmint has dark green lance-shape leaves and red-tinged stems. Its long pointed flower stalks bear pale purple flowers. The home gardener can easily grow spearmint in pots or in a shady damp patch and have the advantage of the fresh leaves. Either fresh or dried the leaves add a pleasant and distinctive flavor to cranberry juice, fruit cup, and such soups as pea soup; they give delicate flavor to meat ragouts or fish; they are good minced and added to cottage and cream cheese and salad dressings; with vegetables such as cabbage, carrots, celery, potatoes, and snap beans; and in jellied salads. Mint sauce, chopped mint and vinegar, is the classic accompaniment to roast lamb, as is mint jelly. Desserts such as custards, fruit compotes, and ice cream are delicious with mint flavor, and fruit beverages and jellies are a natural for its warm taste.

Availability—Fresh spearmint is not commercially available under that name although often what is sold as "mint" is actually spearmint. Dehydrated spearmint flakes are available at the spice counters of food stores. Spearmint extract and oil of spearmint are available.

CANDIED SPEARMINT LEAVES

Wash and dry spearmint leaves. Brush with slightly beaten egg white and sprinkle generously with fine granulated sugar. Put on wax paper to dry. When firm, store between layers of wax paper in airtight containers. Use as a garnish for fruit salads or desserts.

MINTED GREEN PEAS

1 package (1 pound) frozen peas
Salt
Butter or margarine
2 teaspoons chopped fresh spearmint

Cook peas as directed on the package. Add salt and butter to taste. Sprinkle with mint. Makes 4 to 6 servings.

CUCUMBERS WITH MINT

2 medium cucumbers, peeled and thinly sliced
Salt to taste
½ cup malt vinegar
1 tablespoon sugar
2 teaspoons chopped fresh spearmint leaves

Sprinkle cucumbers with salt. Weight down with a plate and let stand in the refrigerator for about 1 hour. Drain off any water. Add vinegar, sugar, and mint. Serve as a relish. Makes 6 servings.

SPICE—This word is applied very loosely to a great variety of vegetable products with aromatic odors and pungent flavors which are used to season foods. Such flavorings as caraway, coriander, and dill can be found on some lists of spices although generally they are classified more specifically as aromatic seeds. Bay leaves, marjoram, sage, and thyme are also spices in the broadest usage of the word, although we are more apt to think of them as herbs. In bygone days even fragrant woods and gums—for example, frankincense, balm, and myrrh—were called spices. But nowadays, the word spice tends to be confined to the following group of products made from various parts (most often other than the seeds or leaves) of plants grown in the tropics: *allspice, red pepper,* and *whole chili peppers,* from dried fruits; *cayenne pepper,* from a ground whole plant; *cinnamon,* from bark; *cloves,* from dried flower buds; *ginger* and *turmeric,* from roots; *mace,* from the dried aril of the *nutmeg,* which itself is the kernel of a fruit; *paprika,* from dried pods; *pepper,* from a dried berry; and *saffron,* from the dried stigmas of a flower.

SPICE

Baked Beans

Seafood Dishes

Ginger Cookies

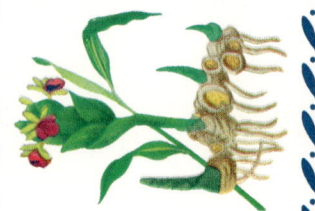

Egg Dishes

Salads

Fish & Fish Sauces

ALLSPICE
It is the berry of the allspice tree, and is sold either **whole** or **ground,** with a flavor which resembles a combination of cloves, cinnamon, and nutmeg. It spices many baked products, puddings, and fruits. Seasons meat, fish, and seafood, duck, sausages, and eggs. Invaluable for mincemeat, pickles, relishes, preserves, and chutneys. Special uses: potpourris and pourris and sachets.

CINNAMON
This spice comes from the bark of the cassia cinnamon tree and has a fruity sweetness and subtle warmth. **Stick** cinnamon is used as a muddler for hot spiced drinks. **Ground** cinnamon flavors cakes, breads, pies, fruits, puddings, soufflés. Seasons pork, ham, stews, casseroles. Used in pickles, preserves, ketchup, chili sauce, chutney. Scents sachets and potpourris.

CLOVES
They are the nail-shape unopened buds of clove trees, warming to the taste. **Whole** cloves stud ham, pork, pomanders; are used in spice bags for meat, stews, fruits, pickles. **Ground** cloves used in baked goods, dessert sauces, spiced fruits, meat, fish, stuffings, stews, meat sauces. Adds flavor to green beans, Harvard beets, sweet potatoes, tomatoes, and carrots.

GINGER
It is a root spice with a strong, piquant, slightly lemony flavor. **Crystallized,** or **preserved,** ginger is a confection. **Cracked** or **whole** is used in pickles, conserves, chutneys, stewed fruits. **Ground** ginger spices gingerbread and other baked products, frostings, and fruits, as well as meat, game, poultry, fish, seafood, soups, vegetables, preserves, pickles, chutneys, conserves, relishes.

MACE
It is a lacy layer covering nutmeg seeds, with a smooth flavor more potent than nutmeg. Used in baked products, puddings, fruits, custards, candies, whipped cream. It enhances chocolate flavors particularly. Seasons sausages, meat loaves, fish and shellfish, poultry, gravies, sauces, chowders, cream soups, vegetables, jellies, pickles, preserves, relishes, and chutneys.

NUTMEG
The seed of the fruit of the nutmeg tree, it has a warm, aromatic, and slightly bitter flavor, and is available both **whole,** for last-minute grating, or **ground.** Used in hot beverages, puddings, baked goods, fruits, sauces, and whipped cream. Seasons chicken, stews, seafood, eggs, soups, salads, sauces, many vegetables, a variety of pickles, conserves, and chutneys.

CHART

Pomander Ball

PAPRIKA
It is ground from the pods of a mild pepper with a pleasant odor, an agreeable, slightly sweet taste, and bright color. Garnishes canapés and appetizers; used in and on beef, pork, veal, lamb, sausage, game, stews, goulash, fish, shellfish, poultry, egg and cheese dishes, soups, salads, vegetables lacking in color, relishes and pickles, ketchup, chili sauce, and chutneys.

BLACK PEPPER
Peppercorns are the dried berries of the pepper vine to be ground in a mill or used in spice bags. Black pepper, the whole berry ground, has a pungent taste. Used more than any other spice, it seasons appetizers, pepper cookies, meats, poultry, fish and seafood, gravies, sauces, eggs, casseroles, soups, salads, vegetables, pickles, relishes, mixed spices, and chutneys.

WHITE PEPPER
This variant comes from the same berry as black, the milder inside of ripe berries after the black hull is removed. In use it is interchangeable with black pepper, but in a little larger quantity. Its special value comes from its being white since it seasons white or light meats, sauces, vegetables, soups, and salads without the black flecks of pepper showing.

Spiced Cider

CAYENNE, RED, and WHOLE CHILI PEPPERS
These south-of-the-border favorites, all members of the capsicum family, have a piquant flavor which varies in intensity. They are used for many meat dishes, especially Mexican, sausages, dressings, gravies, sauces, casseroles, spaghetti, stews, pizzas, chicken, fish, seafood, eggs, cheese, soups, salads, vegetables, pickles, and relishes.

SAFFRON
Although not strictly a spice, it is usually classed with them. 225,000 stigmas of a crocus-like flower make a pound. It has an exotic flavor, pleasantly bitter, is used sparingly, usually sold in specialty food stores. Valued as a coloring in saffron tea, cakes, buns, rolls, biscuits, puddings, pies, and cookies, chicken and seafood dishes, rice and stuffing, curries, fish sauces, soups.

TURMERIC
Available mostly **ground**, this spice is the root of a plant of the ginger family and has a slightly bitter flavor. Used in recipes for cakes, cookies, curried meats, fish, shellfish, poultry, eggs, sauces, gravies, rice, salads, dressings. Its most common uses are in curry powders, pickles, relishes, chowchows, chutneys, and in condiments such as prepared mustard.

Spiced Fruits & Pickles

Clove-Studded Ham

Vegetables

Dessert Sauces

SPICE

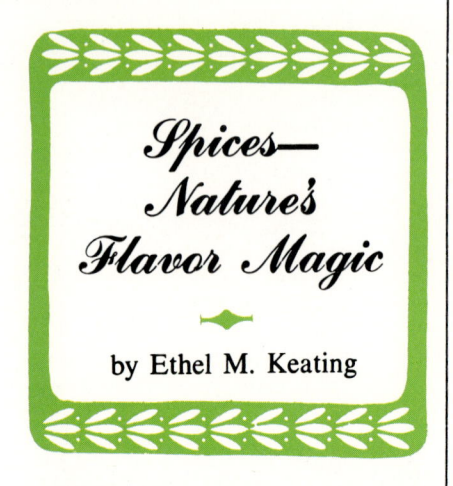

Spices—Nature's Flavor Magic

by Ethel M. Keating

Nobody knows why the ancients prized spices so highly. But, for centuries, men risked their lives on long caravan treks across the Middle East, fought wars, and discovered new worlds so as to possess a few pounds of the spices available in every food store today.

Pepper, cloves, cinnamon, cassia, nutmeg, all were considered necessary for survival. Spices added zest and pungency to the ancients' food and wine; helped mask the odor of sacrifice and of "high" meat and fish. Priests needed spices for incense and anointing oils, for embalming, sacrificial rites, and funerals; doctors for medicines; lovers for potions; and spices gave delight as scent in perfumes and lotions.

The origin of the use of spices is unknown. A Chinese herbal dated 2700 B.C. speaks of cinnamon and in 2800 B.C., people flocked to the Isle of Rhodes for two Grecian delicacies—gingerbread and nougats!

Beginning some seventeen centuries before Christ, the nomadic tribes in the Arabian Desert controlled the spice industry as middlemen and their handsome profits, both from spices and taxes on spices passing through their domains, caused their country to be called *Araby Blest*. Nor would they reveal whence spices came, and kept their secret and control for more than three thousand years. Actually, spices left their East Indies homes by ship for Yemen, the place where Sheba once reigned, and Hadramaut, then made the long trip by camel-back to Macoraba. Here ownership often changed. Loaded on other camels, the pungent bags went to the then-flourishing ports of Tyre and Sidon, whence, reloaded on ships, they were carried to the cities of the Mediterranean.

The Old Testament contains frequent references to spices. In Genesis 43:11 "a little honey, spices, and myrrh, nuts, and almonds." In the thirtieth chapter of Exodus, the Lord gave Moses directions for the preparation of anointing oils, mentioning pure myrrh and cinnamon. The songs of Solomon speak of "the mountains of spices," and in Genesis after the sons of Jacob carried out their plot against Joseph, "behold, a company of Ishmaelites came from Gilead with their camels bearing spicery and balm and myrrh, going to carry it down to Egypt."

During the opulent early Christian era, spices were still used by the wealthy without restraint despite their cost. Nero lavished a year's supply of cinnamon on the funeral rites of his wife Poppaea. And in 410 A.D. Alaris, King of the Goths, demanded 3,000 pounds of pepper as part of the ransom of Rome.

As communications improved, the demand for spices enlarged. Introduced into England about 900 A.D., they were soon in such demand that any of today's common spices were worth their weight in gold. More than ever, Europeans sought ways to wrest the industry away from Arab control.

On to the Spice Islands

If we could only find a direct route to the spice islands," men sighed. Columbus took up the search in behalf of Spain but failed. Five years later the Portuguese Vasco da Gama rounded the Cape of Good Hope, sailed up the Indian Ocean, and discovered the East Indies, the coveted treasure home of spices.

Now leadership in commerce, including the spice trade, went to seafaring Spain and Portugal; but near the close of the 16th century it was wrested away by the Dutch. Soon the English bristled under the high prices the Dutch charged them and to combat them, in 1600, one hundred and twenty-five Englishmen founded the East India Company of Gentlemen Adventurers. Company ships returned from their first voyage richly laden with 210,000 pounds of the finest Sumatra pepper. The actions of the English infuriated the Dutch, who started a war that lasted fifty years, ending with their monopoly broken and England in possession of an Empire.

Pepper

Most valuable of all spices is *pepper*. Throughout the Middle Ages, pepper was a form of wealth used in payment of dowries, taxes, rent, and tributes. In the time of Henry II, a Pepper Guild was formed and the traders were known as "pepperers." Pepper is the dried berry of a perennial vine that once grew wild in northern Sumatra but is now cultivated on large plantations in Malaysia, Ceylon, Thailand, Sumatra, Brazil, and on the Malabar coast of India. Like the grape vine, pepper climbs poles or other supports; currantlike clusters of red berries appear after two or three years and the plants usually mature anywhere from four to seven years. Dried in the sun, the berries become dark-brown to black, hard and wrinkled, and acquire flavor. Differing from other spices, pepper has no aroma to mask the flavor of food; rather, especially when freshly ground, it imparts pungency that enhances and adds zest to the dishes it is used in.

Black pepper refers to berries picked just before fully ripened, dried, cleaned, and shipped to be sold as peppercorns or ground.

White pepper, more attractive to the eye but less pungent to the taste, is prepared by removing the outer coat of fully ripened berries, then grinding the inner white kernel. A pepper grinder is a necessary piece of equipment in every home, for freshly ground pepper has no flavor counterpart.

Cinnamon, Nutmeg, and Mace

When you buy a jar of cinnamon in the United States, unlike any other part of the world, you are most likely getting cassia, for no distinction is made here between the two spices although they are the products of different trees. In fact, the natives of southern China were peeling the bark from cassia trees centuries before "true cinnamon," as it is called in the trade, was known. True cinnamon is premium-priced, milder in flavor and aroma, and is the bark of a species of laurel tree that once grew wild in Ceylon but now is under cultivation.

The most aromatic of the spices, cinnamon (or cassia) was highly prized by the ancients. Its perfume was reserved for oriental women and the candles of kings.

It takes great skill to cut and peel the inner cinnamon bark which is gathered after the May and November rains. When ready for market, it is rolled in pipes or quills which resemble tight rolls of paper with neatly turned-in edges.

Pipes are used in preserving and pickling or as muddlers in hot chocolate, mulled cider or wine. Most cinnamon, however, is ground and used in sweets.

One of the most beautiful trees on earth is found in the Banda group of the Molucca Islands. The majestic *nutmeg* tree sometimes reaches a height of forty feet and has dense black-green foliage which offsets dramatic clusters of fruit resembling large apricots.

When the fruit is ripe, it splits open to reveal a pecan-shape pit covered with a waxy scarlet aril. This aril is *mace*, which is not greatly unlike nutmeg in flavor, perhaps somewhat stronger. The nutmeg is the only fruit that yields two spices. Mace is sun-dried, while nutmeg pits are subjected to several weeks of low heat to dry them until the kernels rattle within their shells. The shells are removed and the nutmegs graded for size.

The first historical mention of nutmeg is in a poem written in 1195 by Petrus d'Ebulo. He tells of the fumigation of the streets of Rome by the burning of nutmegs and other spices for the triumphal entry of Emperor Henry VI.

A century ago ladies and nurses carried little boxes in their pockets which secreted a tiny grater and a nutmeg. They used them to enhance a favorite dish or a cordial.

Spices of the East

In ancient China a courtier who wished to address his emperor was required to hold a *clove* in his mouth. For the Chinese had a predilection for garlic and the rich perfume of the clove was found to sweeten the breath.

Although the strikingly beautiful clove tree, tall, with terminal cymes of crimson flowers, is a native of the Moluccas, most cloves in our markets today come from Zanzibar or Pemba, an island in the Indian Ocean near Zanzibar. The cloves of commerce are the unopened flower buds which are hand-picked when they turn reddish in color and then are sun-dried.

The world's most costly condiment is *saffron*, from India and some Mediterranean countries. The stigma of a purple crocuslike flower, it takes 225,000 of them to make one pound. Saffron has been appreciated by connoisseurs since antiquity. King Solomon had a garden plot to supply saffron for his kitchen; and the legend about crocodile tears is attributed to saffron, for that sweet-smelling spice was said to be the only thing that could move the monster to tears. Its deep orange-yellow color has made it valuable in dyeing and it is also used in perfume.

Ginger is an unimpressive-looking plant which grows two to three feet tall and has small blue and white flowers and reedlike leaves. Its roots provide the spice. Kings of the Orient used to nibble ginger that had been boiled in honey, and in *The Book of 1001 Nights,* it is praised for its stimulating properties. In the days before central heating, English pubs and inns always had a shaker of ginger on the shelf. On cold days it was sprinkled into ale or porter, stirred with a red-hot poker, and drunk sizzling hot, thus producing inner warmth and glow. The resins in ginger provide its pungency, the oils its spicy odor; and the lighter its color, the more bite it has.

Columbus discovered a spice tree growing wild on the island of Jamaica and because of the warmth and pungency of its fruit called it a pepper, while today it is called pimiento. *Allspice,* its more descriptive title, derives from its odor which resembles a bouquet of cinnamon, nutmeg, and cloves. Still growing in Jamaica and Mexico, the pimiento tree soon after blossoming produces small clusters of pea-size fruit. Picked green, they are dried in the sun and after seven or eight days become shriveled, dark-brown in color, and develop a flavor that is highly aromatic.

All these, then, comprise the classic spices of which we use 100,000,000 pounds a year. This figure is even more impressive when we realize that because of their pungency only a dash is needed in any one dish and that all spices are powders and very light in weight. There are, of course, many other spices.

For one dish, curry, spices are purchased already mixed. In many parts of the world the curry recipe is a family or local secret, never entrusted to paper but transmitted only verbally. The curry powder you buy at your food store probably contains varying amounts of coriander, cinnamon, turmeric, cardamom, fennel, fenugreek, ginger, cayenne pepper, allspice, black or white pepper, cloves, and cumin.

The romantic story of spices is thousands of years old, yet their use in our modern kitchens offers never-ending pleasures and novelties of taste.

ROLLED FISH FILLETS WITH SHRIMP SAUCE

6 fillets of sole or flounder
Salt and freshly ground pepper
Freshly grated nutmeg
2 tablespoons fresh lemon juice
¾ cup dry white wine
¾ cup cooked shrimps
Shrimp Sauce

Gently flatten fillets with the flat side of a cleaver; season with salt, pepper, and nutmeg to taste. Sprinkle with lemon juice. Roll up and place in well-buttered baking dish. Pour wine over fillets. Cover with aluminum foil and bake in preheated hot oven (400°F.) for about 15 minutes. On a broilerproof platter, place the rolled fillets; cover with cooked shrimps. Top with Shrimp Sauce. If desired, around edge of platter, place mounds of Duchess potatoes. Place under broiler until nicely browned. Garnish platter with parsley sprigs and lemon wedges if desired. Makes 6 servings.

Shrimp Sauce

Blend 2 tablespoons all-purpose flour into ¼ cup melted butter; add 3 tablespoons cream, liquid from the fish dish, a dash of mace, ¼ teaspoon salt, and freshly ground pepper. Cook, stirring constantly, until thickened and smooth. Remove sauce from heat; stir in 1 egg yolk and 1 tablespoon fresh lemon juice. Cook for 1 minute.

ROAST LAMB WITH HOT CURRIED FRUIT

With a sharp knife cut 5 or 6 slits in leg of lamb; stuff each with a sliver of garlic and a small sprig of parsley. Put on rack in shallow roasting pan. Rub well with powdered ginger; sprinkle with salt and freshly ground pepper. Pour juice of half a lemon over lamb. Roast uncovered in preheated slow oven (300°F.), allowing 25 minutes per pound for rare, 30 minutes per pound for medium, and 35 minutes per pound for well-done lamb. When meat has roasted for 1 hour, add juice of other half of lemon. Baste often. Place roast on heated serving platter; garnish with crisp watercress. Serve with Hot Curried Fruit.

Hot Curried Fruit

Put 8 slices of canned pineapple and 3 tablespoons pineapple juice in shallow roasting pan. Top with 4 bananas, cut into halves lengthwise and across. Melt ¼ cup butter or margarine in skillet; add ⅔ cup firmly packed brown sugar and 2 teaspoons curry powder dissolved in ⅓ cup brandy. Pour over fruit. Bake in preheated slow oven (300°F.) for 1 hour. Baste occasionally. Makes 8 servings.

JAVANESE LAMB

2 teaspoons coriander
½ teaspoon dried ground chili peppers
1 teaspoon cuminseed, pounded
½ teaspoon ground saffron
1 teaspoon ground ginger
2 garlic cloves, minced
2 teaspoons salt
3 pounds boneless lamb, cut into ½-inch cubes
1 cup vinegar
¼ cup cooking oil
½ cup water
Hot cooked rice

Pound together the coriander, chili peppers, cuminseed, saffron, ginger, garlic, and salt. Roll the pieces of lamb in this mixture. Place in a bowl and pour vinegar over the mixture. Marinate for 1 hour. Drain meat and discard vinegar. Heat oil in a saucepan; add meat and brown on all sides. Add the water. Cover and cook over low heat for 30 minutes, or until tender. Serve hot with fluffy white rice. Makes 8 servings.

RHUBARB SAUCE FOR MEATS

1 quart finely chopped onion
1 quart diced rhubarb
1½ pints vinegar
4 cups firmly packed brown sugar
½ teaspoon each of ground cinnamon, allspice, cayenne, and salt

SPINACH

Mix all ingredients in a large saucepan. Slowly bring to boil; simmer for 45 minutes. Pour into hot sterilized jars, and seal. Serve with beef, pork, or chicken. Makes about 4 pints.

SPICED ORANGES

Boil 6 unpeeled California oranges for 20 minutes, allowing 1 teaspoon salt to 2 quarts of water. Drain. Boil in unsalted water for 20 minutes. Drain. Cut into quarters. Pour over oranges the following syrup that has been boiled for 10 minutes:

- 2½ cups sugar
- ¼ cup light corn syrup
- ½ cup water
- 1 cup vinegar
- 12 whole cloves
- ½ cinnamon stick

Bake in an uncovered casserole in preheated slow oven (300°F.) for 1½ hours, or until transparent.

Note: These oranges are excellent with roast meats.

BUTTERED SPICED BEETS

- 8 to 10 small whole beets, cooked
- ¼ cup butter or margarine
- ½ teaspoon salt
- Freshly ground pepper
- ½ teaspoon ground cinnamon
- ¼ teaspoon ginger
- ¼ cup firmly packed brown sugar
- Juice of 1 lemon

Slip skins from cooked beets; dice beets. Put in pan with remaining ingredients. Heat thoroughly until flavors are well blended. Makes 4 servings.

SPICED PRUNES IN LEMON GELATIN SALAD

- 1 pound large meaty prunes
- ½ cup firmly packed brown sugar
- Two 3-inch cinnamon sticks
- 1 teaspoon whole cloves with heads removed
- 1 teaspoon whole allspice
- 1 cup red wine
- Cashew nuts
- 2 packages (3 ounces each) lemon-flavored gelatin
- 2 cups boiling water
- 2 cups ice water

Cover prunes with cold water and let stand overnight. Sprinkle with brown sugar and add spices that have been tied securely in a muslin bag. Simmer until plump and tender, about 30 minutes. Remove spice bag and add wine; simmer for 10 minutes longer. Let cool. Replace prune pits with cashew nuts. Dissolve gelatin in the boiling water and add the ice water. Pour small amount of gelatin into 5-cup mold brushed with oil; refrigerate until set. Arrange prunes on gelatin; pour over enough gelatin to cover; refrigerate until set; add remaining gelatin. Refrigerate. Unmold on large chilled salad plate. Garnish with greens. Makes 8 servings.

CINNAMON-LAYERED QUICK COFFEECAKE

- 1½ cups sugar
- ½ cup chopped nuts
- 1 tablespoon ground cinnamon
- ½ cup butter
- 2 eggs
- 1 teaspoon vanilla extract
- 1 tablespoon fresh lemon juice
- 2 cups sifted all-purpose flour
- ½ teaspoon baking powder
- 1 teaspoon each of baking soda and salt
- ½ pint dairy sour cream

Mix and set aside ½ cup of the sugar, the chopped nuts, and cinnamon. Cream the butter; beat in remaining 1 cup sugar and eggs. Add the vanilla and lemon juice. Sift the flour, baking powder, soda, and salt; add alternately to the butter mixture with the sour cream. Pour half of the batter into a buttered pan (9 x 9 x 2 inches). Sprinkle with some of the cinnamon mixture. Spread the rest of the batter over this and sprinkle with the remaining topping. Bake in preheated moderate oven (350°F.) for 35 minutes. Serve hot.

TOASTED SPICE CAKE

- ¾ cup butter
- 2 cups firmly packed light-brown sugar
- 2 egg yolks
- 1 teaspoon vanilla extract
- 2⅓ cups sifted cake flour
- 1 teaspoon baking soda
- 1 teaspoon baking powder
- 1 teaspoon each of ground cloves and cinnamon
- ¾ teaspoon salt
- 1¼ cups buttermilk
- Meringue
- ½ cup broken nut meats

Cream the butter; beat in the sugar, egg yolks, and vanilla. Sift the cake flour with the soda, baking powder, spices, and salt; add alternately to the butter mixture with the buttermilk. Spread in a buttered pan (13 x 9 x 2 inches) and top with Meringue. Sprinkle with nuts. Bake in preheated moderate oven (350°F.) for 50 to 60 minutes.

Meringue

Beat 2 egg whites until they hold a point when beater is raised, but not until dry. Slowly beat in 1 cup sifted light-brown sugar; continue beating until stiff and smooth.

GINGER COOKIES

- 1 cup molasses
- 1 cup shortening
- ¾ cup sugar
- 1 teaspoon baking soda
- 2 eggs, well-beaten
- 4 cups sifted all-purpose flour
- 1 tablespoon ground ginger
- 1 teaspoon ground cloves
- 1 teaspoon salt

Boil together for 3 or 4 minutes the molasses, shortening, and sugar. Add the baking soda and let cool. Add the eggs and the flour sifted with the spices and salt. Chill. Roll a small amount of dough at a time as thin as possible; cut with a 2-inch cookie cutter. Bake in preheated moderate oven (375°F.) for 8 to 10 minutes. Makes about 10 dozen.

SPICED CIDER

- 12 cups cider
- 12 whole cloves
- 1 cinnamon stick
- ¼ teaspoon ground nutmeg

Bring all ingredients to the boiling point. Strain, and serve hot in mugs.

SPINACH—An annual potherb which originated in southwestern Asia and is grown for its leafy green leaves. It was unknown to the ancient Greeks and Romans and the first written record of it is Chinese; it probably reached China around 647 A.D. It was brought to Spain by the Moors in the 8th century.

Availability—Available year round. It is grown in the South during the winter and in most other areas during spring and fall.

Spinach is sold in bulk by the pound, or washed and trimmed in transparent bags. It is available canned in assorted sizes and frozen as leaf or chopped spinach, creamed spinach, and spinach soufflé.

Purchasing Guide—Choose large, fresh, crisp dark-green leaves; these can be of the flat or crinkled varieties. Avoid decayed, crushed, wilted, insect-injured leaves.

Storage—For bulk spinach trim off the roots; wash in a sink full of warm water. The warm water sends the sand on the leaves to the bottom of the tub. Repeat washings with cold running water; lift spinach out of the water several times to free it from the sand. Drain well; store in a covered container in the refrigerator.

- ☐ Fresh, refrigerator shelf, raw: 3 to 5 days
- ☐ Fresh, cooked; and canned, open, refrigerator shelf: 4 to 5 days
- ☐ Fresh, prepared for freezing; and frozen, refrigerator frozen-food compartment: 3 months
- ☐ Fresh, prepared for freezing; and frozen, freezer: 1 year
- ☐ Canned, kitchen shelf: 1 year

SPINACH

Nutritive Food Values—An excellent source of vitamin A, a very good source of vitamin C and iron, and a fair source of riboflavin. It is low in calories.
- ☐ Fresh, 3½ ounces, raw = 26 calories
- ☐ Fresh; and frozen, chopped, 3½ ounces, boiled and drained = 23 calories
- ☐ Canned, 3½ ounces, regular pack, solids and liquid = 19 calories
- ☐ Canned, 3½ ounces, regular pack, drained solids = 24 calories
- ☐ Canned, 3½ ounces, dietary pack, solids and liquid = 21 calories
- ☐ Canned, 3½ ounces, dietary pack, drained solids = 26 calories
- ☐ Frozen, leaf, 3½ ounces, boiled and drained = 24 calories

Basic Preparation—Rinse in cold running water. If the spinach is to be cooked, drain, and cook with the water that remains on the leaves; spinach to be used raw in salads should be drained and the leaves dried with paper towels.

☐ **To Cook**—Cook in only the water that clings to the leaves; cover the pan; cook for 5 to 10 minutes, until tender; drain; season with butter or margarine, salt and pepper, and fresh lemon juice if desired. Or cook in a small amount of boiling water in an uncovered pan for about 10 minutes, until tender; drain and season.

☐ **To Freeze**—Use only young tender leaves. Wash thoroughly in several changes of water. Remove tough stems. Blanch in boiling water for 1½ minutes. Chill in cold water for 4 minutes. Drain and pack into freezer containers, leaving ½-inch headspace. Seal.

SPINACH-STUFFED FISH FILLETS
- 2 medium onions, chopped
- 1 tablespoon butter or margarine
- 2 pounds frozen sole or flounder fillets, thawed
- 1 pound fresh spinach or 1 package (10 ounces) frozen spinach, cooked and drained
- 1 can (15½ ounces) meatless spaghetti sauce

Cook onions in butter until tender but not brown. Spread each fillet with cooked spinach and sprinkle with onion. Roll up and put in shallow baking dish. Pour on spaghetti sauce; bake in preheated moderate oven (350°F.) for about 20 minutes. Makes 4 to 6 servings.

SPINACH-AND-POTATO PIE
- 1 pound spinach
- 6 medium potatoes
- 1 medium onion
- 3 eggs, beaten
- Dash of pepper
- ¼ cup melted butter or margarine
- 1 teaspoon salt

Wash spinach, chop fine, and set aside. Shred potatoes and onion into eggs; add remaining ingredients, and mix. Spread half of potato mixture in shallow baking dish, spread spinach for second layer, and top with remaining potatoes. Bake in preheated moderate oven (350°F.) for 30 minutes, or until potatoes are browned and done. Makes 6 servings.

BAKED SPINACH RING WITH EGGS
- 2 packages (10 ounces each) frozen chopped spinach
- 3 eggs, beaten
- ¼ cup heavy cream
- ¼ cup melted butter or margarine
- 1½ teaspoons seasoned salt
- ¼ teaspoon pepper
- 1 teaspoon instant minced onion
- ½ teaspoon monosodium glutamate
- 1½ cups soft bread crumbs or cubes
- Creamed Eggs Supreme

Cook and drain spinach. Whirl in electric blender or chop very fine. Mix with next 8 ingredients and pour into well-greased 6-cup ring mold. Set in pan of hot water and bake in preheated moderate oven (350°F.) for 1 hour, or until firm. Unmold on hot platter; fill center with Creamed Eggs Supreme. Makes 6 servings.

Creamed Eggs Supreme
Melt ¼ cup butter or margarine; blend in ¼ cup all-purpose flour. Add 1 teaspoon Worcestershire, 1½ cups milk, and ½ cup heavy cream. Cook, stirring constantly, until thickened. Add a dash of hot pepper sauce, 2 tablespoons chopped parsley, 1 chopped pimiento, and 8 hard-cooked eggs cut into chunks. Heat. Season to taste.

GREEK SPINACH PIE
- 10 sheets phyllo (12 x 15 inches)
- ½ cup butter, melted
- 2 packages (10 ounces each) fresh spinach
- 1 tablespoon salt
- 2 eggs
- 2 cups cottage cheese (small curd)
- 1 cup grated feta cheese
- 3 tablespoons parsley
- 2 green onions with tops, minced
- Salt and pepper

Cut phyllo sheets into halves and place 10 pieces in a buttered pan (7 x 11 inches). Brush each sheet of phyllo with melted butter.

Wash spinach and remove stems. Cut leaves into ½-inch lengths. Sprinkle with salt and let stand for 15 minutes. Beat eggs. Add cheeses, parsley, and onion. Squeeze liquid from spinach. Fold spinach into egg mixture. Season with salt and pepper to taste. Spread mixture over phyllo sheets in pan and top with remaining 10 pieces of phyllo, brushing each sheet with remaining melted butter. Bake in preheated moderate oven (350°F.) for 40 minutes. Cut into squares and serve hot. Makes 6 servings.

GERMAN PANCAKES WITH SPINACH
- Butter or margarine
- All-purpose flour
- Salt and pepper
- Dash of nutmeg
- Milk
- 1 package (10 ounces) spinach
- 5 eggs

Melt 3 tablespoons butter in saucepan, and blend in 3 tablespoons flour, ½ teaspoon salt, dash of pepper, and the nutmeg. Gradually stir in 1 cup milk and cook, stirring constantly, until smooth and thickened. Cook spinach in small amount of boiling salted water until tender, about 5 minutes. Drain very thoroughly and chop fine. Stir into first mixture and set aside. Beat 2 eggs. Add ⅔ cup milk, ½ teaspoon salt, and ½ cup flour. Beat until smooth. Brush an 8-inch or 9-inch skillet with butter. Add one quarter of the batter; tip and tilt pan so that the batter flows evenly over the bottom. Cook quickly. As soon as the pancake browns on one side, turn, and brown other side. Proceed until 4 pancakes are made. Divide spinach mixture between the pancakes and fold over. Put in shallow 1½-quart baking dish. Beat remaining eggs with 1½ cups milk, ½ teaspoon salt, and ⅛ teaspoon pepper. Pour over pancakes. Bake in preheated slow oven (325°F.) for 45 minutes, or until firm and lightly browned. Makes 6 servings.

ITALIAN EGGS FLORENTINE
- 1 package (10 ounces) frozen chopped spinach
- ¼ cup butter or margarine
- 2 tablespoons all-purpose flour
- 1 cup each of milk and light cream
- 8 eggs, poached
- Salt and pepper to taste
- Grated cheese to taste

Cook spinach as directed on package. Make a white sauce with butter, flour, milk, and cream. Put spinach in a shallow baking dish. Arrange drained eggs on top of spinach. Pour white sauce over the eggs. Season with salt and pepper, and sprinkle with grated cheese. Bake in preheated hot oven (400°F.) for a few minutes, or until cheese is browned. Makes 4 servings.

SAG PANEER
An Indian accompaniment for meats, made with spinach and cottage cheese

- ¼ cup butter or margarine
- ½ teaspoon ground turmeric
- 1 teaspoon ground coriander
- 1 teaspoon salt
- 2 packages (10 ounces each) frozen chopped spinach
- ⅔ cup creamy cottage cheese
- 1 tablespoon dairy sour cream

Melt butter. Add turmeric, coriander, and salt. Cook, covered, over low heat for 5 minutes, stirring occasionally. Add spinach. Cook, covered, over moderate heat until spinach is completely thawed. Beat together cottage cheese and sour cream. Stir into spinach. Cook, stirring con-

SPONGECAKE

stantly, until cheese has completely blended with spinach. Serve very hot. Makes 6 servings.

CREAMED SPINACH
- 2 pounds spinach
- 2 tablespoons butter or margarine
- 1 tablespoon all-purpose flour
- Dash of garlic powder
- Salt and pepper to taste
- ¼ cup milk or light cream

Wash spinach and cook, without adding water, until tender; drain. Chop. Melt butter; blend in flour, garlic powder, and salt and pepper. Add milk and cook, stirring constantly, until thickened. Add spinach and heat well. Makes 4 to 6 servings.

SPINACH WITH ALMONDS
- 2 pounds spinach
- ¼ cup chopped blanched almonds
- ¼ cup butter or margarine
- Juice of ½ lemon
- Salt and pepper

Wash spinach. Cook in small amount of boiling salted water for about 5 minutes. Drain and chop. Lightly brown almonds in butter; add lemon juice. Pour over spinach; season to taste. Makes 4 servings.

GERMAN SPINACH SALAD
- 1 pound small fresh spinach leaves
- ½ cup mayonnaise
- ½ cup dairy sour cream
- 6 anchovies, minced
- 1½ tablespoons chopped green-onion tops
- 1½ tablespoons minced parsley
- 1½ tablespoons vinegar
- 1½ tablespoons fresh lemon juice
- ½ garlic clove, minced
- Cheddar-cheese cubes or garlic croutons

Wash and dry spinach. Mix remaining ingredients except cheese and add to spinach. Mix lightly; garnish with cheese. Makes 4 servings.

SPINACH AND CABBAGE SALAD
- 1 small head red cabbage
- 2 pounds fresh spinach
- 3 hard-cooked eggs
- 1 cup French, sour-cream, or Roquefort-cheese dressing
- 2 tablespoons grated onion

Trim cabbage and cut into halves, removing the core. Shred cabbage finely. Wash spinach and trim stems. Tear leaves into bite-size pieces. Toss cabbage with spinach and top with chopped eggs. Beat salad dressing with grated onion. Chill salad until ready to serve. Pour salad dressing over greens and toss lightly just before serving. Makes 8 to 10 servings.

WILTED RAW SPINACH
- 2 tablespoons bacon fat or butter
- 2 tablespoons all-purpose flour
- 1 small onion, minced
- 1 cup water
- ½ teaspoon powdered mustard
- 2 tablespoons vinegar
- ¾ pound fresh spinach, cleaned, drained, and chopped
- Salt and pepper

Melt bacon fat. Stir in flour and onion. Gradually stir in water, mustard, and vinegar. Cook over low heat, stirring constantly, until smooth and thickened. Pour over spinach. Mix well, and season to taste. Serve at once. Makes 4 servings.

SPONGECAKE—A light airy cake with a delicate flavor and texture which is leavened with air incorporated into beaten egg whites. The egg yolks are beaten separately with sugar and folded into the whites. Flour and salt are then carefully folded into batter. Shortening is not generally used in this cake. The cake is baked in an ungreased pan, usually one with a removable bottom, until the top is lightly browned and springs back when touched. It is cooled in its inverted pan. When the cake is cool, it is loosened with a sharp knife or spatula and removed from the pan.

Spongecake is a very old cake, found in the cooking of many nations. In France it is called *génoise* and in Italy *genovese*, since it is said to have originated in the city of Genoa. Old English and Scandinavian cooking also knew the spongecake, as did Jewish cooking. The reason why this cake appears in so many different places is a simple one: it dates back to days when yeast was the only leavening agent known, and since it was unsatisfactory for cakes, they had to be leavened by natural means such as egg whites beaten full of air. Electric beaters have made this task much easier.

Spongecake has many virtues as a cake. It is light and easily digestible, and lends itself admirably to frostings and fillings and to use as the base for *petits fours*. One of the simplest and best ways of serving a spongecake it to fill and frost it with well-flavored whipped cream.

Caloric Value

☐ 3½ ounces = 297 calories

SPONGECAKE
- 1½ cups egg whites (9 to 10 whites)
- ½ teaspoon salt
- 1 teaspoon cream of tartar
- 1⅓ cups sifted granulated sugar
- Grated rind of 1 orange or 1 teaspoon orange extract
- 1⅓ cups sifted cake flour
- ⅔ cup egg yolks (8 or 9 yolks)
- Confectioners' sugar

Beat egg whites until frothy; add salt and cream of tartar gradually, beating constantly. Continue beating until stiff but not dry. Gradually add granulated sugar, beating constantly until all sugar is used and mixture does not run or slip when bowl is stood on edge. Blend in orange rind. Sift flour onto mixture gradually, folding carefully and gently until well blended after each addition. Beat egg yolks until thick and lemon-colored, and gradually fold into first mixture. Pour into ungreased 10-inch tube pan and bake in preheated slow oven (325°F.) for 1¼ hours. Invert cake on rack and let stand until cold before removing from pan. To decorate, dust sifted confectioners' sugar through the holes in a fancy paper doily placed on the top of the cake; then carefully remove doily.

HOT-WATER SPONGECAKE
- 5 eggs (at room temperature)
- 1½ cups sugar
- 2 cups sifted cake flour
- 2 teaspoons baking powder
- ¼ teaspoon salt
- 1 teaspoon vanilla extract
- ½ cup boiling water
- Confectioners' sugar

Beat eggs with rotary beater until very light; gradually beat in sugar. Add dry ingredients slowly, stirring constantly. Stir in vanilla and boiling water. Pour into a medium Turk's-head pan (fluted cake pan with a central tube). Bake in preheated slow oven (325°F.) for 1 hour. Allow spongecake to stand for 1 hour, or until it has cooled. Remove it from the pan and dust with confectioners' sugar, or frost as desired.

CHOCOLATE SPONGECAKE
- 1 cup sifted cake flour
- ⅓ cup cocoa
- ½ teaspoon baking powder
- 1½ cups sifted sugar
- 6 eggs, separated
- ½ teaspoon each of salt and cream of tartar
- ¼ cup water
- 1 teaspoon vanilla extract
- Chocolate Glaze

Sift flour, cocoa, baking powder, and 1 cup sugar. Beat egg whites with salt and cream of tartar until stiff but not dry. Gradually add ½ cup sugar, and beat until very stiff. Combine egg yolks, water, and vanilla; add to dry ingredients, and beat just to blend. Carefully fold egg-yolk mixture into egg whites. Bake in ungreased 10-inch tube pan in preheated moderate oven (375°F.) for about 35 minutes. Cool in pan. Remove, and glaze with Chocolate Glaze.

Chocolate Glaze
Melt together 2 tablespoons butter and 2 ounces (2 squares) unsweetened chocolate. Beat in 2 tablespoons boiling water, 1 cup sifted confectioners' sugar, dash of salt, and ¼ teaspoon vanilla extract.

APPLESAUCE SPONGECAKE
- 3 eggs, separated
- ½ teaspoon salt
- 1 cup sugar

¾ cup hot thick applesauce
1½ cups sifted all-purpose flour
1 teaspoon baking powder
½ teaspoon baking soda
1 teaspoon ground cinnamon
½ teaspoon ground nutmeg
Lemon Cream Sauce

Beat egg whites with salt until foamy. Gradually add ½ cup sugar; beat until stiff but not dry. Beat egg yolks until thick and lemon-colored. Gradually beat remaining sugar into egg yolks. Stir in applesauce. Add sifted dry ingredients, and beat until smooth. Fold in egg whites. Pour into pan (9 x 9 x 2 inches) lined on the bottom with paper. Bake in preheated slow oven (325°F.) for about 45 minutes. Cool in pan. Cut into squares and serve with Lemon Cream Sauce.

Lemon Cream Sauce

In a saucepan beat together ¾ cup sugar, 2 tablespoons cornstarch, ⅛ teaspoon salt, grated rind of 1 lemon, ¼ cup fresh lemon juice, ½ cup water, and 3 egg yolks. Cook over low heat, stirring constantly, until thickened. Cool, and fold in 1 cup heavy cream, whipped.

JELLY SPONGE ROLL

1 cup sifted cake flour
1 teaspoon baking powder
¼ teaspoon salt
3 large eggs
1 cup granulated sugar
⅓ cup water
1 teaspoon vanilla extract
Confectioners' sugar
1 cup soft tart red jelly

Sift first 3 ingredients together. In small bowl, beat eggs until thick and lemon-colored. Pour eggs into large bowl. Gradually beat in granulated sugar. Blend in water and vanilla. Mix in dry ingredients gently, stirring or beating only until batter is smooth. Pour into greased jelly-roll pan (15 x 10 x 1 inches) lined on the bottom with greased brown paper or foil. Bake in preheated moderate oven (375°F.) for 12 to 15 minutes. Loosen edges and immediately turn cake upside down on a towel sprinkled with confectioners' sugar. Carefully peel off paper. Trim off any stiff edges. While cake is still hot, roll up cake and towel from end. Cool on cake rack. Unroll cake and remove towel. Spread with jelly and roll again. If desired, sprinkle with additional confectioners' sugar. Cut into 1-inch slices to serve.

SPOON—This is the oldest and simplest of all eating utensils. Spoons may have many refinements, but basically a spoon is an oval or concave bowl which is fixed to a handle. Throughout many years of use, shapes for various uses have been developed; tea, coffee, sugar, cereal, soup, fruit, dessert, cream soup, thin soup, and serving—each has its own type of spoon.

The earliest spoons were made of wood. As man developed skills in the working of materials he found about him, he developed more elaborate spoons. The early Egyptian ones were elaborately carved of ivory and wood, or made of various metals, finely wrought. The handles were often in the shape of men, women, or animals, and were frequently adorned with lotus blossoms. The spoon was the mark of class in medieval society. Each person had to bring his own eating utensils to the table and children were given a set when they were old enough to eat with company. So to be born with a silver spoon in one's mouth meant that one's family was well-to-do.

In the early days of this country spoons were made of wood, then of pewter and later of silver. The simple colonial patterns of New England were among the best silver spoons made anywhere. In the 19th century, many people collected souvenir spoons upon which memorable scenes of places visited were engraved. The habit still persists.

SPOON BREAD—A famous Southern specialty, this is a baked dish made from white or yellow cornmeal, milk, eggs, and shortening. It is served with a spoon.

The history of spoon bread goes back to the first days of the Virginia Colony when the settlers adapted one of the Indian methods of preparing the native white cornmeal. The Indian's *Suppawn* was a simple porridgelike dish, cooked in pots. The English colonists, recalling the quick breads and porridges eaten in their homeland, refined the dish by adding milk and eggs. Some unknown cook left this mixture in the oven by mistake. Spoon bread was the result.

Spoon bread, and other batter breads made from corn, were especially suited to the colonial way of life. The poorer settlers at first relied more on quick-cooking hoecakes and ashcakes, which could be cooked over a fire rather than in an oven. During the 17th and 18th centuries refinements were introduced which "remain in staunch Favour today among all Classes of Virginians." The batter breads, with their richer ingredients and need of an oven, were developed during this period.

Americans have always eaten many more "quick" breads than have Europeans, largely because of the availability of cheap fuel to make home-baking possible. In continental Europe, conditions demanded that the housewife buy her breads from the village baker or at least take them to him to bake. But in the American South, organized around a central plantation kitchen, spoon bread and its countless relatives could be enjoyed by all.

A recipe for Spoon Bread appears on page 1724.

SPRAT—One of the smallest of the herrings, *Clupea sprattus,* five inches is its normal maximum length. Sprats are caught in abundance in many parts of Europe and extensively eaten there fresh and smoked, both under their own and other names. For example, a sprat is also called a Norwegian sardine or anchovy. In the United States the term sprat is applied to the young of the common herring and to many other small fishes. Sprats are imported canned, under that title, from Denmark and France and are available in specialty food stores and in the gourmet-food sections of many food stores.

SPRITZ—A cookie with a high butter content that is forced out of a special spritz tube. The name comes from the German and it means "to squirt." The spritz cookie dough is squirted out of the cookie press, in interesting patterns, onto an ungreased cookie sheet.

SPRITZ COOKIES

½ cup soft butter or margarine
½ cup shortening
⅔ cup sugar
3 egg yolks
1 teaspoon almond extract
2¼ cups sifted all-purpose flour

Cream butter, shortening, and sugar until light. Beat in egg yolks and flavoring. Add flour, and blend. Fill cookie press and shape fancy cookies on chilled ungreased cookie sheets. Bake in preheated moderate oven (375°F.) for 10 to 12 minutes. Makes 4 to 5 dozen.

CHOCOLATE SPRITZ COOKIES

1 cup soft butter
¾ cup sugar
3 egg yolks
2 ounces (2 squares) unsweetened chocolate, melted
1 teaspoon vanilla extract
2½ cups sifted all-purpose flour
¼ teaspoon salt
Colored tiny candies, colored sugar, bits of candied cherries

Cream butter and sugar; add egg yolks and beat until light. Blend in chocolate and vanilla. Add flour and salt; mix well. Force through cookie press. Decorate. Bake in preheated hot oven (400°F.) for 7 to 10 minutes. Store airtight. Will ship well if not too thin. Makes about 6 dozen.

SPUMONI

ALMOND SPRITZ COOKIES
- ⅔ cup soft butter
- ⅔ cup sugar
- 2 egg yolks, well beaten
- Grated rind of ½ lemon
- Juice of ½ lemon
- ½ teaspoon salt
- ½ cup blanched almonds, grated
- 2 cups sifted all-purpose flour

Cream butter and sugar until light. Add all ingredients except flour. Beat until thick and lemon-colored. Add flour; mix well. Force through cookie press onto cookie sheets. Bake in preheated slow oven (325°F.) for about 15 minutes. Store airtight. Will ship well. Makes 5 dozen.

SPUMONI—Italian molded ice cream with an outer layer of custard containing chopped almonds and an inner filling made with heavy cream, sugar, cherries, and a candied orange peel.

SPUMONI
- 2 cups milk
- 5 egg yolks, slightly beaten
- ⅛ teaspoon salt
- 1 cup sugar
- 1 teaspoon vanilla extract
- 1 cup heavy cream
- 8 maraschino cherries, finely chopped
- 2 tablespoons minced candied orange peel
- 8 slivered blanched almonds
- 2 tablespoons brandy

Turn refrigerator control to coldest setting. In top part of double boiler mix milk, egg yolks, salt, and ¾ cup of the sugar. Cook over simmering water, stirring constantly, until mixture is thickened and coats a metal spoon. Cool; add vanilla. Pour into refrigerator tray and freeze until almost firm. Line a 2-quart melon mold with the mixture. Whip cream until stiff; fold in remaining sugar, the cherries, peel, almonds, and brandy. Fill center of mold, cover, and freeze in freezer or freezing compartment of refrigerator until firm. Unmold on serving plate and cut into wedges. To loosen spumoni from the mold, put a cloth wrung out of hot water on the bottom of mold. Makes 6 to 8 servings.

SQUAB—A young pigeon which has not been allowed to fly. Squabs weigh about one pound and are eaten as a delicacy. They were especially prized in Victorian and Edwardian days, when chickens were not the commercially produced, weight- and quality-controlled birds they are today. In those days, the cook never could be quite sure that even a young chicken would be tender. But squabs were, and this is why they were used for festive dinner parties.

Availability and Purchasing Guide—Available all year in gourmet food stores and specialty stores. They are more plentiful and less costly during the summer months. Frozen squabs are also available in food specialty stores.

Squabs should be plump and firm in appearance.

Storage
- ☐ Refrigerator shelf, raw: 2 to 3 days
- ☐ Refrigerator shelf, cooked: 4 to 5 days
- ☐ Frozen, refrigerator frozen-food compartment: 1 to 2 months
- ☐ Frozen, freezer: 6 to 8 months

Nutritive Food Values—Good source of protein, with some phosphorus and a small amount of calcium.
- ☐ 3½ ounces, raw = 279 calories

Basic Preparation—Squabs can be split and broiled, stuffed and roasted, sautéed, or stewed. They need long, slow cooking and should be served well done. Squabs should be eaten with the fingers as it is impossible to cut off all the meat with a knife and fork.

☐ **To Roast**—If frozen, thaw squab. Season inside and out with salt and pepper. Stuff, if desired, just before cooking, allowing ¼ cup stuffing for each squab. Skewer neck and body openings. Turn back wings. Brush with melted butter and roast on a rack in preheated hot oven (400°F.) for 45 minutes to 1 hour, or until drumstick moves easily in the joint. Brush with more melted butter occasionally during roasting.

☐ **To Broil**—Wash, dry, and split squabs. Or have butcher split them. Put skin side down on a rack in a broiler pan. Brush with melted butter. Season with salt and pepper. Broil 7 to 9 inches from heat for 30 minutes, or until tender, turning squab once during this time. Brush with more butter during cooking.

☐ **To Sauté**—Cut squab into quarters and bread pieces or dip into flour. Season with salt and pepper. Sauté in shallow fat until brown and then continue cooking over low heat for 15 to 20 minutes, or until squab is tender.

☐ **To Freeze**—Eviscerate, wash, and pat dry. Do not stuff before freezing. Wrap in moisture- vapor-proof wrapping, excluding as much air as possible. Seal.

ROAST STUFFED SQUABS
- 1 onion, chopped fine
- Butter or margarine
- 1 cup fine, soft stale-bread crumbs
- 1 cup chopped cooked ham
- ½ cup pine nuts
- ¼ cup chopped parsley
- ½ teaspoon thyme
- 4 cleaned squabs, about 1 pound each
- 4 pieces of fat bacon
- ¼ cup white wine

Sauté onion in 6 tablespoons butter until golden. Mix with next 5 ingredients. Stuff birds with the mixture, close openings with poultry pins and lace with twine. Put, breast sides up, on rack in shallow roasting pan. Cover the breast of each with a piece of bacon. Melt ¼ cup butter and mix with the wine. Roast in preheated slow oven (325°F.) for 1 hour and 15 minutes, basting frequently with the butter-wine mixture. Remove bacon during last 15 minutes of roasting. Makes 4 servings.

SQUASH—A gourd fruit native to the Western Hemisphere, belonging to the genus *Cucurbita*. The Indians called it *askutasquash*, meaning "green thing eaten green" and grew it in Peru as long as 2,000 years ago.

The two main types of squash are summer and winter squash. There are many varieties of each, differing in shape, size, and color:

SUMMER SQUASH—Small, quick growing, with thin skins and light-colored flesh. They are marketed before the rinds and seeds harden. The varieties most common in our food stores are:

- **Scallop, Cymling, or Pattypan**—Disk-shape, with a scalloped edge. The skin is smooth or slightly worted, pale green when young, and turns white as it matures. It is best harvested when half grown or 3 to 4 inches across.
- **Cocozelle**—Cylindrical, with smooth skin slightly ribbed with alternate stripes of dark green and yellow. Similar to zucchini. Best when 6 to 8 inches long and 2 inches in diameter.
- **Caserta**—Also cylindrical but thicker than cocozelle at the tip. The skin has alternate stripes of light and dark green. Best when 6 to 7 inches long and 1 to 1½ inches thick.
- **Chayote**—A pear-shape squash about the size of an acorn squash, light green in color. It has one soft seed in the center. When prepared for cooking, it is cut up unpeeled, without removing the edible seed.
- **Yellow Crookneck**—A squash with a curved neck, larger at the top than the base. The worted skin is light yellow in young squash, turning to a deep yellow when mature. It is best when still light yellow and about half grown. Grows to be 8 to 10 inches long and 3 inches thick.
- **Yellow Straightneck**—Similar to the Crookneck except that the neck is straight and it grows to be much larger, 20 inches long and 4 inches thick when mature.
- **Zucchini**—Sometimes called Vegetable Marrow or Italian Marrow. It is cylindri-

cal but larger at the base. The skin has a lacy pattern of green and yellow that concentrates to give the appearance of stripes. It grows to be 10 to 12 inches long and 2 to 3 inches thick.

WINTER SQUASH—Winter squash has a hard, coarse rough rind that is dark green or orange in color. There are many types of winter squash. The most common varieties in our food stores are:

- **Acorn, Table Queen, or Des Moines**—Acorn-shape and grows to be 5 to 8 inches long and 4 to 5 inches thick. It has a thin, smooth, hard shell which is widely ribbed, and is dark green but changes to orange during storage. The flesh is pale orange and there is a large seed cavity.
- **Buttercup**—Has a turbanlike formation at the blossom end. It grows to be 4 to 5 inches long and 6 to 8 inches thick, with a turban 2 to 3 inches thick. The hard skin is dark green with faint gray pockmarks and stripes and the turban is light gray. The dry sweet flesh is orange in color.
- **Butternut**—Cylindrical in shape with a bulblike base. The skin is smooth and hard and is a light brown or dark yellow color. It grows to be 9 to 12 inches long; at the bulbous end it is often 5 inches in diameter.
- **Warren Turban**—Drum-shape with a turbanlike formation at the blossom end. It grows to be 8 to 10 inches long and 12 to 15 inches in diameter. The hard worted skin is bright orange, the blossom end slightly striped, and the turban a bluish color.
- **Hubbard**—Globe-shape with a thick tapered neck that is somewhat smaller at the blossom end. It grows to be 9 to 12 inches in diameter. The skin may be bronze-green, blue-gray, or orange-red in color; it is hard, worted, and ridged. The flesh is yellowish orange and has a sweet taste.
- **Sugar or Pie Pumpkin**—Green or orange rind with ridges, round or oval-shape, with stem at the top. The flesh is bright orange with many seeds in the center of the pumpkin.

Availability—The varieties of summer squash listed are found in some markets all year round with the peak season May to July.

Among the winter squash, acorn and butternut are available year round, and the other varieties are in food stores from August to December, with the peak season from October to December.

Canned puréed squash is available, as is frozen zucchini and winter squash.

Purchasing Guide—When buying summer squash, look for young squash with fresh tender rinds, free from blemishes, and fairly heavy for their size.

Look for winter squash with a hard rind that is free from blemishes. It should be heavy for its size.

Storage—Purchase summer squash in small quantities and store immediately in the vegetable compartment of the refrigerator.

Place winter squash so that they do not touch in a fairly dry, well-ventilated room with temperatures between 50°F. and 55°F.

☐ Summer squash, fresh, refrigerator shelf or vegetable compartment, raw: 3 to 14 days
☐ Winter squash, fresh, kitchen shelf: 1 to 4 weeks
☐ Fresh, refrigerator shelf, cooked: 4 to 5 days
☐ Fresh, prepared for freezing; and frozen, refrigerator frozen-food compartment: 2 to 3 months
☐ Fresh, prepared for freezing: and frozen, freezer: 1 year
☐ Canned, kitchen shelf: 1 year

Nutritive Food Values—Summer squash provides vitamin C, vitamin A, and niacin. Since summer squash is low in calories and sodium, it may be used frequently in a sodium-restricted diet, reducing, or other special diets.

Winter squash is an excellent source of vitamin A, and has fair vitamin C, riboflavin, and iron.

☐ Summer squash, crookneck and straightneck, 3½ ounces, boiled and drained = 15 calories
☐ Summer squash, scallop, 3½ ounces, boiled and drained = 16 calories
☐ Summer squash, cocozelle and zucchini, 3½ ounces, boiled and drained = 12 calories
☐ Summer squash, other varieties, 3½ ounces, boiled and drained = 14 calories
☐ Winter squash, acorn, 3½ ounces, boiled = 34 calories
☐ Winter squash, acorn, 3½ ounces, baked = 55 calories
☐ Winter squash, butternut, 3½ ounces, boiled = 41 calories
☐ Winter squash, butternut, 3½ ounces, baked = 68 calories
☐ Winter squash, hubbard, 3½ ounces, boiled = 30 calories
☐ Winter squash, hubbard, 3½ ounces, baked = 50 calories
☐ Winter squash, other varieties, 3½ ounces, boiled = 38 calories
☐ Winter squash, other varieties, 3½ ounces, baked = 63 calories

Basic Preparation, Summer Squash—Wash, but do not pare; remove the stem and blossom ends. Leave whole or cut into ¾-inch slices or cubes.

☐ **To Cook**—Cook, covered, in a small amount of boiling salted water (2 to 4 tablespoons) for 10 to 15 minutes, or until tender. Uncover and boil rapidly for a few minutes longer to evaporate excess liquid. Season with salt, pepper, and butter or margarine. A garlic clove or a bouillon cube may be added during cooking, if desired.
☐ **To Freeze**—Use young tender squash with small seeds. Cut squash after washing into ½-inch slices. Blanch in boiling water for 3½ minutes. Chill in cold water for 5 minutes. Drain. Pack into containers, leaving ½-inch headspace. Seal.

Winter Squash—Wash; cut small squash such as acorn or butternut into halves; cut larger squash into individual servings; remove the seeds and stringy portions.

☐ **To Bake**—Dot cut portions with butter or brush with bacon or ham drippings; season with salt and pepper; place in a covered baking dish or wrap in foil. Bake in preheated hot oven (400°F.) for 30 to 60 minutes, or until tender; time varies according to size and type of squash. Remove the cover and unwrap during the last 15 minutes of baking.

Squash may also be baked, uncovered, in a shallow greased pan, cut side down for the first half of the baking period to allow it to steam. Turn up, brush with butter, and season. Continue baking until tender. Allow longer time for baking when using this method.

☐ **To Mash Baked Squash**—Prepare and bake as directed above. When tender, cool slightly and scrape out pulp. Mash pulp, using a potato masher, electric mixer, or blender. Season with salt, pepper, butter, and brown sugar if you wish. Mix well and reheat before serving.
☐ **To Freeze**—Use firm squash. Cut into cubes and remove seeds. Cook, covered, in water to cover and until squash is tender. Remove rind and mash squash. Cool quickly and pack into containers, leaving ½-inch headspace.

If desired, bake squash as above and pack halves or quarters in plastic bags and seal, or wrap in foil. Freeze until firm.

SUMMER SQUASH

SQUASH MANDARIN

2 pounds summer squash
Salt
1 tablespoon butter or margarine
1 can (8 ounces) mandarin oranges
2 teaspoons light-brown sugar
¼ teaspoon ground nutmeg
¼ cup toasted slivered almonds

1 — Butternut
2 — Hubbard
3 — Scallop
4 — Sugar or Pie Pumpkin
5 — Acorn
6 — Summer
7 — Zucchini

SQUASH

Wash squash. Cut, unpeeled, into crosswise slices. Cook in small amount of boiling salted water until just tender; drain and add butter. Keep warm. Pour syrup from oranges into saucepan, add sugar, and bring to boil. Add nutmeg and orange segments. Pour over squash and sprinkle with nuts. Makes 6 servings.

BAKED SUMMER SQUASH
- 1 small onion, minced
- 3 tablespoons butter or margarine
- 3 hard-cooked eggs, chopped
- 3 summer squash, diced
- 2 eggs, well beaten
- 1/3 cup light cream
- 1/4 cup soft bread crumbs

Sauté onion in butter. Combine onion, hard-cooked eggs, and squash. Put mixture in a well-greased 1-quart casserole. Mix beaten eggs with cream and pour over casserole. Sprinkle top with bread crumbs. Bake in preheated moderate oven (350°F.) for about 30 minutes. Makes 6 servings.

SKILLET SQUASH AND ONIONS
- 2 pounds yellow summer squash
- 3 medium onions, sliced thin
- 3 tablespoons butter or margarine
- 1/2 teaspoon salt
- 1/4 teaspoon pepper

Wash squash and dice. Combine all ingredients in skillet. Cover and cook for 20 to 30 minutes, or until squash and onions are tender, stirring frequently. Makes 4 servings.

BAKED CYMLINGS
- 12 tiny cymlings
- 1/4 cup water
- 2 tablespoons butter or margarine
- 1/2 small onion, grated
- 1 tablespoon all-purpose flour
- 3/4 cup light cream
- Salt and pepper to taste
- Buttered crumbs

Wash cymlings and cut into wedges, discarding stems. Add water, cover, and boil until barely tender. Drain, and put into 1½-quart casserole. Melt butter, add onion and flour, and mix. Stir in cream, cook for 2 or 3 minutes, and pour over cymlings. Season with salt and pepper. Top with buttered crumbs. Bake in preheated moderate oven (350°F.) for 20 minutes, or until lightly browned. Makes 4 servings.

SQUASH FRITTERS
- 1½ cups mashed steamed cymling squash
- 1 egg, beaten
- 1/2 cup unsifted all-purpose flour
- 1/2 teaspoon salt
- 1/8 teaspoon pepper
- 1 teaspoon baking powder
- Butter or margarine

Mix all ingredients except butter and drop by spoonfulls into hot buttered skil-

SQUID

let. Cook until golden-brown on both sides. Makes 4 servings.

CHEESE-STUFFED SQUASH
- 3 medium cymling squashes
- 2 onions, minced
- ½ teaspoon each of crumbled dried thyme and sage
- ½ teaspoon salt
- ⅛ teaspoon pepper
- ¼ cup butter or margarine
- 2 celery stalks, minced
- 1 ripe tomato, peeled and diced
- 1½ cups soft stale bread crumbs
- 1 cup shredded Cheddar cheese

Wash squashes, cut into halves crosswise, and scoop out seeds. Cover with boiling water in skillet or kettle and simmer for 5 minutes; drain. Cook onion and seasonings in butter for 3 or 4 minutes. Add celery and tomato. Heat well and stir in crumbs and cheese. Stuff squashes. Put squashes in shallow baking pan and cover bottom of pan with boiling water. Bake in preheated moderate oven (350°F.) for 30 minutes, or until squashes are tender. Makes 6 servings.

BAKED ZUCCHINI
- 2 medium zucchini (about 1 pound)
- Salt to taste
- 1 garlic clove, minced
- 2 tablespoons butter or margarine
- 2 cups bread cubes
- ½ teaspoon poultry seasoning or dried oregano
- Pepper to taste

Wash and cook unpeeled zucchini for 10 minutes in small amount of boiling salted water. Drain and cut into halves lengthwise. Scoop out pulp; chop. Cook garlic in butter for a few seconds. Stir in chopped pulp, bread cubes, poultry seasoning, and salt and pepper. Stuff zucchini with mixture. Put in greased baking dish and bake in preheated moderate oven (350°F.) for 20 minutes, or until zucchini are tender. Makes 4 servings.

SQUASH AND APPLE JAM
- 3½ cups peeled and sliced tart apples
- 4 quarts peeled and sliced summer squash
- 3 pounds sugar
- ¾ ounce whole dried gingerroot*
- 1½ lemons, rind and juice

Cut apples and squash into thin slices. Put in large bowl or enamelware preserving kettle, sprinkling layers with the sugar. Cover and let stand overnight. Tie gingerroot in bag, crush, and put in large kettle with fruit and squash. Add strained lemon juice and thin slivers of lemon rind. Boil only until fruit is clear and tender and liquid jells, about 20 minutes. Pour into jars, cool slightly, and seal. Makes about five ½-pint jars.

*If whole gingerroot is not available, use 1 teaspoon ground ginger. Ground ginger will make a darker jam.

WINTER SQUASH

APPLE-STUFFED ACORN SQUASH
- 2 acorn squashes
- Boiling water
- 3 tart apples
- Melted butter or margarine
- ½ cup maple syrup or honey
- Salt to taste

Wash squashes, cut into halves lengthwise, and scoop out seeds and fiber. Put in baking pan, cut side down, and add ½ inch of boiling water. Bake in preheated hot oven (400°F.) for about 20 minutes. Meanwhile, peel, core, and dice apples. Mix apples with ¼ cup melted butter and the maple syrup. Turn squash halves cut side up and brush cut surfaces with melted butter. Sprinkle with salt. Fill squash with apple mixture. Cover pan with foil and continue baking in hot oven (400°F.) for 30 minutes, or until apples and squash are tender. Makes 4 servings.

BAKED ACORN SQUASH WITH WHIPPED POTATO ROSETTES
- 3 medium-size acorn squashes
- 3 tablespoons melted butter or margarine
- Salt and pepper to taste
- 3 cups seasoned mashed potatoes
- 1 egg, well beaten

Cut squashes into halves and place, cut side up, in a baking pan. Pour ½ inch of boiling water into pan, cover, and oven-steam in preheated hot oven (400°F.) for 40 minutes, or until just tender. Drain water. Brush squash with butter and sprinkle with salt and pepper. Whip potatoes and egg together. Be sure there are no lumps. Force through pastry bag into hollows of squash, using star-shape tip to form rosettes. Or, potatoes can be spooned lightly into squash. Bake in preheated hot oven (400°F.) for 20 minutes, or until thoroughly heated and lightly browned. Makes 6 servings.

GRAPEFRUIT-AND-TANGERINE STUFFED SQUASH
- 2 acorn squashes (about 2 pounds)
- Salt to taste
- ¼ cup firmly packed brown sugar
- 2 tablespoons butter or margarine
- 1 medium grapefruit
- 1 tangerine

Wash squashes and cut into halves lengthwise. Scoop out seeds. Steam for 10 minutes, covered, on top of stove in about 1 inch of salted water; drain. Put in baking pan. Put 1 tablespoon brown sugar, ½ tablespoon butter, and a dash of salt in each center. Bake in preheated hot oven (400°F.) for 15 minutes. Remove from oven; fill centers with peeled fruit cut into segments. Return to oven; bake for 15 minutes longer or until tender. Makes 4 servings.

FRENCH-FRIED SQUASH SLICES
Quarter and peel 1 medium acorn squash; remove seeds and stringy portion. Cut into thin slices and sprinkle with salt, pepper, and brown sugar. Drop all at once into deep hot fat (425°F. on a frying thermometer) and fry for 8 to 10 minutes, or until lightly browned and tender. Makes 3 or 4 servings.

SCALLOPED HUBBARD SQUASH
- 1 onion, chopped
- 1 green pepper, chopped
- 3 tablespoons butter or margarine
- 3½ cups mashed cooked Hubbard squash or 2 boxes (12 ounces each) thawed frozen squash
- Salt and pepper
- ½ cup crushed corn flakes

Cook onion and green pepper in butter until tender. Add squash and season with salt and pepper to taste. Put in shallow baking dish and sprinkle with crumbs. Bake in preheated hot oven (400°F.) for about 30 minutes. Makes 4 servings.

SQUASH CASSEROLE
- 2 cups mashed cooked Hubbard squash
- ¼ cup butter or margarine
- 3 tablespoons brown sugar
- 1 tablespoon prepared mustard
- 1 egg, slightly beaten
- Salt and pepper to taste
- ¼ cup crushed corn flakes

Mix squash with 2 tablespoons each of melted butter and brown sugar, the mustard, and egg; season with salt and pepper. Put in shallow baking dish. Mix corn flakes with remaining melted butter and brown sugar; sprinkle over top. Bake in preheated moderate oven (350°F.) for 20 minutes, or until heated through. Makes 6 servings.

ANISE SQUASH PIE
- ¾ cup sugar
- 1 tablespoon flour
- ½ teaspoon salt
- ¼ teaspoon ground ginger
- 1½ teaspoons crushed aniseed
- ¾ teaspoon fresh lemon juice
- 3 large eggs
- 1½ cups mashed cooked winter squash
- 1 cup milk
- Pastry for 1-crust 9-inch pie, unbaked

Combine first 6 ingredients in mixing bowl. Beat in eggs. Stir in squash and milk. Turn into 9-inch pie pan lined with pastry. Bake in preheated hot oven (400°F.) for 40 to 50 minutes, or until center of pie is firm. Cool before serving. Makes 6 to 8 servings.

SQUID—This odd many-armed salt-water creature belongs to the Cephalopoda, the highest class of mollusks, along with the cuttlefish and octopus. It is found in the North Atlantic. Squid has a group of

WOMAN'S DAY

ten long muscular arms around the front of its head with suckers at the ends, like hands. Squids have a bag of inklike fluid inside which they eject (like working a siphon) when danger is near. The ink clouds the water and protects them.

Availability and Purchasing Guide—Fresh squid is available year round in fish markets in large cities. It should have a sweet fresh odor.

Some canned and dried squid is available in specialty food stores.

Storage—Wrap fresh squid in moisture-proof paper or place in tightly covered dish in coldest part of refrigerator.
- [ ] Fresh, refrigerator shelf: 1 to 2 days
- [ ] Canned, kitchen shelf: 1 year
- [ ] Canned, refrigerator shelf, opened: 3 to 4 days
- [ ] Dried, refrigerator shelf: 2 to 3 months

Nutritive Food Values—High in protein and phosphorus, with some calcium and traces of thiamine and riboflavin.
- [ ] 3½ ounces, raw = 84 calories

Basic Preparation—The best way to clean a squid: turn it so that the back side is up. It may seem difficult to tell which is front and which is back, but the front side does have teeth and eye indications. Starting from the back, cut through, removing the backbone. The inside will then be exposed and you can remove the ink sack, which is usually done by hand.
- [ ] **To Fry**—Cut tentacles into small pieces. Roll pieces in flour. Dip pieces into beaten egg and then into crumbs or into a batter. Fry in deep hot fat or oil (375°F. on a frying thermometer), or sauté in shallow cooking oil until golden-brown. Drain on absorbent paper and add salt and pepper to taste.
- [ ] **To Bake**—Soak cleaned squid in milk to cover. Drain; roll in dry bread crumbs and put in a well-greased shallow baking dish. Season with salt and pepper and dot with butter or margarine. Bake in preheated extremely hot oven (500°F.) for 12 minutes. Serve with tartare sauce or a spicy tomato sauce.

SQUID, ITALIAN STYLE

1½ pounds small squid
½ cup olive oil
1 garlic clove, sliced
Few parsley sprigs
½ teaspoon salt
2 anchovy fillets, chopped
1 tiny piece hot dried red pepper
1 cup dry white wine
½ cup water

Skin squid, remove insides; wash squid well and cut into pieces. Lightly brown garlic in the olive oil. Add remaining ingredients except wine and water. Cook until liquid from squid has evaporated. Add wine and simmer until liquid is evaporated. Add water and simmer for 20 minutes, or until squid is thoroughly cooked. Makes 4 servings.

SAUTÉED STUFFED SQUIDS

½ cup chopped onion
¾ cup olive oil
2 garlic cloves, chopped
4 tomatoes, peeled, seeded, and chopped
½ cup coarsely chopped ripe olives
2 cups buttered soft bread crumbs
1 teaspoon each of salt and pepper
¼ teaspoon ground oregano
6 squids, cleaned

Sauté onion in olive oil until translucent. Add garlic, tomatoes, and ripe olives and cook at a simmer for 15 minutes. Add bread crumbs, salt, pepper, and oregano. Blend well; use this mixture to stuff the cleaned squids. Sauté squids in remaining olive oil until tentacles are crisp. Makes 6 servings.

STEWED SQUIDS IN THE PORTUGUESE MANNER

2 pounds small squids
¼ cup olive oil
2 medium onions, sliced
¼ cup chopped parsley
Pepper
4 tomatoes, peeled and chopped
Salt

Clean squids and wash well in several changes of cold water. Cut into bite-size pieces. Heat olive oil. Cook onions and parsley in it until soft. Do not brown. Season with pepper and add fish. Cover with tomatoes. Simmer, covered, over low heat until fish is tender; cooking time depends on the size of the fish. When cooked, season with salt. This is done last since salt tends to toughen the fish. Serve with rice. Makes 4 to 6 servings.

SQUIRREL—A widely distributed, largely arboreal rodent of the family Sciuridae. Two kinds of squirrels are found in the United States and occasionally eaten as food, particularly in some rural sections of the southern states. These are the red and gray squirrels. The gray squirrel is fatter and the texture and flavor of its meat are superior to that of the red. The flesh of squirrel is light red or pink in color and has a pleasing flavor. The slight gamy taste present in most game meats is not so pronounced in squirrel. Young ones can be fried or broiled the same as rabbits. Only the oldest and toughest animals require parboiling to make them tender.

FRICASSEED SQUIRREL

1 gray squirrel, cleaned and disjointed
½ teaspoon salt
⅛ teaspoon pepper
½ cup all-purpose flour
3 slices of bacon, diced
1 small onion, sliced
1½ teaspoons fresh lemon juice
⅓ cup broth or water

Cut squirrel into 6 or 7 pieces. Rub with the salt and pepper and roll in flour. Fry slowly with the bacon until browned. Add remaining ingredients, cover, and simmer for 1 hour, or until tender, adding more broth or water if necessary. Makes 4 servings.

STARCH—A carbohydrate found in certain grains, vegetables, and roots which is reduced to a white powder or to granules by a complicated chemical process. Starch has no odor or flavor. It acts as a stiffener of liquids, so that in cooking it is used as a thickener. Starches used in thickening must be stirred into a *hot* liquid since they are insoluble in a cold one, which means that they will not swell in it and stiffen it. Starch also absorbs a certain amount of moisture without caking too much; it is added to confectioners' sugar and to baking powder to control moisture which otherwise would be totally absorbed by the sugar or baking powder ingredients, making them impossibly hard.

The best known culinary starches are made from corn, rice, potatoes, arrowroot, and cassava, manioc or tapioca. Some starches are precooked as in instant puddings, pie fillings, and sauce mixes. They require little or no cooking to thicken.

For various kinds of cooking, such as the thickening of sauces and the making of puddings, starches produce better results than flour. They thicken into a softer, more gelatinous, and clearer substance, and they cook more quickly, without the raw taste of flour that has not been sufficiently cooked. Substitutions: 2 tablespoons flour = 1 tablespoon cornstarch, rice starch, potato starch, or arrowroot.

Mix starch with a little cool water to a smooth paste. Stir gradually into hot liquid. Cook, stirring constantly, until liquid has thickened and is clear.

Some starches are used to stiffen clothes; sometimes they are packed in pressurized cans as spray starches.

STEAK—A slice of meat cut from the fleshy part of the carcass of an animal or a cross-section slice of a large fish. When the word steak is used without further specification it generally refers to a beefsteak. However, there are ham steaks, lamb steaks, salmon steaks, etc.

Ground beef, shaped into a patty for cooking, is also called steak, for example: hamburger steak, Salisbury steak.

Steak cuts are usually broiled. For additional information see entries under the specific meats and fishes.

STEAKS, CHARCOAL BROILED
by Philip S. Brown

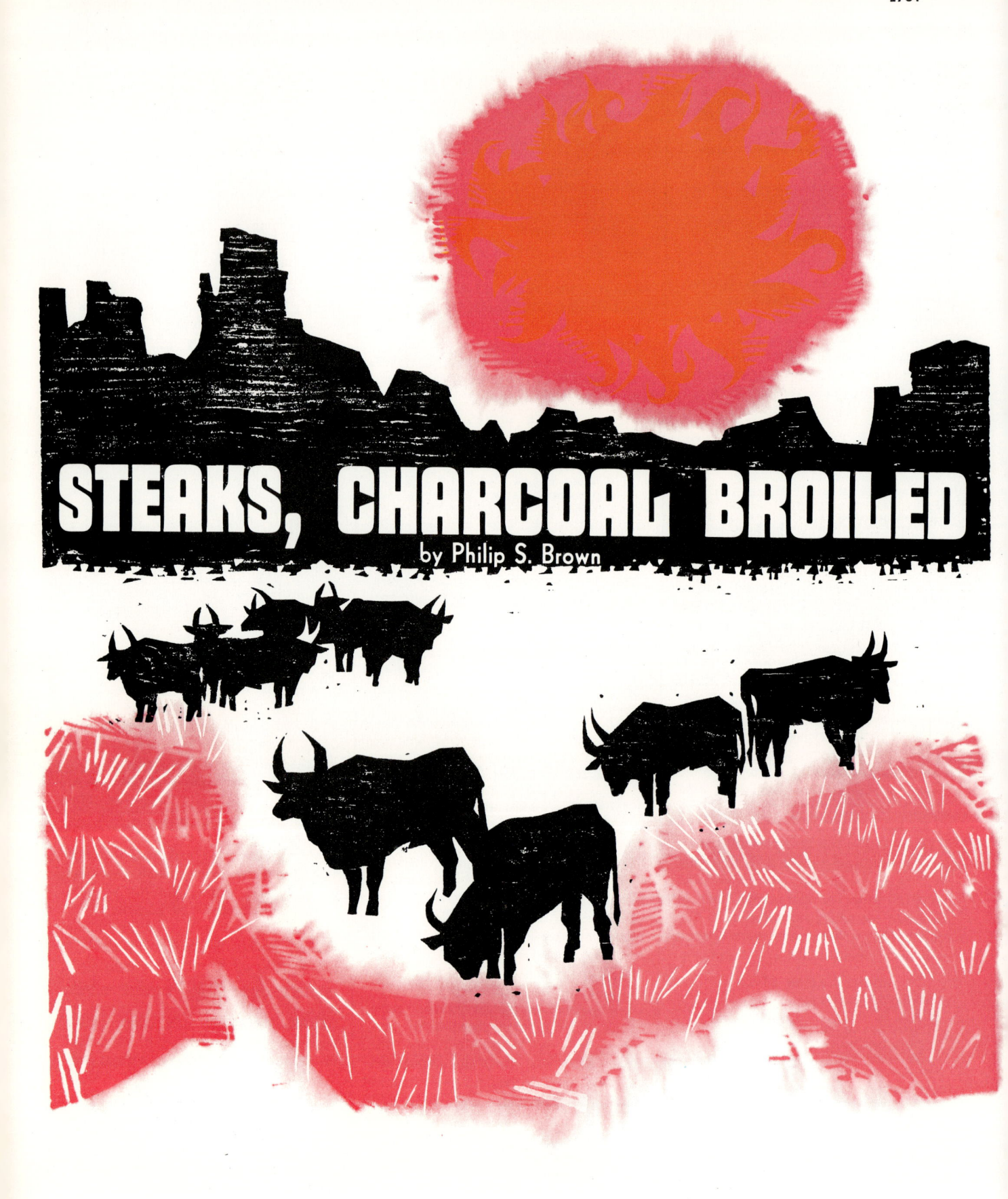

We Americans dearly love steak and our annual consumption of it is a matter of awe and amazement to the rest of the world. Even the English, from whom we got our passion for beefsteaks, think we overdo it a bit, but maybe there is a tiny touch of envy mingled with their scorn. Still, it was the English who started it all with their famous beefsteak clubs. Far and away the most famous of them all was the Sublime Society of Steaks, which was founded by the celebrated theater manager John Rich in 1735, and continued until 1867. In addition to great figures from the literary and theatrical worlds, its membership included brilliant men from all walks of life, even some members of the royal family. In truly democratic fashion all members were on an equal footing; nevertheless, I suspect that membership in The Club was a status symbol of the times.

The French, who had not yet become Kings of the Kitchen, seem to have adopted this English culinary discovery early in the 19th century. Today, of course, travelers in France are everywhere offered the ubiquitous *entrecôte,* as well as *filets* and *aloyaux* (sirloin steaks). But it was the Americans who, in the last century, really took the steak to the family heart. Not at the clubs, not at restaurants serving *haute cuisine,* but in the well-to-do American home, steak was eaten morning, noon, or night, or all three. Steak and eggs was a standard breakfast dish, along with fried potatoes, toast, bacon, and frequently a piece of pie. The trenchermen of the day thought nothing of sitting down, at noon, to a 2-inch, 3-pound T-bone or sirloin steak, then returning home to a family meal of steak and onions.

It has been in this century, however, that steaks have really come into their own. As living conditions have improved, more and more families could afford to splurge on a steak, and the demand grew. Perhaps the greatest impetus given to steak-eating was the discovery that cooking them over glowing coals (the original way of broiling) was still the best. Restaurants began boasting of their charcoal-broiled steaks and before long smart wives figured out that their husbands could do just as good a job in their own backyards. And so they can, if they follow a few simple rules.

Although most of us, including me, mean beefsteak when we say "steak," there are steaks from other animals and fish that are marvelous. The general rules applying to the broiling of beefsteaks apply, with a few slight variations. Veal, pork, ham, lamb, and mutton are all superb, as are fish steaks of various kinds. It's fun to experiment and any of these will be a welcome change, in the unlikely event that you find beefsteaks monotonous.

The Size of Steaks

Steaks vary tremendously in size, shape, tenderness, and beauty. Your steaks should preferably be government-graded Choice at least, and in the case of some less tender cuts (rump, round, flank, and so on), Choice or Prime.

Generally speaking, steaks should be cut no thinner than 1 inch, as it's nearly impossible to control the degree of rareness in a thinner one. Steaks which must be well done, like pork, may be thinner, of course. Personally, I prefer steaks from 1½ to 2½ inches thick, as that's the way to grill them with that crisp brown crackling of the fat and a little crust on the outside, so that each slice is a lovely juicy pink framed in appetizing brown. For boneless cuts, allow at least ½ pound for each diner; 10 to 12 ounces of meat with the bone in. It's a good idea to trim off some of the surplus fat, thus preventing too much flaring with attendant dousing. If you have one of the new slant-grill barbecues, this is no longer a problem, as the fat runs down the grill and not into the fire. While most articles on the subject recommend turning steaks with tongs or a spatula, I find the fork much easier and the resultant holes in the meat close up as soon as the heat reaches them, which is immediately.

How do you know when the steak is done? The easiest way for a novice charcoal cook is to make a slit in the meat with a very sharp-pointed knife and take a peek inside. Here again all the vital juices will not spurt out and the cut will soon be sealed. After a little practice, you should be able to tell by the "feel" of the meat, the way professional chefs do. Press down on the meat with the back of a fork and just wiggle it a little. As the meat cooks it becomes "tighter" and you'll get less reaction to the movement of the fork. As I said, this method requires some practice, but it's a nice professional touch and doesn't impair the appearance of the meat.

How to Start a Charcoal Fire

There are innumerable ways of starting a charcoal fire, and your way is undoubtedly the best for you. The most important thing about fires for steaks is to keep them small. Charcoal is an expensive fuel but a little goes a long way. In general, 12 to 18 briquettes are plenty to cook any steak, although more may be needed if many steaks are being broiled on a large grill area. After igniting, they should be allowed to burn until covered with a thin layer of gray ash; the temperature at the grill level should be around 300°F. for most steaks: this is a medium fire. Most grills in use today have grates or fireboxes which can be raised or lowered for heat control; if yours is fixed in one position, be sure that the fire's right before starting to cook.

As for the grill itself, it can be as simple or elaborate as you like. An old oven grate on two stacks of bricks will produce superb results if the cook knows what he's doing. So use whatever equipment suits you, but understand what you're trying to do. I have cooked steaks on improvised wire-mesh grills, on propane-heated tiles, on electric grills with ceramic "charcoal," and practically every other kind known to man. A couple of minutes devoted to learning the capabilities of the grill will result in perfect steaks every time, and under almost any sort of conditions.

If your steak is 1½ inches thick or more, it should be at room temperature before cooking; if it's thinner than that, better keep it in the refrigerator until just before grilling. A 2-inch steak will take about 3 hours to warm up to 70°F., so if you buy it in the morning, don't refrigerate it; just leave it out. Also remember that the temperature of the air will make a big difference in the time required to cook over an open fire. If there's a cool breeze blowing, not as much heat will reach your steak on the grill, and the top side will not retain its heat as well. If it's a hot summer night, your steaks will cook considerably faster. So consider all these factors, then step up confidently and grill that perfect steak.

BEEFSTEAKS

TENDERLOIN

Tenderloin or *filet* steaks, cut from the long narrow muscle which runs along the backbone in the loin area, cost a pretty penny. Don't let that always stop you, however. Remember that they are boneless and are usually "stretched" with a rich sauce, so they are not always the most expensive meal. Classically the tenderloin is divided into several sections: the Chateaubriand, near the large end; the *filet* steak, a little farther down; the *tournedos,* still smaller, which is the piece of tenderloin found in a T-bone steak; and the *filet mignon,* which is cut from the very smallest part of the tenderloin. Today the terms *filet mignon* and *tournedos* are used to cover just about any steak cut from the tenderloin, while Chateaubriand usually implies a tenderloin steak with Chateaubriand Sauce. Steaks from the tenderloin are usually

STEAKS

cut from 1 to 2 inches thick, but those from the larger end may be cut even thicker, if desired. As they are very lean, larding (weaving strips of fat through the meat) or barding (covering the outside of the meat with a sheet of fat) is usually in order.

CHATEAUBRIAND STEAK

There are a number of stories about what the original Chateaubriand steak was. If you want to go quietly crazy, try to prove which is the right one. Here's the one I prefer, and even though it's seldom seen today it's still a superb idea. A thick slice, 2½ to 3 inches, from the large end of the tenderloin is required. Insert the point of a sharp knife halfway down the outside and move it back and forth to make a pocket. Heat 3 or 4 chopped shallots in beef fat or butter in a skillet, and fill the cavity with this mixture; close the opening with a skewer or toothpicks, or sew it up. Broil for 8 to 10 minutes on a side over a medium fire; it should be quite rare but cooked through. Serve with Béarnaise Sauce or with maître d'hôtel butter. Carve into fairly thin slightly diagonal slices.

A later way with Chateaubriand (at least I think it was later!) was to place the steak between two lesser steaks, then broil it until the outer pieces of meat were black. They were then discarded and the succulent steak within was served with a rich sauce—what glorious extravagance!

A Chateaubriand steak in most modern restaurants is a thick slice of tenderloin, barded with beef fat or bacon, and broiled to the desired degree of doneness (*à point,* as the French say), then served up with Chateaubriand Sauce. This steak should be at least 2 inches thick, and preferably a little thicker. It should be sliced diagonally across the grain, then the sauce poured over the slices. It's a fine luxurious dish for an outdoor party, and each steak will serve at least two, probably more.

CHATEAUBRIAND SAUCE

Cook together 1 cup brown gravy or sauce Espagnole and 1 cup white wine until very thick. Add ½ cup butter, 3 tablespoons fresh lemon juice, 1 tablespoon minced parsley, and salt and pepper to taste. Beat well and serve when the butter is melted. Makes about 1 cup.

TOURNEDOS BÉARNAISE

A *tournedos* is cut from the *filet* after it has been surrounded with a layer of pounded beef fat and tied well. The steak should preferably be cut 1½ to 2 inches thick, and grilled over a medium charcoal fire for about 5 minutes on a side (for rare, that is; allow 7 to 8 minutes on a side for medium, longer if you want to spoil it completely). When done, sprinkle with salt and pepper, and serve with Béarnaise Sauce.

BÉARNAISE SAUCE

In a skillet put 2 tablespoons white wine, 1 tablespoon tarragon vinegar, 2 teaspoons chopped fresh tarragon (or 1 teaspoon of the dried), 2 teaspoons chopped shallot or onion, and ¼ teaspoon freshly ground black pepper. Bring to a boil and cook rapidly until almost all the liquid disappears. Melt ½ cup butter in a small saucepan, but don't let it brown. In the top of a blender put 3 egg yolks, ½ teaspoon salt, a pinch of cayenne, and the wine-tarragon-shallot mixture. Cover and flick the motor on and off high speed. Remove cover, turn motor on high, and gradually add the hot butter, partially covering blender to prevent spattering. It will thicken and become smooth quickly and you'll have ¾ cup Béarnaise Sauce.

TOURNEDOS ROSSINI

This is very rich and very good. The garnishings will be made ready in the kitchen before the meat is cooked. After grilling the *tournedos,* as directed in *Tournedos Béarnaise,* place each one on a round of fried toast, top with a slice of *foie gras* and one of truffle, and pour over Bordelaise Sauce or Madeira Sauce. You can always start that diet tomorrow!

BORDELAISE SAUCE

Cook 2 tablespoons minced shallots or green onions in 2 tablespoons butter. Add ¾ cup red wine and simmer until the liquid is reduced to half. Add 1 can beef gravy or sauce Espagnole, 2 tablespoons each of fresh lemon juice and minced parsley, and salt and cayenne to taste. Heat, add sliced poached beef marrow if you like, and serve. Makes 2 cups.

MADEIRA SAUCE

Heat 1 can beef gravy or sauce Espagnole with 2 beef bouillon cubes. Add ¼ cup Madeira, heat, and serve. Makes about 1¼ cups.

SIRLOIN

The sirloin lies just toward the front of the beast from the rump and round, and to me is one of the most flavorsome of steaks. The whole sirloin contains the large end of the tenderloin, as well as the "top sirloin" and the "sirloin tip." It has a fairly large percentage of bone as well. Frequently the boneless top sirloin is sold separately, but you'll have to dig a little deeper to pay for it. Prime or Choice meat should be selected for these steaks, and they should be cut not less than 1½ inches thick, preferably thicker. Some butchers differentiate between various whole sirloin cuts, depending upon the size and shape of the bone; "wedge bone" and "pinbone" are the usual categories.

WHOLE THICK SIRLOIN FOR A LARGE PARTY

This is my idea of the perfect party steak. Have a whole sirloin cut 2 to 3 inches thick, some of the excess fat removed, and the fat around the edge slashed prettily. Grill over a medium fire for 10 to 15 minutes on a side. If you like a "charred" surface, let the fire flare up around the steak when it is almost done, but remember not to get it really black—the flavor of the fat will be spoiled. Place on a carving board and remove the bone for easier carving. Sprinkle with salt and pepper, top with a goodly hunk of butter, and carve into slices when the butter has melted. The resultant blend of beef juice and butter is really all the sauce you need here. The meat should be carved into slices not more than ½ inch thick, all the way across so that each diner gets some of the top sirloin and some of the tenderloin. The dainty feeders will be happy with a slice or two, while the real trenchermen can indulge in their happy gluttony. Although baked potatoes may seem pedestrian, they are just right with this steak. Serve them simply with butter, salt, and fresh pepper. For a salad, try lettuce with lots of chopped green pepper.

LOIN-STRIP STEAK

This cut is also known as strip steak, shell steak, *contrefilet,* New York cut, or Kansas City cut. It is the strip of loin, usually sold boneless, which is left when

WOMAN'S DAY

the tenderloin is removed from the short loin. A 2- to 2½-inch steak should serve two comfortably, with maybe a little snack left over for breakfast. Grill over a medium fire for 8 to 10 minutes on a side (4 or 5 minutes for a thinner steak) and serve at once. If you're serving individual strip steaks, a good idea, I think, is to roll a bar of butter in finely chopped parsley until it is heavily coated; as the steaks are served, put a slice of this on top of each one, to melt and mingle with the meat juices. There are many sauces that are good with these steaks—Bordelaise or Béarnaise (page 1766), maître d'hôtel butter, or Wine-Shallot Sauce.

WINE-SHALLOT SAUCE

Sauté 1 cup chopped shallots or green onions in ¼ cup butter until soft. Add 1 cup white wine, 2 tablespoons wine vinegar, 1 teaspoon salt, and some freshly ground black pepper, and cook for 5 minutes. Cut in ½ cup butter, cook until melted, and serve the sauce at once.

TOP SIRLOIN STEAK

The top sirloin is really the large end of the loin strip, and is almost always sold boneless. It's a fine steak for serving to several people, sliced and served with butter sauce. Have it cut 2 to 3 inches thick and broil as usual, from 10 to 12 minutes on a side. While it's cooking, prepare the platter or serving board by liberally strewing or spreading it with butter. When the sizzling steak is laid upon this unctuous bed and carved, the melted butter and meat juices will mingle into a harmonious sauce, which is spooned over the meat slices as it is served. You'll want crusty bread to sop up the juices, and perhaps a casserole of corn, tomatoes, and okra.

STEAK AU POIVRE
(French Pepper Steak)

This classic French pepper steak is enjoying a great vogue in the United States. It's one of James Beard's favorites and he cooks it to perfection. For a 2-inch top sirloin you'll need about 1½ tablespoons of peppercorns which should be crushed quite coarsely; or buy "cracked" or "coarse" pepper or seasoned pepper, but be sure it's fresh. Press the pepper firmly into the steak on both sides with the heel of your hand, and let the steak stand for 30 to 45 minutes. Now grill it over a medium fire for 6 to 8 minutes on each side, remove to a hot platter, sprinkle with salt, and place a large chunk of sweet butter on top. Let this melt and run over the surface before carving. Or, if you want to be a classicist, flame it with brandy before serving. Serve with boiled new potatoes rolled in butter and minced tarragon.

PORTERHOUSE, T-BONE, AND CLUB STEAKS

These steaks are all cut from the short loin and it's often hard to tell where one ends and the next one begins. The porterhouse comes from the large end and has more tenderloin; the club steak is from the small end and has no tenderloin; the T-bone lies in between. Porterhouse and T-bone steaks should be cut at least 2 inches thick, while the club should be 1 to 1½ inches. They are cooked in the usual manner and I think they're best as is, with salt, pepper, and butter. To carve them, remove the T-shape bone and slice across, so that each serving has a piece of the tenderloin and a piece of the loin strip.

STEAK WITH ONIONS

One of the great American dishes is steak smothered in onions, and I defy anyone to best it. Traditionally, this is a good-size T-bone, not too thick. Before you cook it, peel and slice 4 to 5 large onions, and cook them very slowly in plenty of butter in a covered skillet, stirring occasionally. They should be golden with little flecks of brown. Grill the steak quickly, put it on a hot platter, and engulf it with the onions. Add salt and pepper and tie into it, eating some onions with each forkful of meat. Such luxury! With it have hard rolls, and ripe tomatoes stuffed with chopped celery and green pepper.

RIB STEAKS

Rib steaks, known in France as *entrecôtes*, can be very good indeed. The ones from the smaller end of the rib are frequently served as "club" steaks. Actually they are next-door neighbors on the hoof, and are definite look-alikes. To my notion, a proper rib steak should be at least 1 bone thick (about 1½ inches), and preferably should have a little extra on each side of the bone. The Spencer or "eye of the rib" steaks have the bone, coarser meat, and fat removed. These should be cut 1 to 2 inches thick and treated like tenderloin.

ENTRECÔTE BERCY

This is an old French classic, still very much in evidence in that country today. Grill the rib steak over a brisk fire, having first sprinkled it with salt and pepper. While it's cooking, heat a platter on the grill and mix 3 tablespoons butter (as it melts) with lots of chopped parsley, chervil, and shallots. Cream them well together and when the steak is done, turn it in the sauce. Put another piece of butter on top and sprinkle with more chopped parsley. Serve with noodles dressed with butter and grated Parmesan, and with green beans vinaigrette.

RIB STEAK BORDELAISE

After the rib steaks have been cooked to perfection, place them on a hot plank or platter and top with thin slices of poached beef marrow. (Cajole your butcher into parting with some marrow bones; put them in a preheated moderate oven (350° F.) for 10 minutes, remove, and slip marrow from bones. Slice marrow ¼ inch thick and poach lightly in a little boiling salted water.) Cover the steaks with Bordelaise Sauce (page 1766). This steak demands good Bordeaux wine and some crusty French bread for sopping up the last drop of sauce. A really good mixed-green salad would be in order, too, perhaps with a little Roquefort cheese crumbled into it.

SPENCER STEAK

This steak, also known as the "eye of the rib," is a rib steak with bone, fat, and coarser outside meat removed. In some parts of the country the Spencer is not trimmed quite as much as the eye of the rib, but in general the terms are interchangeable. It's a very succulent morsel, and should be treated in the same manner as a tenderloin steak, although it won't need extra fat as it's pretty well marbled if of a good grade. They should be cut 1½ inches thick, or a little more. Serve with Béarnaise Sauce (page 1766), and if you wish, baked potatoes and thick slices of red ripe tomato dressed with olive oil, salt, and freshly ground pepper, and sprinkled with minced chives.

RUMP

For some reason or other, rump steaks are not very widely used in this country, at least not for grilling. Choice-grade rump steak is well worth seeking out. It will need marinating or tenderizing before grilling.

MARINATED RUMP STEAK

In the bottom of a dish pour enough olive oil to cover it; about ¼ cup for each steak should do it. Add 1 finely chopped garlic clove and the juice of ½ fresh lemon for each steak, and let 1½-inch rump steaks stand in this for 12 to 24 hours, turning them every once in a while. Add more oil if too much is absorbed. Grill in the usual manner, and add salt and pepper when they are just done. Garnish with sliced sautéed mushrooms: for each steak slice ½ pound mushrooms; sauté slowly in plenty of butter until tender. Serve roasted corn, too, and have cherry tomatoes and other raw vegetables for nibbling.

STEAKS

FLANK STEAKS

Personally, I think this has one of the finest flavors of any steak, bar none. It has the added advantage of being inexpensive, boneless, and easy to cook. Most flank steaks sold in this country are braised endlessly; a great pity, to my notion. Next time you have one, try it this way:

LONDON BROIL

The steak should be of Choice or Prime grade. Have the membrane on the outside pulled off, but do not have the meat scored. In its raw state it will have a maximum thickness of about 1 inch or a little less, but during the cooking it will contract and become considerably more compact and thicker. Have the meat rather cold, brush with a little oil or melted butter, and grill over a hot fire for 3 or 4 minutes on a side: it must be rare to be good. The only trick involved in preparing this excellent steak is in the carving, and that's very easy if you have a sharp knife. Put the cooked steak on a carving board and, starting at the thick end, slice across the grain into very diagonal slices. The knife is held at a very acute angle to the meat, about 25 degrees or less. Thus the slices will be 3 to 4 inches wide, each with a lovely brown frame around the juicy red interior. Salt and pepper are the only sauce needed for the enhancement of this fine steak. A 1½- to 2-pound flank steak will serve 3 or 4 persons. Anything is good with flank steak, but there's nothing better, perhaps, than asparagus and a baked potato.

MINUTE STEAK

These are thin steaks cut from the strip, the sirloin, or the ribs. They won't really cook in a minute, but they don't take very long. They usually weigh 6 to 9 ounces. They should be quite cold before cooking over a good hot fire for about 2 minutes on a side.

DEVILED MINUTE STEAKS

For 4 steaks have ready 1½ to 2 cups toasted buttered crumbs and about ½ cup butter. Grill the steaks quickly, undercooking them a little, then spread them with butter and roll in the crumbs, pressing the crumbs in firmly. Replace them on the grill just long enough for the crumbs to brown and crisp, about 1 minute. Serve with Sauce Diable.

SAUCE DIABLE

Cook 3 tablespoons minced shallots in the same amount of butter until wilted. Add ¼ cup fresh lemon juice or vinegar, 2 teaspoons each of Worcestershire and prepared mustard, a dash of hot pepper sauce, and 1 can beef gravy or sauce Espagnole. Heat well and serve.

ROUND STEAKS

Unless the meat is top grade, round steak needs tenderizing of one kind or another. It may be put through a "tenderizing" machine and made into cube steaks, or treated at home with meat tenderizer. If it is Prime grade, however, there are few cuts which have more flavor than a good top round steak, which should be cooked like a sirloin. Chuck steak may be cooked in the same way as round steak. Cube steaks are usually too thin for proper charcoal-broiling, so round steak on the barbecue is usually in the form of hamburgers, which I'll get to in a few minutes. Hawaiian Teriyaki, which I suppose isn't really a steak, is excellent outdoor fare.

TERIYAKI

Have a 1-inch-thick piece of top round sliced very thin (¼ to ½ inch thick), and marinate in the following mixture: combine ½ cup soy sauce, ½ cup cooking oil, 2 teaspoons sugar, ½ cup fresh orange juice, 1 teaspoon grated fresh gingerroot (or ground ginger if you can't get the fresh), and 1 pressed garlic clove. Let the meat strips remain in this for 1 hour, then weave them back and forth on bamboo or metal skewers. Grill them very quickly over a fairly hot fire, about 30 seconds on a side. Let each guest cook his own.

SKIRT STEAKS

You don't see these too often in markets (I suspect the butchers take them home). If from top-grade beef, they are delicious, and have a flavor and texture all their own. They may be simply grilled, like a London Broil.

MARINATED SKIRT STEAK

Make a marinade of equal parts of soy sauce, sherry, and oil (½ cup of each), to which add 2 tablespoons grated fresh gingerroot or 2 crushed garlic cloves. Marinate the skirt steak in this mixture for 1 or 2 hours, turning frequently. Broil quickly over a hot fire until nicely browned on the outside and rare within, about 3 minutes on a side. Carve like flank steak. Save any marinade for next time. Fried rice is good with this.

DEVILED SKIRT STEAK

Put your skirt steak in a fairly deep pan and grate 1 medium onion over it, spreading it evenly on both sides. Add ½ teaspoon powdered mustard, 1 tablespoon each of vinegar and Worcestershire, 1 teaspoon salt, 1 crushed garlic clove, and some freshly ground pepper, quite a bit of it, say 1 teaspoon. Turn the steak in this mixture several times and let stand for 1 hour. Broil quickly, painting the surface with what's left of the marinade during the cooking. Serve it thinly sliced on buttered toast.

GROUND BEEF

Perhaps the most popular meat in America is the hamburger (oh, all right, maybe the hot dog is!), and tons of them are consumed every day. As with almost everything else, there are two schools of thought (at least) about forming the meat into patties. One group admonishes you to be sure not to handle the meat any more than you can help; form it loosely. The other, to which I belong, believes that the patties should be compact and firmly pressed together. For charcoal grilling this is especially true. A loosely made patty will be apt to disintegrate when you turn it. Lean round, shoulder, rump, or sirloin all make fine hamburgers, but it should be lean. The grill should be greased or the patties brushed with butter, or both, to lessen the danger of sticking. Here again, they're much better if not cooked too much; when well done, they're dry and tasteless.

1 — Porterhouse
2 — Veal Porterhouse
3 — Halibut
4 — Ground Beef
5 — Tournedos
6 — Rib
7 — Club
8 — Lamb
9 — Smoked Ham

STEAKS

HAMBURGER SANDWICHES

Form ground beef into thin cakes about ½ inch thick. Put a slice of onion, of Cheddar cheese, a layer of chopped ripe olives, deviled ham, herb butter, or whatever pleases you on one cake and top with another, pressing firmly together around the edges. Brush with butter and grill quickly over a brisk fire just long enough to warm the filling through. These may be eaten as is, or on toast, or between slices of buttered bread.

STEAK TARTARE EN CROÛTE

A fancy name for a simple sandwich, but awfully good. Mix very lean ground beef with salt and pepper, 1 teaspoon salt and about ¼ teaspoon freshly ground pepper for each pound of meat. Spread evenly about ¼ inch thick on unbuttered bread and top with another slice of bread, also unbuttered. Now brush the outside surfaces of the sandwiches with soft butter and grill over a slow fire until golden-brown, 1 or 2 minutes on each side. You'll find that your guests will eat these as fast as you can cook them, so be sure you have plenty ready for everyone.

OTHER STEAKS

VEAL STEAKS

Young white veal is a real rarity these days, and when you're lucky enough to find it you'll probably roast it or have veal scaloppine or something similar. As it's very lean, it's not the most successful meat for grilling over charcoal, but it can be done well. Most veal steaks are cut from the leg (round), but a porterhouse is very good, too.

MARINATED VEAL STEAK

Have a 1-inch-thick steak cut from the leg, and remove the outside skin. In a shallow dish put ½ cup olive oil and 2 crushed garlic cloves and let the steak marinate in this for several hours, turning occasionally. Broil over a low fire for 7 to 9 minutes on each side. No further basting should be necessary, as the meat will have absorbed enough of the oil to moisten it. Serve with fettuccine and a zucchini and tomato casserole.

PORK STEAKS

Pork is wonderful on the charcoal grill, and the smell of it cooking will stimulate the most jaded appetite. It must be cooked until well done, so a fairly slow fire is in order, but it should develop a slightly charred crust to be perfect. Pork steaks are usually cut from the leg, but a steak from a boneless shoulder butt is also excellent, and economical.

PORK SHOULDER STEAK TERIYAKI

For several people buy a pork shoulder butt, boneless or bone-in, and have it cut into 1-inch slices. You should get 6 or 7 steaks from an average piece. Marinate in the sauce you make for Teriyaki to which you have added an extra crushed garlic clove. (There's a very good bottled Teriyaki Sauce now on the market, from Japan.) Turn the meat in the marinade for about 1 hour. Broil over a brisk fire for 2 minutes on each side; lower heat and cook for 8 to 10 minutes more on each side. This has a real oriental flavor.

FRESH HAM STEAK

This should be cut about 1½ inches thick, and the fat around the edge should be slashed in several places to prevent the steak from curling up. Brush it lightly with butter and place it on the grill, letting it cook slowly. After 10 minutes, turn and cook on the other side, then turn again and give it 5 to 10 minutes more. It should be thoroughly cooked but not dried out in the middle. The fat around the edge will be a crisp dark brown, and the surface of the meat itself a little lighter in color. Salt and pepper are the only adornment needed to make this perfect.

HAM STEAKS

Most smoked ham steaks are too thin for proper grilling. They should be 1 to 1½ inches thick from the center of the ham. Those ½-inch ones, so widely sold, used to be known as "breakfast slices" in the good old days, and one made a nice morning snack along with 2 or 3 fried eggs and some fried potatoes. Alas, those days of free-wheeling eating are long gone, but still there are few things better than a fine ham steak, grilled to perfection over charcoal. Cooking time depends upon how the ham has been processed: a "tenderized" but not fully cooked ham steak, 1 inch thick, will take about 15 minutes on a side over a slow fire; a 2-inch one will take 25 to 30 minutes on a side. An "old-fashioned" ham steak will take about the same length of time. Fully cooked ham steaks need only browning and warming through, so a hotter fire can be used. The fat at the edges should be gashed to prevent curling. It may be brushed with butter before broiling, but that isn't really necessary, as ham has plenty of fat.

DEVILED HAM STEAK

Cover a 1½-inch ham steak with a good coating of English mustard. (Combine 1 tablespoon powdered mustard, ¼ teaspoon salt, and enough vinegar to make a thin paste.) Grill over a low fire, turning fairly often; it should take 40 to 45 minutes. Make a mixture of the mustard and honey (1 teaspoon mustard to 2 tablespoons honey); about 5 minutes before the steak is done, brush both sides with it. Turn the ham several times so that a glaze will form. Remove to a hot platter and slice into medium-thin diagonal slices. Serve with corn bread and coleslaw.

LAMB STEAKS

Lamb or mutton steaks are usually cut from the leg, sometimes from the shoulder. If properly cooked and seasoned, they're among the best meats for charcoal grilling. I think they should be on the rare side, pink at least; like beefsteaks, they become dry and uninteresting when overcooked. They should be cut from 1 to 1½ inches thick. If you need several, buy a whole leg and have the butcher cut the steaks out for you; use the rest for lamb stew or *shashlik*.

GARLIC LAMB STEAKS

Lamb loves garlic and steaks are no exception. Crush a clove of it and let it rest in ½ cup olive oil. Tie some celery leaves, a bunch of parsley, and a good sprig of rosemary or marjoram together in a fagot, and use this to brush the oil on the steaks while they are cooking. Cook the steaks over a brisk fire, from 3 to 6 minutes on a side, basting them with the garlic oil. Season.

FISH STEAKS

There are any number of good-size fish which provide fine steaks for the outdoor cook. Salmon, halibut, and swordfish are the most widely used, but dolphin (the mahimahi of the islands), white sea bass, and albacore are also popular in coastal regions. The main trick to remember is to have the grill and fish both well oiled to prevent sticking. Fish steaks do not take as long as meat to cook, and should be carefully watched so that they don't dry out too much. A 1-inch steak will take about 7 minutes to cook; a 1½-inch steak, 12 minutes; and a 2-inch one about 15 minutes over a moderate fire. They are done when they flake easily and have lost their translucent look. Brush the steaks while they're cooking with melted butter to which lemon juice has been added.

LIVER STEAKS

A properly cooked liver steak, crisply brown on the outside and pink and juicy in the middle, is truly an eating delight. Have the liver (calf's, lamb, or beef) sliced about 1½ inches thick. Butter the outside well and grill over a moderate fire until done to your liking, 7 to 10 minutes on a side. Test by making an incision with a small sharp knife and looking inside. Serve the liver steaks with butter and lemon, or with Béarnaise Sauce (page 1766). Broiled tomatoes are almost a must here, and crisply fried potatoes are good, too.

TURKEY STEAKS

These are a real conversation piece, and can be very good indeed. They're fun and worth a try, I think. Have your butcher cut a frozen young turkey into 1-inch slices (across the bird) on his power saw, from where the wings join the body to the leg joint. (The butcher will probably shake his head at such goings on, but smile sweetly and say nothing.) Or slice a boneless turkey roll; you can find one at most markets. A good-size bird should provide 8 steaks; the ends can be cooked and used for other things. Lay the frozen slices in a large flat pan and let them thaw in a mixture of white wine and melted butter or oil, and use the mixture as a baste when they're cooking. If the slices are too big, divide each into 2 through the section of breastbone. Grill them over a moderate fire for 20 to 30 minutes on a side, turning occasionally and basting frequently, until well done.

STEAM, TO—In culinary language the phrase refers to a method of cooking by exposure to the vapor of boiling water. The food must be above the liquid and never in it. The container is closed during cooking to let the steam accumulate. Steaming is one of the methods used to cook rice, fish, dried fruits, vegetables, breads, puddings, etc. As a cooking technique it has the great advantage of retaining a high proportion of the original flavor and texture of the food so prepared because the nutrients are not dissolved in the cooking liquid as is the case with boiling or poaching. Steaming does have some disadvantages in that it is a more time-consuming way of cooking and the food cannot be browned.

Steaming is the principle used in pressure cooking in which the lid is sealed and the steam accumulates, building up pressure and cooking foods more quickly. There are also available vegetable steamers which resemble two saucepans, one over the other. There are holes in the top one for the steam to enter and cook the vegetable. Steaming can also be done in a double boiler or in an ordinary colander if it fits down inside the kettle and can be covered tightly to prevent steam from escaping. When steaming in vegetable steamers or double boilers, make sure the water is boiling before the top part is placed over the water—not in the water. All steamers and double boilers must have tight-fitting lids and water must be kept boiling during the entire cooking time. If water must be added, it must be boiling water to keep the temperature of the water high.

When steaming fish, the fish should be wrapped in cheesecloth, allowing the long ends of the cheesecloth to hang out on either side of the pan. When the fish is cooked it can be removed by lifting it out by the long ends of cheesecloth. A fish steamer should have a rack which holds the fish above the level of boiling water.

To steam pudding or brown bread it is necessary to put the mixture into a well-greased pudding mold and top it with a tight-fitting lid. The mold should be only two-thirds full. Set the mold on a rack in a kettle. Add boiling water to cover halfway up the sides of the mold. Cover the kettle and keep water boiling for the required length of time, replacing evaporated water with more boiling water. Puddings may also be steamed in a pressure cooker. When the pudding is done, remove the lid and allow it to stand for 10 minutes. Then unmold; if cooled slightly, it will not crack. Puddings cannot be steamed successfully in the top of a double boiler since steam cannot circulate completely around the mold.

STERILIZE—To heat foods or utensils to a high enough temperature to kill harmful microorganisms. The simplest and most successful method is to boil the food or utensil. The time required will depend on the consistency of the food and the size of the containers, for the entire contents must reach the required temperature. Sterilizing by dry heat has also been tried and is still used to some extent, but heat transfer is more rapid in water than in air, therefore sterilization in the home oven requires a longer time with a greater possible change in the food itself. Spores of some types of microorganisms are so heat-resistant that processing long enough to kill them would result in changes in the taste and nutritive values of the food. Chemical sterilization has also been tried, and salting and meat curing may be considered early examples of this kind of process, but other types of chemicals present great hazards even in sterilizing utensils, as residues of the chemical would produce undesirable effects. Sterilization through radiation is as yet a costly process, but this way may be the method of the future. Some food items such as packaged cereals and wheat which are to be stored are successfully sterilized by being passed through an electronic oven. This process takes a much shorter time than any other method. Freezing does not produce sterilization; many organisms simply pass into a dormant stage when frozen. It is for this reason that blanching is necessary before freezing most nonacid foods.

In the home kitchen, sterilizing is chiefly used in preparing canning jars or bottles for a baby's formula. With home equipment it is probably impossible to obtain complete sterilization, but it is possible to reduce organisms to a safe level. To prepare jars or bottles, scrub them with soap and water and rinse well. Immerse the jars in warm water and bring to a boil, keeping the boiling temperature constant. The jars must be completely covered with water throughout. Handle the boiled jars with tongs that have also been boiled. Drain jars upside down on a rack. When cool, turn jars or bottles right side up and fill as soon as possible, or cap with lids that have been sterilized as well.

Processing filled jars or cans is another example of the same procedure. Industry and medicine have developed various techniques for sterilization of materials and instruments. These techniques have been scientifically worked out so that it is possible to have complete sterilization. The nearest approach to this in the home kitchen is the pressure canner.

STEW

Creamy Veal Stew with Mushrooms

STEW

STEW—As a culinary method stewing is the process of long slow cooking of food in liquid in a covered pot. Any dish prepared in this way may be called a stew, although most often the word is reserved for dishes containing meat and one or more vegetables.

BEEF STEW

- 2 pounds beef chuck, cubed
- 3 tablespoons all-purpose flour
- 3 tablespoons shortening
- Salt
- ¼ teaspoon pepper
- 6 cups water
- 12 small white onions, peeled
- 2 cups diced peeled yellow turnip
- 6 carrots, scraped and cut into chunks
- 4 medium potatoes, peeled and cut into quarters
- ½ cup cooked peas

Dredge meat with flour and brown on all sides in shortening in kettle. Add 2 teaspoons salt, the pepper, and water. Bring to boil, cover, and simmer for 1½ hours, or until meat is almost tender. Add remaining ingredients except peas and simmer for 45 minutes, or until vegetables are tender. Season, and sprinkle with peas. Makes 6 servings.

LAMB STEW

- 2½ pounds boned lamb shoulder
- 1 large onion, chopped
- 1 large potato, peeled and chopped
- 2 celery stalks, chopped
- 1 garlic clove, sliced
- 1 teaspoon salt
- Pepper
- Water
- 18 small onions or 3 medium onions
- 2 or 3 large potatoes
- 4 white turnips (optional)
- 6 small carrots

Cut lamb into 1½- or 2-inch cubes and put in a heavy pot with the chopped vegetables, garlic, salt, and a grinding or two of pepper. Add enough water to cover meat and vegetables by ½ inch. Bring to a boil, skim, and turn heat low. Simmer for 45 minutes, or until potato is mushy. Remove meat. Pour liquid through strainer and force as much of the vegetables through as possible. Return to meat, and correct seasoning. Meanwhile prepare the other vegetables. Peel small onions but leave whole. If medium onions are used, cut them into large dice. Cut potatoes into uniform cubes, or into balls using a French vegetable cutter. Do the same with turnips, if you like their assertive flavor. Scrape carrots and cut into 1-inch pieces, or use small scraped French carrots. Put vegetables on top of meat and cover. Add enough water or stock just to cover vegetables, and simmer until the vegetables are tender. Makes 4 to 6 servings.

Brown Lamb Stew

Follow recipe above. Dredge lamb lightly with flour and brown on all sides in 2 tablespoons fat or cooking oil. Proceed as directed.

CREAMY VEAL STEW WITH MUSHROOMS

- 2½ pounds boneless veal, cubed
- 4 cups water
- 1 onion stuck with 3 cloves
- 1½ teaspoons salt
- 1 bay leaf
- 1 carrot, chopped
- 18 small white onions
- 1 pound small mushrooms
- 1 teaspoon fresh lemon juice
- 2 egg yolks
- ½ cup heavy cream
- Minced parsley

Put first 6 ingredients in kettle, cover, and simmer for about 1¼ hours. Remove meat; strain broth over onions; cook until tender. Add mushrooms; cook for 10 minutes. Strain off broth; reduce to one third its volume. Return vegetables and meat to broth; reheat. Mix lemon juice, egg yolks, and cream; stir in ½ cup of hot broth. Add to sauce; heat, stirring, until slightly thickened. Sprinkle with parsley. Makes 4 to 6 servings.

CHICKEN STEW

- 1 stewing chicken (about 5 pounds), cut into pieces
- ½ cup rendered chicken fat or clarified butter
- 1 celery stalk, chopped
- 1 onion, chopped
- 1 carrot, chopped
- Water
- 2 teaspoons salt
- ¼ cup all-purpose flour
- ½ cup heavy cream
- 2 egg yolks

Brown chicken pieces in ¼ cup rendered chicken fat. Put into a heavy pot and add vegetables and water just to cover. Season. Simmer until chicken is just tender, about 1½ hours, depending upon the bird. (Don't let it get dry and stringy.) Remove meat to a hot dish, strain broth, and simmer to reduce to 3 cups. Cook ¼ cup rendered chicken fat and flour together for 2 minutes, add broth, and stir until smooth. Add chicken. Beat cream and egg yolks together. Stir in small amount of hot mixture. Gradually stir into hot mixture left in kettle. Heat, but do not boil, and serve with rice or mashed potatoes. Makes 4 to 6 servings.

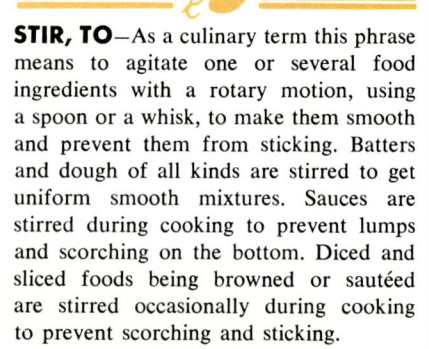

STIR, TO—As a culinary term this phrase means to agitate one or several food ingredients with a rotary motion, using a spoon or a whisk, to make them smooth and prevent them from sticking. Batters and dough of all kinds are stirred to get uniform smooth mixtures. Sauces are stirred during cooking to prevent lumps and scorching on the bottom. Diced and sliced foods being browned or sautéed are stirred occasionally during cooking to prevent scorching and sticking.

The word "stir" involves one of the most important techniques in cooking. To stir constantly means just that. Do not leave the mixture for one second or the resulting product will suffer. To stir occasionally means to stir every few minutes, usually to allow thick food mixtures to cook more evenly. When cooking a sauce it is very important to stir with a rotary motion which cleans the sides and a small part of the bottom of the utensil but it is also important to scrape the entire bottom of the utensil. This is done by pretending to write the figure 8 on the bottom of the pan.

STOCK—A liquid food made by cooking ingredients slowly for a long time so that all the essential flavor and nutrients of the ingredients are dissolved in the liquid. The solid particles remaining are discarded and the liquid may be further concentrated or clarified according to the way it is to be used. Stock is used as a basis, or *fonds,* in the preparation of soups, sauces, and gravies.

The word stock is sometimes used for the liquid in which a food has been cooked, but this is an inaccurate usage. When the purpose of cooking is to prepare a food to be served, it will be cooked just until done. The liquid which remains, which is properly called a broth, may be used for sauces, gravies, or soups; in fact, since it contains many nutrients, it is healthful to use it so. When making stock, however, the food is cooked past the point at which it is done; it is cooked until it is shapeless and almost tasteless since all the value is in the stock. Stock ingredients may include flavorful vegetables or mild herbs, but a cautious hand is used with stock as it may be further concentrated in making sauces or soups and the seasoning would in this case become very strong.

Fish, poultry, meat, game, vegetables—all may be used to make stock and the resulting product is designated accordingly. Also there is brown stock which is usually made from beef and veal as well as vegetables. The ingredients are roasted or browned before being cooked in liquid in order to give the stock a rich brown color. White stock is made from chicken and veal and in this case the ingredients are not browned.

The cook who does not have time to devote to the long slow cooking that is necessary to make stocks may instead use bouillon which is available commercially in the form of canned liquid, cubes, pastes, and granules, but it is necessary to remember that the bouillon will be well seasoned and salted. For fish stock a good substitute is clam broth.

If stock is to be used as a basis for aspics, calf's feet and other veal bones should be added as they are rich in gelatin. Good stock vegetables are carrots, onions, and celery. Parsley and other leaf herbs are possible additions, but remember to use strong-flavored herbs with care as the flavor will be highly concentrated at the end. While it is possible to make stock with the bones of roast meat or poultry, the flavor will be less good unless some uncooked meat or poultry is added. Bones alone cooked for a very long time develop a rather unpleasant taste in the stock. Strained stock with the fat removed may be frozen.

BROWN STOCK
(Bouillon or Beef Stock)

- 1 to 2 pounds cracked marrow bones
- 6 pounds beef shin or other soup meat
- 3 quarts cold water
- 8 peppercorns, slightly crushed
- 6 whole cloves
- 1 bay leaf
- ⅛ teaspoon each of dried thyme and marjoram
- Few parsley sprigs
- 1 carrot, diced
- 1 turnip, quartered
- 1 small onion, diced
- 1 celery stalk, cut into 1-inch pieces
- 1 tablespoon salt

Scrape the marrow from the marrow bones and melt in a large kettle. Remove the lean meat from the shin and cut into 1-inch cubes. Brown half the meat cubes in the marrow. Add remaining meat and bones and the water. Bring to boil and skim off scum. Add remaining ingredients and simmer, covered, for 3 hours. Skim occasionally. Strain stock through a fine sieve. Cool quickly and refrigerate.

■ **To Clear***—When cold, loosen cake of fat on stock with the edge of a knife. Lift off fat. The small quantity of fat which remains can be removed by passing a cloth wrung out of hot water around edge of bowl and over top of stock. Makes about 2½ quarts.

■ **To Clarify**—Taste stock after removing fat. Add seasoning as desired. For each quart add 1 egg white, beaten slightly and mixed with 2 teaspoons cold water. Add broken egg shell. Bring to a boil and boil for 2 minutes, stirring constantly. Let stand for 20 minutes over very low heat. Strain through a fine strainer lined with a double thickness of cheesecloth.

*If stock is to be refrigerated for any length of time, leave fat on as this excludes air and preserves the stock. If stock is to be frozen, the fat should be removed.

WHITE OR VEAL STOCK

- 4 pounds veal knuckle
- Neck and cleaned feet of 1 chicken
- 4 quarts cold water
- 2 medium onions, quartered
- 2 medium carrots, cut into 1-inch pieces
- 1 medium turnip, peeled and quartered
- 1 celery stalk, cut into 1-inch pieces
- 12 parsley sprigs
- 1 thyme sprig
- 2 bay leaves

4 whole cloves
12 peppercorns, crushed slightly
1 tablespoon salt
1 garlic clove

Cut up the meat from the veal knuckle and break the bones into small pieces. Put in kettle with neck and feet of the chicken. Add the water, cover, and let stand in a cool place for 1 hour. Put over low heat and bring slowly to a boil, skimming as the scum rises to the surface. Simmer until clear. Then add remaining ingredients. Bring again to a boil, skim again, and when clear, cover and simmer for 4 to 4½ hours, skimming occasionally as the fat and scum rise. Remove from heat and strain through cheesecloth. Cool quickly and refrigerate. To clear and clarify, see Brown Stock (page 1774). Makes about 3½ quarts.

CHICKEN STOCK

1 stewing chicken, about 5 pounds
  Few chicken feet and necks if available
2 quarts cold water
2 leeks
1 bay leaf
10 parsley sprigs
2 celery stalks, cut into pieces
1 thyme sprig
2 whole cloves
1 medium carrot, quartered
1 small white turnip, peeled and quartered
1 large onion, peeled and quartered
8 peppercorns, crushed slightly
1 small parsnip, halved
2 teaspoons salt

Put chicken with feet and necks in kettle. Add water, bring slowly to a boil, and skim off scum. When clear and free of scum, add remaining ingredients. Bring again to a boil and simmer, covered, for about 3 hours. Remove chicken and strain mixture through cheesecloth. Cool quickly and refrigerate. To clear and clarify, see Brown Stock (page 1774). Makes about 1¾ quarts.

FISH STOCK

2 pounds any white-meated fish with bones and trimmings
2 quarts cold water
1 medium onion, thinly sliced
12 white peppercorns, crushed slightly
1 teaspoon salt
1 large bay leaf
1 large thyme sprig
10 parsley sprigs
1 medium carrot, thinly sliced
2 whole cloves

Bring all ingredients to a boil, lower heat, and simmer, covered, for about 1 hour. Strain through a fine sieve, cool quickly, and refrigerate. Makes about 1¾ quarts.

VEGETABLE STOCK

¼ cup butter or margarine
2 medium onions, diced
3 medium carrots, diced
1 medium turnip, diced
1 celery stalk, diced
1 small head of lettuce, diced
2 large tomatoes, peeled and quartered
1 bay leaf
8 parsley sprigs
1 thyme sprig
8 peppercorns, crushed slightly
1 garlic clove
2 whole cloves
2 vegetable bouillon cubes
1½ quarts boiling water
1 teaspoon monosodium glutamate

Heat butter in kettle. Add next 5 ingredients and cook very slowly, covered, for about 25 minutes, stirring frequently. Add remaining ingredients except monosodium glutamate. Simmer, covered, for about 1½ hours, skimming as skum rises to the top. Strain through cheesecloth. Add monosodium glutamate. Cool quickly and store in the refrigerator. Makes about 1½ quarts.

STOLLEN—A sweet, fruit-filled yeast bread baked in the form of a folded-over roll, like a large Parkerhouse roll. Some cooks put a layer of sugar and cinnamon between the cake layers. The baked loaf is usually frosted and decorated with slivered almonds and with candied cherries. Stollen is traditionally served in Germany for Christmas breakfast. Often thin slices are served with coffee or a glass of wine to guests or callers during the holiday season, as fruit cake is served in England.

STOLLEN

¼ cup water*
1 package active dry yeast or 1 cake compressed yeast
½ cup milk
6 tablespoons sugar
1 teaspoon salt
3 tablespoons soft butter or margarine
2¾ to 3 cups all-purpose flour
1 egg
½ cup chopped blanched almonds
¼ cup each of finely cut citron and candied cherries
1 teaspoon grated lemon rind
½ teaspoon ground cinnamon
  Frosting
  Whole candied cherries
  Slivered blanched almonds

*Use very warm water (105°F. to 115°F.) for dry yeast; use lukewarm (80°F. to 90°F.) for compressed. Sprinkle dry yeast or crumble cake into water. Scald the milk and pour into large mixing bowl. Add 4 tablespoons of the sugar, the salt, and 2 tablespoons of the butter. Cool until just warm. Stir in 1 cup of the flour. Mix in dissolved yeast. Add egg and beat hard. Stir in 1½ cups flour, the chopped almonds, citron, cut cherries, and lemon rind. Sprinkle 2 tablespoons of the remaining flour on board. Turn dough out and knead, adding more flour as needed to make a soft dough. Knead until smooth and satiny, about 5 minutes. Shape into a smooth ball and put in lightly greased bowl. Cover and let rise until doubled, about 2¼ hours. Punch down. Cover and let rest for 5 to 10 minutes. With palms of hands press dough into oval shape about ½ inch thick. Spread half of oval with remaining butter. Mix remaining sugar and the cinnamon and sprinkle on butter. Fold unspread half lengthwise over sugar and cinnamon, making edges even. Lift to lightly greased baking sheet and curve the ends slightly. Press down the folded edge. This helps the loaf to keep its shape as it rises and bakes. Cover and let rise until doubled, about 1¼ hours. Bake in preheated moderate oven (350°F.) for 30 to 35 minutes. Remove to cake rack to cool. Pour Frosting over loaf, letting it drip down the sides. Decorate with whole cherries and slivered almonds.

Frosting

Mix ¾ cup sifted confectioners' sugar and 1 tablespoon milk or cream to make a smooth thick frosting that will just pour.

STRAIN, TO—As a culinary term the phrase is used to describe the process of pouring a food, usually a liquid, through the holes of a sieve or through a cloth to remove lumps or undesirable particles or to clarify the liquid.

Soup stocks are strained after cooking to remove bits of bone and pieces of flavoring vegetables and meats, and to make the stock clear and smooth for both soups and sauces. Tea made from loose tea must be strained before drinking to remove the tea leaves. At times sauces are strained before serving to remove any lumps that may have formed during cooking. In jelly making, the fruit juice must be strained through several thicknesses of cheesecloth without pressing to produce clear jewellike juice.

At times the term can also mean to press a soft or cooked food through the holes of a sieve. Applesauce, cooked fruits, and vegetables are often strained. Strained foods are a part of many special diets and many infant diets. Today a large variety of foods are available already strained. An electric blender can do much to prepare this type of food quickly and with a minimum of waste.

STRAWBERRY

STRAWBERRY—A juicy edible fruit produced by various plants native to the temperate zones of the Old and New World. Strawberries belong to the genus *Fragaria,* a member of the Rose family. The fruits vary in size and even in color; there are whitish or yellowish fruits as well as the much more common red ones. Some strawberries are cultivated, others wild; the wild strawberries are perhaps the most fragrant of all fruits.

Although strawberries have been cultivated to a limited extent in European gardens since early in the 14th century, for the most part Europeans ate the wild strawberry, called the Alpine strawberry, *Fragaria vesca,* which was a native of northern Italy. It is this fruit that was mentioned by the Roman writers Virgil, Ovid, and Pliny. To this day, Frenchmen and Italians prefer these tiny, incredibly delicious wild berries to all others. The French call them *fraises des bois,* "strawberries of the woods," and they serve them simply, with a squeeze of lemon or orange juice and a bit of sugar.

We can thank 18th and 19th century French, English, and American horticulturists for the cultivated species we know today. They are a result of the crossbreeding of a wild strawberry of the eastern seaboard, the Virginia strawberry, *F. virginiana,* which was taken to Europe in the 17th century, with a kind of strawberry found in Chile, *F. chiloensis,* taken to Europe in the early 18th century. In the mid-19th century descendants of these hybrids, reimported into the United States, began being further developed and cultivated on a large scale.

Strawberries have long been eaten plain, or with wine, or with cream. Made into preserves, they are one of the most popular of all jams. Strawberry shortcake is a beloved classic of the strawberry season. But there are other older uses, too, dating from the days before the white people came to this continent. The Indians, and folk people everywhere, made delicious beverages out of the berries. Strawberry wine was a favorite, and the Iroquois' strawberry drink, made with crushed strawberries and water, is still drunk by these Indians today. Roger Williams reports another early use of the berry: "The Indians bruise them in a Morter, and mixe them with meale and make Strawberry bread."

Availability—Fresh strawberries are now available almost all year round in large cities. Peak months are May and June.

Frozen strawberries, packed in water or syrup, sliced or whole, are available, as are a limited quantity of canned strawberries. Strawberry jam, preserves, syrup, gelatin dessert, and pie filling are also available.

Purchasing Guide—Select fresh berries that are bright, fresh, plump, well shaped, and solid in color. The caps should be attached.

Storage—Sort berries and refrigerate. Do not wash until ready to use. Fresh berries are very perishable and should be used as soon as possible.
- Fresh, refrigerator shelf: 3 days
- Canned, kitchen shelf: 1 year
- Canned, refrigerator shelf, open: 4 to 5 days
- Fresh, prepared for freezing; and frozen, refrigerator frozen-food compartment: 2 to 3 months
- Fresh, prepared for freezing; and frozen, freezer: 1 year

Nutritive Food Values—An excellent source of vitamin C. They also contain iron and other minerals.
- Fresh, 3½ ounces, raw and unsweetened = 37 calories
- Canned, 3½ ounces, water pack = 22 calories
- Frozen, whole, 3½ ounces, syrup pack = 92 calories
- Frozen, sliced, 3½ ounces, syrup pack = 109 calories

Basic Preparation—Wash gently before using. Do not allow berries to soak in water. Remove hulls.

- **To Freeze**—Select firm ripe berries. Wash quickly in cold water. Prepare berries as desired—whole, halved, sliced, or crushed. Pack as desired in syrup, in sugar, or unsweetened, or freeze in loose pack.

In syrup: Fill containers with berries to within ½ inch of the top. Fill with a cold syrup of 4 cups water to 4¾ cups sugar.

In sugar: Mix 1 cup sugar with each 4 cups berries until juice is released and sugar is almost dissolved. Pack in containers, allowing ½-inch headspace.

Unsweetened: Fill containers with berries to within ½ inch of the top. Add an ascorbic-acid solution of 4 cups water and 1 teaspoon ascorbic acid.

Loose pack: Put berries in a single layer on a cookie sheet. Put in freezer and freeze until hard. Pour berries into containers, allowing no headspace. Seal.

AVOCADO RING WITH STRAWBERRIES
- 2 boxes (3 ounces each) lime- or lemon-flavored gelatin
- ½ teaspoon salt
- 2 cups hot water
- 1½ cups cold water
- 2 tablespoons fresh lemon juice
- 2 very ripe avocados, peeled, pitted, and mashed
- ⅓ cup mayonnaise
- 3 cups sliced fresh strawberries (reserve ½ cup for Dressing)
- Salad greens
- Honey-Cream Dressing

Dissolve gelatin and salt in hot water. Add cold water and chill until slightly thickened. Pour lemon juice over avocados. Stir avocados and mayonnaise into gelatin, blending well. Pour into 5-cup ring mold and chill until firm. Unmold ring on greens and fill with 2½ cups of the berries. Serve with Honey-Cream Dressing. Makes 6 to 8 servings.

Honey-Cream Dressing
Mix ½ cup each of dairy sour cream and mayonnaise, 1 tablespoon honey, and ½ cup sliced berries.

JELLIED CHEESE AND STRAWBERRY SALAD
- 1 envelope unflavored gelatin
- ¼ cup cold water
- 2 cups (1 pound) creamed cottage cheese
- ¾ teaspoon salt
- ⅛ teaspoon paprika
- Dash of cayenne
- ½ cup milk
- Salad greens
- 1 quart strawberries
- Fresh mint

Soften gelatin in cold water; dissolve over hot water. Mash cheese. Stir in seasonings, milk, and gelatin. Turn into 6 individual molds and chill until firm. Unmold on greens. Wash and hull berries and arrange around salad molds. Garnish with mint sprigs. Makes 6 servings.

STRAWBERRY HARD SAUCE
Cream ⅔ cup soft butter or margarine and gradually beat in 2 cups sifted confectioners' sugar. When thoroughly blended, stir in 1 cup sliced fresh strawberries. Makes 8 servings.

STRAWBERRY VELVET SAUCE
Thaw 1 package (10½ ounces) frozen sliced strawberries. Put berries in container of electric blender and whirl for a few seconds. On low speed, gradually add ½ cup heavy cream, whirling until thick and smooth. Makes about 1½ cups.

STRAWBERRY BETTY
- 1 quart strawberries
- Juice of ½ lemon
- ⅔ cup firmly packed brown sugar
- 4 cups of ½-inch cubes of crust-trimmed white bread
- ¼ cup granulated sugar
- 1 teaspoon grated lemon rind
- 2 tablespoons butter or margarine

Wash and hull berries; mix with lemon juice and brown sugar. Put in shallow 1½-quart baking dish. Mix bread cubes, granulated sugar, and grated lemon rind. Sprinkle over strawberries and dot with butter. Bake in preheated moderate oven (350°F.) for 25 to 30 minutes. Serve warm, with cream. Makes 6 servings.

STRAWBERRY COBBLER
- 3 cups fresh strawberries
- 6 tablespoons water
- 9 tablespoons sugar
- Dash of salt
- 2 tablespoons cornstarch

Fresh Strawberries with Cream

STRAWBERRY

2 tablespoons butter or margarine
1 cup biscuit mix
⅓ cup light cream

Wash and hull berries; mash slightly. Put in 10-inch skillet with cover. Add ¼ cup water, ½ cup sugar, and the salt. Blend cornstarch with 2 tablespoons water and stir into mixture. Bring to boil, stirring frequently, and boil for 1 minute. Dot with butter. Make biscuit dough with 1 tablespoon sugar, the mix, and the cream. Drop by tablespoons onto hot mixture in skillet. Cook, covered, over very low heat for 15 to 20 minutes, or until biscuits are done. Serve warm, plain, or with cream. Makes 4 to 6 servings.

STRAWBERRY MOUSSE
1 egg white
⅛ teaspoon salt
¾ cup confectioners' sugar
1 cup heavy cream
1¼ cups fresh strawberries

Combine egg white and salt and beat until foamy throughout. Gradually add sugar and beat until very stiff. Whip cream until stiff and add to egg white. Wash, hull, and mash berries. Fold into first mixture and pour into refrigerator tray. Freeze, without stirring, until firm. Let stand at room temperature for a few minutes before serving. Makes 4 servings.

STRAWBERRY WHIP

Wash and hull 1 cup strawberries; slice. Put in small bowl of electric mixer with dash of salt, 1 egg white at room temperature, and 1 cup sifted confectioners' sugar. Beat until very stiff. Makes 4 servings.

Note: Serve with custard sauce or as a topping for angel cake or fruit.

STRAWBERRY RICE PUDDING
2 cups milk
½ cup uncooked rice
½ teaspoon salt
¼ cup rum
1 pint strawberries, sliced
1 envelope unflavored gelatin
¼ cup water
3 egg yolks
½ cup sugar
½ teaspoon vanilla extract
1 cup heavy cream, whipped
1 pint strawberries, halved

Scald 1⅓ cups of the milk in top part of double boiler. Add rice and salt and cook, covered, over boiling water until rice is soft. Depending on the quality of the rice used, this may take up to 1 hour. Stir rice occasionally. If rice dries out before getting soft, add more milk. Pour rum over sliced strawberries and chill. Soften gelatin in water. Beat egg yolks with sugar and add remaining ⅔ cup milk. Cook over simmering, not boiling, water until mixture coats spoon. Stir constantly. Add gelatin and blend until gelatin is completely dissolved. Add gelatin-custard mixture to rice and mix thoroughly. Add vanilla. Chill until mixture is slightly thickened. Fold in sliced strawberries and whipped cream. Chill. Pile into sherbet glasses; garnish with berry halves. Makes 6 to 8 servings.

STRAWBERRY-MACAROON CREAM
1 package (10½ ounces) frozen strawberries, thawed
1½ teaspoons unflavored gelatin
Water
¼ cup light corn syrup
Dash of salt
1 cup heavy cream, whipped
½ cup crushed macaroons

Set refrigerator control for fast freezing. Force strawberries through sieve. Soften gelatin in ¼ cup cold water for 5 minutes. Put over low heat and stir until dissolved. Add to strawberries. Add corn syrup and salt. Fold in whipped cream and crushed macaroons. Pour into refrigerator tray and freeze until firm. Makes 4 servings.

STRAWBERRY-ALMOND ROLL
1 package (10 ounces) frozen strawberries, thawed
8 tablespoons sugar
Water
1 teaspoon unflavored gelatin
Red food coloring
3 tablespoons chopped blanched almonds
¼ teaspoon almond extract
½ cup heavy cream, whipped

Turn refrigerator control to coldest setting. Force berries through sieve. Add 5 tablespoons sugar and water to make 2 cups. Sprinkle gelatin on 1 tablespoon cold water, and let stand for 5 minutes. Dissolve over hot water. Stir into berry mixture. Pour into refrigerator tray and freeze until mushy. Add small amount of red food coloring. Beat well, and turn into a 28-ounce can. (It will not fill can.) Put in freezer or freezing compartment of refrigerator until almost firm. Push mixture against sides of can, leaving center hollow. Add remaining sugar, the nuts, and flavoring to whipped cream and pour into center of mold. Cover with wax paper; freeze. To serve, run a spatula around inside of can; wrap in hot cloth until dessert slides out. Cut into slices. Makes 4 servings.

LATTICE STRAWBERRY TARTS
Pastry (2 cups flour recipe), unbaked
1 quart strawberries
1 cup sugar
2 tablespoons cornstarch
2 tablespoons butter or margarine

Cut pastry to fit six 4-inch tart pans. Wash and hull berries. Cut larger ones into halves; leave small ones whole. Add mixture of sugar and cornstarch. Pour into pastry-lined tart pans. Dot with butter. Arrange strips of pastry, lattice fashion, over tarts. Bake in preheated very hot oven (450°F.) for 10 minutes; then reduce heat to moderate (350°F.) and bake for 20 minutes, or until berries are done and pastry is nicely browned. Makes 6 servings.

STRAWBERRY GLACÉ PIE
1 cup biscuit mix
¼ cup butter or margarine
3 tablespoons boiling water
1 quart strawberries
1 cup water
1 cup sugar
3 tablespoons cornstarch
1 package (3 ounces) cream cheese
2 tablespoons heavy cream
¼ teaspoon vanilla extract

Put biscuit mix and butter in bowl. Add boiling water and stir vigorously with fork to form a ball. With fingers and heel of hand, pat evenly into 9-inch pie pan; bring dough up over edge of pan; flute edge. Bake in preheated very hot oven (450°F.) for 8 to 10 minutes; cool.

Wash and hull berries. Simmer 1 cup of the berries and ⅔ cup of the water for 3 minutes, or until berries soften. Blend sugar, cornstarch, and remaining water. Stir into berry mixture and cook, stirring constantly, until thickened. Put remaining berries in pie shell. Cover with cooked mixture and chill for 2 hours, or until firm. Beat cream cheese until fluffy. Add cream and vanilla. Force through pastry tube to garnish pie edge. Makes 6 to 8 servings.

STRAWBERRY SNOWBANK PIE
1 quart strawberries
Pastry for 1-crust 9-inch pie, baked
1¼ cups sugar
½ cup water
½ teaspoon cream of tartar
Pinch of salt
2 egg whites
½ teaspoon vanilla extract

Wash and hull strawberries; arrange in pastry shell, putting prettiest berries in center. Mix sugar, water, and cream of tartar in saucepan. Cover and bring to boil. Uncover and cook until syrup spins long threads (240°F. on a candy thermometer). Add salt to egg whites and beat until stiff. Gradually pour syrup onto whites, beating constantly, until mixture forms stiff peaks. Add flavoring and pile on pie, leaving center uncovered. Cool, but do not refrigerate. Makes 6 to 8 servings.

STRAWBERRY ANGEL-FOOD DESSERT
1 package angel-food mix
2 packages (10½ ounces each) frozen sliced strawberries
1 box (3 ounces) strawberry-flavored gelatin
½ cup sugar
1 cup hot water
1 cup heavy cream, whipped
Whole fresh strawberries, washed and hulled

Prepare cake mix as directed on the package, baking in a 10-inch tube pan. Cool.

Thaw berries; drain, reserving syrup. Dissolve gelatin and sugar in the hot water. Add 1 cup reserved syrup. Chill until slightly thickened. Cut cake into 1-inch pieces. Arrange half in a pan or dish (13 x 9 x 2 inches). Fold drained berries into slightly thickened gelatin. Pour about half of gelatin mixture over cake in dish. Top with remaining cake, then with rest of gelatin. Chill until set. Whip cream and spread on top of dessert. Cut into 15 squares. Serve with a garnish of fresh strawberries. Makes 15 servings.

STRAWBERRY SHORTCAKE

- 3 cups sifted all-purpose flour
- 3¼ teaspoons baking powder
- Sugar (about ⅔ cup)
- 1¼ teaspoons salt
- ½ cup soft shortening
- 1 egg, well beaten
- ⅔ cup milk (about)
- 3 pints strawberries
- Heavy cream

Sift flour, baking powder, 3 tablespoons sugar, and the salt into bowl. Cut in shortening. Add egg and enough milk to make a soft dough, mixing with fork. Knead lightly for about 20 turns on floured board. Divide into thirds. Pat out each third in greased 9-inch layer cake pan. Bake in preheated very hot oven (450°F.) for about 15 minutes. Wash and hull berries. Cut into halves and sweeten to taste. Put shortcake layers together with berries between and on top. Serve with cream. Makes 6 to 8 servings.

STRAWBERRY CAKE ROLL

- 1 cup sifted cake flour
- 1 teaspoon baking powder
- ¼ teaspoon salt
- 3 eggs
- 1 teaspoon vanilla extract
- 1 cup granulated sugar
- ¼ cup water
- ¼ cup sifted confectioners' sugar
- 1 cup sliced fresh strawberries
- 1 pint strawberry ice cream, softened
- 1 package (1 pound) frozen sliced strawberries
- 2 tablespoons brandy (optional)

Sift flour, baking powder, and salt. Beat eggs with vanilla until fluffy and light colored. Gradually beat in granulated sugar. Stir in water. Fold in sifted dry ingredients carefully but thoroughly. Turn into baking pan (1 x 10 x 15 inches) lined with wax paper. Bake in preheated moderate oven (350°F.) for 15 minutes, or until done. Sift confectioners' sugar evenly onto smooth dish towel. Turn hot cake out on towel and carefully peel off paper. Roll up cake from end, jelly-roll fashion; cool. Add fresh strawberries to ice cream. Unroll cake and spread with ice-cream mixture; reroll, wrap in foil, and freeze. Thaw for 10 minutes before serving. When ready to serve, thaw strawberries and mix with brandy. Serve as sauce on sliced roll. Makes 8 servings.

STRAWBERRY-MACAROON TORTE

Blend ½ cup butter, melted, with 1 box coconut-macaroon mix. Using about 1 cup for each, pat mixture thinly and firmly into bottoms of two 9-inch layer-cake pans. Grease sides of pans. Prepare 1 box yellow-cake mix as directed on label. Pour into pans. Sprinkle remaining macaroon mixture evenly over batter. Bake in preheated moderate oven (350° F.) for about 30 minutes. Turn out of pans and cool. Split each layer into halves. Spread Strawberry Cream Filling between layers and on sides of cake, placing bottoms of both layers together in center, and remaining layers, macaroon side out, on top and bottom. Chill in refrigerator for about 2 hours. Makes 8 to 12 servings.

Strawberry Cream Filling

Thaw, drain, and mash 1 box (1 pound) frozen sliced strawberries. Whip 2 cups heavy cream with ¼ cup confectioners' sugar until stiff. Carefully fold in mashed strawberries.

STRAWBERRY ICE CREAM

- 1 quart strawberries (or more to taste)
- ¾ cup sugar
- ¼ teaspoon salt
- 2 cups light cream

Wash and hull berries. Mash well and stir in sugar. Let stand for 20 minutes. Then force through a sieve to remove seeds. Mix with salt and cream and pour into container of crank freezer. Freeze with ice and salt until firm. Makes 1½ quarts.

Note: Two packages (10½ ounces each) frozen sliced strawberries, thawed, can be substituted for the fresh in the above recipe. Stir in ½ cup sugar and force through sieve. Proceed as directed above.

ITALIAN STRAWBERRY ICE

- 2 quarts strawberries
- 1 cup sugar
- 1 cup water
- Juice of 1 small lemon

Wash and hull berries; then purée in a blender. Boil sugar and water together for 5 minutes. Cool. Combine with berry purée and stir in lemon juice. Pour into refrigerator trays and freeze to a mush, stirring occasionally. Makes 4 to 6 servings.

FONDANT-DIPPED STRAWBERRIES

- 1¼ cups water
- 2 cups sugar
- ⅛ teaspoon salt
- 2 tablespoons white corn syrup
- 1 quart strawberries

Combine first 4 ingredients in saucepan. Heat, stirring constantly, until sugar dissolves. Then boil without stirring until a small amount of mixture forms a soft ball when dropped into cold water (238° F. on a candy thermometer). If crystals form on side of pan, remove with fork covered with damp cloth. Pour onto cold wet platter; cool to lukewarm. Beat with fork until white and creamy; knead until smooth. Store in covered jar; let ripen overnight. Melt over hot water. Dip washed and drained berries into fondant; let stand until cool. Serve within a short time.

STRAWBERRY ICE-CREAM SODA

Into a large glass put ⅓ cup frozen or sweetened crushed fresh strawberries, 3 tablespoons milk, and a large scoop of strawberry ice cream. Almost fill glass with chilled carbonated water. Stir.

STRUDEL—A pastry consisting of many layers of paper-thin dough which encases a sweet or savory filling. Strudel is one of the glories of Austrian, Hungarian, and Czechoslovakian baking, and the cooks of those countries produce their crisp, transparent strudel dough in a trice, as a daily food.

Strudel dough resembles *filo*, the equally thin sheets of pastry dough used in much Greek and Turkish cookery. A certain amount of skill is required to make good strudel. But it is not at all impossible to acquire this skill, and the persevering cook will see that her third and subsequent efforts are far superior to her first and second ones.

STRUDEL DOUGH

- 1½ cups sifted all-purpose flour
- ¼ teaspoon salt
- 1 egg, well beaten
- ⅓ to ½ cup lukewarm water
- Filling

Sift flour with salt into a mound on a board. Mix the egg with ⅓ cup water. Make a depression in the center of the flour. Pour in the liquid and stir with a fork until a soft dough is formed. It may be necessary to add a little more water until entire flour is used. Knead the dough on a lightly floured board until it no longer sticks and becomes smooth and elastic. Cover the dough with a bowl and let stand for 20 to 30 minutes.

Cover a table top with a sheet or other cloth. Sprinkle the cloth lightly with flour. Roll out the dough as thin as possible on the cloth. Brush the dough with melted butter to keep the surface from drying. At this point the dough is stretched with the hands until it is about 1 yard square. The dough should be brushed occasionally with melted butter during the stretching process. To avoid making holes with the fingernails put the hands under the sheet of dough palms down, clench the fists, and stretch the dough with the knuckles. When the dough is stretched, cut off the thick outer edge.

STUFF, TO

This dough when stretched can be used for patching the sheet of dough if there are any holes. Fill the dough as specified under each filling.

When ready to roll the strudel, lift one edge of the cloth to allow the dough to roll over itself. Continue rolling until a long roll is shaped. Roll onto a greased cookie sheet and shape into a horseshoe. Brush with melted butter and sprinkle lightly with water. Bake in preheated hot oven (400°F.) for 20 minutes. Brush with additional butter. Then lower heat and continue baking in moderate oven (350°F.) for an additional 10 minutes, or until deep brown. Remove from oven and cool. Sprinkle with confectioners' sugar. Makes 10 to 12 servings.

APPLE STRUDEL

- 8 cups chopped peeled cored tart apples
- Strudel Dough
- ½ cup chopped blanched almonds
- 1½ cups raisins
- 1 tablespoon grated lemon rind
- 1 cup sugar
- ⅓ cup dry bread crumbs
- 3 tablespoons melted butter

Sprinkle apples over the entire surface of Strudel Dough. Sprinkle with almonds and raisins. Mix lemon rind with sugar, bread crumbs, and melted butter. Sprinkle mixture over the apples. Roll up as instructed in dough recipe.

CHERRY STRUDEL

- 8 cups fresh cherries, pitted (An equivalent would be about 6 cups canned pitted dark cherries, drained, with enough juice to make a thick filling)
- Strudel Dough
- Melted butter
- 1 cup blanched almonds, ground finely
- ½ cup sugar
- Grated rind of 1 lemon
- ¾ cup fine dry bread crumbs

Cook fresh cherries until slightly wilted and cooked. Spread cooked cherries over the surface of the dough which has been brushed with melted butter. Combine remaining ingredients and sprinkle them over the cherries. Roll as directed in the dough recipe.

CHEESE STRUDEL

- ¼ cup soft butter or margarine
- 2 cups (1 pound) cottage cheese
- 4 egg yolks
- 1 whole egg
- ⅓ cup sugar
- 1 teaspoon vanilla extract
- Strudel Dough
- 1 egg, well beaten

Combine all ingredients except Strudel Dough and beaten egg. Brush the entire dough with beaten egg. Put the filling in one line down one side of the dough. Roll as directed in dough recipe.

MOHN (POPPY-SEED) STRUDEL

- 2 cups ground poppy seeds
- ½ cup milk
- ½ cup honey
- ½ cup sugar
- ½ cup raisins
- Rind and juice of 1 lemon
- Strudel Dough
- Melted butter

Mix poppy seeds with milk. Add next 4 ingredients. Brush dough with melted butter. Put filling in one line at one side of the dough. Roll as directed in dough recipe.

STRUDEL FILLED WITH PRESERVES

- 1½ cups preserves, such as apricot, raspberry, or pineapple
- ½ cup chopped walnuts
- ⅓ cup chopped blanched almonds
- ¾ cup yellow raisins
- Grated rind of ½ lemon
- ½ teaspoon ground cinnamon
- Strudel Dough
- Melted butter

Combine first 6 ingredients. Brush dough with melted butter. Spread mixture over the dough carefully. Roll as directed in dough recipe.

STUFF, TO—As a culinary term, the phrase refers to filling the hollow of a food with a mixture of other foods. Tomatoes, green peppers, squash, etc., are hollowed and stuffed with meat, bread stuffing, vegetables, etc. Poultry is often stuffed. Some meats such as flank steak, breast of veal, sparerib racks, thick chops, frankfurters, hamburgers, etc., are stuffed. Stuffings can be simple, as single pieces of fruit or vegetables, or can be very complicated, as a forcemeat stuffing.

STUFFING—A savory mixture of foods used to fill fish, poultry, meat, and vegetables. Stuffings, which are also called dressings, keep up the shape of the food that is being stuffed; they also flavor it and make it go further.

Bread, rice, corn bread, potatoes, corn, ground meat, wild rice, sauerkraut, and macaroni can be used as a base for a stuffing. They are seasoned with salt, spices, herbs, and chopped vegetables. Some fat is added to the stuffing such as butter, sausage, bacon, cheese, drippings, etc. Olives, clams, chestnuts, oysters, nuts, mushrooms, apples, prunes, mint, shrimps, pickles, anchovies, etc., may also be added for flavor and texture. Eggs or broth are put in if a moist stuffing is desired.

Stuffings and their ingredients and flavorings are to a large degree a matter of personal taste, but the general rule to remember about stuffings is that rich meats and fish require simple or fruity stuffings and that plain lean meats and fish gain succulence from a rich stuffing. Whatever the kind of stuffing, it should be well seasoned.

Another rule to remember is that all stuffings expand greatly during cooking and that they will burst the meat, fish, or vegetable if they don't have enough room to expand. Excess stuffing should be baked separately; 1 cup stuffing for each pound of meat or fish is ample.

Stuff poultry only just before cooking.

The onion, shallots, or garlic that may be used in a stuffing should always be slightly sautéed in hot butter before being added to the stuffing.

Never use raw pork in a stuffing since it will not cook through. Before being added, raw pork or sausage meat should always be panfried until it loses its raw color.

Many bread stuffings are made commercially. Some frozen already stuffed poultry is sold. Do not attempt this at home. The extremely low temperatures required are not possible in home freezers.

FISH STUFFINGS

NEW ENGLAND CORN-BREAD STUFFING

- 1 small onion, chopped
- 2 tablespoons chopped celery
- ¼ cup butter or margarine
- Few parsley sprigs, chopped
- 2 cups corn-bread crumbs
- ½ teaspoon poultry seasoning
- Dash of ground thyme
- Salt and pepper to taste

Cook onion and celery in the butter until lightly browned. Add remaining ingredients. Use as stuffing for fish. Makes about 2 cups.

VEGETABLE STUFFING

- 2 carrots, shredded
- 2 tablespoons minced parsley
- 2 pimientos, minced
- 2 green onions with tops, chopped
- ⅓ cup melted butter or margarine
- 6 slices of crust-free bread, cubed
- Salt and pepper to taste

Mix all ingredients. Use as stuffing for fish. Makes about 3 cups.

CHEESE STUFFING

- 1 medium onion, thinly sliced
- ¼ cup butter or margarine
- 1½ cups soft stale-bread cubes
- ½ cup grated process American cheese
- Salt and pepper to taste
- ⅛ teaspoon each of ground rosemary and thyme

Cook onion in the butter for 5 minutes. Mix with remaining ingredients. Use as stuffing for fish. Makes 2 cups.

PIQUANT STUFFING

- 1 tablespoon grated onion
- 2 cups soft stale-bread cubes
- ⅓ cup melted butter or margarine
- Juice of ½ lemon

WOMAN'S DAY

Few parsley sprigs, chopped
½ teaspoon celery salt
2 teaspoons capers
Salt and pepper to taste

Cook onion and crumbs in the butter until crumbs are lightly browned. Mix with remaining ingredients. Use as stuffing for fish. Makes 2 cups.

Cucumber Stuffing

Use recipe for Piquant Stuffing; reduce bread cubes to 1½ cups and add 1 cup drained chopped cucumber.

Pickle Stuffing

Use recipe for Piquant Stuffing; add ¼ cup finely chopped sweet or dill pickles.

MEAT STUFFINGS

MINT STUFFING

1 small onion, chopped
¼ cup chopped celery and leaves
¼ cup butter or margarine
½ cup chopped fresh mint leaves or 1 tablespoon dried mint
3 cups soft stale-bread cubes

Cook onion and celery in the butter for 5 minutes. Mix with remaining ingredients. Use to stuff shoulder of lamb. Makes about 3 cups.

SAUERKRAUT STUFFING

About 3½ cups (one 1-pound, 11-ounce can) sauerkraut, drained
2 tablespoons brown sugar
1 garlic clove, minced
1 large onion, chopped
1 tart apple, peeled, cored, and chopped
¼ cup dried currants
1 cup chopped water chestnuts
⅛ teaspoon ground thyme
Salt and pepper to taste

Chop sauerkraut. Add remaining ingredients and mix thoroughly. Use as stuffing for spareribs. Makes about 5 cups.

Stuffed Spareribs

Put stuffing in bottom of baking dish and cover with spareribs cut into serving pieces. Bake in preheated slow oven (325°F.) for 1½ to 2 hours, turning ribs occasionally to brown evenly on all sides.

RAISIN-RICE STUFFING

1¼ cups raw rice
⅓ cup melted butter or margarine
1 medium onion, grated
1 teaspoon salt
1 tablespoon minced parsley
½ teaspoon bouquet garni (a blend of crumbled dried herbs)
Grated rind of ½ orange
¼ cup raisins

Cook rice in boiling salted water until tender; drain. Add to remaining ingredients and mix lightly. Use to fill pocket of breast of veal. Also good in a roasting chicken. Makes about 5 cups.

POULTRY STUFFINGS

BREAD STUFFING

1 cup butter or margarine
1 cup minced onions
1 tablespoon poultry seasoning
1½ teaspoons salt
¾ teaspoon pepper
⅓ cup chopped parsley
¾ cup chopped celery leaves
2½ quarts soft stale-bread crumbs or cubes

Melt butter in skillet and add all ingredients except crumbs. Cook for 5 minutes. Add crumbs. Use as stuffing for turkey. Makes about 9 cups.

Note: Add 2 beaten eggs with the crumbs if desired.

Oyster Bread Stuffing

Follow recipe above. Add 2 cups (1 pint) shucked small oysters, drained and chopped, to the butter with other ingredients. Makes about 10 cups.

Chestnut Bread Stuffing

Follow recipe for Bread Stuffing, reducing crumbs to 2 quarts. Add 1 pound Italian chestnuts, cooked, shelled, and chopped, to stuffing with the bread crumbs. Makes about 10 cups.

CHESTNUT AND SAUSAGE STUFFING

4 dozen Italian chestnuts
2 tablespoons butter or margarine
1 small onion, minced
½ pound sausage meat
2 teaspoons salt
¼ teaspoon pepper
⅛ teaspoon poultry seasoning
1 tablespoon minced parsley
1 cup soft-stale bread crumbs or cubes

Cook and shell chestnuts. Mash half of chestnuts and leave remainder whole. Melt butter in saucepan, add onion, and cook for 3 minutes. Add sausage meat. Cook, stirring constantly, for 5 minutes. Add mashed chestnuts and mix well. Add seasonings and crumbs. Stir in whole chestnuts. Use as stuffing for chicken. Makes 4 cups.

MUSHROOM AND WILD RICE STUFFING

¼ pound mushrooms, chopped
1 small onion, chopped
2 tablespoons butter or margarine
1 cup wild rice, cooked (or 2 cups canned rice)
Salt, pepper, and ground nutmeg

Cook mushrooms and onion in the butter for 5 minutes. Add to rice. Season to taste with salt, pepper, and nutmeg. Use as stuffing for chicken or Rock Cornish hen. Makes 3 cups.

RICE STUFFING

1½ cups raw rice
1 cup butter or margarine
1 cup minced onions
1 teaspoon each of crumbled dried thyme, sage, and marjoram
1½ teaspoons salt
¾ teaspoon pepper
⅓ cup chopped parsley
¾ cup chopped celery and leaves

Cook rice and cool. Melt butter in skillet and add all ingredients except rice. Cook for 5 minutes. Add rice. Use as stuffing for turkey. Makes about 6 cups.

VEAL-AND-VEGETABLE STUFFING

1 pound boneless veal, ground
¾ cup butter or margarine
½ bunch of celery with leaves
2 large onions, peeled
2 tart apples, peeled and cored
3 medium carrots, peeled
4 cups soft stale-bread cubes
2 eggs, beaten
1½ to 2 teaspoons crumbled dried sage
Salt and pepper to taste

Cook veal in butter for 5 minutes. Wash and dry celery. Force through food chopper with onions, apples, and carrots, using medium blade. Add to veal, and cook for 5 minutes longer. Add remaining ingredients and mix lightly. Use as stuffing for turkey or other poultry. Makes about 8 cups.

CELERY-ALMOND STUFFING

1½ cups diced celery
½ cup toasted slivered blanched almonds
1 onion, minced
4 cups soft stale-bread crumbs
⅓ cup melted butter or margarine
⅓ cup chicken bouillon
1 teaspoon poultry seasoning
Salt and pepper to taste

Mix all ingredients. Use as stuffing for chicken. Makes about 6 cups.

SAGE AND ONION STUFFING

1 cup butter or margarine
1 tablespoon crumbled dried sage
1½ teaspoons salt
¾ teaspoon pepper
⅓ cup chopped parsley
¾ cup chopped celery and leaves
2 cups chopped boiled onions
2½ quarts soft stale-bread crumbs or cubes

Melt butter in skillet. Add all ingredients except last two. Cook for 5 minutes. Add onions and crumbs. Use as stuffing for turkey. Makes about 11 cups.

CREAMY BRAZIL-NUT STUFFING

¾ pound shelled Brazil nuts
1¼ cups butter or margarine
2 quarts tiny bread cubes
1 or 2 fresh sage leaves
Heavy cream
Salt and pepper

Cut nuts into small chunks. Brown lightly in ¼ cup of the butter. Dry out bread cubes in oven. Brown in remaining butter. Mix nuts, bread, and sage. Add cream to moisten and salt and pepper to taste. Use as stuffing for turkey. Makes about 8 cups.

Note: If fresh sage is not available, add a tiny pinch of ground sage.

STURGEON

OLIVE STUFFING
12 slices of day-old firm bread
3 medium onions, minced
½ cup chopped parsley
1 cup chopped celery
⅓ cup butter or margarine
¾ cup chopped green olives
2 teaspoons poultry seasoning
1 egg, beaten
Salt and pepper to taste

Trim crusts from bread. Cut bread into small cubes. Cook onions, parsley, and celery in the butter for 8 minutes. Add bread and remaining ingredients; mix lightly. Use as stuffing for poultry. Makes about 8 cups.

VEGETABLE STUFFINGS

MEXICAN-CORN STUFFING
1 small onion, minced
¼ cup chopped green pepper
2 tablespoons butter or margarine
2 pimientos, diced
1½ cups drained canned whole-kernel corn
¼ teaspoon sugar
Dash of cayenne
Salt to taste

Cook onion and pepper in the butter for 5 minutes. Mix with remaining ingredients. Use as stuffing for baked tomatoes, eggplant, or squash. Makes about 1¾ cups.

SYRIAN STUFFING
2 packages (3 ounces each) cream cheese
2 eggs, beaten
Few parsley sprigs, chopped
Salt and pepper
2 tablespoons fine dry bread crumbs

Cream the cheese until softened. Add remaining ingredients except the crumbs and beat well. Fill seed cavities of hot steamed acorn squash halves with the mixture. Sprinkle with crumbs. Bake in preheated moderate oven (375°F.) for 20 minutes, or until filling is firm. Makes enough to fill 4 large squash halves.

ITALIAN CHEESE STUFFING
1 cup cooked rice
¼ cup melted butter or margarine
3 tablespoons grated Parmesan cheese
Few parsley sprigs, chopped
⅓ cup finely diced Mozzarella cheese
Salt and pepper to taste

Mix all ingredients. Use as stuffing for baked tomatoes. Also good in fish. Makes about 1¼ cups.

TURKISH MEAT-AND-RICE STUFFING
1 pound ground raw fatty lamb or beef
1 medium onion, chopped
¼ cup raw rice
1 teaspoon each of chopped fresh mint and dill or crumbled dried herbs to taste
1 tablespoon tomato sauce
Salt and pepper to taste

Mix all ingredients well and use as stuffing for eggplant, zucchini, green peppers, or tomatoes. Makes about 2½ cups.
Note: When stuffing these vegetables, cut off a slice from end of eggplant and zucchini, or top of green pepper and tomato. Scoop out insides, and stuff vegetables. Replace cut-off slice, fasten with toothpicks, and cook upright in covered saucepan with 2 tablespoons butter and 1 cup water. Allow 30 to 40 minutes cooking time.

PIEDMONT STUFFING
Stems of 12 large mushrooms
4 anchovies, minced
1 medium onion, minced
1 tablespoon chopped parsley
2 tablespoons olive oil
¼ cup fine dry bread crumbs
1 egg, beaten
Salt and pepper to taste

Chop mushroom stems. Cook anchovies, onion, and parsley in oil for 5 minutes. Add mushroom stems and cook for 5 minutes longer. Remove from heat and cool. Add remaining ingredients. Use as stuffing for mushrooms.

Stuffed Mushrooms
Stuff 12 large mushroom caps with Piedmont Stuffing. Arrange stuffed caps in shallow pan and add ½ cup olive oil. Bake in preheated moderate oven (350°F.) for about 20 minutes, basting occasionally with the oil in the pan.

STURGEON—Various species of fish of the genus *Acipenser* are known as sturgeon. They are distributed throughout the coastal waters and rivers of the north temperate zone. Most species inhabit the sea for most of the year but ascend rivers to spawn; some are completely freshwater fishes. One related genus, *Scaphirhynchus*, is recognized as a sturgeon; this is the shovelhead, or shovel-nosed, freshwater sturgeon found in the Mississippi and other North American rivers.

Sturgeon have a projecting tapering snout, bony plates, and an asymmetrical tail fin. They range in size from the under three-foot-long snouted sterlet of the Volga River to the huge beluga of the Black and Caspian Seas where sturgeon is king among fish. This last fish is the largest of all fresh-water fish: it has been measured at twenty-six feet long, weighing 3,221 pounds. Although sturgeon was once plentiful on the West Coast, in the Great Lakes, and in some eastern rivers of the United States, it is now very scarce in American waters.

Fresh sturgeon steaks are a prized delicacy, and the flavor is so distinctive that they require little seasoning. Smoked sturgeon is a delicious but expensive treat. Even more of a delicacy is the roe of the sturgeon, called caviar, which is usually served chilled with lemon juice and toast or dark bread.

Another product of the sturgeon is isinglass, made from the swim bladder of the fish. It is used nowadays as a clarifying agent and in making jellies and glues.

Availability—Smoked sturgeon and caviar are available in specialty food stores.

Storage
☐ Refrigerator shelf: 2 to 3 months

Nutritive Food Values—High in protein.
☐ Smoked sturgeon, 3½ ounces = 149 calories
☐ Caviar, granular, 3½ ounces = 262 calories
☐ Caviar, pressed, 3½ ounces = 316 calories

SHERRY SMOKED STURGEON IN RAMEKINS
½ pound smoked sturgeon
¾ cup butter or margarine
¼ cup all-purpose flour
¼ teaspoon salt
½ teaspoon celery seed
⅛ teaspoon ground nutmeg
2 teaspoons minced parsley
2 cups half-and-half (half cream, half milk)
¼ cup sherry
2 hard-cooked eggs, chopped
½ cup coarse dry bread crumbs

Cut sturgeon into 1-inch cubes. Melt ½ cup butter and blend in flour, salt, celery seed, nutmeg, and parsley. Gradually add half-and-half, stirring constantly. Cook, stirring, until smooth and thickened. Add sherry, eggs, and sturgeon; remove from heat. Divide mixture into 6 individual ramekins. Sprinkle lightly with crumbs and dot with remaining butter. Bake in preheated hot oven (400°F.) for 5 minutes, or until browned. Makes 6 servings.

SMOKED-STURGEON DEVILED EGGS
1 teaspoon fresh lemon juice
¼ teaspoon powdered mustard
1 tablespoon mayonnaise
4 hard-cooked eggs
Pinch of cayenne
½ cup finely flaked smoked sturgeon
1 celery stalk, minced
1 tablespoon minced green pepper
Salad greens
Radishes, sliced cucumber

Blend lemon juice and mustard. Stir in mayonnaise. Cut eggs into halves lengthwise and remove yolks. Mash yolks and blend with mayonnaise mixture, cayenne, fish, celery, and green pepper. Fill egg whites with the mixture and arrange on salad greens. Garnish with radishes and cucumber slices. Makes 4 servings.

SUCCOTASH—A native American dish consisting of corn and beans, usually Limas, combined after cooking and served together.

The word comes from the language of the Narraganset Indians; *msakwatas* means "something broken into pieces." The dish is a truly indigenous one, discovered by the early settlers who learned it from the Indians.

Different versions of succotash have been developed over the years, some containing tomatoes and other vegetables besides the Lima beans and corn. In addition to the homemade variety, canned and frozen succotash are widely available.

SUCCOTASH

2 cups cooked Lima beans (fresh, frozen, or canned)
2 cups whole kernel corn (fresh, frozen, or canned)
2 tablespoons butter
1 teaspoon salt
½ teaspoon sugar
¼ teaspoon pepper
¼ cup water
½ cup heavy cream (optional)

Combine all ingredients except cream. Simmer, covered, over lowest possible heat for 5 minutes. Stir occasionally and check for moisture; if necessary, add a little more water. Add cream, if desired, and heat through. Makes 4 to 6 servings.

SUCKER—A name popularly applied to various types of fresh-water fish closely related to carp that are, with two Asiatic exceptions, native to North America. Suckers live and feed near the bottom of streams. Their flesh is lean and they are eaten where they are abundant. Generally speaking, they are the kind of fish caught by youngsters on fishing expeditions and brought home for their mothers to prepare.

Suckers can be cooked in any way fish is cooked. If broiled, they must be well spread with oil or butter to counteract their leanness. Poached, braised, or pan-fried, they profit from a sauce such as mayonnaise, tartare, hollandaise, etc.

Caloric Value

☐ 3½ ounces, raw = 104 calories

SUET—The hard fat around the kidneys and loins in beef, mutton, and other carcasses which yields tallow. In cookery, unless the word is otherwise qualified, the reference is always to beef suet which has a bland taste. It is widely used in British cooking as a shortening for pastry and for savory and sweet puddings, to which it gives a rich smooth quality. For this purpose it is shredded or diced. Suet can also be melted down, strained, and used like any other solid fat. Although it has a low smoking point, suet can be used for shallow frying.

Suet is sold in meat markets by the pound in large pieces, or it is sold by weight and sliced and ready to be used for barding meats. Large pieces of suet can be finely cubed or shredded with a sharp knife, or they can be ground through the coarse blade of a meat grinder.

Caloric Value

☐ Suet (beef kidney fat), 3½ ounces, raw = 854 calories

SUET PUDDING

1¼ cups sultana raisins
1¼ cups dried currants
1 cup raisins
1 cup mixed chopped candied fruits
½ cup chopped blanched almonds
2 cups sifted all-purpose flour
1 nutmeg, grated
½ teaspoon each of ground allspice and ginger
10 ounces suet, finely chopped
2¼ cups (1 pound) dark brown sugar
6 cups soft bread crumbs
6 eggs
½ cup each of milk and brandy

Chop large raisins and mix with other fruits and nuts. Mix flour with spices, suet, sugar, and bread crumbs. Beat eggs with milk and brandy. Stir into dry ingredients. Beat in fruits and nuts. Spoon mixture into two 6-cup molds which have been greased. Cover the top of the mold with paper that has been greased or with greased aluminum foil. Set molds in a large kettle filled with boiling water that comes halfway up the mold. Boil puddings for 7 to 8 hours, adding more boiling water to keep up the level of the liquid. Remove molds from the water. Remove paper and cover puddings with dry paper or foil. Store puddings until ready to use. Some puddings are kept for as long as a year, which improves their flavor. When ready to serve, boil pudding again for 2 to 3 hours. Stick a branch of holly with berries into the top of each pudding. Serve with brandy set aflame, rum butter, or cream. Makes 16 to 20 servings.

SUGAR—A sweet substance, capable of being crystallized, which is colorless or white when pure. It occurs in many plant juices and forms an important element of human food. Sugar as we usually think of it is, more specifically, cane sugar, which may also be called sucrose or saccharose. By extension, sugar also means any of a class of sweet, soluble compounds comprising the simpler carbohydrates. In addition to cane sugar these carbohydrates or natural sugars are: dextrose or grape sugar, levulose or fruit sugar, lactose or milk sugar, and maltose or malt sugar.

The chief sources of sugar are the sugar cane and the sugar beet, the completely refined products of which are identical and form the granulated sugar, loaf, or cube, sugar, etc., found in the food stores. Cane sugar is made by expressing the juice from the sugar cane. It is then treated with lime to remove impurities, filtered, and evaporated to crystallization. The mother liquor, or molasses, is removed, usually in a centrifuge. The crude yellowish or brown sugar thus obtained is refined by redissolving, clarifying, decolorizing, and recrystallizing. In the case of beet sugar, the sugar is removed by extraction with water and carried to the refined state in one operation. Crude cane sugar is often sold as brown sugar but crude beet sugar has an unpleasant flavor.

Sugar cane was used in India as long ago as 1000 B.C. At that time the sugar cane was chewed because of its sweet taste. It was not until about 500 B.C. that the sweet juice in the center of the cane was processed in any way. It was then made into *gur*, a crude substance of sugar crystals and molasses. This is still found in some parts of modern India. Sanskrit, an ancient Indian language, called sugar *sakara*, which also meant gravel or pebble. The modern word "sugar" is derived from the Sanskrit through the Arabic *sukkar*, although modern refining has made the table sugar a fine, scarcely "gravelly" product.

People of the Mediterranean area heard of the delicious sweet sugar of India through the armies of Alexander the Great in the early 4th century B.C., but it was not until 1,000 years later that sugar cane was brought to the Middle East, North Africa, and southern Europe with the conquering Moslem armies.

At one time the merchants of Genoa had almost a monopoly on the sugar trade. They hired the young Christopher Columbus to ship sugar from Madeira to Genoa. Columbus was already familiar with the valuable cane because his first wife's mother owned a sugar plantation. With a thorough knowledge of the plant and its value, it is no wonder that he brought it to the New World in 1493 on his second voyage. Originally planted in Santo Domingo, the sugar cane spread

SUNDAE

quickly to Puerto Rico, Cuba, and various countries in Central and South America. It brought enormous fortunes to its planters.

The early colonists of America had to pay high prices for their sugar, if they could get it at all. It was imported from the West Indies in solid cone-shaped loaves wrapped in blue paper. Special sugar shears had to be used to cut it into small pieces, each worth its weight in gold. Because it was so expensive, many people had to make do with molasses, or other products such as honey. In the middle of the 18th century sugar cane was introduced into Louisiana. But it was not until the 19th century that modern methods of refining made it no longer a luxury.

Much younger is the sugar-beet industry. The Chinese have made a crude sugar from beet juice since very early days but the European discovery of the sugar content of the beet is attributed to Margraff, a German scientist, in 1747. No successful method of extraction was devised, however, until fifty-two years later in France. Improvements were made from time to time and by 1900 western civilization was consuming two pounds of beet to one pound of cane sugar. The pendulum has since swung the other way. Sugar-beet cultivation was first introduced into the United States in 1880. Colorado, Michigan, Utah, California, and Nebraska are the chief producing states.

TYPES OF SUGAR

Granulated sugar is the product for general use. The terms "granulated," "fine granulated," and "extra fine granulated" are used. They are all universally available in different size packages.

Superfine or **powdered** sugar is a very fine granulated sugar for use in cold drinks, for fruits and cereals, and for special cake baking. Use in recipes which need a quick-dissolving sugar; 1 cup superfine equals 1 cup granulated.

Confectioners' sugar is granulated sugar that is crushed very fine and mixed with cornstarch to prevent caking. X's may be used to indicate grade. There is only a slight difference between the 10X or ultra-fine, and the 4X or very fine. Confectioners' sugar is used for frostings, confections, hard sauce, and dusting; 1¾ cups confectioners' sugar equals 1 cup granulated.

Brown sugar is also called soft sugar and consists of extremely fine crystals that are covered with a film or coating of molasses. This coating gives the sugar the characteristic color and taste which is of primary value. At one time, 15 grades of soft sugar were produced ranging in color from white to yellow to brown. Now, fewer grades are produced. Common household grades are light brown and dark (old-fashioned) brown. Sometimes a medium brown is available. It may be made from the syrup that remains after the sugar is extracted from sugar cane or sugar beet, or by adding refined syrups to white sugar crystals.

The light brown sugar is milder in flavor and is used in baking, icings, and candy. The dark brown sugar is used in cookies, cakes, gingerbread, mincemeat, plum pudding, and baked beans.

Brown sugar often hardens. To avoid this, keep sugar in airtight container in refrigerator. To restore hardened sugar, heat in oven at low temperature until it is soft enough to crumble. The sugar may be rolled and sifted or crumbled in an electric blender. Or piece of apple, lettuce, or fresh bread may be placed on a piece of wax paper and put in the container of brown sugar for 2 days. Replace if necessary.

When measuring, pack brown sugar firmly into container; it should retain the shape of the container when it is removed.

Also available is *brownulated* sugar which pours freely. Use substitution table on the package when using brownulated sugar instead of regular brown sugar.

Maple sugar is made from the sap of the sugar maple, concentrated and crystallized into sugar. It is sold loose or pressed into cakes or decorative molds.

Rock candy is made by immersing a string in a supersaturated solution of sugar and water. The sugar solution is not stirred, allowing large sugar crystals to form on the string. Also sold crystallized on small sticks for drink swizzle sticks.

Colored sugars are available and are used for decoration.

Cinnamon sugar, a combination of granulated sugar and ground cinnamon, is also sold. It is used for flavoring toast, cookies, coffeecakes, etc.

Storage—Lasts indefinitely; store in an airtight container to prevent caking or lumping.

Nutritive Food Values—Sugar is almost 100 per cent carbohydrate and is the most efficient source of energy that can be used by the human body.
- Brown, 3½ ounces = 373 calories
- White, granulated or powdered, 3½ ounces = 385 calories

NONNUTRITIVE SWEETENERS

People who must restrict their intake of sweets turn to the nonnutritive sweeteners. As the name indicates, these organic compounds are a substitute for sugar and contain no calories. They are used in the manufacture of dietetic food products only, and may also be purchased for home use.

The chemical names are calcium cyclohexyl sulfamate, calcium saccharin, saccharin, sodium cyclohexyl sulfamate, and sodium saccharin. The calcium compounds can also be used by persons who are on a sodium-restricted diet. Saccharin is 300 times sweeter than sucrose.

Sucaryl comes in two forms, sucaryl sodium and sucaryl calcium.

The Association of Food and Drug Officials of the United States has recommended that diet foods be separated from normal foods, that the dietary nature be emphasized, and that the labels state the dietary nature and list the true contents.

The nonnutritive sweeteners may be in liquid or tablet form. There are several brands.

Saccharin should not be used for cooking as it produces a bitter flavor. One eighth teaspoon noncaloric sweetener equals 1 teaspoon granulated sugar.

SUNDAE—A dish consisting of ice cream topped with a sauce or sauces, with the optional addition of such garnishes as nuts, cherries, fruits, and whipped cream. There is no limit to the variations possible in sundaes.

SUNFISH—One of a large group of freshwater fish which are closely related to the perches and include the black bass, crappie, and calico bass, commonly called "sunnies." Their bright coloring and interesting shapes as well as their courage make them an excellent game fish for fishermen. They are not fished commercially.

Sunfish are generally panfried or broiled.

PANFRIED SUNFISH WITH DILL SAUCE
   4 sunfish, cleaned
      Undiluted evaporated milk
   ¼ cup each of all-purpose flour
      and cornmeal
   ½ teaspoon salt
      Dash of pepper
      Cooking oil
      Dill Sauce

Wipe fish with a damp cloth or paper towel. Dip into evaporated milk and roll in mixture of flour, cornmeal, and seasonings. Fry in small amount of hot oil for 3 to 5 minutes on each side, turning carefully with fork or flat turner. Add more oil as needed. Do not overcook. Serve with Dill Sauce. Makes 4 servings.

Dill Sauce
Melt 2 tablespoons butter or margarine and blend in 2 tablespoons all-purpose flour. Gradually add 1 cup milk and cook, stirring constantly, until thickened. Add 3 tablespoons minced fresh dill and season to taste.

Swedish Cookery
by Nika Hazelton

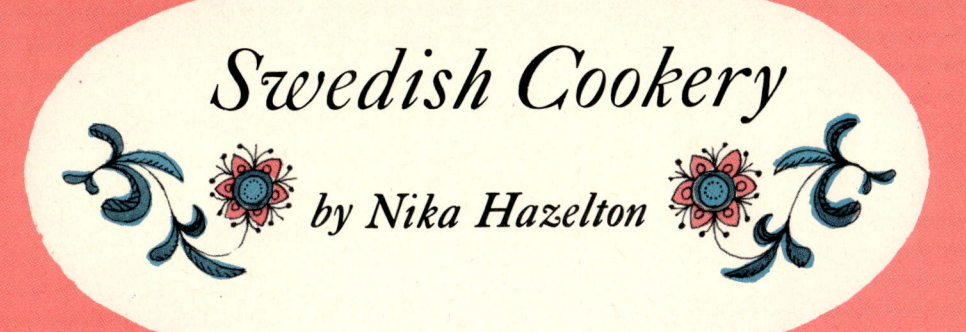

Sweden's fame for flavor is seen in recipes for hearty soups; meats and seafood; piquant sauces; tasty vegetables and salads; custard cream and fruit tortes; and the famous glögg.

SWEDISH COOKERY

Sweden is a very prosperous country, and her high standard of living is reflected in her food, which is by far the richest and most varied of all Scandinavian food. The Swedes eat well. Although their food is bland, as is all Scandinavian food, it is not nearly as bland as that of the other countries. The Swedes like flavorings; anchovies are much admired, dill is the national food plant, cardamom and spices are used in baking. The Swedes are also fond of sweetened foods. In all of Scandinavia sugar is used far more in nonsweet cooking than it is in America, but the Swedes use much more sugar than other Scandinavians.

The one thing the Swedes don't serve any more is the enormous smorgasbord that we Americans find in our Swedish restaurants and on such festive occasions as weddings, church suppers, or club socials. At a dinner party, the usual smorgasbord consists of four or five appetizers at the outside. There will be herring in some form or other, smoked salmon, a homemade liver pâté, and a cheese.

The Swedes eat a good many nourishing soups, including fruit soups, and much fish and seafood. The salmon is excellent, and so is the fresh-water fish such as pike. Lobsters are highly thought of, and boiled crayfish, which look like miniature lobsters and are not shrimps, are the national passion. Their season is August to September, and they are the reason for most congenial parties, open-air ones preferably, held under a shiny moon, with much *akvavit,* beer, and all-round merriment.

Far more meat is eaten at everyday family meals in Sweden than in the other Scandinavian countries. Pork, lamb, and veal are boiled, pot-roasted, or minced in the ubiquitous meatballs. Oven roasts, such as we and the English like, are not common, and beef is not as good as in the United States. The meats, of course, come with rich, delicious cream gravies. Chicken, as in all Scandinavia, is a party dish and a treat, although it is becoming less expensive. Goose, on the other hand, is a national bird, roasted with a stuffing of apples and prunes. Game and game birds, from the enormous Swedish forests, are common, and they are usually pot-roasted with bacon and cream.

The variety and excellence of baked foods is staggering. The American visitor in a Swedish home, especially in the country districts, finds it almost impossible to believe that Swedish women can bake so much, so well, and so often. Swedish home baking, to be consumed with coffee, is about the best in the world.

Sweden's present food habits are in an interesting state of transition between the old and the new. On one hand we have a national cuisine of traditional foods, to be eaten in a ritual manner especially on holidays. Among them are the sausages, the Shrove Tuesday buns, the Christmas lutfisk, to mention a few—all of them dishes which for the conservative Swedes have an almost mystical significance. On the other hand, these same Swedes—very prosperous, very traveled, and well versed in foreign affairs—are the producers and consumers of the most modern canned and frozen foods. They are also thoroughly sophisticated in their restaurant food, which is French influenced, as is the restaurant food in all of Scandinavia. In the clear air of the North, their cuisine seems infinitely richer than other European countries, with combinations of meats and vegetables, or fish and vegetables, and a predilection for cream sauces that are typically Swedish.

APPETIZERS

FÅGELBON
(Bird's Nests)

12 to 16 anchovy fillets, chopped
4 raw egg yolks
4 tablespoons minced onion
2 tablespoons capers
4 tablespoons minced parsley
4 tablespoons minced pickled beets

Make nests on a large platter or on 4 individual serving plates. Allowing one-fourth of the ingredients for each serving, arrange each ingredient in a circle. First, arrange anchovies, leaving space for an egg yolk in the center. Surround anchovies with a circle of onion. Then follow with circles of capers, parsley, and beets. Drop an egg yolk into center of each. If nests are on a large platter, the first person served mixes the ingredients together well. If on individual plates, each person mixes his own. Makes 4 servings.

GRAVAD LAX MED SENAPSSÅS
(Marinated Salmon with Mustard Sauce)

3-pound middle-cut piece of salmon
6 tablespoons salt
3 tablespoons sugar
3 teaspoons coarsely crushed white peppercorns
1 large bunch of fresh dill
Lemon wedges, freshly ground pepper, and dill for garnish
Mustard Sauce

Cut fish along the back into 2 fillets. Carefully remove backbone. Wipe fillets with damp paper towel. Mix salt, sugar, and crushed pepper. Rub part of mixture into fish fillets. Put a thick layer of dill sprigs in the bottom of a dish about the size of salmon fillets. Put 1 fillet, skin side down, on dill layer. Sprinkle with salt mixture. Add more dill sprigs. Put remaining fish fillet, skin side up, on dill. Sprinkle with remaining seasonings and dill. Put a board or plate on top of fish and weight down. Refrigerate for 16 to 24 hours. Scrape fish and cut away from the skin into ⅛-inch slices or ½-inch slices if served as a main dish. Arrange on platter and garnish with lemon wedges, pepper, and dill. Serve with the Mustard Sauce. If desired, serve salmon with tiny, piping hot dill potatoes, or with toast. Keeps for 2 weeks in refrigerator. Makes 8 to 10 servings.

Note: The skin is delicious cut into ½-inch-wide strips and panbroiled for 5 or 6 minutes, or until crisp and well browned.

Senapssås
(Mustard Sauce)

With wire whisk, blend 3 tablespoons prepared mustard, 3 tablespoons sugar, 1 tablespoon vinegar, 3 tablespoons salad oil, and ¼ teaspoon salt. Add freshly ground pepper to taste. Chill. Just before serving, add 3 tablespoons finely chopped fresh dill.

SMÅ KÖTTBULLAR
(Small Meatballs)

2 tablespoons fine dry bread crumbs
⅓ cup water
⅓ cup light cream
¾ pound ground lean beef
¼ pound ground veal
1 teaspoon salt
Freshly ground pepper
1 teaspoon cornstarch
1 tablespoon grated onion
⅓ cup butter or margarine

Mix crumbs, water, and cream and let stand for 10 to 15 minutes. Add remaining ingredients except butter and mix

SWEDISH COOKERY

well. Dip hands into cold water and shape meat into small balls about ¾ inch in diameter. Fry a few at a time in browned butter, shaking pan now and then to make balls round and browned on all sides and of desired doneness. Serve warm in a chafing dish, or cold for sandwiches. Makes about 5 dozen meatballs.

SILL OCH SKINKSALLAD
(Herring and Ham Salad)

- 1 salt herring
- 1 cup each of diced cooked potatoes, pickled beets, and diced apples
- 1 cup diced cooked ham (optional)
- ½ cup diced dill pickles
- ¼ cup minced onion
- ¼ cup liquid from pickled beets
- 2 tablespoons sugar
  Freshly ground pepper
- 2 hard-cooked eggs, chopped
  Parsley
- 1 cup dairy sour cream
  Hot toast

Clean the herring and cut into boneless fillets. Cover generously with cold water and let stand for 10 to 12 hours. Drain and rinse; drain. With scissors, cut fish into ⅛-inch pieces. Combine fish, potatoes, beets, apples, ham (if used), pickles, and onion. Mix lightly but thoroughly. Mix liquid from beets with sugar and pepper. Gently stir into fish mixture. Pack into a 1-quart mold rinsed with cold water. Chill. Unmold and garnish with chopped egg and parsley. Serve with sour cream and toast. Salad may be arranged on lettuce, if desired. Makes 6 to 8 servings.

SOUPS

BRUNKÅLSSOPPA
(Brown Cabbage Soup)

- 1 large head cabbage, cored and shredded
- ¼ cup butter or margarine
- 3 tablespoons brown sugar
- 4 cups beef bouillon or more, depending on thickness of soup desired
- 1 teaspoon salt
- ½ teaspoon pepper
- ¼ teaspoon ground allspice

In a deep kettle brown cabbage in hot butter on all sides. The color should be a light brown. Stir occasionally. Add sugar and cook, stirring constantly, until sugar is completely dissolved. Add bouillon, salt, pepper, and allspice. Simmer, covered, for about 1 hour. Serve with dumplings. Makes 6 to 8 servings.

ÄRTER OCH FLÄSK
(Yellow Pea Soup)

- 1 pound dried yellow Swedish peas*
- 3 quarts water
- 1 pound fresh pork shoulder
- 1 smoked ham shank, about 2 pounds
- 1 large onion
- 1 celery stalk
  Salt
- 3 whole cloves
  Prepared mustard
- ½ teaspoon ground ginger
- ½ teaspoon dried thyme leaves

Wash peas and put in heavy kettle. Add the water and let stand overnight. Do not discard water. Bring quickly to boil and boil vigorously for about 10 minutes. Remove any scum or skins from top. Reduce heat and simmer for 2 hours. Add meats, whole onion, celery, 3 teaspoons salt, and cloves. Simmer for 1 hour longer, or until meat and peas are tender. Remove meat, cut into slices, and serve separately with prepared mustard. Season soup with ginger, thyme leaves, and more salt, if necessary. If too thick, add a little water. Makes about 2 quarts.
*Dried yellow Swedish peas are available in Scandinavian food stores. Dried yellow split peas can be substituted.

ÄPPELSOPPA
(Apple Soup)

- 6 juicy fairly tart apples
- 1½ cups dried apples, washed and soaked
- 7 cups water
  Thin peel of ¼ lemon
- 1 cinnamon stick
- ⅔ cup sugar
- 1½ to 2 tablespoons cornstarch or potato flour
- ¼ cup Madeira, white wine, or fresh lemon juice
  Whipped cream
  Rusks
  Garnish: mint sprig, cluster of ripe currants, or cherry

Wash apples, drain, core, and cube; combine with drained soaked dried apples in enamelware saucepan; add water and bring to boil. Add lemon peel and cinnamon stick. Cook only until apples are tender; put through wire sieve. Reheat with sugar. When boiling, mix the cornstarch with ½ cup cold water and stir into the boiling soup. Stir and boil for 3 minutes, or until clear. (With potato flour, let boil for about 10 minutes.) Add wine. Remove from heat. Chill thoroughly. Serve in iced bowls, with dab of whipped cream and rusks. Garnish each serving as desired. Makes 6 or more servings.

FISH

STEKT SILL ELLER STRÖMMING
(Fried Herring or Smelt Fillets)
Excellent also when made with filleted mackerel

- 2 pounds herring or smelt fillets
- 1 teaspoon salt
- ¼ teaspoon white pepper
- ½ cup butter or margarine
- 1 cup chopped parsley or ½ cup chopped dill
- 2 eggs, beaten
- 2 cups fine dry bread crumbs

Wash fish fillets in ice water. Dry on absorbent paper. Sprinkle with salt and pepper. Blend ¼ cup of the butter with the parsley. Spread on fish fillets and put together like a sandwich. Dip fish sandwiches into beaten eggs and roll in bread crumbs. Shake free of excessive crumbs. Chill for 15 to 30 minutes. (This is not strictly necessary, but fish fries more easily.) Melt remaining butter and fry fish sandwiches in it until golden on all sides. Serve with mashed potatoes and a salad. Makes 6 servings.

KOKT LUTFISK
(Boiled Lutfisk)

A must for a Swedish Christmas. Lutfisk is cod treated with lime, and in the old days this treatment took place at home. But now the Swedish housewife buys her lutfisk ready for cooking. In America, Scandinavian delicatessens will have lutfisk at Christmas time.

- 3 pounds prepared lutfisk, cut into serving pieces
  Salt
- ½ cup (about) boiling water
  Pepper
  Powdered mustard
  Ground allspice

Lutfisk is delicate to handle and it is best to place the pieces in a piece of cheesecloth, tying the ends.

Boil salt and water in large deep frying pan. Add lutfisk, either wrapped in a cheesecloth or in pieces, skin side down. Cover pan and bring to simmering, not boiling, point. Simmer for 10 to 15 minutes, or until fish flakes easily. Lift out fish carefully and drain well. Place on hot platter and remove skin and fins. Serve with pepper, a dash of powdered mustard, and a dash of ground allspice; good with boiled potatoes and a cream sauce. These are the classic Swedish Christmas foods to go with lutfisk. Makes 6 servings.

ENCYCLOPEDIA OF COOKERY

SWEDISH COOKERY

FISKGRYTA
(Fish with Onions and Tomatoes)

- 2 medium onions, sliced
- 2 tablespoons butter or margarine
- 1½ pounds fillet of sole, cod, or flounder
- 1 tablespoon fresh lemon juice
- 1 teaspoon salt
- 4 medium tomatoes, sliced ¼ inch thick
- Pepper
- ¼ cup white wine
- 3 tablespoons chopped parsley or dill

In a heavy saucepan, sauté onions in the butter until soft and golden. Wipe fish with a damp cloth and cut into serving pieces. Sprinkle with the lemon juice and salt. Arrange fish pieces on top of onions. Cover with tomato slices and sprinkle with pepper. Pour wine over top, cover, and simmer for 10 to 15 minutes. Add parsley. Good with riced potatoes. Makes 4 to 6 servings.

MEAT

BIFF À LA LINDSTRÖM
(Beef Lindström)

- 2 pounds steak, ground
- 3 egg yolks
- ¾ cup mashed potatoes
- 2 teaspoons salt
- ½ teaspoon pepper
- ¼ cup heavy cream
- ¾ cup finely chopped cooked beets or pickled beets
- ⅓ cup finely chopped onion
- ⅓ cup chopped capers
- Butter

Blend together meat, egg yolks, mashed potatoes, and salt and pepper. Gradually beat in cream. Combine beets, onion, and capers, and blend into mixture. Shape into large flat patties and fry quickly in butter on both sides. Makes 6 to 8 servings.

Note: In Sweden, Beef Lindström is often served with a fried egg on top.

SLOTTSSTEK
(Royal Pot Roast)

- 4 pounds beef, chuck or round
- 2 teaspoons salt
- 1 teaspoon ground allspice
- ½ teaspoon pepper
- 3 tablespoons butter or margarine
- 3 tablespoons brandy or whiskey
- ⅓ cup hot beef bouillon
- 2 medium onions, sliced
- 3 minced anchovy fillets or 1 teaspoon anchovy paste
- 2 bay leaves
- 2 tablespoons white vinegar
- 2 tablespoons molasses or dark syrup
- Gravy

Rub meat with salt, allspice, and pepper. Heat butter and brown meat in it on all sides. Pour brandy over hot meat and flame. Add all other ingredients except Gravy and blend. Simmer, covered, over very low heat for about 2 hours, or until meat is tender. Remove meat to hot serving platter and keep hot. Make Gravy. Slice meat and surround with little mounds of buttered peas, carrots, and cauliflowerets, and decorate with tomato and cucumber slices and parsley. Pour a little of the gravy over the meat and serve the rest of the gravy separately. Makes 6 to 8 servings.

Gravy

Make gravy from pan drippings in usual manner. Flavor with ¼ teaspoon anchovy paste and fold in 1 cup heavy cream, whipped.

KALVKOTLETT À LA OSCAR
(Veal Cutlet à la Oscar)

This combination of the tenderest veal, lobster, asparagus, and Béarnaise sauce is a specialty of first-class Scandinavian restaurants. The asparagus used in Sweden is snow white and very tender. This kind of asparagus can be bought here in specialty stores imported in glass jars.

- 2½ pounds boneless rump of veal, ¾ inch thick
- 1 teaspoon salt
- ¼ teaspoon white pepper
- ¼ cup butter or margarine
- 12 stalks of hot cooked asparagus, tender part only
- 1½ cups cut up cooked lobster meat
- 1½ cups Béarnaise Sauce (page 1766)
- Parsley sprigs

Cut meat into 6 round serving pieces and trim away all fat and gristle. Rub meat with salt and pepper. Melt butter in large skillet. Over medium heat cook meat until golden on both sides. Reduce heat and simmer, covered, for 10 to 15 minutes, or until meat is tender and cooked through. Arrange meat on hot serving platter. Place 2 asparagus spears on top of each round. Top with lobster. Cover with Béarnaise sauce and decorate with parsley sprigs. Serve with browned potatoes and a tossed green salad. Makes 6 servings.

KOKT LAMM MED DILLSÅS
(Boiled Lamb with Dill)

This very popular and excellent dish must be made with fresh dill, which can be bought all the year round in many American markets, and in all Scandinavian and Jewish vegetable stores.

- 3 pounds breast or shoulder of lamb
- Boiling water
- 1 tablespoon salt to each quart of water
- 4 white peppercorns
- 1 bay leaf
- 5 dill sprigs
- Dill Sauce

Trim meat of excess fat. Scald quickly in boiling water. Drain, place in casserole or Dutch oven, and add boiling salted water to cover. Bring to a boil and skim. Add next 3 ingredients. Simmer, covered, for 1 to 1½ hours, or until meat is tender. Drain and reserve broth. Cut meat into serving pieces. Place on hot platter and garnish with more dill sprigs. Serve with Dill Sauce and boiled potatoes. Makes 4 to 6 servings.

Dill Sauce

- 2 tablespoons butter or margarine
- 2 tablespoons all-purpose flour
- 1½ to 2 cups broth from lamb
- 2 tablespoons chopped dill
- 1½ tablespoons white vinegar
- 2 tablespoons sugar
- Salt to taste
- 1 egg yolk, beaten

Melt butter, add flour, and stir until smooth. Add hot broth gradually, and cook until mixture is thickened and smooth. Simmer, covered, for 10 minutes, stirring frequently. Add dill, vinegar, sugar, and salt to taste. Remove from heat and stir in beaten egg yolk. Serve hot.

JULSKINKA
(Christmas Ham)

Allow about 3½ weeks for a home-cured ham, or use a cured ham for baking.

Curing for Ham

- 1 fresh ham (10 to 12 pounds)
- 1 cup salt
- ¼ cup sugar
- 2 teaspoons saltpeter (from the drugstore)

To cure ham, prepare a large stone crock or a deep enamelware pan. Do not use aluminum. Combine salt, sugar, and saltpeter. Wipe fresh ham with a cloth. Rub salt mixture into the ham on all sides. Sprinkle any remaining salt mixture over ham. Place ham in crock. Let stand in a cool place or refrigerator for 3 days.

Brine

- 3 cups salt
- ½ cup firmly packed brown sugar
- 1 tablespoon saltpeter
- 2 teaspoons whole cloves
- 4 to 5 quarts boiling water

Add salt, sugar, saltpeter, and cloves to boiling water. Boil for 2 minutes. Cool.

WOMAN'S DAY

SWEDISH COOKERY

Kalvkotlett à la Oscar

SWEDISH COOKERY

Pour brine over ham in crock. Do not remove the previous salt mixture from ham. The ham should be completely covered by the brine. Place a plate weighted with some heavy objects on the ham to keep it down in the brine. Cover crock. Let ham stand for 3 weeks. Makes 8 to 10 servings.

Seasonings for Cooking Ham
Boiling water
3 bay leaves
12 peppercorns
12 whole allspice
1 medium onion

Remove ham from brine. Wash and drain thoroughly. Place ham in deep kettle and cover with boiling water, bay leaves, peppercorns, allspice, and onion. Simmer, covered, until ham is tender, 4 to 5 hours. Do not boil ham, but keep liquid just at simmering point. Remove ham from heat and let cool in liquid. Drain cooled ham. Trim off skin and excess fat. Place ham on rack in roasting pan.

Glaze
2 egg whites
2 tablespoons sugar
2 tablespoons powdered mustard
⅓ cup fine dry bread crumbs

To glaze ham, beat egg whites until they stand in soft peaks. Beat in sugar and mustard. Brush mixture over ham, fat side up, and cover well on all sides. Cover thinly but evenly with bread crumbs. Bake ham in preheated moderate oven (350°F.) for 35 to 45 minutes, or until glaze is brown. Remove ham to platter.

Garnish
Paper frills, parsley, soft butter

To garnish ham, garnish bone of ham with a paper frill and surround with parsley sprigs.

Note: If the ham is to be served cold, fill smallest pastry tube with softened butter and pipe decorative swirls and loops on ham. You might also write on it: *God Jul*, that is, Merry Christmas!

PYTT I PANNA
(Swedish Hash)
6 tablespoons butter or margarine
3 medium onions, diced
3 cups diced peeled boiled potatoes
3 cups diced leftover meat
Salt and pepper to taste
Fried eggs
Cucumber pickles, sliced

Heat 2 tablespoons of the butter and cook onions in it until soft and golden. Transfer to hot plate. Brown potatoes in 2 tablespoons butter and transfer to hot plate. Brown meat in remaining butter. Return onions and potatoes to skillet and mix thoroughly with meat. Season with salt and pepper and heat through. Arrange on hot platter and garnish with fried eggs (1 for each serving) and sliced cucumber pickles. Makes 4 to 6 servings.

FYLLD BLOMKÅL
(Stuffed Cauliflower)

The dish is good family fare and can be made with any favorite meat-loaf combination.

2 medium cauliflowers
1 pound ground meat (beef, pork, veal, or any combination)
½ cup fine dry bread crumbs
¾ cup chopped parsley
1 egg
1½ teaspoons salt
½ teaspoon pepper
Dash of hot pepper sauce
Aluminum foil
⅔ cup butter or margarine

Trim cauliflowers of green leaves. Turn upside down and with sharp knife scoop out main stalk to make cavity. Take care not to break off buds. Wash cauliflowers and cook in boiling salted water until just tender. Combine next 7 ingredients and blend thoroughly. Line baking dish with aluminum foil and butter heavily with half of butter. Fill cauliflower cavities with meat mixture. Place on aluminum foil, meat side down. Dot with remaining butter. Cover tightly with more aluminum foil so that cauliflower is completely covered. Bake in preheated moderate oven (350°F.) for 30 to 40 minutes. Place on hot platter and serve with tomato, mushroom, or curry sauce. Makes 6 servings.

VEGETABLES AND SALADS

SKÅNSK POTATIS
(Swedish Creamed Potatoes)
6 tablespoons butter or margarine
2 medium onions, sliced thin
6 cups diced peeled raw potatoes
1½ teaspoons salt
¼ teaspoon white pepper
1 cup light cream, or more*
3 tablespoons minced parsley or fresh dill

Heat 2 tablespoons of the butter in skillet and cook onions in it until soft and golden. Transfer onions to casserole. Heat remaining butter and sauté potatoes in it until golden-brown and half cooked. Transfer potatoes to casserole. Season with salt and pepper and mix thoroughly with onions. Add cream. Simmer, covered, over lowest possible heat for about 15 minutes, or until potatoes are done. The cream should be absorbed and the potatoes creamy. Stir occasionally and check for dryness; if necessary add more cream, a little at a time. Before serving, sprinkle with parsley. Makes 6 servings.

* It is impossible to give accurate amounts for cream. Different kinds of potatoes will absorb different amounts of cream, and the absorption of cream depends also on the shape of the casserole. However, the dish is very easy to make; all it needs is a little attention.

POTATIS OCH SVAMP
(Potatoes and Mushrooms)
4 cups hot mashed potatoes
2 eggs, beaten
1 teaspoon salt
½ teaspoon pepper
⅛ teaspoon ground cardamom
1 pound mushrooms, sliced
¼ cup butter or margarine (hot)
2 tablespoons melted butter
⅓ cup chopped chives or parsley

Combine potatoes, eggs, salt, pepper, and cardamom and mix thoroughly. Sauté mushrooms in hot butter until just limp. They must be still firm. Place mushrooms into the bottoms of 4 individual well-buttered baking dishes (4½ x 6 inches). Top with a border of mashed potatoes piped through a tube in decorative swirls. Or else, use a fork and score the border with the fork to make a pattern. Paint potatoes with melted butter and sprinkle with chives. Bake in preheated hot oven (425°F.) for about 15 minutes, or until potatoes are slightly browned. Or broil under medium broiler for about 5 minutes. Makes 4 servings.

RÖDBETSSALLAD MED ÄPPLEN
(Beet Salad with Apples)
1 jar (1 pound) pickled sliced beets
2 medium tart apples
2 tablespoons mayonnaise
1 tablespoon sugar
⅛ teaspoon salt
Freshly ground pepper
2 tablespoons chopped parsley

Drain beets and cut into strips ¼ inch thick. Peel apples and dice finely. Mix beets, apples, mayonnaise, sugar, salt, and pepper to taste. Toss ingredients lightly together. Garnish with chopped parsley. Serve with meat or fish. Makes 4 to 6 servings.

WOMAN'S DAY

KÅLSALLAD MED LINGON
(Cabbage Salad with Lingonberries)

- 2 cups finely shredded white cabbage
- ¾ cup lingonberries

Mix ingredients and toss lightly. Serve with any kind of meat. Especially good with broiled or fried liver, also with fried fish. Makes 4 servings.

SAUCES

SAUCES FOR FISH AND MEATS

Swedish cooks are famous for their sharp dill-flavored sauces and those in which mustard and wine combine for pungent good flavor. Many Scandinavian sauces are well known to American cooks, such as currant-jelly sauces for game, caper sauces for boiled fish, wine sauces for ham and game. But their piquant sauces created for shellfish and smoked salmon are among the great sauces of the world's cuisine. Here is the famous *Skarpsås* which is served with any cold fish or shellfish, and as dressing for meat and fish salads.

SKARPSÅS
(Sharp Dill Sauce)

- 1 cup wine vinegar
- 1 tablespoon fresh lemon juice
- ¼ cup sugar
- Dash of hot pepper sauce
- 1 tablespoon onion juice
- 1 tablespoon powdered mustard
- ⅛ teaspoon cayenne
- 2 tablespoons chopped fresh dill

Combine all ingredients in wide-mouthed bottle or glass jar and shake it well. Chill. Shake sauce again before using. Makes about 1½ cups.

KAPRISSÅS
(Caper Sauce)

For pork chops and for fried fish and meats

- 1 small onion, chopped
- 1 tablespoon butter
- 3 anchovy fillets, minced, or 2 teaspoons anchovy paste
- 3 tablespoons capers
- 3 tablespoons chopped parsley
- 1½ teaspoons all-purpose flour
- ½ cup chicken bouillon
- ½ cup mild vinegar

Brown onion in butter. Add anchovies, capers, and parsley. Stir in flour. Add bouillon and vinegar and simmer, covered, for 10 minutes, stirring frequently. (For a thinner sauce, add a little more bouillon.) If made for pork chops, pour sauce over chops before serving. If for fried fish or meats, serve separately. Makes about 1⅓ cups.

BREADS, DUMPLINGS, AND PANCAKES

RÅGBRÖD
(Rye Bread)

A very good, easy bread

- 1 cup milk
- 1 package active dry yeast or 1 cake compressed yeast
- 2 tablespoons sugar
- 1 cup water*
- 4½ cups all-purpose flour
- ¾ cup dark corn syrup
- 1 teaspoon fennel seeds
- 1 teaspoon aniseed
- ⅓ cup butter or margarine
- Grated rind of 1 orange
- 1½ teaspoons salt
- 3 cups rye flour
- Lukewarm water

Scald milk and cool to lukewarm. Sprinkle or crumble yeast and sugar into water. *Use very warm water (105°F. to 115°F.) for dry yeast; use lukewarm (80°F. to 90°F.) for compressed. Let stand for a few minutes, then stir until dissolved. Stir in milk. Beat in 3 cups of the all-purpose flour. Cover and let rise until doubled in bulk, 1 to 1½ hours. Combine syrup, fennel, and aniseed in saucepan and bring to boiling point. Cool to lukewarm. Beat syrup, butter, orange rind, and salt into risen batter. Stir in rye flour and 1 cup of the remaining all-purpose flour. Use remaining flour for kneading. Sprinkle some of remaining flour on bread board and turn dough onto it. Knead with floured hands until smooth and elastic. Place in greased bowl, turn to grease on all sides, and let rise until doubled in bulk, 30 minutes to 2 hours.

Shape dough into 2 loaves. Grease 2 bread loaf pans (9 x 5 x 3 inches) and place loaves in pans. Cover and let rise until doubled in bulk, about 50 minutes. Bake in preheated moderate oven (375°F.) for 35 minutes. Brush with lukewarm water and bake for 5 minutes longer.

SEMLOR
(Shrove Tuesday Buns)

Traditionally served on Shrove Tuesday and throughout Lent, and often accompanied by hot milk with cinnamon

- 1 package active dry yeast or 1 cake compressed yeast
- ¼ cup water*
- 1 egg, slightly beaten
- ⅔ cup light cream, lukewarm
- ¼ cup sugar
- 1 teaspoon salt
- ½ teaspoon ground cinnamon
- ½ cup butter or margarine, at room temperature
- 3 to 3¼ cups sifted all-purpose flour
- Almond paste
- Whipped cream
- Confectioners' sugar

Sprinkle or crumble yeast into water. *Use very warm water (105°F. to 115°F.) for dry yeast; use lukewarm (80°F. to 90°F.) for compressed. Let stand for a few minutes, then stir until dissolved. Stir in half of beaten egg (reserve other half), the cream, sugar, salt, cinnamon, and butter. Mix thoroughly. Add flour, a little at a time, and beat to make a soft dough. Turn out dough on floured surface and knead for about 10 minutes, or until dough is smooth and elastic. Place dough in greased bowl and turn to grease on all sides. Cover and let rise until doubled in bulk, 1 to 1½ hours. Punch down risen dough and knead on floured board until smooth. Shape dough into 10 or 12 round buns. Place buns on greased cookie sheet. Cover and let rise until almost doubled in size. Brush with reserved egg. Bake in preheated hot oven (400°F.) for 10 to 12 minutes, or until golden-brown. Cool on racks. Cut off tops of buns with a sharp knife. Insert a wafer-thin piece of almond paste into each bun. Top with whipped cream. Replace top of bun and sprinkle with confectioners' sugar. Makes 10 or 12.

POTATISBULLAR
(Swedish Potato Dumplings)

For soup or as a main course, served with butter or a sauce

- ¼ cup butter or margarine
- 2 egg yolks
- ½ cup fine dry bread crumbs
- ½ cup firmly packed cooked mashed potatoes
- ¼ teaspoon salt
- 1 cup ham or luncheon meat, diced into ½-inch cubes

Cream butter and beat in egg yolks. Stir in bread crumbs, potatoes, and salt. Mix thoroughly. Knead and shape into a long roll. Cut off pieces about the size of a walnut. Flatten each piece in the hand and place a cube of ham in middle. Shape into a round dumpling enclosing ham completely. Cook, uncovered, in simmering soup or simmering water for

ENCYCLOPEDIA OF COOKERY

SWEDISH COOKERY

10 minutes. Cover and cook for 5 minutes longer. Makes 6 servings.

PLÄTTAR
(Pancakes)

The delicious small pancakes served in Swedish restaurants in America are almost as popular as the smorgasbord specialties. Special plättar *pans are now available in our housewares and kitchen supply shops, and by mail order; some are tagged with a little booklet containing recipes for these delicate dessert pancakes. Here is the recipe which serves 6 people.*

- 2 eggs
- 3 cups milk
- 3 teaspoons sugar
- 1⅓ cups sifted all-purpose flour
- 1 teaspoon salt
- Melted butter for plättar pan

Beat eggs and combine with milk, beating well; add sugar, flour, and salt gradually, beating well. Heat pancake pan slowly; brush with melted butter. Stir batter, pour into depressions in pan, and bake until browned on one side. With small spatula turn cakes to brown other side. Cakes should be thin, with crisp edges, and delicately browned all over. For each serving arrange 6 hot pancakes in a circle on a warmed plate; put a mound of confectioners' sugar in the center. Serve lingonberries or lingonberry jam, Swedish pack if possible. Makes 2¾ cups batter, about forty 3-inch pancakes.

CAKES, PASTRIES, AND COOKIES

MARÄNGSUISSE
(Cream Meringue Torte)

Meringue confections are one of the glories of Swedish baking. This torte can be put together with a cream filling or with sweetened whipped cream and fruit, such as raspberries, strawberries, or blueberries.

Cake
- ¾ cup butter or margarine
- ¾ cup sugar
- 6 eggs (yolks are used for cake, whites for meringue)
- 1 teaspoon vanilla extract
- ½ teaspoon almond extract
- 1¼ cups plus 1 tablespoon sifted all-purpose flour
- 1½ teaspoons baking powder
- ¼ teaspoon salt
- ½ cup milk
- Meringue
- Orange Filling or Fancy Lemon Filling
- Whipped Cream Topping
- 1 cup toasted slivered almonds

With electric blender at low speed cream together butter and sugar for 3 minutes. Beat in egg yolks, one at a time, and then beat for 3 minutes longer. Stir in vanilla and almond flavorings. Sift together flour, baking powder, and salt. Add to batter alternately with milk. Grease and flour three 9-inch layer-cake pans. Distribute batter among pans and smooth with knife or spatula. Spread Meringue evenly on top of the cake batter in the 3 pans. Bake in preheated slow oven (300°F.) for 45 to 50 minutes, or until cakes test dry. Cool on racks. Remove carefully from pans and brush free of crumbs.

Meringue
- 6 egg whites
- 1 cup sugar
- ½ teaspoon vanilla extract
- ½ cup finely ground almonds or walnuts

Beat egg whites until stiff and dry. Use an electric beater. Gradually beat in sugar. Fold in vanilla and ground nuts.

Orange Filling
- ⅓ cup all-purpose flour
- 1 cup sugar
- ⅛ teaspoon salt
- ¼ cup water
- 1½ cups fresh orange juice
- ¼ cup fresh lemon juice
- 2 tablespoons grated orange rind
- 1 tablespoon grated lemon rind
- 4 egg yolks, beaten

Combine flour, sugar, salt, and water and blend until smooth. Add fruit juices and rinds. Cook until mixture thickens and is smooth and almost transparent, stirring constantly. Stir a small amount of the hot filling into the egg yolks. Return to saucepan and cook over low heat for 3 minutes longer, stirring constantly. Remove from heat and beat until cool.

Fancy Lemon Filling
- 1 tablespoon cornstarch
- ½ cup sugar
- ½ cup water
- Grated rind and juice of 2 small lemons
- 4 egg yolks, beaten

Combine cornstarch and sugar. Blend with water to a smooth paste. Stir in lemon rind and juice. Blend in beaten egg yolks. Cook over lowest possible heat until filling is thick, stirring constantly. Beat until cooled.

Whipped Cream Topping
- 1½ to 2 cups heavy cream, chilled
- 2 tablespoons sugar
- 2 teaspoons vanilla extract

In chilled bowl and with chilled beater whip cream until stiff. As cream begins to thicken, beat in sugar and vanilla.

■ **Assembling the Meringue Torte**—Just before serving, place 1 cake layer on cake plate, meringue side up. Cover with ⅓ of the Orange Filling. Top with second layer, meringue side up. Repeat process, always placing layers meringue side up. Frost the top and sides of the torte with Whipped Cream Topping and sprinkle with toasted slivered almonds. Serve as soon as possible, and keep under refrigeration until serving time. Makes about 8 servings.

TUSENBLADSTÅRTA
(Thousand Leaves Torte)

A rich, handsome, and worthwhile Swedish specialty. It is important that the layers be very thin and crisp and that the applesauce used be made of tart and well-flavored apples. If the apples are too mild in flavor, the Torte will be too bland.

Torte
- 2 cups sifted all-purpose flour
- 1 cup cold butter
- 4 tablespoons ice water

Sift flour into mixing bowl. With pastry cutter or 2 knives, cut in butter until pieces are of the size of peas. While mixing with fork, add ice water gradually. Toss until dough just holds together. With hands, and handling as little as possible, shape into a ball. Chill for 30 minutes to 1 hour. Meanwhile, prepare both fillings.

Applesauce Filling
- 1½ cups thick, tart, and well-flavored applesauce

Custard Cream Filling
- 1½ teaspoons unflavored gelatin
- 2 tablespoons cold water
- 2 egg yolks
- 3 tablespoons sugar
- 1½ tablespoons cornstarch
- 1 cup light cream
- 1 teaspoon vanilla extract
- 1 cup heavy cream, whipped

Sprinkle gelatin on cold water to soften. In top part of a double boiler combine egg yolks, sugar, cornstarch, and light cream. Cook over simmering, not boiling, water until smooth and thick, stirring constantly. Remove from heat and beat in gelatin and vanilla. Stir until gelatin is dissolved. Cool, beating occasionally. Fold in heavy cream. Chill. While Custard Cream Filling is chilling, make Lemon Icing.

Lemon Icing
- 2 tablespoons fresh lemon juice
- 1 cup sifted confectioners' sugar

Stir lemon juice gradually into confectioners' sugar, a little at a time, beating constantly, until spreading consistency has been achieved.

■ **Assembling Thousand Leaves Torte**— Divide chilled dough into 6 portions. Use 1 portion at a time; keep others in refrigerator until used. Roll each portion between 2 sheets of wax paper to a 9-inch circle. Use a 9-inch layer-cake pan to measure circle, and trim off excess dough. Slide each layer onto a cookie sheet and peel off carefully the top sheet of wax paper. Prick with fork all over or layers will bunch during baking. Brush layers with iced water and sprinkle with 1 tablespoon sugar. Bake in preheated hot oven (425°F.) for 6 to 8 minutes, or until golden-brown. Cool on cookie sheets. Carefully peel off the bottom sheet of wax paper. Sandwich layers together by spreading first layer with Applesauce Filling, second layer with Custard Cream Filling, third layer with Applesauce, fourth layer with Custard Cream Filling, and fifth layer with Applesauce. Reserve top layer.

■ **Garnishing Thousand Leaves Torte**
- ½ cup candied orange peel
- ½ cup blanched almonds
- 1 cup heavy cream
- 1 teaspoon sugar
- ½ teaspoon vanilla extract

Cut orange peel into strips. Ice top layer with Lemon Icing and place on top of other torte layers. Arrange orange peel strips in star pattern in the middle of the top layer. Toast almonds and chop coarsely. Sprinkle almonds around outer edge of cake. Whip cream with sugar and vanilla. With a pastry tube make rosettes of whipped cream on sides of torte, or frost sides with a spatula. Makes 10 to 12 servings.

MAZARINTÅRTA
(Mazarin Torte)

One of the most famous of Swedish cakes

Dough:
- 1⅓ cups sifted all-purpose flour
- 1 teaspoon baking powder
- ⅓ cup sugar
- ½ cup butter
- 1 egg

Into deep bowl sift together flour, baking powder, and sugar. Cut in butter and add egg. Mix together and knead with hands or spoon into a smooth dough. Chill while preparing Filling.

Filling:
- ½ cup butter
- ⅔ cup sugar
- 1 cup ground blanched almonds
- ½ teaspoon vanilla extract
- 2 eggs
- ⅔ cup raspberry jam

Cream butter; add sugar gradually and beat until fluffy. Add almonds and vanilla. Add eggs, one at a time, beating well after each addition.

■ **Assembling Mazarin Torte**—Roll out chilled dough between 2 sheets of wax paper to fit bottom of 9-inch springform pan. Cut remaining dough into a strip and line sides of pan with it. Bring the dough at the bottom of the pan and the dough on the sides together so that they are tightly joined. This is done to prevent filling from oozing out during baking. Spread ⅓ cup of the raspberry jam over dough at bottom of the pan. Top with filling. Bake in preheated moderate oven (350°F.) for about 50 minutes, or until torte tests done. Cool torte for 10 minutes. Remove sides of springform pan and let torte cool entirely. When cold, spread with remaining ⅓ cup jam. Dribble Lemon Icing (at left) over top of jam. Makes 10 servings.

RÅGKAKOR
(Rye Rings)

The amount of rye flour may have to be increased a little since different flours have different rates of absorption of liquids.

- 1 cup butter or margarine
- ½ cup sugar
- 1 cup rye flour
- 1½ cups (about) sifted all-purpose flour

Cream butter and gradually add sugar. Stir in rye flour first; mix thoroughly. Then add other flour. Chill dough for 30 minutes. Work with a little of the dough at one time; keep remaining dough in refrigerator until ready to handle. Knead dough slightly and roll out as thinly as possible between 2 sheets of wax paper. Prick surface with fork all over. Cut out rounds with 2- or 3-inch cookie cutter. Cut center from cookies with thimble. Place cookies on buttered and floured cookie sheet, using spatula. Bake in preheated moderate oven (350°F.) for 8 to 10 minutes, or until golden. Cool on cookie sheets. Makes about thirty 3-inch cookies.

PUNSCHKAKOR
(Punch Rings)

- ½ cup butter or margarine
- 1¼ cups sifted all-purpose flour
- 2 tablespoons Swedish punch or rum
- 1 egg, beaten
- ½ cup finely chopped almonds
- 2 tablespoons sugar

Cream butter until fluffy. Add flour and Swedish punch. Mix thoroughly with spoon or with hands. Roll out on wax paper to strips ½ x 4 inches. Shape strips into rings. Brush with egg. Combine almonds and sugar and sprinkle on top of cookies. Bake on buttered and floured cookie sheets in preheated moderate oven (350°F.) for 8 to 10 minutes, or until golden. Makes about 9 dozen.

MORMOR'S SYLTKAKOR
(Grandmother's Jelly Cookies)

A traditional Swedish Christmas cookie, consisting of a large cookie topped with a smaller one

- ½ cup butter, at room temperature
- ⅓ cup sugar
- 1 egg, separated
- 1¼ cups sifted all-purpose flour
- ¼ teaspoon salt
- ¼ cup finely chopped blanched almonds
- ¼ cup sugar
- Currant jelly

Cream butter and gradually add sugar. Beat in egg yolk, flour, and salt. Blend thoroughly. On floured surface roll out to about ¼-inch thickness. The dough must be rolled thinly. Divide dough. Cut one portion of the dough with 2⅓-inch round cookie cutter. Cut the other portion of the dough with a round or scalloped 2-inch cookie cutter. Remove center of 2-inch cookies with a thimble. Beat egg white slightly. Combine almonds and sugar. Brush each 2-inch cookie (those with the hole) with egg white and sprinkle with almond-sugar mixture. Place on buttered and floured cookie sheets almond side up. Bake all cookies in preheated moderate oven (375°F.) for 6 to 8 minutes. Do not let brown. Cool cookies on racks. Place about ½ teaspoon currant jelly on bigger cookie and top with smaller cookie, almond side up. The jelly should appear in the hole in the center of the top cookie. Makes about 12 cookies.

SWEETBREAD

KANELKAKOR
(Swedish Cinnamon Cookies)

These cookies are not the usual Central European cinnamon stars which are made with white of egg. They are very tender and flavorful cookies.

- ⅔ cup butter
- 1 cup sugar
- 1 egg
- 1 teaspoon vanilla extract
- 1⅓ cups sifted all-purpose flour
- 1 teaspoon each of baking powder and ground cinnamon
- ½ cup walnuts, finely chopped
- 2 tablespoons each of ground cinnamon and sugar, mixed

Cream butter and gradually add 1 cup sugar. Beat in egg and vanilla. Sift flour with baking powder and 1 teaspoon cinnamon. Add to egg mixture and blend thoroughly. Chill for 30 minutes. Combine walnuts and mixed cinnamon and sugar. Roll chilled dough into balls the size of walnuts. Roll each ball in walnut-cinnamon sugar. Place cookies on greased and floured cookie sheets about 3 inches apart. Bake for about 12 minutes in preheated moderate oven (350°F.). Makes about 3 dozen cookies.

GLÖGG
(This is the Swedish Christmas drink.)

- 3 whole cardamoms
- 8 whole cloves
- 1 cinnamon stick
- 4-inch strip of orange rind (yellow part only)
- 1⅓ cups water
- ¼ cup blanched almonds
- ½ cup golden raisins
- 1 bottle (24 ounces) Bordeaux wine
- 1 bottle (24 ounces) port
- ½ bottle (1-pint size) brandy
- Sugar to taste

Tie cardamoms, cloves, cinnamon, and orange rind in a cheesecloth bag. Place in water and bring to a boil. Simmer, covered, for 10 minutes. Add almonds and raisins and simmer for 10 minutes longer. Add Bordeaux wine, port, and brandy and bring to a quick boil. Remove from heat immediately. Cool, and store, covered, overnight. At serving time, remove spice bag. Heat *Glögg* but do not boil. Add sugar to taste. Serve in heated mugs or glasses, with a few almonds and raisins in each glass. Makes about 20 punch-cup servings.

SWEETBREAD—The thymus glands of lamb, veal, or young beef (under 1 year; the thymus disappears in mature beef). Sweetbreads consist of two parts: the heart sweetbread and the throat sweetbread. Lamb and veal sweetbreads are white and tender; beef sweetbreads are redder in color and a little less tender.

Availability and Purchasing Guide—Widely available year round fresh and frozen.

Fresh sweetbreads should be absolutely fresh when purchased; this means firm and clear in appearance.

Storage—Sweetbreads are very perishable and should be used at once. They may be precooked and kept covered in the refrigerator but even so they should be used quickly. If frozen, keep frozen until ready to use.

☐ Fresh, refrigerator shelf, raw or cooked: 1 day
☐ Frozen, refrigerator frozen-food compartment: 2 to 3 weeks
☐ Frozen, freezer: 3 to 4 months

Nutritive Food Values—A good source of protein.

☐ Young beef, 3½ ounces, raw = 207 calories
☐ Young beef, 3½ ounces, cooked = 320 calories
☐ Veal, 3½ ounces, raw = 94 calories
☐ Veal, 3½ ounces, cooked = 168 calories
☐ Lamb, 3½ ounces, raw = 94 calories
☐ Lamb, 3½ ounces, cooked = 175 calories

Basic Preparation—Sweetbreads should be precooked before using them in recipes. Put in a saucepan with water to cover. Add 1 teaspoon salt and 1 tablespoon vinegar or fresh lemon juice for each 4 cups of water used. (The acid helps to keep the sweetbreads white and firm.) Simmer for 20 minutes. Then, hold sweetbreads under cold running water and slip off membrane with fingers. Cut out dark veins and thick connective tissue. Cut very thick sweetbreads into halves lengthwise. Use at once or refrigerate.

☐ **To Broil**—Precook sweetbreads as directed above. Split them and brush with melted butter or cooking oil. Sprinkle with salt and pepper. Then broil about 3 inches from broiler unit until golden-brown, 4 to 6 minutes on each side. Spread with soft butter or margarine.

☐ **To Sauté**—Precook sweetbreads as directed above; then split. Dip into fine dry bread crumbs or cracker crumbs, then into beaten egg, then again into crumbs. Sauté in hot butter or margarine in skillet until delicately browned on both sides. Serve with lemon quarters.

CREAMED SWEETBREADS

- 1 pair large sweetbreads
- 1 large onion, minced
- 12 medium mushrooms, sliced
- 6 tablespoons butter or margarine
- ¼ cup all-purpose flour
- 1 teaspoon salt
- ½ teaspoon curry powder
- 2½ cups light cream
- 1 tablespoon brandy
- ¼ cup sherry

Prepare sweetbreads as in Basic Preparation (at left). Break into pieces. Cook onion and mushrooms in the butter for 5 minutes. Blend in flour and seasonings. Gradually add cream and cook, stirring constantly, until thickened. Add sweetbreads, brandy, and sherry; heat. Makes 4 servings.

SWEETBREADS, NORMANDY STYLE

- 3 pairs sweetbreads
- ½ pound mushroom caps
- 6 tablespoons butter
- Salt and pepper to taste
- 3 ounces Calvados or applejack
- 1 cup light cream
- 2 egg yolks
- Sautéed Apples

Prepare sweetbreads as in Basic Preparation (at left). Cut into ¼-inch slices. Slice mushroom caps. Melt butter in a large skillet. Add sweetbreads and let them sauté for 10 minutes. Add mushrooms, and continue cooking until mushrooms are tender. Season with salt and pepper. Remove to a hot platter. Add Calvados to the pan, then the cream mixed with egg yolks. Stir until thickened, being careful mixture does not boil. Pour over the sweetbreads, and serve with Sautéed Apples. Makes 6 servings.

Sautéed Apples

Peel 5 cooking apples; slice thinly. Sauté in butter until soft but not mushy.

SWEETBREAD AND CUCUMBER SALAD

- 1 pair sweetbreads
- Salted water
- 1 onion, sliced
- 2 whole cloves
- ⅓ bay leaf
- 1 parsley sprig
- 1 lemon slice
- 2 cucumbers
- 3 celery stalks, chopped very fine
- Mustard-flavored mayonnaise
- Green pepper and pimiento, chopped (optional)

Poach sweetbreads in salted water, together with the onion, cloves, bay leaf, parsley, and lemon, for 20 minutes. Remove sweetbreads. Hold under cold running water and slip off membrane with fingers. Cut out dark veins and thick connective tissue. Cut sweetbreads into bite-size pieces and chill. Peel and seed 1 cucumber and cut into small dice. Add the celery and sweetbreads and toss with a mayonnaise flavored lightly with mustard. Arrange on greens and garnish with the second cucumber, peeled, seeded, and chopped. Chopped green pepper and pimiento can be added if desired. Makes 4 servings.

WOMAN'S DAY

SWEET CICELY (Myrrhis odorata)—A perennial plant with aromatic leaves which are excellent, finely chopped, in salads and stews. The leaves have a mild aniselike flavor. The seeds can be eaten fresh. This herb is said to improve the flavor of all other herbs with which it is combined. The seeds are especially good in beverages and cordials, fruit salads, and fruit cups.

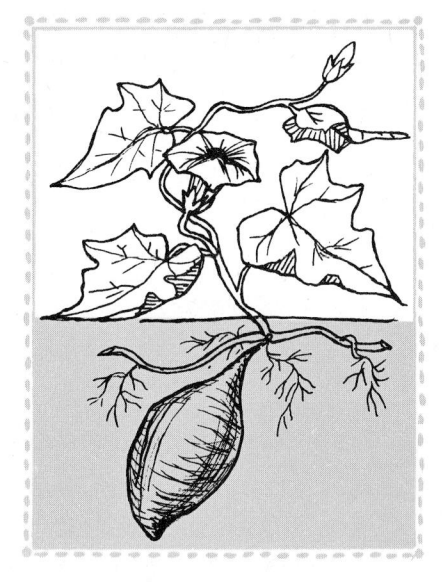

SWEET POTATO—The enlarged or swollen roots of a perennial vine of the morning-glory family. There are hundreds of varieties with skins of many colors although yellow tones predominate. They can be slender or globular, forked or beet-shape. The flesh is usually yellow-red, but some sweet potatoes are white. The majority are sweet, but there are also sweet potatoes which are no sweeter than a white potato. Some sweet potatoes have a jellylike consistency, while others are so dry that they have to be moistened with butter or a lubricant in order to be swallowed.

The sweet potato, *Ipomoea Batatas*, is often confused with the yam which it resembles. Yams, however, belong to the completely different botanical genus *Dioscorea*. For the cook, sweet potatoes and yams are interchangeable in recipes.

The sweet potato is a truly native American vegetable, from the tropical parts of the continent. The Indians cultivated them long before the coming of the white man. Sweet potatoes grew in colonial gardens in the South. From the Americas they traveled to such countries as the South Seas, China, Japan, and Indonesia, where they have become an indispensable and basic food. Sweet potatoes have given the name "potato" to the white variety, but in tropical America *Batatas* invariably means the sweet potato. The same is true for our southern states, where sweet potatoes are an important staple food. There, a "potato" is a sweet potato and a white potato is an "Irish potato."

Availability and Purchasing Guide—All year round fresh, canned, dehydrated, and also frozen. There are two main types of sweet potatoes, the dry meaty type and the moist-flesh type. Varities of the dry meaty type are: Little Stem Jersey, Big Stem Jersey, Yellow Jersey, Gold Jersey. Varieties of the moist-flesh type are: Nancy Hall, Puerto Rica. The dry meaty type is of a very light yellow or orange flesh. The moist-flesh type ranges from light yellow to orange-reddish tint and is much sweeter.

Select smooth plump potatoes that are clean, dry, and uniform in shape and color.

Storage—Refrigerate; or store at room temperature if a cool dry place is available.
- Refrigerator shelf, raw: 1 month
- Refrigerator shelf, cooked and covered: 4 to 5 days
- Refrigerator frozen-food compartment, prepared for freezing: 2 to 3 months
- Freezer, prepared for freezing: 1 year
- Canned, kitchen shelf: 1 year
- Canned, refrigerator shelf, opened but covered: 4 to 5 days
- Dried, kitchen shelf: 6 to 8 months

Nutritive Food Values—Excellent source of ascorbic acid and vitamin A.
- 3½ ounces, baked in skin = 141 calories
- 3½ ounces, boiled in skin = 114 calories
- 3½ ounces, candied = 168 calories
- Canned, 3½ ounces, syrup pack = 114 calories
- Canned, 3½ ounces, dietary pack = 46 calories
- Dehydrated, 3½ ounces, reconstituted with water = 95 calories

Basic Preparation—Scrub and trim off woody or bruised portions. Sweet potatoes are usually cooked before peeling.
- **To Boil**—Cook in boiling salted water to cover. Cover and boil until tender, 20 to 30 minutes. Drain; remove skins. Cooked potatoes are then mashed, candied, glazed, etc.
- **To French-Fry**—Boil for 10 minutes only; drain, peel, and cut into strips.
- **To Bake**—Grease the skins of clean potatoes and bake in preheated hot oven (400°F.) for 30 to 40 minutes. Potatoes that are greased before baking peel easily.
- **To Charcoal-Broil**—Grease sweet-potato skins. Wrap double foil loosely around potatoes. Cook in coals for about 45 minutes. Keep warm on edge of grill.
- **To Panroast**—Peel sweet potatoes and cover with boiling salted water. Cook for 10 minutes. Drain and put in pan with meat for 1 hour before meat is done. Baste 4 or 5 times with pan drippings.
- **To Freeze**—Wash potatoes and cook by any method until just tender. Dip cooled slices or whole sweet potatoes into a solution of ½ teaspoon ascorbic acid and 5 cups cold water. Add 2 tablespoons fresh orange or lemon juice to each 4 cups mashed sweet potatoes. For candied sweet potatoes, after dipping pieces or whole potatoes, roll them in brown or granulated sugar.

Pack into freezer containers, leaving ½-inch headspace.

SWEET POTATO COOK BOOK

SOUPS

CHICKEN AND SWEET-POTATO SOUP
- 1½ quarts chicken bouillon
- 1 cup diced cooked chicken
- 2 carrots, diced
- ¾ cup diced celery
- 1 onion, thinly sliced
- 4 medium sweet potatoes, peeled and diced
- ⅛ teaspoon each of ground thyme and poultry seasoning
- Seasoned salt and pepper to taste

In kettle mix all ingredients except salt and pepper. Bring to boil. Simmer, covered, for about 25 minutes. Season with salt and pepper. Makes about 2 quarts.

SWEET POTATO GUMBO
- ¼ cup ham drippings
- 1 large onion, chopped
- 4 chicken bouillon cubes
- 3½ cups water
- 2⅓ cups (one 1-pound, 3-ounce can) tomatoes
- 2 cups (one 1-pound can) sliced okra, drained
- 2 cups (one 1-pound can) peas, undrained
- 4 sweet potatoes, cooked, peeled, and diced
- ½ teaspoon crumbled dried thyme

SWEET POTATO COOK BOOK

Heat drippings in kettle. Add onion and cook until golden. Add remaining ingredients; simmer, covered, for 30 minutes. Makes 2½ quarts.

CREAM-OF-SWEET-POTATO SOUP
- 3 sweet potatoes
- 2 cups chicken bouillon
- 1 teaspoon sugar
- ⅛ teaspoon each of ground nutmeg and cloves
- 1½ cups milk
- Salt to taste

Peel and slice potatoes. Add to bouillon and bring to a boil. Simmer, covered, for about 20 minutes, or until tender. Force through food mill or purée in blender. Reheat with remaining ingredients. Serve hot, or chilled with a dollop of sour cream. Makes 1 quart.

MAIN DISHES

VEAL WITH SWEET POTATOES IN SOUR-CREAM SAUCE
- 2 pounds veal cutlet, cut ¼ inch thick
- 1½ teaspoons salt
- 3 tablespoons all-purpose flour
- 3 tablespoons butter or margarine
- 1 onion, chopped
- ¼ cup chopped parsley
- 1 teaspoon paprika
- 2 teaspoons prepared mustard
- 1 chicken bouillon cube
- 1½ cups boiling water
- 6 sweet potatoes, peeled and halved
- 1 cup dairy sour cream

Cut veal into serving pieces and dredge with seasoned flour. Brown on both sides in hot butter. Add onion and brown lightly. Add parsley, paprika, mustard, and bouillon cube dissolved in water. Cover and simmer for about 35 minutes. Add potatoes. Cook, covered, for 30 minutes longer, or until meat and potatoes are tender. Remove to a hot platter. Add cream to liquid in skillet and heat. Pour over meat and potatoes. Makes 6 servings.

TURKEY AND SWEET-POTATO CASSEROLE
- 3 tablespoons butter or margarine
- 3 tablespoons all-purpose flour
- 1½ teaspoons salt
- ¼ teaspoon pepper
- ⅛ teaspoon poultry seasoning
- 2 cups milk
- 1 cup grated Cheddar cheese
- 2 cups diced cooked turkey
- 12 small white onions, cooked
- 6 sweet potatoes, cooked, peeled, and halved

Melt butter and blend in flour and seasonings. Gradually add milk and cook, stirring constantly, until thickened. Add cheese. Stir until melted. Fold in remaining ingredients and put in 2-quart casserole. Bake in preheated moderate oven (350°F.) for 30 minutes. Makes 6 servings.

PORK-CHOP AND SWEET-POTATO SKILLET
- 4 pork chops
- 1 tablespoon shortening
- Salt and pepper to taste
- ¼ teaspoon each of ground thyme and marjoram
- 1 onion, sliced
- 4 sweet potatoes, peeled, and sliced
- 1 green pepper, cut into rings
- 2⅓ cups (one 1-pound, 3-ounce can) tomatoes

Brown chops on both sides in shortening in skillet. Season with salt, pepper, and herbs. Top with onion, potatoes, and green pepper; add tomatoes. Cover; cook slowly for 45 minutes. Makes 4 servings.

BAKED CHICKEN AND SWEET POTATOES
- 1 frying chicken (about 3 pounds), cut up
- Salt and pepper to taste
- Fine dry bread crumbs
- 1 egg
- 3 tablespoons water
- 4 sweet potatoes, cooked and peeled
- ½ cup butter, melted

Sprinkle chicken with salt and pepper. Roll in crumbs. Beat egg and water together. Dip chicken into egg mixture and roll again in crumbs. Put in shallow baking dish or pan without piling up pieces. Put sweets around chicken. Baste with half of butter. Bake in preheated hot oven (400°F.) for about 1 hour, basting several times with remaining butter. Makes 4 servings.

SAUSAGE-APPLE BAKE
- 3 cups mashed cooked sweet potatoes
- 1 cup applesauce
- 2 eggs, beaten
- ½ teaspoon salt
- ½ teaspoon ground cinnamon
- ¼ teaspoon ground nutmeg
- 1 pound link sausages

Mix all ingredients except sausages. Put in shallow 1½-quart baking dish. Cook sausage until browned. Arrange on ingredients in baking dish. Bake in preheated moderate oven (350°F.) for about 30 minutes. Makes 4 servings.

SWEET-POTATO AND ROAST-BEEF HASH

Mix 2 cups chopped cooked sweet potatoes and 2 cups chopped cooked roast beef. Season to taste with salt and pepper. Add ¼ cup roast-beef gravy. Brown on both sides in a little shortening. Makes 4 servings.

CANDIED SWEET POTATOES AND HAM BALLS
- 1 egg
- ½ cup water
- ⅓ cup instant powdered cream
- 1½ cups soft stale-bread crumbs
- 1 teaspoon powdered mustard
- 2 cups ground cooked ham
- 4 sweet potatoes, cooked, peeled, and halved
- ¾ cup firmly packed brown sugar
- ¼ cup vinegar

Beat egg lightly; add ⅓ cup of the water, the cream, crumbs, ½ teaspoon mustard, and the ham. Mix well and shape into 12 balls. Put in large shallow baking dish, making 1 layer only. Arrange potatoes around edge. Mix sugar, remaining mustard and water, and the vinegar. Pour over ham balls and potatoes. Bake in preheated moderate oven (375°F.) for about 45 minutes, basting several times with the syrup in bottom of dish. Makes 4 servings.

SIDE DISHES

BROWN-SUGAR CANDIED SWEET POTATOES
- 4 medium sweet potatoes
- Salt
- ¾ cup firmly packed brown sugar
- ⅓ cup water
- 2 tablespoons butter or margarine

Cook sweet potatoes until tender. Peel, halve, and sprinkle with salt. In skillet mix sugar, water, and butter. Bring to boil. Put potatoes in syrup and cook over low heat, turning occasionally, until potatoes are candied, about 15 minutes. Makes 4 servings.

Maple-Candied Sweet Potatoes
For syrup in above recipe substitute ½ cup maple syrup and ¼ cup butter or margarine. Add 1 teaspoon aromatic bitters to syrup with potatoes.

Flambéed Sweet Potatoes
Follow recipe for Candied Sweet Potatoes. Just before serving, lightly heat ½ cup brandy. Pour over the sweet potatoes and ignite.

SWEET-POTATO SOUFFLÉ
- 1 cup milk
- ½ teaspoon salt
- 2 teaspoons sugar
- 2 tablespoons butter or margarine
- 2 cups mashed sweet potatoes
- 2 eggs, separated
- ½ cup raisins
- ½ teaspoon ground nutmeg
- ½ cup chopped walnuts
- 15 marshmallows

Scald milk with salt, sugar, and butter. Add to potatoes and beat well. Beat egg yolks and add to potato mixture. Stir in raisins, nutmeg, and nuts. Beat egg whites until stiff and fold into mixture. Pour into 1½-quart casserole. Top with marshmallows. Bake in preheated slow oven (325°F.) for 45 minutes, or until set. Makes 6 servings.

SWEET-POTATO TOURNEDOS
Select sweet potatoes about 2 inches in diameter, or use canned. Cook fresh potatoes until tender; peel, and cut into pieces 2 inches long. Wrap a thin slice of bacon around each potato slice and fasten with a toothpick. Put in shallow baking

SWEET POTATO COOK BOOK

pan and bake in preheated very hot oven (450°F.) for 15 minutes; turn once.

CREAMED SWEET POTATOES
- 2 cups diced cooked sweet potatoes
- 2 tablespoons butter or margarine
- 1½ tablespoons all-purpose flour
- ⅛ teaspoon each of pepper and paprika
- ½ cup milk
- 1 bouillon cube
- ½ cup hot water

Cook sweet potatoes in butter for 5 minutes. Sprinkle with flour, pepper, and paprika. Add milk and bouillon cube dissolved in hot water. Simmer, covered, for 20 minutes. Makes 4 servings.

ALMOND PORCUPINES
- 4 cups mashed cooked sweet potatoes
- 2 tablespoons butter or margarine, melted
- 1½ teaspoons salt
- ½ teaspoon ground cinnamon
- 1 egg
- Slivered blanched almonds
- ½ cup apple butter

Beat together potatoes, butter, salt, cinnamon, and egg. Shape into 8 mounds with spoon, or from pastry bag, on greased cookie sheet. Insert a few almond slivers in each. Bake in preheated hot oven (400°F.) for about 20 minutes. Put a spoonful of apple butter in center of each. Makes 8 servings.

Brazil-Nut Porcupines
Cover 3 or 4 shelled Brazil nuts with cold water, bring to boil, and simmer for 2 or 3 minutes. Drain and cut into slivers. Substitute for almonds in recipe above.

ORANGE SWEET POTATOES
- 4 medium sweet potatoes
- ¼ cup firmly packed brown sugar
- 2 tablespoons butter or margarine
- Grated rind of 1 orange
- ¼ cup fresh orange juice
- ½ teaspoon salt
- ⅛ teaspoon pepper

Cook sweet potatoes. Peel and mash while hot. Add brown sugar, butter, orange rind and juice, salt, and pepper. Whip. Put in baking dish. Brown lightly under broiler. Makes 4 servings.

SCALLOPED SWEET POTATOES AND APPLES
- 2 cups sliced peeled cooked sweet potatoes
- 2 tart apples, peeled and sliced
- ½ cup firmly packed brown sugar
- ¼ cup butter or margarine
- 1 teaspoon salt

Put alternate layers of potatoes and apples in shallow baking dish. Sprinkle each layer with sugar. Dot with butter and sprinkle with salt. Cover and bake in preheated moderate oven (350°F.) for 45 minutes. Uncover and bake for about 10 minutes longer. Makes 4 servings.

SCALLOPED SWEET POTATOES AND CHESTNUTS
- 4 medium sweet potatoes
- 1 pound chestnuts
- Salt
- ¾ cup firmly packed brown sugar
- ¼ cup hot water
- ¼ cup butter or margarine

Cook, peel, and halve sweet potatoes. Cover chestnuts with boiling water. Simmer, covered, for about 20 minutes. Rinse in cold water and remove shells and skins. Keep nuts in large pieces and arrange with sweets in shallow baking dish. Sprinkle with salt. Bring to boil brown sugar and hot water. Add butter. Pour over ingredients in casserole. Bake, uncovered, in preheated moderate oven (350°F.) for 30 minutes. Makes 4 to 6 servings.

SWEET-POTATO MARSHMALLOW BALLS
- 2 pounds sweet potatoes
- Salt to taste
- ¼ teaspoon ground cinnamon
- Dash of ground nutmeg
- 1 tablespoon all-purpose flour
- 6 marshmallows
- Fat for deep frying

Cook, peel, and mash potatoes. Add salt, spices, and flour. Cool; shape mixture around marshmallows to form balls. Fry in deep hot fat (375°F. on a frying thermometer) until browned. Makes 3 or 4 servings.

SCALLOPED SWEETS AND CRANBERRIES
- 6 sweet potatoes
- 1½ cups whole-berry cranberry sauce
- ¾ cup water
- ½ cup firmly packed brown sugar
- ¾ teaspoon grated orange rind
- ¾ teaspoon ground cinnamon
- 1½ tablespoons butter

Cook and drain potatoes. Peel; cut into halves lengthwise and arrange in baking dish. In saucepan mix remaining ingredients except butter. Simmer, uncovered, for 5 minutes. Add butter; stir until butter is melted. Pour over potatoes and bake, uncovered, in preheated moderate oven (350°F.) for 20 minutes, or until glazed and hot. Makes 6 servings.

SWEETS À LA RECTOR
- 8 medium sweet potatoes, cooked
- ½ cup firmly packed brown sugar
- 2 tablespoons butter or margarine
- ½ teaspoon salt
- ¼ teaspoon paprika
- ½ cup sherry

Peel and slice potatoes. Arrange in shallow baking dish. Sprinkle with sugar and dot with butter. Add seasonings and sherry. Bake in preheated moderate oven (350°F.) for about 30 minutes. Makes 6 servings.

HOME-FRIED SWEET POTATOES
Cook 4 medium sweet potatoes. Peel and slice about ¼ inch thick. Melt ¼ cup margarine in skillet, add potatoes, and cook slowly, turning to brown evenly. Sprinkle with salt, and a little sugar if desired. Makes 4 servings.

SWEET POTATOES WITH TOMATOES
Line a greased pie pan with mashed sweet potatoes and cover with halves of peeled tomatoes. Season with salt, pepper, and celery salt to taste. Cover with more sweets and dot with butter. Bake in preheated slow oven (325°F.) for 1 hour.

MASHED SWEET POTATOES AND YELLOW TURNIPS
Cook 2 cut-up peeled medium sweet potatoes and 3 cups diced yellow turnips in boiling salted water until tender, about 25 minutes. Drain and mash. Add salt and pepper to taste, 3 tablespoons butter or margarine, and ¼ cup hot milk. Beat until smooth. Makes 4 servings.

SWEET POTATOES WITH MINCEMEAT
Bake 6 medium sweet potatoes as directed for Baked Sweet Potatoes, page 1795. Remove pulp from shells and mash with 1 tablespoon butter and 1 teaspoon salt. Add 1 cup prepared mincemeat. Fill custard cups with mixture and bake in preheated slow oven (325°F.) for 30 minutes, or until lightly browned. Makes 4 to 6 servings.

PEANUT SWEET POTATOES
- 4 medium sweet potatoes
- ⅔ cup milk
- ¼ cup peanut butter
- ½ teaspoon salt
- ½ cup chopped salted peanuts

Wash sweet potatoes, and bake in preheated moderate oven (350°F.) for 45 minutes, or until done. Cut potatoes into halves and remove potato from shells. Reserve shells and mash potato. Beat in milk, peanut butter, and salt. Refill shells with the mixture and sprinkle with chopped peanuts. Put on baking sheet and brown lightly in oven. Makes 4 servings.

BREADS, PANCAKES, AND STUFFING

LOUISIANA PANCAKES
- 1½ cups sifted all-purpose flour
- 3½ teaspoons baking powder
- 1 teaspoon salt
- ½ teaspoon ground nutmeg
- 1¼ cups mashed cooked sweet potatoes
- 2 eggs, beaten
- 1½ cups milk
- ¼ cup butter, melted

Sift dry ingredients into bowl. Combine remaining ingredients and add to flour. Mix only until blended. Drop by tablespoonfuls onto hot greased griddle and fry until browned. Makes 24 pancakes.

SWEET-POTATO BISCUITS
- 1½ cups sifted all-purpose flour
- 4 teaspoons baking powder
- ¾ teaspoon salt
- ½ cup shortening
- ¼ cup milk
- 1¼ cups mashed cooked sweet potatoes
- 5 slices of crisp bacon, crumbled

SWEETSOP

Sift dry ingredients; cut in shortening. Combine remaining ingredients and add to first mixture. With fork, mix until soft dough is formed. Roll or pat to ½-inch thickness on floured board. Cut with floured 2½-inch cutter. Bake in preheated hot oven (425°F.) for 15 minutes, or until golden. Makes 10 to 12.

SWEET-POTATO DOUGHNUTS
- 2 eggs, beaten
- ¾ cup sugar
- 3 tablespoons shortening
- ¾ cup mashed cooked sweet potatoes
- ¼ cup milk
- 3½ cups sifted all-purpose flour
- 4 teaspoons baking powder
- ½ teaspoon salt
- ¼ teaspoon each of ground nutmeg and cinnamon
- Fat for deep frying

Combine first 4 ingredients and beat until well blended. Add milk and sifted dry ingredients; mix well. Chill for 1 hour, or until firm enough to roll. Roll on lightly floured board to ½-inch thickness and cut with floured 3-inch cutter. Fry in deep hot fat (375°F. on a frying thermometer) until golden-brown and done. Drain. Makes 30.

SWEET-POTATO WAFFLES
- 2 cups sifted all-purpose flour
- 3 teaspoons baking powder
- 1 teaspoon salt
- ¼ teaspoon ground cinnamon
- 3 eggs, separated
- 1½ cups milk
- ¾ cup mashed cooked sweet potatoes
- ¼ cup butter or margarine, melted
- ⅓ cup chopped nuts
- Maple syrup

Sift together flour, baking powder, salt, and cinnamon. Beat egg whites until stiff. Beat egg yolks; add milk and potatoes. Beat until blended. Add to dry ingredients with butter and mix well. Fold in egg whites and nuts. Bake. Serve hot with syrup. Makes 4 to 6 servings.

SWEET-POTATO SAVORY STUFFING
- ½ pound sausage
- 1 onion, minced
- ½ cup diced celery
- ¼ teaspoon poultry seasoning
- ½ teaspoon salt
- Dash of pepper
- 1½ cups soft stale-bread cubes
- 2 cups mashed cooked sweet potatoes

Cook sausage until half done, breaking up meat with fork. Add onion, celery, poultry seasoning, salt, and pepper. Cook, stirring constantly, until sausage is cooked. Add bread cubes and potatoes. Mix well. Use as stuffing for poultry or pork. Makes 4 cups.

DESSERTS

SWEET-POTATO APPLE CRISP
- 2½ cups (1-pound, 4-ounce can) apple slices
- 2 cups very thin slices of peeled sweet potatoes
- 1 teaspoon ground cinnamon
- ½ teaspoon salt
- 2 tablespoons fresh lemon juice
- ½ cup unsifted all-purpose flour
- ½ cup firmly packed brown sugar
- ⅓ cup butter or margarine

Drain apples; add enough water to juice to make 6 tablespoons liquid. Alternate layers of apples and potatoes in shallow 1½-quart baking dish. Sprinkle with mixed cinnamon and salt. Mix liquid and lemon juice; pour over first mixture. Combine flour and sugar; cut in butter. Sprinkle over top. Cover and bake in preheated moderate oven (350°F.) for 30 minutes. Uncover and bake for 15 minutes longer. Makes 6 servings.

SPICY SWEET-POTATO PUDDING
- 6 sweet potatoes
- ¾ cup cane or corn syrup
- 1 egg
- 3 tablespoons butter or margarine, melted
- 1 cup milk
- ½ cup all-purpose flour
- ½ teaspoon ground nutmeg
- 1 teaspoon ground cinnamon
- ¾ teaspoon salt

Peel and grate potatoes, 1 cup at a time. Add syrup to prevent darkening. There should be 4 cups in all. Add egg, butter, and milk. Sift in dry ingredients and mix well. Pour into 1½-quart casserole. Bake, uncovered, in preheated slow oven (300°F.) for about 2½ hours, stirring every 30 minutes for first 2 hours. Makes 4 to 6 servings.

GOLDEN CHEESECAKE
- 1⅔ cups fine graham-cracker crumbs
- ⅓ cup butter or margarine, melted
- 2 envelopes unflavored gelatin
- ½ cup water
- ¾ cup sugar
- ½ teaspoon salt
- ⅓ cup milk
- 3 eggs, separated
- 2 packages (8 ounces each) cream cheese
- 1¼ cups puréed cooked sweet potatoes
- 1 cup heavy cream
- 2 teaspoons vanilla extract
- 1 teaspoon grated orange rind

Mix crumbs and butter; reserve ¼ cup and press remainder onto bottom of 9-inch springform pan. Chill. Soften gelatin in cold water in top part of a small double boiler. Add ½ cup sugar, the salt, milk, and slightly beaten egg yolks. Cook, stirring constantly, over boiling water until slightly thickened. Pour over cheese and potatoes; beat until smooth and blended. Cool. Beat egg whites until foamy; add ¼ cup sugar and beat until stiff. Whip cream and fold into first mixture with egg whites. Add flavorings. Pour into prepared pan. Sprinkle with reserved crumbs. Chill until firm.

SWEET POTATO-PECAN PIE
- ¼ cup soft butter
- ¼ cup firmly packed brown sugar
- ⅛ teaspoon salt
- 3 eggs
- ¾ cup dark corn syrup
- 1¼ cups mashed cooked sweet potatoes
- 1 teaspoon vanilla extract
- 1½ cups pecans
- Pastry for 1-crust 9-inch pie, unbaked

Cream butter and sugar. Beat in salt, eggs, corn syrup, sweet potatoes, and vanilla. Add 1 cup of the nuts and pour into pastry-lined pie pan. Sprinkle remaining nuts over top. Bake in preheated moderate oven (375°F.) for 50 to 55 minutes. Cool. Makes 6 to 8 servings.

MOLASSES DROP COOKIES
- ½ cup butter or margarine
- ¼ cup sugar
- 1 egg
- ½ cup light molasses
- 1 cup grated raw sweet potatoes
- 1 teaspoon grated orange rind
- 2 cups sifted all-purpose flour
- ½ teaspoon each of salt and baking soda
- 1 teaspoon baking powder
- ½ teaspoon ground ginger
- ⅓ cup buttermilk
- 1 cup sliced pitted dates
- ½ cup chopped nuts

Cream butter and sugar. Beat in egg, molasses, sweet potatoes, and orange rind. Sift together flour, salt, baking soda, baking powder, and ginger. Add to egg mixture alternately with buttermilk. Mix well. Add dates and nuts. Drop by teaspoonfuls onto greased cookie sheets. Bake in preheated moderate oven (375°F.) for 12 to 15 minutes. Makes 48 cookies.

SWEETSOP—A small tropical American tree and its sweet pulpy fruit. Also called the sugar apple, the skin of the heart-shape fruit is yellow-green, thick and rough. It is custardlike and very sweet, similar to the cherimoya but not so piquant in flavor. Numerous dark-brown or black seeds are embedded in the pulp. The sweetsop is eaten raw, and used for desserts and ices.

Grown in southern Florida and California, the fruit is in season from midsummer to about December and is available in limited supplies in local food stores in the areas where it is grown.

SWISS CHARD—Another name for chard, a type of beet which does not develop the fleshy roots of ordinary beets. It is grown for its large leaves which have thickened midribs and are used as are other green vegetables.

SWISS COOKERY

by James A. Beard

Jellied open-faced sandwiches; fish and meats; cheese, egg, and potato dishes; tempting pastries; all acquire a unique flavor in Switzerland's cosmopolitan cuisine.

SWISS COOKERY

Eating the Swiss way is an interesting and varied experience, for the cuisine of Switzerland is most cosmopolitan. Although the Swiss have for centuries been a firmly independent people, peacefully cultivating their mountain-rimmed valleys and minding their own business, they are a people banded together from three distinct national cultures. There are German Swiss, French Swiss, and Italian Swiss. There is also a fourth Switzerland, Romanic or Romansh Switzerland, to use the local dialect. It is part of the Grisons, in the eastern part of the country, centered in the region that contains the famous resort of St. Moritz. The people of these valleys speak a distinctive language derived from Latin, and they have many original recipes.

In spite of the many generations of being united, the country is still trilingual and Swiss cooking is trilingual, too. Around Lausanne and Geneva the cuisine is similar to French. Around Bern and Zurich it has overtones of German and Austrian cooking. In the Savoy region, bordering on the lakes, it takes on a distinct Italian flavor. In addition, Switzerland has developed some special and unique favorites of her own. Being a lush dairy country, Swiss cuisine includes many dishes lavish with cheese, cream, and butter. Veal and young beef liver are exceptionally good and used in interesting ways. And the Swiss make tasty unusual dishes with fine beef.

OPEN SANDWICHES

SWISS OPEN-FACE SANDWICHES

Among the most attractive foods found in all sections of Switzerland are the open sandwiches. They are served in Zurich, in Bern, in Lausanne, in practically every town. They are made with squares or rounds of rye bread, firm white bread, pumpernickel, almost any good bread you choose. The pieces of bread are topped with a great variety of meats, fish, cheese, and garnishes and then each one is delicately coated with a gelatin aspic to keep it firm and fresh. An array of these sandwiches is a most appetizing and colorful mosaic.

To make, spread the bread with a seasoned butter, add toppings of your choice, and an appropriate garnish. (See suggestions below.) Chill the sandwiches well, and then brush each lightly with meat-flavored aspic made with canned beef broth or jellied consommé with a little more gelatin added to make it firm. Do not cake the sandwich heavily with aspic; give it just a gentle coating so that it will have a sparkling finish. A wide pastry brush or paint brush does a good job.

Seasoned Butters

Cream butter before spreading on bread and add one of the following to ½ cup soft butter:

- 2 teaspoons powdered mustard and 1 teaspoon prepared mustard
- 1 teaspoon finely chopped sweet or sour pickle
- 2 teaspoons anchovy paste or finely chopped anchovy
- 2 teaspoons chopped onion and 2 teaspoons finely chopped green pepper
- 2 teaspoons finely chopped peeled seeded tomato and ½ teaspoon fresh or crumbled dried basil
- 1 finely chopped garlic clove and 2 teaspoons minced parsley
- ½ teaspoon fresh or crumbled dried rosemary and 2 teaspoons minced onion
- 2 tablespoons finely chopped cooked shrimps and 1 tablespoon finely chopped parsley with 1 teaspoon fresh lemon juice

TOPPINGS

- Paper-thin slices of prosciutto with a green-olive garnish
- Thin slices of baked ham with a garnish of 2 tiny asparagus tips
- Slices of thinly cut salami arranged in a pattern and garnished with a tiny gherkin or pickled onion
- Slices of white meat of chicken, garnished with a tiny wedge of tomato or a green-pepper ring centered with a slice of stuffed olive
- Small shrimps nicely arranged on a thin spread of mayonnaise and topped with a tiny rosette of mayonnaise and a tiny sprig of parsley
- Thin slice of rare roast beef with a small bowknot of pimiento and a slice of gherkin
- Anchovy fillets with a slice of hard-cooked egg and a caper
- Thin slices of smoked salmon with an onion ring and capers
- Rolls of thinly sliced bologna with black and green olives speared on a toothpick
- Thin slices of chicken-liver pâté topped with a small pickle
- Whole boneless skinless sardines with a slice of lemon and a slice of hard-cooked egg
- Thin slices of smoked sturgeon with a dash of red caviar and a cucumber slice
- Thin fillets of herring with a thin slice of dill pickle
- Alternating slices of tongue and Swiss cheese with prepared mustard and a thin slice of tomato
- Fillets of smoked eel with a bit of chopped onion, parsley, and capers
- Thin rounds of lobster with a green-pepper ring and a slice of hard-cooked egg
- Rare roast beef on a spread of mustard butter and topped with a rosette of mustard butter

Garnishes

- Stuffed egg
- Crisp fried onion rings
- Switzerland Emmentaler or Gruyère cut into fine julienne strips
- Roquefort-cheese-flavored mayonnaise
- Tiny pickled capers
- Slices of raw mushroom

FISH AND MEAT

BASLER LACHS
(Sautéed Salmon)

2 medium onions, thinly sliced
6 tablespoons butter
All-purpose flour
4 salmon steaks
Salt and pepper to taste
Juice of ½ lemon
Sherry
Lemon slices

Sauté onions in 4 tablespoons of the butter until evenly browned. Remove onions and keep warm. Add remaining butter. Lightly flour salmon steaks, season, and brown evenly on both sides in the hot butter. Cook until fish flakes easily when tested with a toothpick or fork. Add lemon juice and transfer fish to hot platter. Add a little sherry to the pan to rinse it. Spoon onion on salmon steaks and pour sauce over all. Garnish with lemon slices. Makes 4 servings.

POISSON EN PAPILLOTE
(Fish Baked in Foil)

In Switzerland the fish might be perch or trout or other lake or stream fish. Choose any local fresh fish that is available.

Foil or parchment
Cooking oil
6 to 8 small whole fish, cleaned
3 tablespoons chopped parsley
¼ cup chopped mushrooms
Salt and pepper to taste
2 tomatoes, peeled and sliced
6 to 8 lemon slices

Cut 6 to 8 heart-shape pieces of foil large enough to hold the fish with some room left for expansion. Place a well-oiled fish to one side of each piece of paper. Sprinkle with parsley, mushrooms, and salt and pepper. Top with a slice of tomato and a slice of lemon. Fold over the other half of the foil or parchment to envelop the fish, and crimp the edges together to make the package airtight. Arrange the *papillotes* in a baking pan and bake in preheated hot oven (400°F.) for 20 to 25 minutes. Place the fish in their envelopes on plates and serve. Makes 6 to 8 servings.

Ramequins au Fromage

Croquettes au Fromage

Bernerplatte

SWISS COOKERY

THON EN SALADE
(Tuna Salad Plate)

- 2 cans (7 ounces each) tuna fish
- ¾ cup mayonnaise
- Lettuce
- 4 tomatoes, peeled
- 8 ripe olives
- 4 hard-cooked eggs
- 1 garlic clove
- 1 teaspoon paprika or curry
- Parsley or capers

Break up tuna with fork. Toss with ¼ cup mayonnaise and form into a mound in center of serving plate. Surround with lettuce, tomato wedges, olives, and quartered eggs. Crush garlic and mix with ½ cup mayonnaise. Sieve the dressing and add paprika. Pour over tuna and garnish with parsley. Makes 4 servings.

STUFATO
(Braised Beef)

A beef dish from southern Switzerland

- 1 teaspoon crumbled dried rosemary
- 2 cups dry red wine
- 1 teaspoon salt
- 1 onion stuck with 2 cloves
- 1 bay leaf
- 1 celery stalk
- 1 parsley sprig
- 3 to 4 pounds of bottom round or chuck roast, rolled and tied
- 1 marrowbone
- 2 or 3 bacon strips, cut into small bits
- 1 small onion
- All-purpose flour
- Broth, wine, or water
- 3 tablespoons butter, melted
- 3 tablespoons all-purpose flour
- 1 cup dairy sour cream

Combine rosemary, red wine, salt, onion stuck with cloves, bay leaf, celery, and parsley. Marinate the meat and the marrowbone in this mixture overnight or at least for 8 to 10 hours. The longer it marinates, the better. Render the bacon pieces. Remove the bits and reserve. Brown the second onion in the remaining fat. Remove the meat and bone from the marinade and wipe them dry. Dust with flour and brown in the onion-flavored fat. Remove the meat. Pour off the fat. Strain the marinade.

Place the meat on a rack in a kettle. Add the marinade, bacon bits, and enough broth to cover. Simmer, covered, on top of stove or in preheated slow oven (300°F.), allowing 30 to 35 minutes per pound. Turn the meat twice during cooking. When it is tender remove it to a hot platter. Take the marrow from the marrowbone. Reduce the sauce over high heat until it measures about half of its original amount. Skim off the excess fat, add the marrow, and thicken with butter and flour blended. Taste for seasoning. Then stir in the sour cream, and heat. Pass the sauce separately and serve sautéed mushrooms and boiled potatoes. Makes 6 to 8 servings.

Note: *Stufato* is also excellent when cooled, pressed, and served cold.

FILET DE BOEUF À LA SUISSE
(Roast Beef)

- 1 filet of beef (3 to 4 pounds)
- Cooking oil
- 1 cup dry red wine
- Salt and pepper

Heat the oven to very hot (475°F.). Rub the filet well with oil and arrange on a rack in a roasting pan. Roast for 15 minutes and then baste with the wine. Season to taste. Roast for another 15 minutes. Baste with the pan juices and additional red wine. Roast for 10 minutes more. Baste again and let stand for 10 minutes. Makes 8 to 12 servings.

BIFTECKS TARTARE
(Tartar Sandwiches)

- 1 pound filet of beef without fat
- Thin slices of pumpernickel
- Mustard butter
- Onion rings
- 1 hard-cooked egg

Accompaniments:
- Minced onion
- Capers
- Chopped parsley
- Mustard
- Worcestershire
- Salt and pepper

Chop the beef fairly fine. Spread the bread slices, toasted or not as you choose, with mustard butter and then spread on very smoothly the chopped raw beef. Garnish each with an onion ring and a slice of egg and serve with the accompaniments. Makes 4 servings.

■ **Variation**—You can combine the beef with the seasonings and blend in 1 raw egg. Mix well and spread on bread or toast. Garnish with onion ring, sliced egg, capers, and chopped parsley.

ROGNONS BOLO
(Flambéed Kidneys)

- 3 tablespoons butter
- 2 tablespoons cooking oil
- 4 veal kidneys with most of the fat removed, cut into ½-inch slices
- All-purpose flour
- Salt and pepper to taste
- ⅓ cup brandy
- 1 teaspoon Dijon mustard
- Juice of ½ lemon
- Hot cooked rice

Heat butter and oil in a chafing dish or skillet until very hot. Dust kidneys lightly with flour and brown quickly on each side. Season with salt and pepper and flame with heated brandy. Remove to a hot serving dish and add mustard and lemon juice to the pan. Blend and spoon over the kidneys. Serve with rice. Makes 4 to 6 servings.

BERNER LEBERLI
(Sautéed Liver Bernese)

- 8 thin slices (1½ pounds) young beef liver
- 2 cups milk
- All-purpose flour
- 8 slices of bacon
- ¼ cup butter
- Salt and pepper
- Juice of ½ lemon
- 8 leaves of fresh sage
- 8 lemon slices

Soak liver in milk for 30 minutes. Remove, wipe dry, and roll in flour. Sauté bacon and keep warm. Pour off fat. Melt butter in same skillet and heat until bubbly. Sauté the liver gently, turning once to brown on both sides. Season to taste. Remove to a hot platter. Add lemon juice to pan. Pour over liver. Garnish with bacon, sage, and lemon slices; serve with Rösti (page 1804). Makes 4 servings.

GESCHNETZELTES
(Minced Veal)

- ⅓ cup butter
- 3 tablespoons minced onion
- 1½ pounds veal cutlet, ½ inch thick, cut into 1-inch strips
- All-purpose flour
- Salt and pepper to taste
- 1 teaspoon chopped fresh or ¼ teaspoon crumbled dried tarragon
- ½ cup dry white wine
- 1 tablespoon fresh lemon juice
- ½ cup dairy sour cream

Heat butter in a heavy skillet. Sauté onion in it until just wilted. Dredge veal strips lightly with flour and add them to the pan. Brown evenly. Season with salt and pepper and add tarragon and wine. Cover and cook gently for 4 minutes. Add lemon juice. Toss the veal in the seasonings and sauce and test for tenderness. When done, slowly stir in sour cream. Heat through, but do not boil. Makes 6 servings.

Note: This dish should be served with noodles, dressed with butter and chopped parsley.

CÔTELETTES DE PORC AU FROMAGE
(Pork Chops with Cheese)

Allow 2 pork chops per person and sauté them until nicely browned on both sides and done through. Grill the same number of thick slices of tomato and top with thin slices of Swiss or Gruyère cheese to melt at the last minute. Serve each chop with a tomato on top and a little cream sauce if you like.

BRATWURST
(Cooked Sausage)

This sausage appears on almost every Swiss menu. It is of very fine texture, delicately flavored, and varies in size from 4 to 7 inches. It may be broiled until crisply browned or sliced and sautéed in butter. It is sometimes sold in the streets of Zurich with big hard rolls to accom-

SWISS COOKERY

pany it and good mustard, a delicious snack on a brisk day.

I find bratwurst available in many areas of this country. Try it the Swiss way, sautéed, served with onions sautéed in butter until brown and tender, mashed potatoes, and sometimes sauerkraut. Or try it as a tasty addition to your outdoor grill menus. Grill it over charcoal and serve with mustard, fresh corn on-the-cob, and hot French bread.

BERNERPLATTE
(The Dish from Bern)

This is the Swiss version of the French choucroute garnie. *In short, it is sauerkraut surrounded with a variety of smoked meats and sausage.*

For 6 persons, drain and rinse 3 pounds fresh sauerkraut. Place in a large pot lined with strips of salt pork or bacon, add 5 or 6 juniper berries, some pepper, 1 cup beer or white wine, and 1 cup broth or water. Bring to a boil, cover the pot, lower the heat, and simmer for 2 to 3 hours. Heap the sauerkraut on a large platter; surround it with any or all of the following meats, and serve with boiled potatoes and a variety of mustards.

1. Smoked loin of pork, sliced. This can be purchased in most areas across the country. Roast it in preheated slow oven (325°F.) for about 15 minutes per pound.

2. Slices of boiled or baked ham.

3. Half-inch slices of cooked salt pork or pickled pork. For the last 1½ hours of cooking add to the sauerkraut a 2-pound piece of the pork with even streaks of fat and lean.

4. A selection of sausages. In Switzerland, the selection would probably include bratwurst, simple coarse pork sausages, and perhaps *saucisson de Frankfort,* which to us is frankfurter. The sausages can be braised or added to the sauerkraut. Cooking time varies from 30 minutes for large sausages to about 10 minutes for the frankfurter.

MIXED GRILL

This is one of the most popular of all Swiss entrées and is found in all sections of the country. Its combinations may vary but it always has a selection of 4 or 5 broiled meats usually with a broiled mushroom cap and a broiled tomato for garnish.

1. A small half slice of beef filet grilled rare; a slice of veal cutlet grilled to well done; Brockwurst or other sausage, grilled; a kidney (lamb or veal), grilled; a strip of bacon.

2. A cut of calf's liver, grilled; a small pork chop, well done; 2 or 3 mushroom caps; a small lamb chop.

3. Veal sweetbreads; a cut of filet of beef; chicken livers; a pork sausage; 1 or 2 slices of bacon.

Note: These are usually served with watercress and *Rösti* (page 1804). The mixed grill may also be prepared on an outdoor grill.

GEFÜLLTES BROT
(Stuffed Bread)

- 2 cups ground cold meat (rare beef, ham, pork, veal, or a combination; or a combination of ground chicken, gizzards, and livers)
- 2 pickles, finely chopped
- 3 tablespoons minced onion
- 3 tablespoons minced parsley
  Dash of hot pepper sauce
- 2 hard-cooked eggs, chopped
- 1 tablespoon Worcestershire Mayonnaise
- 1 large loaf well-crusted French or Vienna bread
  Butter

Mix ground meat with next 6 ingredients. Bind well with mayonnaise so that you have a stiff paste. Cut both ends from the loaf of bread; with fork, remove the crumbs, leaving a shell about ½ inch thick. Brush the interior well with soft butter and then force the meat mixture into the bread firmly so that it has no air holes in it. Wrap in foil and keep in refrigerator for several hours before slicing. Makes 6 servings.

FONDUES

FONDUE
(Melted Cheese Dish)

- 1 garlic clove
- 2 cups dry white wine
- 1 pound Swiss cheese, finely cut
- 1 teaspoon cornstarch
- 3 tablespoons kirsch, brandy, applejack, or vodka
  Pinch of ground nutmeg
  Dash of hot pepper sauce
- 2 loaves Italian or French bread with hard crust, cut into bite-size pieces, each of which must have at least one side of crust

Rub an enameled metal casserole with garlic. Pour in wine and set over low heat. Heat until air bubbles rise to the surface. Add cheese by handfuls, stirring constantly with a wooden spoon or fork. Keep stirring until the cheese is melted. Dissolve cornstarch in kirsch and add it to the cheese mixture. Stir again for 2 or 3 minutes and season with nutmeg and hot pepper sauce. Place casserole on the table on a hot plate, over an alcohol burner, or on a hot tray to keep it faintly bubbling. Guests spear pieces of bread on fondue forks and dip them into the cheese. Tradition says that if a lady drops bread into the fondue the men at the table may kiss her; if a man drops bread into the cheese, he may kiss any girl he chooses. Makes 6 servings.

FONDUE BOURGUIGNONNE
Tiny cubes of beef sautéed in peanut oil, then dipped into sauce

- 1 cup butter and 1 cup peanut oil or 2 cups oil and no butter
- 2½ pounds filet of beef, well trimmed and cut into ½-inch cubes

Melt butter in a fondue pan over an alcohol burner or in an electric skillet. Add oil and heat thoroughly. Give each guest 2 long-handled, two-pronged fondue forks (one for cooking and one for eating). Warn them not to eat with the fork they use in cooking or they may burn themselves severely. Each guest spears a piece of meat and cooks it to suit his taste; rare, medium, or well done. He then dips the meat into any of several sauces and eats. Sauces may include Béarnaise or Bordelaise (page 1766), barbecue sauce, or any favorites that you choose. With this meat dish go potatoes and a good salad. Allow a generous ¼ pound of beef per person. This recipe serves 6 to 8. Prepare at least 1 cup of each kind of sauce.

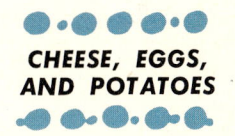

CHEESE, EGGS, AND POTATOES

CROQUETTES AU FROMAGE
(Cheese Croquettes with Green Noodles)

- ½ pound green noodles
- ⅓ cup butter
- ½ pound Gruyère, cut into strips 2 inches by 1 inch
- 1 egg, beaten
  Fine dry bread crumbs
  Olive or peanut oil
- ½ cup grated Romano cheese
- 2 tablespoons chopped parsley
  Pine nuts
  Paprika

Cook noodles in boiling salted water until just tender. Drain and combine with butter. Dip strips of cheese into egg and roll in crumbs. Brown in hot oil. Sprinkle Romano cheese and parsley on noodles in a serving dish. Arrange cheese croquettes on the noodles and sprinkle with pine nuts and paprika. Makes 4 to 6 servings.

STEAK DE FROMAGE
(Batter-Fried Cheese)

- 1 pound Swiss or Gruyère cheese
  Beer Batter
  Butter
- 8 eggs
- 2 teaspoons water
  Dash of hot pepper sauce
  Salt and pepper to taste

Cut slices of cheese 3 x 5 inches and ½ inch thick. Dip into Beer Batter and sauté in butter to brown on both sides. Arrange in a baking pan (15 x 10 inches). Beat eggs well; add remaining

SWISS COOKERY

ingredients. Pour over cheese and bake in preheated moderate oven (375°F.) for about 12 minutes. Makes 6 servings.

Beer Batter

Combine 2 slightly beaten eggs, ⅔ cup beer, and ¼ teaspoon hot pepper sauce. Slowly beat in 1 cup all-purpose flour, ½ teaspoon salt, and 2 tablespoons cooking oil.

KÄSESALAT
(Cheese Salad)

- ½ pound Swiss cheese (Emmentaler)
- 6 hard-cooked eggs
- ¾ cup dairy sour cream
- 1½ teaspoons Dijon mustard
- ½ teaspoon powdered mustard
- 1 teaspoon prepared horseradish
- Salt and pepper to taste
- 1 teaspoon grated lemon rind
- 1 teaspoon caraway seeds
- Greens

Cut cheese into ½-inch cubes; chop eggs coarsely. Combine and toss with sour cream and seasonings. Arrange on a bed of greens. Makes 4 servings.

OEUFS AU FOUR
(Baked Eggs)

- 6 eggs
- 2 large onions
- ¼ cup butter
- 2 cups rich cream sauce
- 2 tablespoons fresh lemon juice
- 3 tablespoons chopped parsley or
- ⅔ cup grated Swiss cheese

Hard-cook the eggs and remove the shells. Keep the eggs hot. Slice the onions rather thickly. Cook in butter for 10 to 12 minutes, or until just tender. Drain, reserving drippings. Prepare the rich cream sauce using the onion drippings as part of the liquid. Arrange eggs and onions in buttered casserole. Add the lemon juice to the sauce and pour over the mixture. Top with parsley and bake in preheated moderate oven (375°F.) for 15 to 20 minutes. Makes 4 servings.

OEUFS À LA CRÈME
(Eggs with Cream Sauce)

- Butter
- 8 eggs
- 8 tablespoons heavy cream
- Salt and fine pepper to taste
- 1 cup grated Swiss cheese

Use shirred-egg dishes or small individual casseroles and butter them well. Into each dish break 2 very fresh eggs. Pour 2 tablespoons heavy cream over the whites in each dish. Season with salt and pepper and sprinkle a wreath of grated cheese over each egg white. Bake in preheated moderate oven (350°F.) for 15 to 20 minutes. Makes 4 servings.

GNOCCHI
(Dumplings)

- 1 recipe Pâte à Choux
- 2 cups rich cream sauce
- ¼ pound (1 cup) Swiss or Gruyère cheese, grated

Drop teaspoonfuls of Pâte à Choux (or force it through a pastry bag with a plain tube, cutting off 1-inch pieces) into boiling salted water. Poach for about 5 minutes, or until puffy and cooked. Drain well. Put in a baking dish. Pour cream sauce over and sprinkle with grated cheese. Bake in preheated moderate oven (375°F.) for 15 to 20 minutes, or until cheese is melted and lightly browned. Makes 4 servings.

Pâte à Choux

Place ¼ cup butter and ½ cup hot water in a heavy saucepan over medium heat; when butter melts and water boils, add ½ cup all-purpose flour and ¼ teaspoon each of salt and sugar. Stir vigorously until the mixture leaves the sides of the pan. Beat in 2 eggs, one at a time, until the mixture is waxy and shiny.

RÖSTI
(Home-Fried Potatoes)

New, very waxy potatoes should be boiled in their jackets or baked, although the former is desirable as baked ones will require much more butter. Cool the cooked potatoes, peel, and grate them coarsely. A rounded-edge 8-inch skillet or sauté pan is the preferred one. The small black iron pans are excellent. Melt a little lard or shortening in the pan. Add 1½ to 2 cups of the grated potatoes and cook over brisk heat, shaking the pan from time to time. Add bits of butter, in all about 1 tablespoon, to the potatoes and push the potatoes over the butter with a spatula, lifting the edge of the potatoes to see if they are becoming too brown on the bottom. Continue shaking the pan. When they are nicely browned on the bottom, turn the potatoes with a heavy spatula and continue in the same manner on the other side. You may have to add additional butter. Press the potatoes more firmly so that you have a beautifully browned cake which will slide out of the pan easily. Each cake will serve 2 or 3.

Note: Sometimes a little grated onion is added to the Rösti; at other times, grated Gruyère or sapsago cheese.

PASTRIES

KUCHENTEIG
(Tart Pastry)

Use for tart shells or open fruit pies

- 2 cups unsifted all-purpose flour
- 3 tablespoons sugar
- ¾ cup butter or margarine
- 1¼ teaspoons grated lemon rind
- 3 hard-cooked egg yolks, mashed
- 2 raw egg yolks
- ½ teaspoon salt

Make a well in center of flour, working on a table or in a bowl. Put all remaining ingredients in well. Butter should not be ice cold, nor so soft it is oily. Using fingertips, make a paste of center ingredients, gradually incorporating flour to make a firm smooth ball of paste. Work as quickly as possible so butter won't become greasy. When bowl or table top has been left clean, chill dough until firm enough to roll between sheets of wax paper.

Note: To use this pastry for quickies, hors-d'oeuvre, etc., omit the sugar and lemon rind.

RAMEQUINS AU FROMAGE
(Cheese Tartlets)

- Standard pastry, 2-cups flour recipe, unbaked
- 2 cups grated Swiss cheese
- 1 cup milk
- 2 eggs
- ¼ teaspoon salt
- ¼ teaspoon powdered mustard
- Dash of hot pepper sauce

Line well-greased 3-inch tartlet pans, 1 inch deep, with pastry. Beat together cheese, milk, eggs, salt, mustard, and hot pepper sauce. Half fill tartlet shells with mixture. Bake in preheated hot oven (425°F.) for 15 minutes. Makes 16.

BEIGNETS SOUFFLÉS
(Fritters)

Prepare 1 recipe of Pâte à Choux (at left). Heat cooking oil in a deep fryer to 370°F. on a frying thermometer. Drop in the dough by spoonfuls, or make small balls with lightly floured hands. Fry in hot oil until brown and puffy. They may be kept warm in a medium oven until ready to serve, but are best served freshly made. Roll in granulated sugar and serve quite hot, or serve with a raspberry syrup, or flambé with heated brandy and additional sugar. Makes 16.

REHRUECKEN
(Chocolate Almond Torte)

This torte is sometimes called a "larded saddle of venison" because it is baked in a loaf pan with a rounded bottom, and when inverted its shape and brown color resemble a saddle of meat. The traditional boat-shape rehruecken *pan comes in 10½ inches or double that size. If you do not have such pans use regular loose-bottomed layer-cake pans.*

- Butter (about ⅓ cup)
- Fine dry bread crumbs
- 5 eggs, separated
- 2 whole eggs
- ½ cup granulated sugar
- ½ teaspoon ground cinnamon
- 2½ tablespoons finely chopped citron
- ¼ pound blanched almonds, grated (¾ cup)
- ⅓ cup grated unsweetened chocolate
- 4 ounces (4 squares) unsweetened chocolate
- ¼ cup boiling water
- 2 cups sifted confectioners' sugar
- ⅛ teaspoon salt
- ½ teaspoon vanilla extract
- Slivered blanched almonds

Rehruecken

Fondue Bourguignonne

ENCYCLOPEDIA OF COOKERY

SWORDFISH

You need two 10½-inch *rehruecken* pans or one large one; or you can use two 9-inch loose-bottomed layer-cake pans. Butter the pans well and dust with bread crumbs. Shake out excess crumbs. Combine egg yolks, whole eggs, and granulated sugar; beat until light and lemon-colored. Add cinnamon, citron, grated almonds, and grated chocolate. Mix well. Beat egg whites until stiff but not dry. Fold into chocolate mixture until whites are no longer visible. Pour into pans and bake in preheated moderate oven (350° F.) for about 30 minutes for small pans, or 45 minutes for large. Remove from pans and cool on a rack. To make glaze, melt together ¼ cup butter and 4 squares chocolate. Beat in boiling water and next 3 ingredients. Spread smoothly over cakes, let harden slightly, and stud with slivered almonds.

APFELTORTE
(Apple Tart)

Kuchenteig (page 1804) or plain pastry, unbaked
⅓ cup butter
8 large cooking apples, peeled and cut into eighths
Sugar (about ½ cup)
1 teaspoon vanilla extract
2 apples, peeled and sliced thin
1 cup water
Juice of 1 lemon
1 egg
3 to 4 tablespoons heavy cream
Apricot preserves, melted (optional)

Line a 10-inch flan ring or pie pan with pastry, and chill. Melt butter in skillet and add 8 apples. Cover and cook, stirring occasionally, until apples are just soft. Add ⅓ cup sugar and the vanilla and break the apples into small pieces. Cool slightly and spoon into pastry-lined pan. Cook thinly sliced apples in water with lemon juice for about 5 minutes. Drain apples and dry. Arrange slices in a pattern on top of pie. Sprinkle with sugar. Bake in preheated hot oven (425° F.) for 10 minutes. Reduce heat to moderate (350°F.) and bake for 20 minutes longer. Beat egg and cream and pour over tart. Bake for about 10 minutes longer. Serve warm. If desired, glaze top with preserves melted over hot water. Makes 8 to 10 servings.

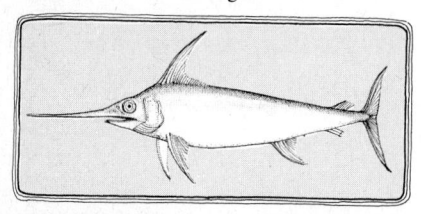

SWORDFISH—An oceanic food and sport fish of heroic proportions; swordfish may weigh between 200 and 600 pounds. Strong muscles, a powerful forked tail, a sail-like dorsal fin and other strong fins, as well as the characteristic flattened "sword," which is a prolongation of the forepart of the skull, make the swordfish a very fast swimmer as well as a powerful predator on lesser fish.

The swordfish is a fish of the Atlantic and Mediterranean. Occasionally it is found in the Pacific. It is numerous in the eastern Atlantic from Nova Scotia to the Antilles.

Swordfish are among the world's best game fish; they are also fished commercially. Their flesh is red, meaty, and rich.

Availability—Fresh swordfish is available from April to September, sold as steaks. Frozen swordfish steaks are available year round. Some swordfish is sold canned.

Storage

☐ Fresh, refrigerator shelf, raw: 1 to 2 days
☐ Fresh, refrigerator shelf, cooked: 3 to 4 days
☐ Fresh, prepared for freezing; and frozen, refrigerator frozen-food compartment: 2 months
☐ Fresh, prepared for freezing; and frozen, freezer: 1 year
☐ Canned, kitchen shelf: 1 year

Nutritive Food Values—Good source of protein and vitamin A.

☐ Fresh, 3½ ounces, broiled = 174 calories
☐ Canned, 3½ ounces, solids and liquid = 102 calories

Basic Preparation

☐ **To Sauté**—Cut swordfish steaks into serving pieces and sauté in hot butter or margarine until well browned on both sides and fish flakes easily with a fork. Remove to a hot platter and season with salt and pepper. Add a little more butter to the pan, and a little wine, if desired. Heat and pour over fish. Serve with lemon wedges.

☐ **To Broil**—Put slices of swordfish in shallow pan. Brush with melted butter or margarine. Broil under medium heat for 5 to 7 minutes on each side, basting with drippings in pan; be careful not to let fish become dry. Spread lightly with mayonnaise. Season with salt and pepper and sprinkle top with fine dry bread crumbs; baste again with drippings. Broil for a few minutes longer, or until crumbs are crisp and brown.

☐ **To Bake**—Cut swordfish steaks into serving pieces and season with salt and pepper. Dip into a mixture of ¼ cup melted butter or margarine and 2 tablespoons fresh lemon juice. Put in a shallow baking dish and pour any remaining butter mixture over top. Bake in preheated moderate oven (350°F.) for 25 to 30 minutes, or until fish flakes easily with a fork. Sprinkle with paprika, if desired.

☐ **To Freeze**—Clean fish and eviscerate. Cut fish into steaks. Dip pieces of fish into a solution of 4 cups water and 1 tablespoon ascorbic acid for 20 seconds. Wrap pieces of fish in moisture-vapor-proof wrapping, excluding as much air as possible. Seal.

SWORDFISH AMANDINE

½ cup chopped almonds
½ cup butter
Parsley
1 lemon
4 swordfish steaks
Sherry
Pepper
2 green onions, chopped
8 slices of crisp bacon, crumbled
Paprika

Brown almonds lightly in 2 tablespoons of the butter. Melt remaining butter; add few parsley sprigs, chopped, and grated rind and juice of ½ lemon. Put fish on foil-covered broiler pan. Put 1 tablespoon sherry over each steak, and sprinkle with pepper. Spoon some of butter mixture over each. Broil under medium heat for 10 minutes, basting with sherry-butter mixture. Turn fish; baste. Broil for 10 minutes longer. Sprinkle with almonds, green onions, and bacon. Garnish with lemon slices and paprika. Makes 4 servings.

DEEP-FRIED SWORDFISH

1½ pounds swordfish steaks
2 eggs
3 tablespoons water
Fine dry bread crumbs
Cooking oil or shortening for deep frying
Salt

Cut steaks into bite-size chunks. Dip into eggs and water beaten together, then into crumbs. Fry until golden-brown in deep hot oil (375°F. on a frying thermometer). Drain on absorbent paper; sprinkle with salt. Serve very hot with tartare sauce. Makes 4 servings.

SWORDFISH WITH TOMATO SAUCE

1½ pounds swordfish, 1½ inches thick
7 tablespoons olive oil
1 cup finely chopped parsley
2 garlic cloves, minced
Juice of 1 lemon
1 can (8 ounces) tomato sauce
Salt and pepper to taste

Cut fish into serving pieces; put in baking dish. Simmer next 3 ingredients for 10 minutes. Add lemon juice and sauce; heat. Season and pour over fish. Bake in preheated hot oven (425°F.) for 25 minutes. Makes 3 or 4 servings.

MAYONNAISE SWORDFISH

Season 2 pounds swordfish with salt and pepper. Spread generously with mayonnaise and sprinkle lightly with instant minced onion, then with packaged corn-flake crumbs, fine dry bread crumbs, or cracker crumbs. Bake in preheated hot oven (400°F.) for about 30 minutes. Makes 4 servings.

WOMAN'S DAY

SYLLABUB—A drink or dessert made with milk or cream and a wine or liquor. It is of two kinds: curdled and fresh. In the curdled kind, which an 18th-century Williamsburg writer described as "everlasting," the milk or cream is curdled with wine or other acid. The best-known type of syllabub, however, is the frothy kind, made by beating the milk or cream to a foam (sometimes made with egg white, although this is not the classic method) and flavoring it with wine of some sort. This type should be served immediately.

The origin of the word is unknown, but it is thought that it may have come from a kind of wine of the Champagne district, Sill or Sille, and the Elizabethan slang word "bub," which meant a bubbling drink. Syllabub is thought to have been made with Sille and frothing cream, hence, to make a Sille Bub. Whatever the correct origin is, the spelling of the word is anything but consistent. It may be spelled sillabub, sillebub, sulebubbles, or even sillybubbles. The drink is probably of English origin, and has been popular since pre-Elizabethan times. The early colonists of this country brought with them their love of the foaming drink or dessert, and it was popular through the 19th century. There are as many recipes for syllabub as there are spellings of the word, but they fall into the two main categories mentioned above.

OLD ENGLISH SYLLABUB

- 2 cups heavy cream*
- 1 cup sugar
- ½ cup sherry
- Grated rind and juice of 1 lemon

Combine ingredients in deep bowl. Beat with rotary beater or whisk in the same direction for 30 minutes. Or use an electric beater at medium to high speed for about 6 minutes, or until stiff but not curdled. The mixture should be very stiff. Set a large, very fine sieve over another bowl. Pour mixture onto sieve. Refrigerate for about 1 hour. Spoon the froth that remains on the sieve into sherbet glasses. Serve with thin crisp cookies. Makes about 6 servings.

*The cream should be very thick; use heavy cream that has been refrigerated for 3 to 4 days.

SYRUP or SIRUP—A sweet, thick, sticky liquid made from a concentrated solution of sugar and water, with or without the addition of a flavoring agent such as chocolate; or from a concentrated solution of sugar and the juice of a plant, for example, corn syrup; or from the concentrated juice of such plants, as sugar cane, etc., which results in cane syrup and molasses, the sugar maple from which maple syrup is made, and the sugar sorghum from which sorghum syrup is made.

The word comes from the Arabic *sharab*, "drink."

Many commercial syrups are widely available in food stores: maple syrup and blends of maple and cane syrup, cane syrup, sorghum cane syrup, corn syrup (both light and dark), and molasses (both light and dark). These syrups are used for pancakes, waffles, etc. Other syrups for use in making beverages are chocolate syrup, and fruit syrups such as lemon, lime, orange, pineapple, and raspberry.

SUGAR SYRUPS FOR STEWED FRUITS
These syrups can be used to great advantage when stewing fruit, since fruit stewed in a hot syrup will preserve its shape and not become mushy. Make the syrup appropriate for the fruit to be stewed. Drop a few pieces of fruit into the hot syrup; they should not crowd each other. Simmer gently until fruit is just tender. Remove with slotted spoon and put in serving dish. Repeat until fruit is used. Pour remaining syrup over fruit.

	Sugar Cups	Water Cups	Yield in Cups
Thin—for apples, grapes, rhubarb	2	4	5
Medium—for apricots, berries, cherries, figs, grapefruit, grapes, peaches, pears, plums, prunes	3	4	5½
Heavy—for berries, figs, peaches, plums	4¾	4	6½

To make syrup: Add sugar to water, cover, and bring to a boil. Remove cover, lower heat, and simmer for 3 minutes.

CHOCOLATE SYRUP

- 3 squares (3 ounces) unsweetened chocolate
- ⅔ cup water
- ½ cup sugar
- Dash of salt
- ½ cup corn syrup
- ½ teaspoon vanilla extract

Put chocolate and water in saucepan. Bring to boil and simmer until thick and well blended, stirring constantly. Add sugar and salt; bring to a boil and boil gently for 2 minutes, stirring. (For a thicker syrup, boil for 4 minutes.) Add corn syrup and bring again to a boil. Remove from heat, cool slightly, and add vanilla. Pour into a jar and cover tightly. Keep in refrigerator. Serve hot or cold as sauce or for use in chocolate drinks. Makes about 1½ cups syrup.

Note: For chocolate drinks, use 2 tablespoons syrup to 1 cup milk.

COCOA SYRUP

- 1 cup unsweetened cocoa powder
- ¾ cup sugar*
- ½ cup corn syrup*
- ¼ teaspoon salt
- 1¼ cups cold water
- ½ teaspoon vanilla extract

Mix first 4 ingredients in saucepan. Gradually add water, put over low heat, and stir until smooth. Then boil gently for 3 minutes, stirring constantly. Add vanilla. Pour into jar and cover tightly. Serve hot or cold as sauce or use in making drinks. Makes about 2 cups.

*Syrup can be made with 1½ cups sugar instead of sugar and corn syrup.

Note: For drinks use 2 tablespoons syrup to 1 cup milk.

ORANGE SYRUP

- Grated rind of 1 orange
- ½ cup fresh orange juice
- 1 cup sugar
- Dash of salt
- Sections from 1 orange

Mix grated rind, orange juice, sugar, and salt and boil until the consistency of maple syrup, 4 or 5 minutes. Add orange sections free of seeds and membrane. Serve hot or cold on pancakes or waffles. Makes 1 cup.

HOT SPICED SYRUP

- 2 cups maple or maple-blended syrup
- 1 cup butter or margarine
- 1 teaspoon ground cinnamon
- ¼ teaspoon each of ground allspice and mace

Combine all ingredients in saucepan. Boil for 2 or 3 minutes over medium heat. Beat with rotary beater until blended. Serve hot on pancakes or waffles. Makes about 3 cups.

T

TAFFY—An old-fashioned homemade candy made by boiling sugar, molasses, or some other syrup with water and perhaps a flavoring agent until they are caramelized, and then pulling the mixture apart until it becomes light and fluffy.

MOLASSES TAFFY

In a 2-quart saucepan put 1 cup molasses, 1 cup sugar, and 1 tablespoon butter. Cook over low heat, stirring frequently, until sugar has dissolved. Increase heat and cook until the syrup, when dropped into very cold water, forms threads which are hard but not brittle (268 to 270°F. on a candy thermometer). Pour syrup onto greased platter and wait. As edges cool, fold toward center or they will harden before the rest is ready for pulling. When candy is cool enough to handle, press into ball with lightly buttered fingers. Stretch ball into a rope about 18 inches long. Double the strand and stretch again. Repeat the stretching until the candy turns light and the ridges hold their shape. Pulling may take anywhere from 5 to 20 minutes depending on how energetic you are. Put the candy rope on a board covered with confectioners' sugar or cornstarch and stretch it into a thin rope. Cut with scissors into pieces of the desired size. Wrap each piece separately in wax paper or plastic wrap.

CHOCOLATE TAFFY

- 2 cups dark corn syrup
- ¼ cup water
- 2½ ounces (2½ squares) unsweetened chocolate
- ¼ teaspoon salt
- 1 tablespoon butter
- ¼ teaspoon vanilla extract

Combine first 4 ingredients in saucepan and cook over high heat, stirring, until mixture boils. Continue cooking, stirring almost constantly, until 260°F. registers on candy thermometer, or until a little of mixture dropped into cold water forms a hard ball. Remove from heat. Add butter and vanilla, stir, and pour onto greased platter. When cool enough to handle, butter hands lightly and pull candy until light in color and too hard to pull further. Stretch out into long rope ½ inch in diameter; cut with scissors into 1-inch pieces. Wrap in wax paper. Makes about 1 pound.

TAMALE—A basic Mexican food, consisting of a highly seasoned ground meat, cheese, or other filling, encased in a dough made from cornmeal. It is then wrapped in corn husks and steamed. Tamales are a very popular food throughout the Southwest.

Tamales should be made with *masa*, which is itself made by soaking dried corn in a lime solution until the husks can be rubbed off. The corn is then ground while still wet. The *masa*-making process is probably as old as the Mexican Indians; to this day it is made by hand in many villages. Commercially made *masa* is also available, usually in 5-pound bags, in specialty food shops. Tamales are also available canned.

TAMALES DE MAÍZ CON POLLO
(Green Corn-Husk Tamales with Chicken Filling)

- 1¾ cups masa
- 1 cup warm water
- ½ teaspoon salt
- ¼ cup lard
- Fresh corn husks
- 1 cup minced cooked chicken
- ¼ cup finely chopped almonds
- 1 tablespoon chopped capers
- ½ teaspoon salt
- 2 tablespoons cooking oil

Mix together the first 4 ingredients and beat until very creamy and smooth. Trim the thick bottom part from corn husks and wash well, removing any silk. For each tamale, take 2 corn husks, pointed part at top, and paste together at one side with some of the *masa* mixture. This makes the husk wider. Now spread another tablespoon of the mixture on the inside, about 1 inch from the bottom and extending about 2 inches up the husk. Top with 2 teaspoons of the filling, made by combining the last 5 ingredients. Fold husk around filling, paste with a little more *masa,* then fold bottom toward top so that the pointed arms extend a little above the bottom or trimmed end. Stand open side up in a steamer, and steam for 1 hour. These may be frozen and reheated over steam. Makes about 1 dozen.

TAMARA—A powdered spice combination used in Italian cookery. It generally consists of aniseed, fennel seed, cinnamon, cloves, and coriander. Tamara is not generally available in the United States.

TAMARIND—A tall tropical shade tree native to the upper Nile region of tropical Africa and possibly southern Asia as well. Its name is derived from the Arabic *tamr hindi,* "Indian date." The tamarind is widely cultivated in all of the Orient as an ornamental and shade tree and in India its hard yellowish wood is used for making furniture, while its leaves and red-striped flowers are eaten. It is a favored tree in the West Indies and Florida, since it is one of the best hurricane resistant plants.

Tamarind pulp is used in preparing chutney, curries, and preserves. Before use the pulp is generally soaked in water and the liquid strained off; or the pulp is simmered for a few minutes, then strained. The juice is used in pickling fish and in making a syrup. This syrup, when diluted with water, makes a cold drink with a mild laxative quality.

Availability—Tamarind is available in specialty food stores packaged much like dates. It is in a pulp, however, rather than separate pieces as dates are. It also contains seeds.

Tamarind juice is put up in cans in Puerto Rico and sold here in some specialty food stores.

Caloric Value
☐ 3½ ounces, raw = 239 calories

FRIED FISH WITH TAMARIND SAUCE
1- to 2-pound red snapper
⅓ cup lard
1 garlic clove, crushed
3 tablespoons soy sauce
1 teaspoon sugar
2 tablespoons tamarind pulp
1 tablespoon water
1 tablespoon shredded fresh gingerroot
3 scallions, cut into 1-inch pieces
2 shallots, minced and fried

Clean fish and prepare for cooking. Fry in lard until light brown. Remove and reserve. Brown garlic in the same lard. Add soy sauce, sugar, tamarind pulp, and water. Return fish to mixture. Add gingerroot and scallions. Cook for 5 minutes. Place on hot serving dish. Sprinkle with the fried shallots. Makes 2 to 4 servings.

TANGELO—A member of the citrus family which is a hybrid of the tangerine and grapefruit. They were crossed in 1897 to produce the new fruit. The name is derived from the words "tangerine" and "pomelo," another name by which the grapefruit is known. Tangelos have an orange rind and pale yellow flesh with a pronounced acid flavor. Their size is medium to large. Two of the most successful varieties differ considerably in shape (pear or round) and in peel (thin and smooth or rough and thick).

Tangelos are available from late October through January with peak months in November and December. They are eaten out-of-hand or used in salads. They are also squeezed for juice. Buy and store as any citrus fruit.

Caloric Value
☐ Juice, 3½ ounces = 41 calories

TANGERINE—A citrus fruit that is a descendent of the mandarin orange. Tangerines are smaller than oranges. Like all mandarins, tangerines have thin skins which peel off readily and segments that can be easily separated from the pulp. The color of the skin is a rather intense orangy-yellow, and the flavor of the fruit delicate, yet a little spicy and tart. They are named after the North African city of Tangiers, although their original home is China. They are extensively cultivated in China, Japan, in Mediterranean Europe, and in our own Gulf States.

Tangerines are eaten raw and are used in salads. Peeled and segmented, they can be served with a cheese tray; combined with Tokay grapes or blueberries and sprinkled with coconut; or used in gelatin. The rind can be used grated as a flavoring.

Availability—Tangerines are in season from December to April. Some are available canned, usually called "mandarin oranges." Canned and frozen concentrated tangerine juice is available.

Purchasing Guide—Select fruit that is deep orange to red in color, shiny skinned, clean, and heavy for its size.

Storage—Keep tangerines in the refrigerator. Freezing is not recommended.
☐ Fresh, refrigerator shelf: 1 to 2 months
☐ Canned, kitchen shelf: 1 year
☐ Canned, refrigerator shelf, opened: 5 to 6 days
☐ Frozen juice, refrigerator frozen-food compartment: 3 weeks
☐ Frozen juice, freezer: 1 year

Nutritive Food Values—A good source of vitamin C.
☐ Fresh, 3½ ounces = 46 calories
☐ Juice, fresh; and canned, unsweetened, 3½ ounces = 43 calories
☐ Juice, canned, 3½ ounces, sweetened = 50 calories
☐ Frozen concentrate, unsweetened, 3½ ounces, undiluted = 162 calories
☐ Frozen concentrate, unsweetened, 3½ ounces, diluted with 3 parts water = 46 calories

TANGERINE COMPOTE
6 medium tangerines
½ cup sugar
1½ cups water
⅛ teaspoon salt
2 tablespoons fresh lemon juice
¼ teaspoon whole cloves
2 cinnamon sticks

Peel tangerines, remove all white fiber, and break into sections. In a saucepan mix together sugar, water, salt, cinnamon, and cloves. Boil for 3 minutes. Remove cinnamon and cloves with slotted spoon. Add lemon juice and tangerine sections. Cool. Refrigerate overnight. Makes 6 servings.

FRESH TANGERINE AND APPLE SALAD
5 medium tangerines
3 large fresh eating apples
½ head lettuce
1 cup (8-ounce package) cottage cheese
Mayonnaise or French dressing

Peel tangerines, remove stringy membrane, and separate into sections. Wash apples, core, cut into eighths, and arrange with tangerine sections over head lettuce on salad plates. Top each salad with cottage cheese. Serve with mayonnaise. Makes 6 servings.

TANSY (*Tanacetum vulgare*)—A coarse-growing perennial herb which reaches a height of two to three feet and has distinctive flowers that look like little yellow buttons, and leaves divided like ferns. A variant, known as fern-leaved tansy, *T. vulgare*, var. *crispum*, is a smaller plant, with more delicately fernlike leaves of a darker green color.

At one time the leaves were much used as a seasoning, especially in omelets and puddings; witness the tansy pudding which was a traditional English Easter Sunday dish, and they were also used for medicinal preparations. The taste, however, is very harsh to the modern palate and in large amounts tansy is said to be poisonous. Consequently, it is no longer in favor as a culinary herb.

TAPIOCA—A valuable farinaceous food made by heating the starch obtained from the roots of the manioc, one of the chief tropical food plants. Under the action of the heat the starch grains burst and are converted into small irregular masses. This product, after baking to remove all moisture, is flake tapioca. The pellet form of pearl tapioca is obtained by forcing the moist starch through sieves of various sizes. Tapioca is also marketed in several sizes of granulated (made by grinding flake tapioca). An example of this is the quick-cooking tapioca sold in packages in food stores. This is the most widely available form, but pearl tapioca is also available in specialty stores and some tapioca flour is available in health-food stores. The pearl is used for desserts primarily. The quick-cooking can be used for desserts, meat loaves, and for thickening gravies. Also available are packaged pudding mixes, among them chocolate, orange coconut, and vanilla tapioca pudding mixes.

Nutritive Food Values—A carbohydrate food, very easily digested.
- Pearl or quick-cooking, 3½ ounces, raw = 352 calories
- Cream pudding, 3½ ounces = 134 calories

TAPIOCA TUNA SOUP
¼ cup pearl tapioca
½ cup water
1¼ teaspoons salt
⅛ teaspoon each of pepper and paprika
1 teaspoon powdered mustard
1 tablespoon minced onion
3 cups milk
1 cup light cream
1 cup (6½- to 7-ounce can) tuna, drained and flaked
2 tablespoons butter or margarine

Soak tapioca in the water for 1 hour, or longer. Water should be absorbed. Combine tapioca and remaining ingredients except last 2 in top part of a double boiler. Put over rapidly boiling water and cook for 10 to 15 minutes, stirring frequently. Add tuna and butter and mix well. Keep over hot water for 15 to 20 minutes to heat thoroughly and blend flavors. Makes about 5 cups.

Note: If preferred, substitute 2 tablespoons quick-cooking tapioca for the pearl. Omit water. Proceed as directed.

TOMATO BEEF LOAF
2 pounds ground beef
⅓ cup quick-cooking tapioca
1 medium onion, minced
2 teaspoons salt
¼ teaspoon pepper
¼ teaspoon dried savory or oregano
1½ cups canned tomatoes, mashed

Combine all ingredients and mix well, lightly but thoroughly. Pack into loaf pan (9 x 5 x 3 inches) and bake in preheated moderate oven (350°F.) for 1 to 1¼ hours. Let stand for a few minutes before turning out of pan. Makes 6 to 8 servings.

TAPIOCA CREAM PUDDING
1 egg, separated
⅓ cup sugar
3 tablespoons quick-cooking tapioca
⅛ teaspoon salt
2 cups milk
1 teaspoon vanilla extract

Beat egg white until foamy. Measure 2 tablespoons sugar from the ⅓ cup. Gradually add the 2 tablespoons to egg white and beat until soft peaks are formed. Mix remaining sugar and other ingredients except vanilla in heavy saucepan. Cook, stirring constantly, until mixture comes to a full boil. Very slowly add to the beaten egg white, stirring rapidly to blend. Add vanilla. Cool, stirring once after 20 minutes. Serve warm or chilled. Makes 4 servings.

■ **Variations**—Serve pudding with chocolate or fruit sauce. Or fold in diced fruit.

BUTTERSCOTCH TAPIOCA CREAM
2 eggs, separated
Brown sugar
½ cup butter
4 cups milk
⅓ cup quick-cooking tapioca
¼ teaspoon salt
1 teaspoon vanilla extract

Beat egg whites until foamy. Add ¼ cup packed brown sugar, 2 tablespoons at a time, beating until mixture stands in soft peaks. Set aside. Melt butter in a saucepan. Add ⅔ cup packed brown sugar and cook, stirring, until sugar is dissolved. Mix egg yolks, milk, tapioca, and salt in a saucepan. Cook, stirring, over medium heat until mixture comes to a full boil, about 8 minutes. Add butterscotch mixture and mix well. Pour a small amount of hot mixture gradually into the meringue, blending well. Quickly stir in remaining tapioca mixture. Add vanilla. Let stand for 15 to 20 minutes; stir. Serve warm or cold. Makes 8 servings.

TARO—A plant of the subtropics and tropics, grown for its large underground tuber which has a high starch content and is very easily digested. Its large "elephant-ear" leaves can be eaten as greens when young. The large starchy corm or bulb and tuber are boiled, fried, baked, or used in soup. However, they have an acrid taste when raw. Poi, a staple food of the Pacific, particularly Hawaii, is made from taro root. Canned poi is available in Hawaii and in some specialty food stores in the continental United States. Dasheen, a variety of taro, is grown in southern and tropical climates as a substitute for potatoes. Dasheens have been grown as a commercial crop in the southern United States since 1913. They are available year round in vegetable stores in Spanish neighborhoods.

TARRAGON (*Artemisia dracunculus*)—This perennial shrublike herb which is often called French tarragon grows over eighteen inches tall. Its dark-green leaves are long, narrow, and pointed, and they are one of the most distinctive of the culinary leaf herbs. Fresh or dried, they add a slightly aniselike flavor to chicken livers, vegetable juices, chowders, and consommés; pheasant, sweetbreads, tongue, veal, and especially chicken or turkey dishes; broiled fish, shellfish; scrambled eggs or omelets; butters, marinades, mustards, mayonnaises, sauce béarnaise, and tarragon vinegar; asparagus, beans, beets, broccoli, cabbage; tossed green, tomato, fish, or jellied salads. It can be seen from this list that tarragon is an extremely useful herb, but it should be used with some care. Its distinctive flavor tends to dominate dishes, so it should not be used in herb bouquets of delicate herbs such as chervil, savory, and parsley.

Tarragon's botanical name, *dracunculus*, as well as its French name *estragon*, means "little dragon." It is said that this was chosen because of the way the roots twist about like serpents.

Unknown to the Egyptians, Greeks, or Romans of the ancient world, tarragon was mentioned in the 13th century by an Arab doctor, who said that Indian kings mixed it with fennel juice for medicinal effect. The Syrians, he reported, ate the cooked tops of the plant with vegetables. The good doctor claimed tarragon would sweeten the breath and should be taken before drinking medicine because it would dull the taste.

The powerful taste of tarragon has always been one of its distinguishing characteristics. Gerard, the English herbalist, wrote not long after its introduction in the middle part of the 16th century: "Tarragon is not to be eaten alone in sallades, but joyned with other herbs, as Lettuce, Purslain, and the like, that it may also temper the coldnesse of them."

Tarragon was introduced into the United States some time before 1806. It may not have been one of the first herbs to cross the ocean, but once it did gourmets rejoiced. Nineteenth-century cooks liked to use it in dishes which sounded exotic to them, such as sauce tartare and sauce béarnaise. The Americans of the 20th century, led on by their nutritionists to appreciate tossed green salads, have found tarragon the perfect accompaniment, as Gerard suggested centuries before.

TART—A pastry filled with fruit, jam, custard, eggs, meat, cheese, or other fillings. The pastry may be of various kinds and the filling may be sweet or nonsweet. Tarts may serve as main dishes or appetizers as well as desserts. They may be baked after being filled, or the pastry may be baked separately and then filled with a cooked or uncooked filling. They may be served hot or cold. Often tarts are topped with whipped cream, a glaze of fruit sauce or preserves, or some other garnish. Tarts may be of any size, but the individual tart is a favorite since it eliminates the bother of cutting and serving a large pie. Small tarts are often called tartlets. Appetizer tarts must be very small, like hot canapés, so that they may be eaten in no more than two bites.

APPETIZER BEEF TARTLETS
1 cup very finely diced cooked beef
⅛ teaspoon fresh lemon juice
1 teaspoon grated onion
2 dashes of hot pepper sauce
Dash of cayenne
Leftover or canned beef gravy
Salt
12 tiny unbaked Tart Shells (page 1814), made with Standard Pastry (page 1814)
Parsley sprigs

Mix beef and next 4 ingredients. Add gravy to moisten and salt to taste. Fill tart shells with the mixture. Heat in preheated moderate oven (375°F.) for 10 minutes. Garnish with parsley sprigs. Makes 12.

EGG AND ANCHOVY TARTLETS
Prepare and bake 12 tiny Tart Shells (page 1814), using Standard Pastry (page 1814). Mash 2 hard-cooked eggs with 2 tablespoons soft butter and ½ teaspoon prepared mustard. Add 1 can (2 ounces) anchovy fillets, cut into small pieces, and 1 tablespoon grated onion. Fill tart shells and sprinkle with paprika. Makes 12.

CURRIED CHICKEN TARTLETS
Prepare 12 tiny unbaked Tart Shells (page 1814), using Standard Pastry (page 1814). Chop finely enough cooked chicken to make 1 cup. Add 1 teaspoon curry powder, 1 teaspoon minced almonds, 1 teaspoon chopped chutney, mayonnaise to moisten, and salt and pepper to taste. Fill tart shells and sprinkle with paprika. Makes 12.

EGG TART
1 package (10 ounces) piecrust mix
Oeufs Brouillés
3 egg whites
3 tablespoons grated cheese

Use piecrust mix to line an 8-inch pie pan, fluting a high edge. Bake piecrust in preheated hot oven (400°F.) for 10 to 12 minutes, or until lightly browned. Let cool a little; then fill with *Oeufs Brouillés*. After filling pie shell, top with stiffly beaten egg whites mixed with cheese. Bake in preheated moderate oven (375° F.) until lightly browned, about 10 minutes. Makes 6 servings.

Oeufs Brouillés
Melt a little butter in top part of a double boiler and brush the sides of it before you put in the eggs. Beat 6 eggs with a fork, but very lightly. Add salt and pepper. Add 1 teaspoon cold water. Pour mixture into buttered pan and cook over hot, not boiling, water. Stir constantly with a wooden spoon, scraping bottom and sides of pan. Remove from heat while still quite liquid, like heavy cream. Continue stirring, adding 1½ tablespoons fresh butter. If desired you can add 2 tablespoons heavy cream.

TWO-CHEESE MEAT TARTS
⅓ cup shortening
¾ cup shredded process Cheddar cheese
1¾ cups sifted all-purpose flour
¼ teaspoon salt
3 tablespoons cold water
1 cup diced luncheon meat
½ cup crumbled cooked bacon
1 package (3 ounces) cream cheese
2 tablespoons undiluted evaporated milk
Parsley sprigs

Cut shortening and Cheddar cheese into flour and salt. With fork, lightly mix in water. Divide into 16 pieces, and roll out each to form a round about 3½ inches in diameter. Fit into muffin pans. Mix luncheon meat and bacon; put a spoonful into each pastry-lined muffin pan. Mix cream cheese and evaporated milk; spread on meat. Bake in preheated very hot oven (450°F.) for about 15 minutes. Garnish with parsley. Makes 12 tarts.

ONION CHEESE TARTS
Prepare and bake 6 large Tart Shells (page 1814) using Standard Pastry (page 1814); cool. Melt 2 tablespoons butter or margarine in a saucepan over low heat. Add 2 medium onions, sliced; cover tightly and steam over low heat for 10 to 12 minutes, or until soft. Drain and remove to tart shells. Top with ⅔ cup grated American cheese. Beat lightly 5 eggs and 1½ cups milk or light cream and season with salt, pepper, and a dash of ground nutmeg. Pour over onions and cheese. Bake in moderate oven (375°F.) until just set, 25 to 35 minutes. Serve warm with sliced steak. Makes 6 tarts.

HOT TUNA TARTS
Combine 1 can (7 ounces) tuna fish, flaked, with 1½ to 2 cups medium cream sauce seasoned with sherry, herbs, or spices. Heat 4 large baked Tart Shells (page 1814), made with half recipe for Standard Pastry (page 1814). Fill with creamed tuna. Garnish tops to suit your imagination and taste. Makes 4 servings.

FRANKFURTER CUSTARD TARTS
2 eggs, well beaten
1 cup dairy sour cream
½ teaspoon salt
Dash of pepper
½ pound frankfurters, cubed
6 large unbaked Tart Shells (page 1814), made with Standard Pastry (page 1814)

Beat eggs, sour cream, salt, and pepper. Add frankfurters. Fill pastry-lined tart pans. Bake in preheated hot oven (425° F.) for 20 minutes. Makes 6 tarts.

TONGUE AND EGG TARTS
Prepare half recipe for Standard Pastry (page 1814). Line 12 small or 6 larger tart shells with the pastry. Combine 1 cup minced cooked tongue, 3 chopped hard-cooked eggs, 3 raw egg yolks, 1 cup light cream, and salt, pepper, and onion powder to taste. Brush tart shells with egg

TART

white, allow to dry, and fill with the mixture. Bake in preheated moderate oven (375°F.) until nicely browned. Makes 12 small or 6 large tarts.

FRENCH APPLE TART
Half recipe for Standard Pastry (page 1814), unbaked
¼ cup all-purpose flour
½ cup firmly packed brown sugar
Apples, quartered and peeled
½ cup granulated sugar
2 tablespoons butter
Ground cinnamon
¼ cup heavy cream or milk

Line pie pan with pastry. Put flour and brown sugar in pastry. Top with quarters of apples. Sprinkle granulated sugar on top. Dot with butter. Sprinkle with cinnamon. Pour cream over top. Bake in preheated moderate oven (350°F.) for about 50 minutes, or until apples are tender. Makes 6 to 8 servings.

APPLE-RAISIN-NUT TARTS
1¾ cups sugar
¾ cup water
4 tart apples, peeled, cored, and cut into eighths
½ teaspoon ground cinnamon
¼ teaspoon ground nutmeg
⅛ teaspoon salt
½ cup butter or margarine
2 large eggs, beaten
1 cup seedless raisins
½ cup coarsely chopped nuts
1 tablespoon fresh lemon juice
Twelve baked 2½-inch Tart Shells (page 1814), made with Standard Pastry (page 1814)

Mix ¾ cup sugar and water; bring to boil. Add apples and cook, covered, stirring occasionally, until tender. Drain and cool. In top part of double boiler, mix 1 cup sugar, spices, salt, and butter. Add beaten eggs and mix well. Add remaining ingredients except tart shells and cook over hot water, stirring, until thickened. Cool. Put apples in baked tart shells and cover with mixture. Makes 12 servings.

APRICOT-JAM TART
2 cups sifted all-purpose flour
1 cup butter
1 cup confectioners' sugar
½ cup ground almonds
½ teaspoon ground cinnamon
¼ teaspoon salt
3 egg yolks
Juice and grated rind of ½ lemon
Apricot jam

Knead together all ingredients except jam; chill in refrigerator. Remove half to two-thirds of the dough and roll to ½-inch thickness. Place in a flat 8-inch pan. Cover with ½-inch layer of apricot jam. Roll remaining dough and cut into strips about ⅜ inch wide; arrange lattice fashion over jam. Bake in preheated moderate oven (350°F.) for 50 minutes. Cool. Fill lattice openings with more jam to produce a really opulent effect. (Raspberry or sour-cherry jam may be substituted.) If you use the latter, increase sugar. Makes 6 to 8 servings.

BANANA CHRISTMAS TARTS
3 tablespoons cornstarch
⅔ cup sugar
¼ teaspoon salt
2 cups milk
3 eggs, beaten lightly
1 teaspoon vanilla extract
4 bananas
1 teaspoon fresh lemon juice
6 baked 4-inch Tart Shells (page 1814), made with Standard Pastry (page 1814)
2 to 3 tablespoons currant jelly
Whipped cream, sweetened

Mix first 3 ingredients together in top part of a double boiler. Gradually stir in 1¾ cups of the milk. Cook and stir over hot water or low direct heat until thick and bubbly. Combine remaining milk with eggs. Add a small amount of hot sauce to egg mixture. Return to double boiler. Continue cooking until very thick, about the consistency of mayonnaise, stirring constantly. Stir in vanilla extract. Remove from heat. Chill. Mash 1 banana with lemon juice until puréed. Stir into chilled custard. Spoon filling into cooled tart shells. Arrange remaining bananas, sliced ⅛ inch thick, over filling. Melt currant jelly over hot water. Spoon a thin layer over top of tarts for a glaze. Chill. Garnish with whipped cream. Makes 6 servings.

GLAZED CHERRY TARTS
Prepare 1 recipe Sweet Pastry (page 1814). Make and bake 8 large Tart Shells (page 1814). Make Vanilla Cream Filling (at right). Substitute 1 teaspoon vanilla extract and ½ teaspoon almond extract for the 2 teaspoons vanilla extract. Drain 2 cups (one 1-pound can) pitted red sour cherries, reserving ¾ cup juice. In saucepan mix ¼ cup sugar, 2 tablespoons cornstarch, and ⅛ teaspoon salt. Add cherry juice; cook, stirring constantly, until thickened. Add cherries and 1 tablespoon fresh lemon juice. Add red food coloring to tint desired shade. Cool. Before serving, fill tart shells, and top with cherry mixture. Makes 8 tarts.

GLAZED FRUIT TARTS
Different fruit combinations may be used
2 packages (3 ounces each) cream cheese, softened
¼ cup milk
8 large baked Tart Shells (page 1814), made with Sweet Pastry (page 1814)
Fresh or frozen strawberries, peach slices, and blueberries
Currant jelly, melted

Mix cream cheese and milk until smooth and blended. Spread in cooled tart shells. Cover with berries and fruit; top with a glaze of melted jelly. Makes 8 large tarts.

PEACH CREAM TARTS
Prepare 1 recipe Sweet Pastry (page 1814). Make and bake 8 large Tart Shells (page 1814). Cool, and remove from pans. Prepare and chill Vanilla Cream Filling (below). Before serving, fill the shells, and top with a small well-drained peach half. Spread with peach preserves; put chopped nuts around edge. Makes 8.

STRAWBERRY CHIFFON TARTS
1 quart strawberries
½ cup sugar
1 envelope unflavored gelatin
¼ cup cold water
1 tablespoon fresh lemon juice
Dash of salt
2 egg whites
¼ cup sugar
8 large baked Tart Shells (page 1814), made with Sweet Pastry (page 1814)

Wash berries; reserve 8 for garnish. Decap remainder and force through sieve. Measure; if necessary, add water to make 2 cups; add sugar. Soak gelatin in cold water for 5 minutes; dissolve over hot water; add lemon juice, and combine with berries. Chill until partially set. Beat salted egg whites until stiff; add sugar, 1 tablespoon at a time, beating after each addition until dissolved. Fold meringue into berry mixture; pour into tart shells; chill until set. Garnish with whole berries. Makes eight 4-inch tarts.

DEVONSHIRE BERRY TARTS
Use half of recipe for Sweet Pastry (page 1814) substituting 1 egg yolk for the whole egg. Add just enough milk to hold mixture together. Prepare and bake 6 large Tart Shells (page 1814). Wash and hull 1 quart strawberries; put half through sieve. Add enough water to sieved berries to make 1½ cups. Mix ¼ cup cornstarch, dash of salt, and ¾ cup sugar. Stir in sieved berries. Cook, stirring constantly, until thickened. Cool. Mix 1 package (3 ounces) cream cheese with 2 tablespoons milk; spread in tart shells. Cover with whole berries, tips up. Top with sieved-berry glaze. Chill. Makes 6 tarts.

VANILLA CREAM FILLING
3 cups milk
¾ cup sugar
6 tablespoons cornstarch
½ teaspoon salt
3 eggs, beaten
1 tablespoon butter
2 teaspoons vanilla extract

Scald milk in top part of a double boiler over boiling water. Mix sugar, cornstarch, and salt. Stir into milk. Cook, stirring constantly, until thick. Cover; cook for 10 minutes longer. Add small amount of mixture to eggs; return to double boiler; cook for 5 minutes. Add butter. Put in bowl, and sprinkle small amount of sugar over top to prevent skin from forming. Chill; add vanilla, and stir. Makes about 3½ cups, or enough for 8 to 12 tarts.

Chocolate Filling
Use recipe for Vanilla Cream Filling. Melt 3 ounces (3 squares) unsweetened

Strawberry Chiffon Tarts

Apricot-Jam Tart

Tongue and Egg Tart

Two-Cheese Meat Tarts

TASTE

chocolate in milk, and beat until smooth. Proceed as directed. Makes about 3½ cups, or enough for 8 to 12 tarts.

STANDARD PASTRY
For two 9-inch shells, 8 large individual pies or tarts, or 24 tiny tarts:
- 2 cups sifted all-purpose flour
- 1 teaspoon salt
- ⅔ cup plus 2 tablespoons lard or hydrogenated shortening
- ¼ cup cold water

Mix flour and salt. Cut in lard with pastry blender or 2 knives until ingredients are well blended and mixture resembles coarse meal. Sprinkle with the water, 1 tablespoon at a time, mixing lightly with a fork until all the dry ingredients are moistened. Gather dough together with fingers so it cleans the bowl. Press firmly into a ball.

SWEET PASTRY
For two 9-inch shells, 8 large individual pies or tarts, or 24 tiny tarts:
- ⅔ cup soft shortening
- 2 cups sifted all-purpose flour
- ½ teaspoon baking powder
- ¼ cup sugar
- ½ teaspoon salt
- 1 egg, beaten with 2 tablespoons milk

Cut shortening into sifted dry ingredients. With fork, lightly mix in egg mixture. Chill until ready to use.

TART SHELLS
Prepare Standard Pastry or Sweet Pastry (above). Divide pastry into 6 to 8 equal parts. Roll each part into a 4-inch round or a 4-inch square. Fit pieces of pastry over backs of muffin cups or custard cups, making pleats so pastry will fit close. (Pastry may be rolled into rounds and fitted into individual tart pans. Do this when filling unbaked tart shells for later baking. Prick with fork to prevent puffing during baking. Put the pastry-covered cups or lined pans on baking sheet. Bake in preheated very hot oven (450°F.) for 8 to 10 minutes. Cool and remove from pans. Fill with any desired pie filling or Vanilla Cream Filling (page 1813). Makes 6 to 8 large tart shells.

■ **For Tiny Tart Shells**—Divide pastry into 24 pieces. Roll each into a round or square. Fit over backs of tiny muffin cups. Proceed as directed in above recipe. Makes 24 tiny tart shells.

TASTE—One of the senses of man, located in the mouth, by which he perceives the different qualities of substances.

The taste buds are located in the tongue and soft palate, and are in general receptive to four main sensations: sweet, sour, salty, and bitter. These four basic tastes range themselves into an infinite number of combinations of varying strength and degree. There are also other sensations, such as smelling, hearing, and feeling which, although distinctive, register simultaneously with taste in the brain, and give us what we call the taste of whatever we put in our mouth.

Taste is a very complex matter, one that has intrigued scientists and inspired a great deal of philosophical speculation. Scientifically speaking, the sense of taste has not been as extensively studied as the sense of seeing, perhaps because the sources of taste are more elusive and individual. It is known, however, that we can distinguish the distinctive taste of a substance better when it is cold than when it is hot, and that a particular taste may be reinforced by the introduction of a dash of its opposite: sweet things are likely to taste sweeter because of the addition of some salt, for example.

TEA—The name given to an evergreen shrub or small tree, *Thea sinensis;* the leaves of this shrub; the drink made from these leaves; and the light afternoon meal or social occasion at which this drink is served.

The tea plant is native to China and has long been cultivated there, and in Japan, India, and southeastern Asia. Some tea is now also grown in Africa. The tea plant is related to the magnolia and, like its relative, would produce blossoms and grow to a great height if it were not pruned. But the plant must be kept to the size of a bush so that the young leaves, which make this universal beverage, may be easily plucked off as they grow. If properly cared for and pruned, a tea plant may be productive for up to seventy years.

The principal difference in teas comes from the treatment of the leaves once they are picked. *Black tea,* by far the most popular, is made by allowing the dried and rolled tea leaves to ferment before they are fired. Black teas, which make an amber-colored beverage, are produced in China, Formosa, India, Ceylon, Indonesia, Japan, and Africa.

Green tea, produced in China, Japan, India, Ceylon, and Indonesia, is dried, rolled, steamed, and fired, without being allowed to ferment. The leaves retain their greenish color and the resulting beverage is a greenish-yellow color and rather bitter.

Oolong tea, from China, Formosa, and Japan, has leaves which are partially fermented, giving the beverage the aroma of black tea and the "bite" of green tea.

Besides these three main types of tea there are special teas which are scented and spiced. The leaves are combined with jasmine, gardenia, mint, orange, or spices.

Within the main categories of tea there are many varieties. A list follows:

BLACK TEAS
Assam—A full-bodied robust India tea of high quality grown in Assam Province in Northeast India.

Ceylon—"High-grown" teas. Grown at a height of more than 4,000 feet, these teas are considered the best quality, especially those from the district of Uva in Ceylon. They are delicate and fragrant.

Darjeeling—This tea is grown in the Himalaya Mountains and has an excellent flavor and aroma. It is considered the best and most delicate of all India teas.

Earl Grey—A mixture of black teas from India and Ceylon which gives a hearty aromatic brew.

English Breakfast—A mellow and fragrant blend of a China character.

Keemum—Mild yet hearty China tea.

Lapsang Souchong—A black tea, originally produced in Formosa, with a unique smoky flavor. It is very strong.

Sumatra—Generally used in tea blends; comes from Sumatra and Java.

Black teas are also graded by the size of the leaf: Orange Pekoe, Pekoe, and Pekoe Souchong are the larger leaves. Smaller leaves and cut leaves are referred to as Broken Orange Pekoe, Broken Pekoe Souchong, Fannings, and Dust. It is Fannings which are used in tea bags, as the water penetrates them more quickly.

GREEN TEAS

Basket Fried—A light gentle tea from Japan.

Gunpowder—A type of green tea in which each leaf is rolled into a little pellet. Considered the highest grade of green tea, it makes a delicate light-colored brew.

OOLONG TEAS

Formosa Oolong—This semifermented tea has subtle flavor.

Jasmine—Flavored and scented with white Jasmine blossoms, this tea has delicate flavor.

Tea has a long and colorful history; its origins are surrounded with legend and myth. Basically, the reason for its popularity arose from the fact that the inhabitants of the Far East discovered early that they must boil their water in order to keep healthy. Boiled water has a flat taste, especially when hot. The addition of the tea leaves made a drink that was healthy, stimulating, warming, and good tasting as well.

The first history of tea was written about 800 A.D. by a Chinese scholar Lu Yu; it reported that tea had been used as a beverage as early as the 6th century. By 793 it was valuable and its use widespread enough to be taxed. From China, tea drinking spread to Japan where it was surrounded with elaborate ceremonies, still practiced today.

Europeans were not to have the pleasure of the refreshing brew until the early 17th century. The first tea load was brought by the Dutch in 1610. The English, who were to make tea famous, at first had to import their supply from Holland; it was not until the end of the century that the East India Company of England began to import tea directly from China.

In the 18th century Jonas Hanway, the Englishman who invented umbrellas, waxed furious against the new beverage in his "An Essay on Tea; considered as pernicious to Health; obstructing industry; and impoverishing the Nation." The famous Dr. Johnson no less fiercely replied that Hanway was wrong; for he, Johnson, was a "hardened and shameless tea drinker ... who with tea amuses the evening, with tea solaces the midnight, and with tea welcomes the morning."

The majority of Englishmen now agree with Dr. Johnson, and modern investigation has shown that the combination of caffeine and tannin that tea contains is indeed healthful. Today, throughout Great Britain, the tea break, especially afternoon tea, is an established custom.

It is not strange that a beverage with such a widespread reputation should come to the young American Colonies. The first tea drinkers were not the English settlers here, but rather the colonists in New Amsterdam, later New York. From there the habit spread throughout the colonies.

Tea, in fact, was partly responsible for the War of Independence that was to change the Colonies into the United States. By the 18th century tea was a popular drink and the colonists imported it from England. When the British Parliament, without the consent of the colonists, taxed tea in 1773, and later permitted the East India Company to export tea directly to America without the help of American importers, patriotism and commercialism banded together in rebellion. The famous Boston Tea Party was only the first of many "dumpings" of tea by the angry Americans.

It was unthinkable that any patriotic American would drink tea after all this, and many substitutes from native roots and barks were devised.

In modern America we have certainly forgotten our early hatred of imported tea. We have even made contributions to the art of tea drinking, for iced tea was first made at the St. Louis Fair in 1904. There a merchant, distressed that the hot customers did not want his steaming cups of tea, thought of putting it over ice. Today iced tea is one of our most popular summer beverages.

Americans are also responsible for the tea bag. About the turn of the century an enterprising New York importer sent around his wares in tiny silk bags. The idea caught on and now more than half of America's tea is bought in tea bags. If made with boiling water in a pot, tea bags make as good tea as loose tea, in spite of the objections of purists. Modern Englishmen, in fact, are taking more and more to the tea-bag habit.

There are as many ways of drinking tea as there are countries that drink it. The Russians favor very strong tea, drunk in glasses rather than cups. The traditional Russian way of brewing it is to mix a little very strong tea essence with boiling water from a samovar which is present in all Russian households. Some Russians put jam in their tea to sweeten it, and others drink it through a piece of sugar held in the mouth. The Chinese and Japanese favor tea with no additional flavoring, and drink it out of handleless cups. The Americans drink their tea in all ways; milk and sugar are popular, and we have added the slice of lemon, sometimes studded with a clove.

Whichever way tea is made, one thing is absolutely essential: that the water be *boiling*. Good tea cannot be made with either hot or near-boiling or gently simmering water. The water *must* be at a full rolling boil, or the tea won't be any good.

Availability—Black tea in leaf or tea-bag form is universally available. A wide variety of other teas are available in gourmet and specialty food stores.

Instant tea is available in jars. It consists of equal parts of pulverized tea and malto-dextrin to protect the flavor. It dissolves in either hot or cold water. Instant tea is also available in vacuum-sealed foil packages. This contains sugar and powdered lemon juice and is used mainly for iced tea, although it can also be prepared as hot tea.

1 pound tea makes about 200 cups. 1 tea bag = 1 teaspoon loose tea.

Storage—Store in tightly covered container on the pantry shelf away from cooking odors and spices.

☐ Kitchen shelf: 6 months

Nutritive Food Values—Tea has no nutritive value except when sugar, milk, or cream are added. Tea contains a stimulant called theine which is identical with caffeine in coffee.

Basic Preparation—The best tea is made in a pot. Pots of china, pottery, or glass hold the heat better than metal pots. Metal may also give a metallic flavor to the beverage.

Water should be freshly drawn and boiled.

Scald teapot to warm it.

The usual proportion of tea is 1 teaspoon tea or 1 bag per cup (8 ounces) of boiling water. For iced tea use 50 per cent more tea to allow for melting ice. Brew or steep tea for 3 minutes. Never boil.

Very soft water extracts the flavor of the tea more quickly than hard water. Very hard water may cause tea to be cloudy.

☐ **To Make Iced Tea**—Fill tall glass full of cracked ice or cubes. Brew tea, using 1½ teaspoons per 8-ounce cup of water, and pour hot tea directly over the ice to cool and to avoid loss of flavor by evaporation.

HOT SPICED TEA

Boiling water
4 or 5 teaspoons tea
1 teaspoon whole cloves
1 cinnamon stick
¼ cup fresh orange juice
2 tablespoons fresh lemon juice
4 strips of lemon rind

Heat china, glass, or earthenware teapot with boiling water; drain. Measure tea and spices into the hot pot. Add 3 cups rapidly boiling water. Stir at once into teacups, or into another hot teapot for serving. Never allow tea leaves to remain in the tea after it is brewed. Add lukewarm fruit juices and lemon rind. Serve with sugar if desired. Makes 4 servings.

LEMON ICED TEA

Dilute 1 can (6 ounces) frozen lemonade concentrate according to directions on can. Pour into ice-cube tray of refrigerator and freeze. Make double-strength tea by pouring 1 cup boiling water over 2 teaspoons tea for each glass of iced tea desired; let steep for 5 minutes; strain. Pour into tall glass filled with lemonade ice cubes.

MINTED ICED TEA

Make double-strength mint tea by pouring 4 cups boiling water over 8 teaspoons tea and sprigs of mint, chopped. Steep for 5 minutes; strain. Pour into large ice-filled pitcher. Add ⅓ cup superfine sugar dissolved in ½ cup fresh lemon juice. Press a few lemon slices into the tea mixture. Mix well. Garnish with sprigs of fresh mint. Makes about 6 large glasses.

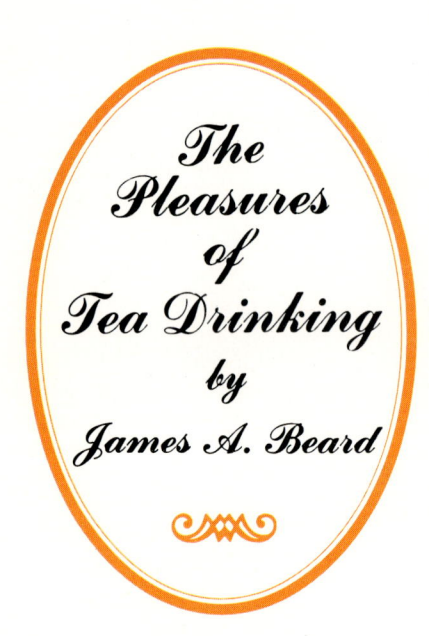

The Pleasures of Tea Drinking
by James A. Beard

"Thank God for tea! What would the world do without tea?—How did it exist? I am glad I was not born before tea." This warm appreciation for the cup that cheers was expressed by Sidney Smith, English writer and wit of the early 19th century. I heartily agree with Mr. Smith. The era B.T.—Before tea—must have been bleak.

English tea, or tea as we know it in this country, is actually a fairly recent addition to our menus. Of course, in the Orient it has been a ritual for thousands of years. Just when the first samples of tea were brought to Europe no one knows for sure. Perhaps they were carried sometime during the Middle Ages by one of the adventurous silk merchants who plied the caravan routes to the Far East. At any rate, little notice was taken of this strange plant until centuries later.

Tea first came to England about the middle of the 17th century, but was not immediately popular. It was extremely expensive and no one knew how to brew it properly. In fact, when it arrived in Boston shortly after, housewives boiled the leaves for hours and made a black, bitter drink and, curiously enough, then served the drained leaves to be eaten with butter and salt!

The Dutch apparently had more information on the use of this exotic plant, for tea was an immediate success in the New Amsterdam colony, now New York City. Fashionable ladies of the colony offered their guests a choice of several brews, and served it with sugar and little bowls of saffron and peach leaves to be added for flavor. The Dutch housewife took great pride in her array of teapots, one for each type of brew, and her silver teaspoons and sugar bowl.

It may be that the English learned how to prepare tea from their Dutch neighbors for, by the 18th century, the drink had caught on in England and was considered a "must" at elegant dinner parties. It was served after the meal in the drawing room, where the hostess presided at the tea table. The proper hour for dinner in the mid-18th century was 4 P.M. After dinner, the ladies retired to the drawing room, and the gentlemen joined them there about 7 o'clock for hot tea, cordials, liqueurs, and thin slices of bread and butter. In later years, fashion decreed that the dinner hour should be moved into the evening, and teatime at 5 o'clock in the drawing room became the pleasant custom.

Being an import from the Orient, tea was always dear. Yet, in spite of high cost, tea drinking soon spread from the elegant homes to all classes. Servant girls refused to take jobs unless they were granted a daily tea ration, or tea money in addition to wages. Cooks reserved the right to appropriate used tea leaves, which they dried and resold to poorer people. Laborers and cottagers were drinking tea three times a day. Social reformers of the time wrote tracts complaining bitterly that the working classes were being corrupted! They spent money on tea that should be used for nourishing broths. But their protests were ignored. After all, what broth could give the warming lift to the spirits that a steaming cup of tea brought? And so tea ceased to be a luxury. It became a household necessity and a firm tradition.

The English are the most noted European tea imbibers, but the pungent drink is popular all over the Continent. In Russia the samovar, and the hot glass of tea are as much a part of everyday life as the English kettle and teapot. Here in America, millions of us carry on the tea-drinking tradition, and an afternoon tea is still one of the most gracious ways to entertain.

I was brought up in a tea-drinking family. My Chinese amah consumed tea all day long—fragrant China tea, clear amber in color and scalding hot—sipping it from tiny, handleless porcelain cups. My mother, whose background was English, was what I call a "teatotaller." Tea drinking for her lasted from before breakfast until bedtime. She had a collection of teapots, one for each time of day, and special ones for elegant tea parties. Hers was no "standard" tea. It was a blend of the choicest teas from both China and India. She labored long to get just the right combination of aroma and flavor, mixing and sampling many brews to achieve perfection. After a blending session, she stored her mix in decorative tins. A few precious pounds of the tea went to very special friends who would appreciate its rare qualities.

Afternoon tea, with guests invited, became a most elaborate ritual, and one that took days of preparation. During this time the house was in an uproar, but oh, what fine smells! What food! Madeira cake, fruity, buttery, and blessed with a touch of fine wine, was one of her favorites. Another great specialty of our house was seedcake, which, to my mother, was a poundcake laden with caraway seeds, and cut into thin, thin slices. It was incredibly fragrant, soft, and pungent to the taste buds.

Afternoon tea also called for shortbread molded into fancy shapes; scones baked on a "girdle"; paper-thin oatcakes; and potato scones. I was especially fond of currant bread, a yeast dough enriched with butter, sugar, and sultana raisins. This last, sliced thin and toasted, smelled fruity and buttery. Then there were my mother's teacakes—oven scones dotted with currants which had been soaked in sherry or brandy before they were swirled into the dough. We also had paper-thin sandwiches of tomato on watercress, or made with various pastes and fillings; and sometimes, just for a big splash, a huge, iced white mountain cake.

Guests came around 3 o'clock, the tea table was unveiled around 4, and everyone went on talking and chewing and drinking until 5:30 or 6. These party tea drinkers ate with gusto and relish, tasting

WOMAN'S DAY

each thing, enhancing it with jams, jellies, or preserves, and discussing the merits of every bite.

To my mother, tea was much more than drink and ritual. It was an aid to the troubled heart, the quick picker-upper after a session with dentist, corset fitter, or dressmaker, the perpetual soother to be called upon in every difficulty. Tea was a kind friend.

I am happy that I was able to visit and know England when the long afternoon-tea ceremony was still a general rule. My early recollections of London revolved around tea at the Ritz in Piccadilly, at shops along Bond Street, or at the now-departed Victoria and Metropole hotels on Northumberland Avenue. Sunday-afternoon tea at the Ritz was particularly exciting. Here one found music, famous people, and gay, fashionable people. It was pure joy to sit in the 18th-century French Room, and have a beautiful tea service placed by you, and perfectly trained waiters pass lavish trays of small asparagus sandwiches, *foie gras* nestling between moist slices of good bread, leaves of mustard and cress peering out from well-buttered sandwiches; or, if you preferred, they would rush you fragrant, buttery toast on heated plates. Then there were trays and trays of pastry; éclairs no longer than an inch-and-a-half; miniature tartlets; *barquettes* with the most delectable fillings.

And always, of course, there was tea—strong, hot, pungent, and stimulating.

Teas in the countryside often meant luscious huge strawberries just picked, and warm still from the sun. These came with stems intact, to be picked up and dipped into sugar, or sometimes anointed with Devonshire cream. With the fruit, we ate rich scones, muffins, crumpets, and maids-of-honour.

In country homes there was nigh tea, which for many took the place of dinner. This was a simple, hearty meal that might include bacon and eggs or sausages or dropped eggs, with buns or crumpets or biscuits and cake. Such plain tasty fare, spread out on a tea table in front of a cozy fire, is to me in the very best English tea-drinking tradition. Of such a country tea the British poet, William Cowper, wrote:

Now stir the fire, and close the shutters fast,
Let fall the curtains, wheel the sofa round,
And while the bubbling and loud-hissing urn
Throws up a steamy column, and the cups
That cheer but not inebriate wait on each,
So let us welcome peaceful evening in.

On a recent trip to England, I found, to my sorrow, that the leisurely teatime is fast disappearing. Tea as a drink is just as popular, just as necessary, but the war brought changes. Nowadays most people have time for only a quick cup of tea and a biscuit. It's rare to find a country inn or hotel where tea as a relaxed ceremony is available. When I stopped by inns the same story was told to me over and over: "Tea is economically unsound. No one wants it any more."

Already, since the war years, a muffin, or what we in America call an English muffin, has all but dropped from the English scene. While I was there I noticed a long correspondence in the London newspapers on this subject, and I (and also two others in the know) finally advised the readers that, should they wish muffins, they would probably have to take a trip to the United States to find them!

Not only are muffins and other tea breads becoming more and more difficult to find in their native land, but even the village bakery that used to boast of homemade maids-of-honour, tartlets, rock cakes, and simnel cakes, is fast disappearing. A food-conscious couple in London, Mr. and Mrs. Drage, have invested in a small bakery in Shepherd Market, and here one can still find all the traditional tidbits associated with the tea ritual. It is heartening to know that this shop serves over 7,000 customers a week with ginger cakes, Genoa cakes, scones, and muffins.

Don't misunderstand. The English still love their favorite drink and everywhere one finds good tea, well brewed, and a fine selection. You can choose from the smoky Lapsang Souchong, the Oolong, the scented Earl Grey blend, the sturdy Darjeeling, and many, many others from India, Ceylon, Formosa, China, and Japan. Indeed, one cup I had on my visit I will remember as the best I ever sipped. I spent a frigid morning on an oyster boat near Colchester, seeing the beds from whence come some of the finest oysters of the world. We were warmly dressed, but a cold, damp wind penetrated everything, and chilled us almost to rigidity. Just as I thought I could stand it no longer, for there was no shelter on the boat, a crewman brought me a cracked, stained cup of tea, hot enough to scald. It was black, it was cloudy, it was frighteningly strong, but one sip and I knew it was the greatest drink I had ever experienced. It warmed me; it thawed me; it was a lifesaver. Don't ask me if it was Lapsang, Oolong, or Darjeeling. It was just good, hot tea, and nothing ever tasted better!

So, even though the old custom of a relaxing teatime is gradually slipping away, the English still know how to brew a fine pot of tea. Here in this country, in spite of the fact that millions of us drink tea daily, it is almost impossible to get it properly made, especially in restaurants.

If others can make good tea, so can we. Here are some suggestions: First, there are many types of tea, each with its own flavor and aroma. As with wine, so with tea, one learns by tasting. Try the different varieties and compare them. Now for making the brew: Tea must be made in a china pot. Never, never try to make it in a teacup. Tea does not steep in the cup, and all the finest flavors and aromas escape. Fill the teapot with boiling water to heat it before you make the tea. Then empty it, and put in the tea leaves. The usual amount is one teaspoon of leaves per cup; some people who like very strong tea use a little more. If you like weak tea, don't cut down on the leaves, for you will sacrifice flavor and aroma. Instead, add a little hot water to the tea after you pour it into the cup.

The water must be boiling, a round bubbling boil, when you pour it over the tea leaves in the pot. Clap the lid on quickly before any steam escapes, and cover the pot with a tea cozy. This holds in the heat while the tea steeps. Allow about five minutes for this process. Then pour it, and drink!

I like my tea piping hot and without any additions. The English usually take milk, never cream. They claim milk does not smother the tea flavor, whereas the richer cream does. Some people like a slice of lemon or lime, and sugar, and an old favorite is something we used to call Russian tea; tea with sugar, lemon, and a dash of rum, a fine choice on a cold winter day.

Iced tea is a great summer bracer. Don't make the tea ahead of time and let it get cold before using it. Make it fresh and extra strong, and then pour it, while hot, over ice cubes. The flavor and aroma will be far better.

Scalding hot or icy cold, tea not only stimulates and revives, but has a subtle way of conjuring up the richness of a romantic past. An obscure poet has written:

Thy amber-tinted drops bring back to me
Fantastic shapes of great Mongolia towers,
Emblazoned banners, and the booming gongs;
I hear the sound of feast and revelry,

And smell, far sweeter than the sweetest flower
The kiosks of Pekin, fragrant of Oolong!

—Francis Saltus Saltus,
"Flasks and Flagons."

CRUMPETS

A cold day, a brisk fire in the grate, crumpets to toast and smother with butter and eat dripping with preserves between sips of hot, steaming tea! This is one of the great gastronomical treats. Most English, and yet it grows more and more difficult to find them there. Some strong-minded Britishers must form a Society for the Preservation of the Crumpet!

To make these you will need special crumpet rings, metal hoops that are placed on the griddle to hold the crumpet batter in shape.

- ¾ cake compressed or 1½ teaspoons active dry yeast*
- 2 cups warm milk
- 4 cups all-purpose flour
- ½ teaspoon of salt
- Butter

Dissolve the yeast in ½ cup warm milk. *(If dry yeast is used, dissolve it in ¼ cup warm water. Decrease milk by ¼ cup.) Sift the flour and salt into a warmed bowl and let stand in a warm place for 15 to 20 minutes.

Make a well in the center of the flour. Combine the yeast and milk with 1½ cups warm milk and pour this into the well. Stir it into the flour, mixing thoroughly. The batter should be thin. If the flour absorbs the milk too much, add more warm milk. Cover the batter with a clean towel and stand in a warm place to rise for about 45 to 60 minutes.

Grease a griddle and place the crumpet rings on it. Heat well. Fill each ring with batter to a depth of about ½ inch. Cook until the crumpets are nicely browned on the bottom, then turn them to finish cooking on the other side. The second side will be porous in texture and not as brown. To eat, toast the crumpets and butter lavishly on the porous side. Makes about 4 dozen.

CURRANT BREAD

This is one of my special delights on baking day and, for two or three days after, it brought joy to the breakfast and tea tables. On trips to England, I occasionally run across a tiny inn where they still serve currant bread, and I never fail to indulge myself. You will find that it makes a delicious base for walnut sandwiches, and is very elegant served with prune conserve or quince honey for tea.

- 1½ cups dried currants
  Rum or sherry
- 1 cup milk
- 3 tablespoons sugar
- 2½ teaspoons salt
- 6 tablespoons butter
- 1½ packages (or cakes) of yeast
- 1 cup warm water
- 6 cups all-purpose flour
- ½ cup sugar
- ½ cup softened butter

Cover the currants with rum or sherry, and set aside to soak for 1 hour or more.

Scald the milk and stir in 3 tablespoons of sugar, 2½ teaspoons of salt, and 6 tablespoons of butter. Let cool to lukewarm. Meanwhile, dissolve the yeast in 1 cup of warm water. Add this to the lukewarm milk mixture and stir in 3 cups of sifted flour. Beat until thoroughly smooth, and gradually add another 3 cups (approximately) flour, or enough to make a smooth, kneadable dough. Turn out on a lightly floured board and knead until thoroughly blended and elastic. (This will take about 10 to 12 minutes.) If you have an electric mixer with a dough hook, use this for the job and it will take 5 to 6 minutes. Put dough in a buttered bowl, cover with a clean towel or napkin, and set in warm place to stand until doubled in bulk.

Punch the dough down, turn it out onto the board again, and knead in ½ cup sugar, ½ cup softened butter, and the dried currants. Form the dough into 2 loaves and put these into buttered bread pans (9 x 5 x 3 inches). Brush with melted butter and let stand in a warm place until light. Bake in preheated hot oven (400°F.) for 50 minutes, or until done and nicely browned.

GINGER CAKES

My mother made her ginger cakes from an old Middlesex recipe. She baked them in round layer-cake pans and cut them into finger-shape pieces while they were still warm. Sometimes she added bits of chopped, crystallized ginger to the mixture, but I preferred plain ginger cakes.

- 2 cups all-purpose flour
- 1 cup firmly packed brown sugar
- 1 tablespoon ground ginger
- 1 teaspoon baking soda
- ¼ teaspoon salt
- 1 cup butter

Mix the dry ingredients well; then, with hands, combine them with the butter until well blended and crumbly. In a 9-inch layer-cake pan, put ½-inch thickness of the mixture and bake in preheated moderate oven (325°F.) for 45 to 60 minutes. Cut the ginger cake into finger-shape pieces while it is still warm. Remove the pieces carefully with a spatula and store in covered tins.

HOT OATCAKES

I remember watching with fascination as my Aunt Lizzie rolled out oatcakes and cut them into farls, or small sections, to bake on her floured "girdle." My reward for patient waiting was a goodly supply of the cakes—hot, crisp, and nicely curled at the edges. Traditionally, oatcakes, like potato scones, are served cold, but I find them far more delicious piping hot.

For this recipe, you must use the Scotch or the Irish oatmeal, not the regular rolled oats commonly found in our food stores.

- 1 pound Scotch or Irish oatmeal, and a little extra
- ¾ teaspoon salt
- ½ teaspoon baking soda
- 2 tablespoons fat (butter, beef drippings, or bacon fat)
- 1 cup hot water

Mix 1 pound of the oatmeal, salt, and soda and add the melted fat and hot water. Blend with wooden spoon until the dough is moist and will hold together. Sprinkle a board with a little oatmeal and roll out the dough into thin round cakes, about 8 inches in diameter. Dust the tops of these with a little oatmeal and cut each cake into 8 small triangles. Bake on a hot griddle dusted with oatmeal, turning the cakes several times to cook them on both sides. They should be very crisp.

Oatcakes may be baked in the oven, but they are better if made the old-fashioned way. If you bake them in the oven, arrange them on an ungreased cookie sheet and bake in preheated moderate oven (350°F.) for 20 minutes, turning them several times as they cook.

Serve these little cakes hot with butter and jam. Makes about 9 dozen.

POTATO SCONES

These were originally very simple peasant fare, often cooked over an open fire outdoors, or on the hearth. Later they became a fine snack for tea. I consider them a delectable Scottish specialty. They are traditionally served cold at tea; I prefer them served hot with plenty of butter.

- 1 cup warm mashed potatoes
- ⅓ cup melted butter
- 1 teaspoon salt
- ½ cup all-purpose flour

Mix all the ingredients until thoroughly blended. Divide the dough into thirds and roll each third out into a circle about ¼ inch thick. Cut each circle into sixths and bake on a hot floured griddle, or in a hot floured skillet, for about 5 minutes, turning once to brown on both sides. Makes 18.

SEEDCAKE

This favorite item was always kept on hand in a red tin box in our larder. I well remember sneaking a nice thick slice now and then. Although the theft was always detected, it was well worth it.

- 1 cup butter
- 1 cup sugar
- 5 eggs
- 2 cups all-purpose flour
- ½ teaspoon salt
- 1 teaspoon baking powder
- 1 teaspoon vanilla extract
- 1 to 2 tablespoons caraway seed

Cream the butter and sugar together. Add the eggs, one at a time, beating the mixture thoroughly after each addition. Add the rest of the ingredients and beat for 4 or 5 minutes by hand, or if you have an electric mixer beat the mixture with this for 2 minutes at low speed. Butter and flour a 9-inch tube pan and pour batter into this. Bake in preheated moderate oven (350°F.) for 45 minutes, or until cake tests done with a straw.

SHORTBREADS

We baked our shortbreads in squares, in rounds, and in fancy-shape molds. They always had elaborate fruit decorations on top. I still think these shortbreads are one of the tastiest of confections.

- 3 cups sifted all-purpose flour
- ½ cup sugar
- 1 cup soft butter
- 1 egg yolk

Mix first 3 ingredients very thoroughly with hands. Add egg yolk, kneading dough well after addition. Divide into 4 parts, and roll each into a square or circle about ½ inch thick. Prick with fork. Bake in preheated moderate oven (350°F.) for 15 minutes. Reduce heat to 300°F., and bake for about 30 minutes longer. Cut into eighths, and return to oven until edges are browned. Makes 32.

WHITE MOUNTAIN CAKE

This was a real specialty at our house.

- 1 cup butter
- 2⅔ cups sifted cake flour
- ½ teaspoon salt
- 1 teaspoon vanilla extract
- ¼ teaspoon cream of tartar
- 7 egg whites
- 1¾ cups sugar

Set the oven for 350°F. and butter a 9-inch tube pan. Add a sprinkling of flour to the buttered pan and shake it about to cover butter lightly; shake out excess flour.

Cream butter with 1⅓ cups flour and the salt until really fluffy. Add vanilla. Add cream of tartar to egg whites and beat until they form soft peaks. Add sugar gradually and continue beating until stiff. Carefully fold into butter mixture, alternating with remaining flour. Pour the batter into the tube pan and bake in preheated moderate oven (350°F.) for 50 minutes, or until cake pulls away from sides of the pan. Cool on a rack and turn out gently onto a decorative cake plate. Ice lavishly with your favorite white icing.

TEQUILA or TEQUILLA—A Mexican liquor distilled from the fermented sap of a century plant, the *Agave tequilana*.

TERRAPIN—A name given to several species of edible North American turtles which live in fresh or brackish waters. Terrapin is an adaptation of the old Indian name for the diamondback turtle that lives in the coastal swamps and rivers of the eastern seaboard. Growing to seven or eight inches long, it is considered by people of Baltimore and Philadelphia as one of nature's greatest delicacies. Around the turn of the century terrapin was the de luxe dish of all de luxe dishes, and even then it was very expensive. Now few terrapins come into the market and other turtles are marketed as substitutes.

Caloric Value

☐ Diamondback terrapin, 3½ ounces, raw = 111 calories

MARYLAND DIAMONDBACK TERRAPIN STEW

Fill a large kettle with water and bring to a boil. Toss live terrapin into boiling water. Boil for 5 minutes. Remove from water and rub it in a coarse towel to take off the skin of the feet and head. Fill kettle with fresh boiling salted water. Cook terrapin until shell cracks and feet fall off. Remove from broth and put it on its back. Reserve broth. Let terrapin cool.

Remove nails from feet. Cut meat out of shell. Remove carefully, without damaging them (so as not to taint flesh), gall bladder, sandbags, and large intestines. Throw them away. Cut meat into 1- to 2-inch strips. Cut liver and small intestines into small pieces and add to meat. If there are any eggs in the terrapin, add them to meat. In saucepan combine meat and about 1 cup of reserved broth. Simmer, covered, for 30 minutes. Add ¼ cup butter, and season with salt and pepper. If desired, add a dash of hot pepper sauce.

Combine about ½ cup heavy cream with 2 beaten egg yolks. Remove stew from heat and stir cream mixture into it. Return to heat and heat through, but do not boil. Remove from heat and stir in ⅓ cup sherry or Madeira. Makes 3 servings.

TERRINE—A dish, originally of earthenware, in which a *pâté* or similar food is prepared. Sometimes the food is sold in the same dish. Another meaning is: a kind of ragout cooked and served in the same dish, such as the French *terrine de boeuf*, similar to a *daube*. The term may also apply to a dish of several meats braised together and served in a terrine. A soup tureen is sometimes called a terrine.

TETRAZZINI—A main dish of cooked chicken baked with spaghetti in a rich cream sauce. The dish was named for Luisa Tetrazzini, a world-famous Italian coloratura soprano of the first part of the 20th century, who loved to eat well.

CHICKEN TETRAZZINI

- ¾ pound mushrooms, sliced
- 1 small green pepper, slivered
- ¼ cup butter or margarine
- 3 tablespoons all-purpose flour
- 2 teaspoons salt
- ¼ teaspoon pepper
- 2½ cups light cream
- 4 cups diced cooked chicken
- 2 pimientos, chopped
- 2 tablespoons sherry
- 6 ounces fine spaghetti, cooked
- 2 egg yolks, beaten
- Grated Parmesan cheese

Cook mushrooms and green pepper in butter for 5 minutes. Blend in flour and seasonings. Add cream and cook, stirring constantly, until thickened. Add next 3 ingredients, and heat. Divide spaghetti among 6 broilerproof baking dishes or put in large shallow baking dish. Add small amount of chicken or turkey mixture to egg yolks; stir into remaining mixture. Pour over spaghetti, and sprinkle with cheese. Bake in preheated slow oven (300°F.) for about 45 minutes. Put under broiler to brown lightly. Serve with tomatoes filled with vegetable salad on bed of greens. Makes 6 servings.

THANKSGIVING

Thanksgiving

by Sophie Kerr

If you were asked, on a quiz program perhaps, which is the only purely American holiday which is also an all-family celebration, would you answer instantly it is Thanksgiving Day? Oh yes, we have other purely American holidays, such as Fourth of July for Independence, Decoration Day in remembrance of our honored soldier dead, Columbus Day for the Great Admiral, Washington's and Lincoln's birthdays for our noblest statesmen, but Thanksgiving Day is different. It is a gathering of blood kin, a reunion of the generations. Since it is an autumn festival when the harvests are reaped and winter is drawing near, it is also a good time to look around us and within ourselves and think some penetrating thoughts on what we are doing and where we are going, what we are and what we aren't, what we have and what we haven't, and how much do we like ourselves.

And it is also a good time to recall those people who gathered together to celebrate the first Thanksgiving in New England, and observe how strongly the tradition of that day is still active among us, and among our morals and mores, all the way along to our menu. Make no mistake, the first Mayflower tourists are present on Thanksgiving Day, our unseen and unsuspected guests.

It was a group of obstinate, persevering, industrious, devout human beings who sat down to that feast of thanks for what they had achieved, and for the first solid hope of survival and progress. They had come through three years of bitter hardship, their number was smaller than when they landed, their needs no less. If today, as we look back on their meager living and note how little they had in comfort and security such as we take for granted, we might wonder what they had to be thankful for. We ourselves, we realize perhaps a bit shamefaced, wouldn't consider that we had anything at all to be thankful for if we had no more than Elder Brewster's valiant band. But then comes the blazing beautiful truth that although they had no steam heat, tiled baths, wall-to-wall carpet, or television, they did have courage, will power, and faith without limit, and these items add up to that one invaluable possession, character. Character can't be bought, can't be sold. It has to be built, a tiny scrap at a time, by those who would possess it.

WOMAN'S DAY

ENCYCLOPEDIA OF COOKERY

THANKSGIVING

So let's put at the top of our list of what we're thankful for the great and illuminating fact that the first Americans who had a Thanksgiving were people of great and illuminating character. They were not high-rolling adventurers hunting gold and gems. No, they were hunting freedom of spirit and belief for themselves and their descendants, and they were willing to work and sacrifice to get it. On that memorable feast day they sat down to eat with no great assurance that there'd be any food before them on the morrow. But they were free, and freedom is a magic sauce for the poorest dish. It is relish and sustenance for the soul. Brewsters, Bradfords, Carvers, Winslows, Cushmans, Allertons, John Alden the carpenter, Miles Standish the captain, what a dauntless company! All of us have inherited some of their passion for freedom. For this we can give thanks on this holiday which they unknowingly bequeathed to us.

The assembling of all the Plymouth colonists in one party for Thanksgiving (they had no babysitters) is the forerunner of the assembling of families for the holiday. Young and old, rich or poor, pretty or plain, families come together on The Day. There are dissenting opinions on the charm of this occasion, mutterings of: "Look, I didn't choose my family and I don't fancy having them all barge in on me en masse." My dear peevish brother, it is all too true, we didn't choose our families and obviously our families didn't choose us, either, and might very likely prefer as kin some quite different types from ourselves.

Nevertheless, they are our families. Perhaps some of them could be nicer, less critical, more agreeable, better-looking, more fun, but there they are, our families, and this is Thanksgiving coming up, the day when we sit at one table and eat and talk together and consider the strange and unexpected scions and sprouts of the family tree. Let's hit the philosophic note: Maybe Cousin Englebert isn't such a crabby old grouch after all, maybe Great-aunt Aggie is imposing-looking rather than overbearing, maybe sister Zoe's children are growing up to be almost human, and, given a little distance and atmosphere, the family makes a fair to good showing of citizens. And it wasn't at all a bad idea to have them all together and look them over. We actually like them better. We think maybe they like us better, too.

At the beginning of this little paper I noted that the early Thanksgiving celebrators had set a style for the feast's menu which has held through all these years. The colonists ate wild turkey and venison. Now, unless we have a hunter in the family, most of us aren't likely to eat venison, but the colonists' wild turkey has merely changed to the domestic turkey. Turkey is Thanksgiving fare, the day's main dish, but the accompaniments vary. A proper New Englander tells me that a proper New England Thanksgiving dinner consists of roast stuffed turkey, cranberry sauce or cranberry jelly, mashed potatoes, creamed onions, mashed turnips, and possibly Hubbard squash, with baked Indian pudding or pumpkin pie to follow. Farther South, when I was a small girl, we were more lavish, and at the Thanksgiving dinner at my grandparents' house in Maryland a big roast stuffed turkey was in the middle of the table, but there was a clove-studded baked ham at one end and a huge round dish of escalloped oysters at the other. There were two tall glass holders filled with celery, and some half dozen vegetables including super-delicious dried sweet corn; a whole fleet of sauceboats filled the spaces around these main dishes, with sweet-and-sour pickles, jelly, and spiced fruits of which I recall particularly the spiced whole crab apples. For dessert, there was pumpkin pie, homemade ice cream, and a seven-tiered chocolate cake. Yet let me say right here and now, there wasn't a fat person in the family, although my Aunt Cora, a mere in-law married to my Uncle Tom, was a pleasantly plump figure.

Grant that such Thanksgiving fare was not in the Puritanical style, the spirit of the day was reverent and there was nothing ostentatious or greedy about that crowded dinner table. Everything on it but the seasoning, spices, and sugar had been raised right there on the farm, and the oysters had been tonged up from the deep tidewater river flowing so quietly beside it. It was a peaceful and decorous feast, shared in thankful affection, as the prayer that preceded the meal attested. Elder Brewster and his congregation would have been at home with my grandparents who felt that all good that had come to them in life should be openly named and acknowledged. Moreover, they felt there was no soul alive who had nothing to be thankful for. They used the old-fashioned phrase "count your blessings," and they counted theirs and rejoiced that their neighbors had as much.

Yet, there are, and were always, people who never thought of listing what they possess to be thankful for! They are missing something exciting. It can give a new angle on the complication of today's living. Try it some time. You'll be surprised.

Last of all there are, and were always, people who resent the belief that thanksgiving is universal; people who honestly believe that they have nothing whatever to give thanks for. Perhaps these sad and resentful ones have suffered cruel bereavement, sickness, betrayal, losses so heavy and persistent and unjust that they feel stripped bare of all good, with nothing left even to hope for. To these unhappy spirits I offer the wonderful words of the gypsy to his despairing friend: "There's night and day, brother, both sweet things; sun, moon and star, brother, all sweet things; there's likewise a wind on the heath. Life is very sweet, brother."

I think Elder Brewster himself never said words of thanksgiving more touching and more true.

MENU

MUSHROOM CONSOMMÉ AND
CHEESE STRAWS
ROAST TURKEY WITH SAVORY
STUFFING, GIBLET GRAVY
WHOLE CRANBERRY SAUCE
CRANBERRY MOLD
DUCHESSE POTATOES WITH
YELLOW TURNIPS
ALMOND CANDIED YAMS
BUTTERED BROCCOLI
WHOLE GREEN BEANS
ONIONS AND CELERY IN CREAM
PEAS, MUSHROOMS, AND PIMIENTO
CELERY HEARTS, ASSORTED OLIVES
WATERMELON AND CANTALOUPE
PICKLES
ESCALLOPED OYSTERS
CHOICE OF PUMPKIN PIE TOPPED
WITH GINGER ROSETTES
MINCE TARTS
AMBROSIA IN
FROZEN ORANGE SHELLS
ROASTED NUTS
COFFEE

(Each recipe serves 6)

MUSHROOM CONSOMMÉ
To 2 cans beef consommé, add 1 can (3 or 4 ounces) canned chopped mushrooms, a pinch of instant minced onion, 1 tablespoon fresh lemon juice, and salt and pepper to taste. Heat. A dash of sherry can be added just before serving, if desired.

CHEESE STRAWS
Add ½ cup grated sharp Cheddar cheese and 1 egg yolk to ½ package prepared piecrust mix. Roll ⅛ inch thick; sprinkle with paprika. Cut into strips, 3 x ½ inches. Bake in preheated hot oven (425° F.) for 8 to 10 minutes.

ROAST TURKEY
Buy a ready-to-cook turkey, allowing 1 pound per person. Remove neck and giblets in the cavity of the bird. Wash the turkey inside and out, removing any bits of lung or kidney, and wipe dry.

THANKSGIVING

The turkey should be stuffed just before you're ready to roast it. Allow about 1 cup of stuffing per pound of drawn bird. (If any stuffing remains, put it in a baking pan, and after the turkey is cooked, spoon some of the turkey drippings over the stuffing and bake in preheated hot oven (425°F.) until well browned.) With a large bird, consider making 2 stuffings, one for the neck cavity and one for the body cavity.

If you want to add giblets to the stuffing, or make a giblet gravy, wash giblets and cook them, including the neck, heart, and gizzard, for about 2 hours in boiling salted water with an onion and a few celery leaves. Add liver during last 20 minutes. Drain, reserving broth for gravy. Remove meat from neck, chop with heart, gizzard, and liver. Add to stuffing or gravy.

Rub the turkey's neck and body cavities with salt. Lightly fill body cavity with stuffing. Tie the legs together with string. Stuff neck cavity lightly; draw skin of neck over cavity to the back, and fasten with a skewer. Fasten wings behind back by bending tip ends under.

The turkey can be roasted in an open pan or can be wrapped in foil.

To roast in an open pan, use preheated moderate oven (325°F.). Place turkey, breast side up, on wire rack in shallow pan. If you have a roasting thermometer, insert it between the thigh and the body, avoiding the bone. Cover bird with a piece of cheesecloth dipped in melted butter. If cheesecloth dries during cooking time, spoon some of the drippings in pan over it. Roast until thermometer registers 190°F., or until drumsticks can be moved up and down easily. When bird is done remove string, and place turkey on a large hot platter. Let stand for about 20 minutes before cutting, so the meat will absorb its own juices.

To roast wrapped in foil, use preheated very hot oven (450°F.). Put unstuffed turkey on its back in center of large piece of heavy-duty 18-inch wide foil. (To wrap a bird over 12 pounds, it may be necessary to use 2 strips of foil joined with a tight double fold. Open and press flat to prevent leaks.) Bring foil from one side up and over breast of turkey. Bring second side up, and lay over the first with an overlap of 3 inches; do not fold edges. Fold foil at ends of turkey, pressing close to body. Fold edges of side sections of foil together with edges of lower section over edge of upper section. The top of last fold should be 3 inches or more above bottom of pan to prevent drippings from running over top of fold. Place turkey in roasting pan. Roast in preheated very hot oven (450°F.) for the time indicated in roasting chart below. About 20 minutes before roasting time is up, open and fold back foil. Let juices run into the pan to brown for the gravy. When roasting time is ended, test for doneness in the same manner as for the unwrapped birds. Then remove bird and foil from the pan.

To make Garnish for Turkey: Cut large peeled carrots in half lengthwise. With vegetable peeler, strip off thin lengthwise slices. Put in ice water to curl. Put several on toothpicks to form flowers. Put a broccoli flower or sprig of parsley in centers. Arrange around turkey with watercress.

SAVORY STUFFING
Use one of the recipes for turkey under Poultry Stuffing, page 1781.

GIBLET GRAVY
For 6 cups gravy pour drippings from roasting pan into bowl. Skim off fat and put ½ cup fat in saucepan. Blend in ½ cup all-purpose flour and cook until bubbly. Measure skimmed drippings and enough of the broth reserved from cooking giblets to make 6 cups. Add, with giblets, to fat in saucepan and cook until thickened, stirring constantly. Season to taste with salt and pepper.

WHOLE CRANBERRY SAUCE
Mix 1 cup each sugar and water. Bring to boil, and boil for 5 minutes. Add 2 cups (½ pound) cranberries which have been picked over and washed. Cook for 5 minutes, or until cranberries stop popping. Do not stir. Cool in pan.

CRANBERRY MOLD
Cook 1 pound fresh cranberries in 2 cups water for 5 to 10 minutes, or until all skins pop open. Strain through fine sieve, pressing pulp through with juice. Stir in 2 cups sugar and boil for about 3 minutes. Pour into 1-quart mold and refrigerate for several hours, or until set. Unmold at serving time.

DUCHESSE POTATOES WITH YELLOW TURNIPS
Cook, and mash 6 medium-size potatoes with 2 tablespoons butter and ⅓ cup milk. Beat in 2 egg yolks. Put in casserole, making a nest. Bake in preheated hot oven (400°F.) for 20 minutes, or until lightly browned and hot. Fill center with 3 cups hot cooked Julienne-cut yellow turnips, seasoned with salt, pepper, and butter. Sprinkle with chopped parsley.

ALMOND CANDIED YAMS
Heat ¾ cup dark brown sugar, ½ cup water, and 3 tablespoons butter. Add 6 to 8 yams. Cook slowly until syrup is absorbed, turning potatoes several times. Sprinkle with toasted slivered almonds.

BUTTERED BROCCOLI
Cook 3 packages (10 ounces each) frozen broccoli according to package directions. Season to taste with salt, pepper, and butter.

WHOLE GREEN BEANS
Cook 3 packages (10 ounces each) frozen whole green beans according to package directions. Season with salt, pepper, and butter.

ONIONS AND CELERY IN CREAM
Slice 1 cup celery and cook in small amount of salted water until just tender. Add 2 cans (16 ounces each) drained onions and ½ cup medium cream; heat.

PEAS, MUSHROOMS, AND PIMIENTO
Cook 3 packages frozen peas and mushrooms (10 ounces each) according to package directions, and add 1 cut-up pimiento.

ESCALLOPED OYSTERS
Butter a 1½-quart baking dish. Crush fine enough crackers to make 2 cups cracker crumbs, and mix with ½ cup melted butter. Put crumbs in layers with 2 pints of oysters (reserve ⅓ cup of crumbs for top). Sprinkle each layer with salt and pepper. Mix 1 cup cream with oyster liquid and dash of mace. Pour over all. Sprinkle crumbs on top. Bake in moderate oven (350°F.) for about 40 minutes.

PUMPKIN PIE TOPPED WITH GINGER ROSETTES
In saucepan, mix 1½ cups canned pumpkin, ¾ cup light brown sugar, ½ teaspoon each of salt and ginger, 1 teaspoon

ROASTING TIME CHART

OPEN PAN (Stuffed)			IN FOIL (Unstuffed)	
Oven Temperature	Approximate Roasting Time	Drawn Weight	Oven Temperature	Approximate Roasting Time
325°F.	3 hrs.	8 lbs.	450°F.	2¼ hrs.
325°F.	3½ hrs.	10 lbs.	450°F.	2¾ hrs.
325°F.	4 hrs.	12 lbs.	450°F.	3 hrs.
325°F.	4½ hrs.	14 lbs.	450°F.	3¼ hrs.
300°F.	5½ hrs.	18 lbs.	450°F.	3½ hrs.
300°F.	6½ hrs.	25 lbs.	450°F.	3¾ hrs.

THICKEN, TO

cinnamon, dash of cloves, 1 can (14½ ounces) evaporated milk, and 2 tablespoons butter. Heat until butter is melted. Pour over 1 egg and 1 egg yolk, slightly beaten. Add ½ teaspoon lemon extract. Fold in 1 stiffly beaten egg white; cool. Pour into unbaked 9-inch pastry shell. Sprinkle with nutmeg. Bake in preheated extremely hot oven (500°F.) 8 minutes. Reduce heat to moderate (325°F.); bake for 30 minutes longer, or until set. Cool. Decorate with whipped-cream rosettes and candied ginger.

MINCE TARTS

Line tart shells with pastry. Fill with prepared mincemeat and crisscross with strips of pastry. Bake in preheated hot oven (400°F.) for 25 minutes, or until pastry is done. Serve with cheese, if desired.

AMBROSIA IN FROZEN ORANGE SHELLS

With sharp knife cut oranges zigzag about one-third of the way down from top. Scoop out pulp. Freeze shells (or chill). Combine pulp with chunks of pineapple. Fill shells and sprinkle with grated coconut. Garnish each with small leaf, if desired.

ROASTED NUTS

Buy nuts in shell, and heat in slow oven (300°F.).

THICKEN, TO—The culinary process of making a liquid food thicker or denser in consistency. Flour is one of the most common thickening agents, and cornstarch, tapioca, potato flour, bread crumbs, grated potato, cream, fats, and eggs are often used. Thickening agents that must be cooked in order to expand and thicken, like flour or cornstarch, should be mixed with a little cold water or liquid before being stirred slowly into the food. This prevents lumping. When adding cream or egg yolks to thicken a sauce, remove sauce from heat, stir in thickening agent, and return to heat. Bring to just below boiling point; don't boil, or sauce will curdle.

THYME—There are a number of varieties of this popular culinary herb. Garden and English thyme, *Thymus vulgaris*, are bushy little perennials, with gray-green leaves; garden thyme's leaves are broad, while the wild or creeping thyme, *T. serpyllum*, is a firmly matted ground cover. The wild thyme's leaves may be many colors other than green; two varieties have white striped or greenish-yellow leaves. Whether from wild or garden thyme, and no matter what their color, the pungent and sweetly fragrant leaves are widely used in cooking. Fresh or dried thyme flavors vegetable juices, soups, meat and poultry dishes, fish, cheese, stuffings, sauces, vegetables, cream and custard desserts, and jellies. It is traditional in New England clam chowder and much of Creole cooking. It is a relatively powerful herb with a distinctive flavor. Dried thyme is widely available in leaf or ground form. It is also found in herb combinations such as poultry seasoning.

HERBED CHICKEN CASSEROLE
1 frying chicken (3 pounds), cut up
¼ cup soft butter
1 tablespoon paprika
1 teaspoon ground dried thyme
1 teaspoon salt
½ teaspoon pepper
1 large carrot, sliced
2 slices of bacon, diced
½ cup consommé

Wash and dry chicken. Mix butter with seasonings and spread on chicken pieces. Put in casserole. Add remaining ingredients. Cover and bake in preheated hot oven (400°F.) for 1 hour, or until chicken and carrot are tender. Makes 4 servings.

TIMBALE—A word of French derivation meaning literally "kettle-drum." One culinary meaning is a custard or forcemeat mixture containing forcemeat, fish, or cheese, baked in individual timbale molds or custard cups, and unmolded; then served plain or with a béchamel or other sauce.

Another meaning is that a timbale is the edible mold itself and is made of pastry or even cooked macaroni, taken out of the dish it was baked in and filled with a meat, fish, cheese, or other mixture, even with spaghetti and sauce. Individual timbale cases to hold various mixtures are made with timbale irons which can be bought in various shapes and sizes: heart, round, square, and jumbo round. The irons are heated in fat, dipped in a fritter-like batter, and put back in the fat until cooked. Then they are pushed off the iron. They form pastry cases which can be filled with creamed mixtures or even with fruit for dessert. These timbale irons are sometimes called Swedish timbale irons and are available in stores selling Scandinavian kitchen equipment.

CREAMED CRABS AND SHRIMPS IN TIMBALE CASES
1 small onion, minced
3 tablespoons butter or margarine
3 tablespoons all-purpose flour
1 teaspoon seasoned salt
¼ teaspoon seasoned pepper
½ teaspoon steak sauce
½ teaspoon grated lemon rind
1½ cups milk
½ cup light cream
1 can (4½ ounces) shrimps, drained and rinsed
1 can (6½ ounces) crabmeat
1 can (3 ounces) sliced mushrooms, drained
2 tablespoons sherry
Salt and pepper to taste
Timbale Cases

Cook onion in the butter until golden. Blend in flour and seasonings. Add lemon rind, milk, and cream and cook, stirring constantly, until thickened. Add shellfish and mushrooms; add sherry, season, and serve in Timbale Cases, allowing 2 cases for each serving. Makes 4 to 6 servings.

Timbale Cases
Special timbale irons are necessary for making these

¾ cup all-purpose flour
½ teaspoon salt
1 teaspoon sugar
¾ cup milk
2 egg yolks, slightly beaten
Cooking oil

Mix dry ingredients. Stir in milk, egg yolks, and 1 tablespoon oil. Mix only until smooth. Let stand for several hours so that air bubbles disappear. Put enough oil in a small heavy pan to cover timbale iron completely. Put the iron into the cold oil and heat to 375°F. on a frying thermometer. Lift out the iron, drain slightly on absorbent paper, and dip into the batter to about three-quarters of its depth. Lift out, lower into the hot oil, and fry for 1 to 1½ minutes, or until delicately browned. Pry off timbale case with a fork. Drain upside down on absorbent paper. Proceed until all of batter is used. Makes about 18.

Note: Leftover cases may be frozen.

EGG TIMBALES WITH CURRY SAUCE
6 eggs
¾ teaspoon salt
Dash of pepper
Little grated onion
1½ cups milk
Curry Sauce

Beat eggs slightly; add seasonings, onion, and milk. Pour into 4 custard cups. Bake in shallow pan of hot water in preheated moderate oven (350°F.) for 20 minutes. Serve with Curry Sauce. Makes 4 servings.

Curry Sauce
1 small onion, minced
1 tablespoon butter
2 teaspoons curry powder
¼ cup ketchup
¼ cup milk
¼ teaspoon salt
½ cup water
1 tablespoon undiluted evaporated milk
1 tablespoon fresh lemon juice

Brown onion lightly in butter; add curry powder. Combine ketchup, milk, salt, and water and add gradually. Cook until thick. Add evaporated milk and lemon juice.

CHEESE TIMBALES
4 eggs
1½ cups milk
¾ cup soft stale-bread crumbs
1 cup shredded sharp Cheddar cheese
¾ teaspoon salt
⅛ teaspoon pepper
1 teaspoon Worcestershire

WOMAN'S DAY

Beat eggs and milk until well mixed. Add remaining ingredients. Turn into 4 custard cups. Set in pan of hot water. Bake in preheated moderate oven (350°F.) for 30 to 40 minutes, or until set. Makes 4 servings.

TIME, TO—The phrase, when applied to foods, means to prepare or cook them for a specified length of time. Foods are marinated for so many hours or days, they are cooked or baked for so many minutes or hours, etc.

Accurate timing is one of the essentials of good cooking, since the success of the dish depends on it. Much of it can be learned from following recipes carefully. But some knowledge of timing comes only from experience; no recipe can cover every possible contingency in cooking. Meats, for instance, may vary in the ways they are cut, the age of the animal, whether they were frozen, etc., and all of these factors affect their timing. Experience also counts in being able to time all the various dishes in a meal so that they will be ready at the same time. A timer is a most valuable little kitchen accessory. It is wound and set like an alarm clock, and it goes off like one, reminding the cook to look after her food. Modern kitchen stoves are often equipped with timers.

TINT, TO—As a culinary phrase this means to add a coloring substance to foods in order to intensify or change their color. The tinting is done either by natural means, such as using spinach juice to make green noodles, or with artificial food colorings. These contain United States certified colors, and are sold in little bottles. Since they are very concentrated, they must be used cautiously, drop by drop, or results can be dismaying.

Most commonly, tinting is used in frostings, candies, and other sugar cookery, and in commercial baking.

TOAST—A slice of bread, thick or thin, put under the broiler or in an electric toaster and browned or toasted on both sides.

TOAST COOK BOOK

By JEANE ELAM

APRICOT-HONEY TOAST
2 eggs, beaten
⅔ cup apricot nectar
Honey
8 slices of white bread
Butter, bacon fat, or cooking oil

Combine eggs, apricot nectar, and 2 tablespoons honey in bowl. Dip each bread slice into apricot mixture, turning to coat both sides. Grill or panfry bread on both sides in hot butter. Serve with additional honey.

BACON-CHEESE TOAST
8 lean bacon strips, minced
½ pound mellow Cheddar cheese, grated
Butter
Sliced white bread

Add minced bacon to grated cheese and blend well. Spread on lightly buttered bread. Broil on cookie sheet until cheese is melted.

BANANA TOAST
2 bananas, sliced
4 slices of buttered toast
2 tablespoons brown sugar
Salt to taste

Arrange banana slices on toast and sprinkle with brown sugar and salt. Broil, watching carefully, until banana cooks and sugar bubbles.

CALLIE-TOAST
Take oval-shape toast and spread with Mustard Butter, page 1829. Border the edges with a line of finely chopped and very red smoked tongue. Garnish the middle of each with chopped white chicken meat and, in the center, drop a pinch of chopped truffle.

CARAMEL-CARDAMOM TOAST
16 slices of bread
1 cup firmly packed brown sugar
½ cup butter or margarine
¼ teaspoon ground cardamom

Toast bread on one side, remove crusts, and spread untoasted side generously with mixture of remaining ingredients. Toast spread side in broiler until bubbly and brown. Cut into fingers before serving.

CHEESE TOAST ROLL-UPS
2 cups soft sharp cheese
½ teaspoon salt
Dash of cayenne
1 teaspoon prepared mustard
3 tablespoons heavy cream
Thin slices of white bread, crusts removed

Combine all ingredients except bread, and stir to a smooth paste. (Grate cheese if necessary.) Spread on bread and roll the slices. Secure with toothpicks. Put on cookie sheet and bake in preheated hot oven (400°F.) until cheese is melted. Remove toothpicks and serve roll-ups piping hot.

CHEESE TOAST SPECIAL
2 tablespoons butter or margarine
1½ tablespoons all-purpose flour
½ cup milk
½ cup grated Switzerland Swiss cheese
3 tablespoons dry white wine
½ teaspoon powdered mustard
1 garlic clove, minced
1 egg, beaten
Salt and white pepper to taste
Diagonal slices of French bread

Melt butter and blend in flour. Add milk and cook, stirring constantly, until thick and smooth. Cool for 15 minutes. Then stir in remaining ingredients except bread. Toast bread on one side. Spread untoasted side with the cheese mixture, making the layer of spread about ½ inch thick. Put under broiler until heated and lightly browned.

CHOPPED BEEF TOAST
½ pound chopped beef
¼ teaspoon onion salt
½ teaspoon monosodium glutamate
4 slices of white bread
2 tablespoons butter or margarine

Mix first 3 ingredients. Spread bread with half of butter and toast on one side. Spread untoasted side to edges with the chopped beef; dot with remaining butter and broil for 5 or 6 minutes. Makes 2 servings as a luncheon dish or snack.

CINNAMON TOAST DE LUXE
1-pound loaf fresh white bread
1 cup butter or margarine
1 cup fine granulated sugar
1 tablespoon ground cinnamon

Cut slices of bread diagonally. Sauté half of slices slowly, 2 or 3 at a time, adding butter gradually until each piece is golden-brown on each side, but not dark. Remove slices from skillet and drop into a clean unglazed brown-paper bag containing a mixture of sugar and cinnamon. Shake gently and serve warm. Makes 24 to 32 pieces. To pick up less sugar, put toast on a paper towel to dry for a minute after browning in butter.

Note: For variety, combine sugar and cinnamon and add a little water to make a paste. Dip bread into paste and sauté

TOAST COOK BOOK

in butter until browned. The sugar and butter caramelize and give the toast a delicious crisp crust. Serve while hot.

CROUTONS
Trim crusts from bread slices and dice bread. Sauté in butter until an even brown. Or butter slices of trimmed bread, cut into dice, and brown in preheated moderate oven (350°F.)

DANISH TOAST
Lightly toast (do not grill) slices of dark or whole-rye bread equal in thickness; spread with Horseradish Butter (page 1829). Then cover with alternate strips of smoked salmon, caviar, and herring fillets marinated in white wine.

DEVILED TOAST
- 2 tablespoons butter or margarine
- ½ teaspoon cayenne
- 1 teaspoon prepared mustard
- 1 teaspoon pickle relish
- Hot toast rounds

Mix first 4 ingredients and spread on hot toast. Good, too, topped with sliced cooked sausage or broiled kidney.

DUTCH RASPBERRY TOAST
- 12 slices of stale bread, without crusts
- ⅓ cup butter or margarine
- Raspberry syrup
- Ground cinnamon
- 1 cup heavy cream, whipped

Sauté bread in the butter. Pour some of the raspberry syrup over a layer of cooked bread. Sprinkle with cinnamon. Cover with another layer of the fried bread slices, pour some sauce over it, and continue in this way until toast is used. Let stand for several hours at room temperature. Serve with whipped cream.

EGG AND CHEESE TOAST
Make well seasoned scrambled eggs. Toast 1 slice of bread for each serving and spread with chutney or tomato ketchup. Heap the scrambled eggs on the toast and cover thickly with grated Cheddar cheese. Put under broiler to brown lightly. Sprinkle with chopped parsley or garnish with narrow strips of green pepper alternating with strips of pimiento.

FLUFFED BRANDY TOAST
- Unsliced white bread
- 2 eggs
- 1 cup milk
- ¼ cup brandy
- ¼ cup butter or margarine
- 3 tablespoons sugar

Cut 6 slices of bread 1 inch thick; trim off crusts. Beat together eggs, milk, and brandy; soak bread for 5 minutes in this mixture. Melt butter in skillet; brown one side, turn, and sprinkle with the sugar. Brown underside.

FRENCH TOAST
- 2 eggs, beaten slightly
- ⅔ cup milk
- ½ teaspoon salt
- 8 slices of white bread
- Butter or margarine
- Sugar

Combine eggs, milk, and salt. Dip bread into the mixture and brown each side in well-buttered griddle or skillet. Serve hot, sprinkled with sugar.

FRIED TOAST WITH ANCHOVIES
- ½ pound Mozzarella cheese, sliced thin
- 8 anchovy fillets
- 16 slices of bread, ½ inch thick, from long French loaf
- ½ teaspoon pepper
- ½ cup all-purpose flour
- 2 eggs, beaten
- Olive oil

Put a slice of Mozzarella and 1 anchovy fillet on each of 8 slices of bread. Sprinkle with pepper and cover with another slice of bread. Dip into cold water and roll in flour. Then dip into beaten eggs and fry in olive oil until golden-brown on each side.

GARLIC TOAST, ITALIAN STYLE
- 1 loaf Italian bread
- ¼ cup garlic-seasoned oil
- Grated Parmesan cheese
- Paprika

Split loaf of bread lengthwise. With knife, score cut sides crisscross fashion. Brush with garlic oil and sprinkle with cheese. Put under broiler until golden-brown. Sprinkle with paprika and cut diagonally into serving pieces.

GOLDENROD TOAST
- 4 eggs, hard-cooked
- 2 cups white sauce
- 6 to 8 slices of white bread, toasted
- Parsley

Separate yolks and whites of eggs and chop whites. Add whites to the sauce. Heat thoroughly and pour over toast. Sprinkle with riced egg yolks and garnish with parsley.

HERBED TOAST
- 1 loaf French bread
- ½ cup sweet butter, softened
- 1 tablespoon finely minced parsley
- 1 teaspoon each of finely minced chives, chervil, and tarragon
- ½ teaspoon finely minced basil

Cut bread into slices 1 inch thick. Combine butter and herbs, creaming thoroughly with a fork. Spread one cut surface of each slice with the herbed butter, spreading it well to the edges. Bake for 10 minutes in preheated very hot oven (450°F.). (One large garlic clove, minced, may be added to herbs before creaming with butter.) If dry herbs are used, use half the amounts and soak them in a little vermouth, white wine, or water for 10 minutes. Squeeze out extra moisture before mixing with butter.

HONEY PECAN TEA TOAST
Spread white bread with butter, then with honey. Sprinkle with crushed pecans and broil until browned. Top each with a tiny dab of red jelly. Delicious with afternoon tea or a fruit salad plate.

ISLAND TOAST WITH BACON
- 2 eggs
- 1 cup pineapple juice
- ½ teaspoon salt
- 4 slices of stale bread, ½ inch thick
- 8 slices of bacon
- 4 slices of drained pineapple, cut into halves

Beat eggs until light; stir in pineapple juice and salt. Dip bread into mixture and soak well. Sauté bacon and set aside on hot platter. Fry the bread in the bacon drippings until browned on both sides. Remove bread to platter with bacon. Sauté pineapple in the bacon drippings. Garnish platter with bacon and pineapple.

ROLLED JAM TOAST
- Sliced white bread
- Butter
- Jam

Remove crusts from bread. Spread bread with butter, then with jam. Roll slices and secure with toothpicks. Put on baking sheet and toast under broiler. Turn to brown evenly.

LEMON TOAST
Toast 6 slices of white bread on one side. Cream ¼ cup butter or margarine with 1 teaspoon fresh lemon juice and 1 teaspoon grated lemon rind. Spread on untoasted side of bread and broil until golden-brown. Serve with fish entrées. Or add 2 tablespoons sugar to mixture, spread, and broil as directed. Serve as tea toast.

MELBA TOAST
Cut white bread or other bread into the very thinnest possible slices and remove crusts. Put bread in a barely warm oven until crisp and slightly browned. Cool, and store in a tightly closed container in cool place or refrigerator.

1 — Rolled Jam Toast
2 — Honey Pecan Tea Toast
3 — Dutch Raspberry Toast
4 — Cheese Toast Roll-Ups
5 — Goldenrod Toast
6 — Callie Toast
7 — Shrimp Toast
8 — Toast Luncheonettes
9 — Pineapple Finger Toast
10 — Sour-Cream Date Toast
11 — Spiced Marmalade Toast
12 — Waffle Toast with Cinnamon-Nut Topping

TOAST COOK BOOK

MILK TOAST
Cut bread ¾ inch thick and toast lightly on each side. Spread lightly with butter and sprinkle with salt to taste. Put in bowl and pour 1 cup hot milk over top.

PEACH PUDDING TOAST
- 1 package (3 ounces) vanilla pudding and pie filling
- 2 eggs
- 1 cup milk
- ⅛ teaspoon ground cardamom
- 8 slices of white bread
  Butter, bacon fat, or cooking oil
- 1 package (12 ounces) frozen peaches, thawed
- 1½ teaspoons fresh lemon juice

Combine pudding mix, eggs, milk, and cardamon. Dip bread slices into mixture and brown in butter on griddle or in skillet. Mix peaches and lemon juice and serve over toast.

Note: Juice from peaches can be mixed with 1 teaspoon cornstarch and cooked until thick. Cool, and combine with peach slices mixed with lemon juice.

PINEAPPLE FINGER TOAST
Unsliced white bread
Pineapple spears, drained
Brown sugar and cinnamon (3 parts sugar, 1 part cinnamon)
Butter or margarine

Remove crusts and cut bread into strips 3 inches x 1½ inches and 1½ inches thick. Toast on 3 sides. Put strips on baking sheet with untoasted side up, laying pineapple stick on top. Sprinkle well with sugar and cinnamon mixture. Dot with butter. Brown under broiler.

PRALINE TOAST
- 1 cup firmly packed brown sugar
- ¼ cup melted butter or margarine
- ½ cup finely chopped pecans
- 12 thin slices of white bread

Mix brown sugar and butter, add pecans, and blend thoroughly. Spread mixture on bread and brown in preheated hot oven (400°F.) for 5 to 10 minutes.

PUFFED TOAST SQUARES
- ½ pound Cheddar cheese, softened
- ½ cup butter or margarine, softened
  Prepared mustard
  Curry powder
  Caraway or celery seeds
  Salt, and pepper or paprika to taste
  White bread, cut into 1½-inch cubes

Blend cheese, butter, and seasonings to taste. Cover bread cubes with the cheese spread. Keep chilled until ready for use. Put on cookie sheet and put in preheated moderate oven (375°F.) until browned and puffed.

Note: Any of the following seasonings are also delicious creamed with the butter: chili powder, dillseed, grated lemon rind, parsley, or pimiento.

PULLED TOAST
Remove the crusts from a small loaf of bread and pull the bread apart into irregular pieces with 2 forks. Put in preheated slow oven (300°F.) until dry and light brown. Good with soups or salads.

RAISIN SCRAMBLE TOAST
- 8 slices of day-old raisin bread
  Butter or margarine
- 5 eggs
- ⅓ cup half-and-half or milk
- 1 teaspoon seasoned salt

Toast raisin bread until dry and golden-brown. Butter each slice, then cut into small cubes; shake off excess crumbs. Beat eggs lightly with half-and-half and salt. Heat 2 tablespoons butter in large skillet. Add eggs and cook over low heat, stirring occasionally, until eggs are creamy and begin to thicken. Add toast cubes. Stir gently just until set but still moist.

RUM-CINNAMON TOAST STICKS
White bread, unsliced
Rum
Butter or margarine, melted or creamed
- 1 part ground cinnamon and 3 parts granulated sugar, or ½ cup confectioners' sugar, ½ cup firmly packed brown sugar, and 1 tablespoon ground cinnamon

Cut bread into ¾-inch slices. Then cut slices into ¾-inch strips. Sprinkle with rum. Dip strips into butter and roll in either of the sugar mixtures. Toast strips on 4 sides or put in preheated hot oven (400°F.) for 8 minutes. These are especially good put together with applesauce.

SALT STICKS
Cut sliced white bread into ½-inch strips. Brush with melted butter or margarine. Toast in preheated hot oven (400°F.) for 8 to 10 minutes, or until lightly browned. Sprinkle with coarse salt.

SESAME TOAST
- 3 tablespoons sesame seeds
- 3 tablespoons soft butter or margarine
- 2 garlic cloves, peeled and crushed (optional)
- 1 long loaf Italian or French bread

Spread sesame seeds in a pan and brown lightly in preheated hot oven (400°F.). Combine seeds with butter and garlic, if used. Cut bread into thick slices. Butter each slice. Put in hot oven (400°F.) for 15 to 20 minutes.

SHRIMP TOAST
Cover toast rounds with Shrimp Butter, page 1829, and garnish with a border of shelled shrimp tails with a caper in the center of each round.

SOUR-CREAM DATE TOAST
- 1 cup dairy sour cream
- 1 cup chopped pitted fresh dates
- 12 slices of white bread
- 2 eggs
- ¾ cup milk
  Dash of salt
  Bacon fat
- 12 crisp bacon slices

Mix sour cream and dates. Spread on 6 slices of bread and cover with remaining 6. Beat eggs with milk and salt. Dip bread into mixture and brown on both sides in bacon fat. Serve hot with crisp bacon slices.

SPICED MARMALADE TOAST
- 1 loaf French bread, about 12 inches long
- ⅓ to ½ cup soft butter or margarine
- ½ cup orange marmalade or apricot or cherry preserves
  Ground cinnamon

Cut bread into 1- to 1½-inch diagonal slices. Spread generously with butter, then with marmalade. Sprinkle cinnamon over top. Put slices, marmalade side up, in shallow pan and bake in preheated hot oven (400°F.) until edges are crisp.

TEXAS-STYLE ONION TOAST
Put slices of bread on a long shallow baking pan or ovenproof dish. Drizzle olive oil or cooking oil over slices and brown on one side under broiler. Turn slices and top untoasted sides with thinly sliced Bermuda onion. Drizzle more oil over top and brown under broiler. Sprinkle lightly with grated Parmesan cheese and return to broiler for a few seconds. Good with roast beef or steak.

TOAST BOXES
Cut stale bread into 2½-inch cubes. Trim off all crusts and hollow out center, leaving sides of box ½ inch thick. Toast in preheated hot oven (400°F.) until delicately browned, but not dried. Remove from oven and brush with butter. Fill with any desired filling.

TOAST CUPS
Preheat broiler. Cut crusts from bread slices, spread one side with soft butter

and press buttered side to fit into muffin-pan sections. Brush top sides with butter and place on a low shelf under the broiler until golden-brown. Use instead of patty shells when serving creamed dishes.

TOASTED ROUNDS AND STICKS

Cut white bread with a doughnut cutter. Cut any kind of dark bread into sticks. Toast in oven until lightly browned. Put sticks through holes in rounds. Serve hot with butter or margarine.

TOAST LUNCHEONETTES

Spread hot toast rounds lightly with butter. On each round, put a thick slice of tomato. Cover the tomato with chopped onion and chopped green pepper. Season with salt and pepper to taste. Or put on each buttered round a slice of American cheese and a piece of partially cooked bacon. Crisp the bacon under the broiler.

TOMATO-SOUP TOAST

    2 eggs
    ½ teaspoon salt
    ¼ teaspoon paprika
    ½ cup condensed tomato soup
    6 slices of bread
      Butter or drippings
      Parsley or chives, minced

Beat first 4 ingredients until light. Dip bread into this mixture and sauté in hot butter until browned. Serve sprinkled with minced parsley.

TOWN TOAST

    ½ cup butter or margarine
    ½ cup grated Gruyère cheese
    ½ cup grated Parmesan cheese
    2 tablespoons heavy cream
      Dash each of salt and cayenne
      Toast rounds
      Lyons sausage or cervelat, very
        thinly sliced
      Gruyère cheese, sliced

Mix butter, grated Gruyère and Parmesan, cream, and seasonings. Spread thickly on toast rounds. Top with thin slices of sausage and slices of Gruyère cheese.

WAFFLE TOAST WITH CINNAMON-NUT TOPPING

    Butter or margarine
    8 slices of white bread
    1 egg, slightly beaten
    ¾ cup milk
      Dash of salt
      Sugar, ground cinnamon, and
        chopped nuts

Spread butter lightly on bread. Mix egg, milk, and salt. Dip each bread slice into egg-milk mixture. Drain, then put in heated waffle iron. Bake until golden-brown. Serve hot with mixture of sugar and cinnamon, and chopped nuts.

NONSWEET TOAST BUTTERS

• **Anchovy**—Wash 12 to 15 salt anchovies in cold water and dry them thoroughly. Remove the fish from the bones, pound smoothly with ½ cup butter, and rub through a fine sieve. Chill. Canned anchovies can be substituted for the salt fish, if preferred.
• **Caper**—Mix ¼ cup soft salt butter and 2 tablespoons minced capers. Chill.
• **Caviar**—Mix ¼ cup soft salt butter, 2 teaspoons caviar, ¼ teaspoon grated onion, and a few drops of fresh lemon juice.
• **Chive**—Mix ¼ cup soft salt butter and 2 tablespoons minced chives. Chill.
• **Crayfish**—Pound ¼ cup cooked crayfish with ½ cup soft salt butter. Rub through a fine sieve; chill.
• **Garlic**—Mix ¼ cup soft salt butter and 2 crushed garlic cloves; chill.
• **Horseradish**—Mix 2 tablespoons soft salt butter and 1 tablespoon freshly grated horseradish. Use at once as this turns dark on storage.
• **Lemon**—Mix 3 tablespoons soft salt butter, 1 teaspoon fresh lemon juice, ½ teaspoon grated lemon rind, and 1 teaspoon minced parsley; chill.
• **Mustard**—Mix 3 tablespoons soft sweet butter, 1 teaspoon minced onion, and 1 tablespoon prepared mustard; chill.
• **Nut Butter**—Mix ¼ cup sweet butter and 2 tablespoons finely minced salted nuts.
• **Olive Butter**—Mix ¼ cup soft sweet butter, 2 tablespoons chopped olives, and a few drops of onion juice.
• **Paprika**—Mix 3 tablespoons soft sweet butter, 2 teaspoons paprika, and ½ teaspoon onion juice; chill.
• **Samsoe**—Mix 2 tablespoons each of soft salt butter and grated Samsoe cheese; chill.
• **Shrimp**—Pound ½ cup cooked shrimps with ½ cup soft salt butter. Rub through a fine sieve; chill.

SWEET TOAST BUTTERS FOR TEA TOAST

• **Honey**—Cream ½ cup sweet or salt butter and ½ cup to 1 cup honey. Chill.
• **Orange**—Cream ½ cup salt or sweet butter, ½ cup firmly packed brown sugar, 2 teaspoons grated orange rind, and 2 teaspoons fresh orange juice. Chill. Chopped nuts can be added if desired.
• **Orange-Brandy**—Cream ¼ cup salt or sweet butter, ½ cup sifted confectioners' sugar, ½ teaspoon grated orange rind, and 1 tablespoon orange or plain brandy.

TODDY—An alcoholic drink, hot or cold, made from a basic liquor such as whiskey or rum, with the addition of hot water or ice, sugar, and such spices as cinnamon, nutmeg, and cloves.

The original toddy was an Asian drink made from the fresh or fermented sap of several kinds of palm trees, chiefly East Indian varieties. The word is of Hindustani origin, from *tari*, "juice of palmyra palm." In India the sap is also used as a leavening substance for bread. Toddies are not limited to India, but are made throughout southeastern Asia, Brazil, Africa, etc., always from some type of palm sap.

The word toddy came into English use through the British traders of the Far East, who applied it to their potions. The colonists brought the word to the New World, along with the drink. Toddies were very fashionable in polite 18th-century society, and today both the word and the drink have a delightful old-fashioned connotation.

A hot whiskey or rum toddy is made by dissolving sugar to taste in half a tumbler of boiling water. Add 1 jigger whiskey or rum or more to taste, a twist of lemon peel, and a pinch of ground cinnamon or ground nutmeg.

TOFFEE—A brittle but chewy candy made by cooking together sugar and butter or cream, with the possible addition of such other ingredients as nuts and chocolate.

TOFFEE

    2 cups firmly packed brown sugar
    ¼ cup butter
    1 tablespoon vinegar
    2 tablespoons boiling water
    1 teaspoon vanilla extract

Combine ingredients in heavy saucepan. Bring to a boil and cook until mixture reaches 290°F. on a candy thermometer, or the hard-crack stage, that is, when a little of mixture, dropped into cold water, will separate into hard brittle threads. Pour into a pan (8 x 14 inches). Cool a little. When lukewarm, mark into squares with the point of a sharp knife. Makes about 1 pound toffee.

TOMATO—The fruit of a plant of the genus *Lycopersicon*, native to South America. It grows on vines which sprawl, bush, or clump, according to training and environment. The semiwild tomato of Peru has vines that are twenty to fifty feet long and climb all over trees and bushes. The cultivated tomato is usually not quite so vigorous. Tomatoes come in many shapes and colors. They may be yellow, green, or whitish, or even vari-

TOMATO

colored, as well as the best-known red. They may be ribbed, round, pear shape, or cherry shape. The small green varieties are often used in pickles, while the large ripe red ones are most popular in sauces. The deep-red pear-shape tomato is a specialty of Italian tomato pastes, and is often canned with basil.

The tomato was first found wild thousands of years ago by the pre-Incan civilizations of Peru and Ecuador. It was carried north by these people as they migrated to Central America and Mexico. The Spanish explorers who came to Mexico took the fruit which the Nahuatl Indians called *tomatl* back with them to Europe in the early 16th century. There the Italians and Spaniards ate them, usually stewed or in sauces. Their northern neighbors, the English, thought the fruits pretty, but disdained to eat them. At the end of the 16th century a famous English herbalist, Gerard, got seeds from Spain and Italy so he could grow plants as curiosities. He remarked disparagingly of eating tomatoes: "They yield very little nourishment to the bodie, and the same naught and corrupt."

This doubting attitude prevailed for some time. Tomatoes were thought by some people to be poisonous, and by others to be a powerful aphrodisiac.

Time broke down some of the English prejudice, and by the middle of the 18th century one observer commented that tomatoes were "much used in soups." These early tomatoes were probably only palatable cooked in stews or sauces. They were of the ribbed kind, and considerably smaller and harder than the juicy sweet varieties we know today, which had not yet been bred.

In this country tomatoes were grown in Virginia as early as 1781, but only as a curiosity. Around the turn of the century they were brought to various cities by immigrants. A refugee from the Haitian revolt against the French is said to have introduced them to Philadelphia in 1798; an Italian painter carried them to Salem, Massachusetts. Although looked upon as curiosities tomatoes had their partisans such as the Maine editor who advised in 1835 that the tomatoes were a "useful article of diet and should be found on every man's table." But it was not until after 1840 that tomato cultivation became widespread.

The Maine editor's "every man" could not have tomatoes on his table until the end of the 19th century. The fruit is a tropical one, and it cannot be grown in the North during the winter, for it dies at the first frost. Tomato growing was introduced to Florida during the 19th century, and the produce was shipped north by refrigerated cars. However, it was not until the Spanish-American war at the end of the century that the tomato canning and preserving industry developed to such an extent that tomatoes became one of the most used fruits.

Availability—Fresh tomatoes are now available all year round with greatest supplies from May through August. Most commonly found are: *beefsteak,* large, red, and slightly elliptical in shape, for eating raw; *red cherry,* cherry-size and shape, bright red, excellent for eating raw, pickles, and preserves; *San Morzano,* intense red, plum-shape, for eating raw, tomato pastes, and purées; *yellow plum,* plum-size and shape, bright yellow, for eating raw and preserves.

Canned whole tomatoes, tomato juice, purée, paste, sauce, and soup are all universally available, as are pickled green tomatoes. Bottled tomato ketchup and chili sauce are available. Spaghetti sauces based on tomatoes are available canned, frozen, or dehydrated. Dehydrated tomato soup is also available.

Purchasing Guide—Tomatoes are best in flavor if ripened on the vine in nearby areas. Those shipped long distances must be picked green and so are less juicy and flavorful when ripened and sold in our markets. Look for tomatoes that are a good color for their variety, firm, rounded, and free from blemishes. If they are not all to be used immediately include a few that are a little underripe. Tomatoes should be heavy for their size.

Storage—If fully ripe, refrigerate. The slightly underripe tomatoes will keep for 8 to 12 days, ripening while refrigerated. Green tomatoes should be kept at room temperature so they will continue ripening. To store peeled tomatoes, wrap in wax paper, plastic wrap, or foil and refrigerate. Tomatoes should not be frozen raw, only as a cooked food.

☐ Fresh, ripe, refrigerator shelf, raw: 2 to 3 days
☐ Fresh, underripe, refrigerator shelf, raw: 8 to 12 days
☐ Fresh, cooked; and canned, opened, refrigerator shelf: 4 to 5 days
☐ Canned, kitchen shelf: 1 year
☐ Fresh, in cooked dishes, refrigerator frozen-food compartment, prepared for freezing: 2 to 3 months
☐ Fresh in cooked dishes, freezer, prepared for freezing: 1 year

Nutritive Food Values—A good source of vitamins and minerals, especially vitamins A and C. Tomatoes are low in calories.

☐ Fresh, 3½ ounces, raw = 22 calories
☐ Fresh, 3½ ounces, boiled = 26 calories
☐ Canned, 3½ ounces, regular pack, solids and liquid = 21 calories
☐ Canned, 3½ ounces, dietary pack, solids and liquid = 20 calories
☐ Ketchup, 3½ ounces = 106 calories
☐ Chili sauce, 3½ ounces = 104 calories
☐ Canned tomato juice, 3½ ounces = 19 calories
☐ Canned tomato juice cocktail, 3½ ounces = 21 calories
☐ Canned tomato paste, 3½ ounces = 82 calories
☐ Canned tomato purée, 3½ ounces = 39 calories

Basic Preparation—Wash and cut out stems. Peel if desired. To peel, dip into boiling water for about ½ minute, then into cold water to chill. The skin will slip off easily. Or hold a tomato on a fork over an open flame or high heat until skin splits; peel. Or stroke the skin lightly with the back of a knife; then slip off the skin.

☐ **To Stew**—Cook, covered, with no water (a few slices of onion may be added) for 8 to 10 minutes. Season with any of the following: salt, pepper, celery salt, 1 or 2 teaspoons sugar, a piece of bay leaf. Butter and a few bread crumbs or toast cubes may be added before serving.

☐ **To Broil**—Cut out core from stem end of firm tomatoes. Cut into halves. Put on cookie sheet. Make crisscross cuts on top surface of each. Dot with butter and sprinkle with salt, pepper, and onion salt. Or use any of the seasonings listed below. Broil under moderate heat for 10 minutes, or until tomatoes are tender and topping is lightly browned. If preferred, tomatoes can be baked instead, in preheated hot oven (425°F.) for 10 to 15 minutes.

Seasonings for Broiled Tomatoes
Spread with soft butter, and add one of the following combinations:
- Bread crumbs, onion salt, ground sage, and thyme
- Thinly sliced onion and paprika
- Grated cheese and soft bread crumbs
- Grated Parmesan cheese
- Crushed dry cereal and shredded cheese
- Chopped green onion or chives
- Chopped fresh herbs such as thyme, rosemary, marjoram, dill, basil, or sage

Omit butter, and top with one of the following:
- Garlic spread
- Anchovies and oil from can
- Peanut butter and chopped crisp bacon
- French dressing or mayonnaise
- Cheese spread
- Prepared mustard and a dash of Worcestershire

TOMATO COOKBOOK

In soups, salads, vegetable dishes, sauces, spicy relishes and preserves, the tomato is a colorful and nutritious asset to any meal.

TOMATO COOK BOOK

APPETIZERS AND SOUPS

CUCUMBER TOMATO COCKTAIL
- 1 medium cucumber
- 2¼ cups tomato juice
- 2 tablespoons chopped green onions and tops
- 1 teaspoon Worcestershire
- Juice of 1 lemon
- 2 teaspoons prepared horseradish
- ½ teaspoon salt
- ⅛ teaspoon pepper
- Dash of hot pepper sauce
- Lemon wedges

Peel cucumber and grate. Add remaining ingredients except lemon wedges. Cover and refrigerate for 2 hours. Strain through a coarse sieve, and garnish with lemon. Makes 4 servings.

HOT APPLE-TOMATO APPETIZER
- 2 cups apple juice
- 2 cups tomato juice
- 8 whole cloves
- 1 teaspoon fresh lemon juice
- ½ teaspoon Worcestershire

Mix all ingredients and simmer for 5 to 8 minutes. Strain to remove cloves and serve hot in mugs. Or chill and serve as a cocktail. Makes 4 cups.

SPICED TOMATO COCKTAIL
- 1 cucumber
- 5¾ cups (one 1-quart, 14-ounce can) tomato juice
- 3 green onions, chopped
- 3 tablespoons fresh lemon juice
- Dash hot pepper sauce
- 1 tablespoon Worcestershire sauce
- 1 tablespoon bottled horseradish, drained
- Salt and pepper to taste

Peel and grate cucumber. Add to tomato juice. Add remaining ingredients. Mix thoroughly. Cover and let stand in refrigerator for about 2 hours. Strain through a coarse sieve. Makes 8 servings.

SHERRIED TOMATO-SHRIMP BISQUE
- 4⅔ cups (two 1-pound, 3-ounce cans) tomatoes
- 2 cups beef broth (or use beef bouillon cubes and water or canned beef bouillon)
- 1 cup cut celery and leaves
- 2 small onions, sliced
- 2 small carrots, sliced
- 2 parsley sprigs
- 4 whole cloves
- 6 peppercorns
- Small piece of bay leaf
- Pinch of ground thyme
- 2 teaspoons salt
- 3 tablespoons uncooked rice
- 1½ pounds shrimps, cooked and cut into pieces
- 2 cups light cream
- Sherry
- Croutons
- Thin slices of lemon and chopped parsley

Put tomatoes, broth, vegetables, seasonings, and rice in kettle; bring to boil. Cover, and simmer for 1 hour. Force through fine sieve, or put in blender, and whirl until smooth. Just before serving add shrimps; heat. Heat cream and add to tomato mixture. Season to taste. Serve at once with dash of sherry and a sprinkling of croutons. Garnish with lemon slices and finely chopped parsley. Makes about 2½ quarts.

CHILLED CREAMY TOMATO SOUP
- 1 can (18 ounces) tomato juice, chilled
- ¾ teaspoon salt
- ¼ teaspoon ground basil
- Pinch of ground marjoram
- ½ cup dairy sour cream
- 1 tablespoon chopped chives or green onion

Mix all ingredients except chives. Blend with beater or in blender. Sprinkle with chives. Makes 4 to 6 servings.

SPICY TOMATO BOUILLON
- 2⅓ cups (one 1-pound, 3-ounce can) tomatoes or 2 cups chopped ripe tomatoes
- 1 can (10½ ounces) beef broth
- 1 small onion, sliced
- ¼ teaspoon each of celery seeds and peppercorns
- 3 whole cloves
- Salt
- Chopped parsley

Heat all ingredients except salt and parsley. Simmer for about 10 minutes. Season to taste with salt. Serve topped with parsley. Makes 4 servings.

TOMATO-AND-HERB SOUP ON THE ROCKS
- 2 beef or chicken bouillon cubes
- 1 cup boiling water
- 3 cups tomato juice
- 1 onion, grated
- 1 cup chopped celery
- 1 green pepper, minced
- 1 teaspoon salt
- 1 garlic clove
- 3 tablespoons fresh lemon juice
- Dash of hot pepper sauce
- 2 tablespoons minced fresh herbs (parsley, basil, savory, etc.)
- ½ cucumber, sliced
- 2 peeled ripe tomatoes, sliced

Dissolve bouillon cubes in water; cool slightly. Combine bouillon, tomato juice, onion, celery, green pepper, and salt. Cut garlic into halves and put toothpick through both halves; then add to mixture. Mix lightly. Chill, covered, in refrigerator for several hours, or overnight. Just before serving, remove garlic; add the remaining ingredients, and more salt if needed. Put 2 cubes of ice in each serving. Makes 1½ quarts.

CREAM-OF-FRESH-TOMATO SOUP
- 2 cups chopped ripe tomatoes
- 1 medium onion, sliced
- ½ bay leaf
- ½ teaspoon salt
- ⅛ teaspoon pepper
- 2 tablespoons butter or margarine
- 2 tablespoons all-purpose flour
- 2 cups milk
- Chopped fresh basil or mint

Simmer tomatoes with onion, bay leaf, salt, and pepper for about 10 minutes. Strain. Melt butter and stir in flour. Add milk and cook, stirring constantly, until thickened. Slowly stir in hot tomatoes. Sprinkle with herb. Makes 4 servings.

HOT DISHES

STEWED GREEN TOMATOES AND PEPPERS
- 1 large onion, sliced
- 3 tablespoons butter or margarine
- 2 medium green peppers
- 6 large green tomatoes
- Salt and pepper to taste

Cook onion in butter in skillet for 3 minutes; do not brown. Wash and core peppers and tomatoes; cut into eighths lengthwise. Add to onion. Simmer, covered, stirring often, for 20 minutes, or until peppers are just tender. Season with salt and pepper. Makes 4 servings.

TOMATOES, CORN, AND OKRA
- 1 medium onion, chopped
- 2 tablespoons butter or margarine
- 1 pound okra, sliced
- 4 medium tomatoes, peeled and quartered
- Salt, pepper, and paprika
- 1 cup corn, cut from cob or canned

Cook onion in butter until yellow. Add okra and cook for about 5 minutes, stirring. Add tomatoes and cook until okra is tender. Season to taste with salt, pepper, and paprika. Add corn; cook for 5 minutes longer. Makes 4 servings.

SAVORY TOMATOES, BEANS, AND SQUASH
- 1 large onion, sliced
- 1 garlic clove, minced
- ¼ cup minced parsley
- 2 teaspoons salt
- ¼ teaspoon each of pepper, ground thyme, and ground sage
- 2 tablespoons cooking oil
- 1 pound green or wax beans, cut
- 3 large tomatoes, diced
- 2 cups diced yellow squash

WOMAN'S DAY

Cold Tomatoes Stuffed with Shrimp Salad

Cook onion, garlic, parsley, and seasonings in oil in large skillet for about 3 minutes. Add remaining ingredients. Add water to half the depth of mixture. Cover and simmer for 20 minutes, or until beans are tender. Makes 4 to 6 servings.

FRIED TOMATOES WITH CREAMY GRAVY

Remove ends from 4 large tomatoes, and cut into halves. Season tomatoes, and dredge with flour. Brown on both sides in 3 tablespoons bacon fat. Remove to hot platter. Blend 1 tablespoon flour into drippings in pan. Add 1½ cups milk. Cook until thickened, stirring constantly. Add more seasoning if necessary. Pour over tomatoes; serve at once. Makes 4 servings.

FRIED GREEN-TOMATO AND CUCUMBER SLICES

- 2 large green tomatoes
- 1 large ripe (yellow) cucumber
- Salt and pepper to taste
- Undiluted evaporated milk
- Quick-cooking rolled oats
- Cooking oil

Slice tomatoes about ½ inch thick. Peel cucumber, slice, and remove seeds. Sprinkle with salt and pepper. Dip slices into milk, then into oats; rub oats between hands to make them fine. Fry slowly in hot oil until brown and tender. Makes 4 servings.

EGG-AND-TOMATO SCRAMBLE

- 6 eggs, beaten
- 2 medium tomatoes, chopped
- ½ teaspoon salt
- ⅛ teaspoon pepper
- Few fresh basil leaves, chopped
- 2 tablespoons butter or margarine

ENCYCLOPEDIA OF COOKERY

TOMATO COOK BOOK

Combine eggs, tomatoes, and seasonings. Melt butter in skillet; add egg mixture and cook, stirring occasionally, until scramble thickens. Makes 4 servings.

BAKED STUFFED TOMATOES
- 4 large ripe tomatoes
- 1 can (10½ ounces) cream-of-mushroom soup
- Salt and pepper to taste
- Stuffing
- Buttered soft bread crumbs

Cut a thin slice from stem end of unpeeled tomatoes. Scoop out centers, leaving outer wall. Reserve centers. Pour soup into shallow baking dish and put tomato shells in dish. Sprinkle inside of tomatoes with salt and pepper. Fill with any one of the following stuffings. Then sprinkle with buttered bread crumbs. Bake in preheated moderate oven (375°F.) for about 30 minutes. Makes 4 servings.

Corned-Beef Hash Stuffing
Cook 1 chopped onion in 2 tablespoons shortening for 5 minutes. Add tomato centers, and cook until thick. Add 1 can (1 pound) corned-beef hash and 2 tablespoons chopped parsley. Mix well, and fill tomatoes.

Savory Crumb Stuffing
Cook 1 chopped onion and ¼ cup chopped celery in ¼ cup butter for about 5 minutes. Add tomato centers, and simmer for about 10 minutes. Add 4 cups soft bread crumbs, 1 teaspoon poultry seasoning, salt to taste, and a dash of cayenne. Mix well, and fill tomatoes.

Macaroni or Rice Stuffing
Cook 1 chopped onion, ½ chopped green pepper, and ¼ cup chopped celery in 2 tablespoons shortening for about 5 minutes. Add tomato centers, and cook for 10 minutes. Combine with 2 cups cooked macaroni or rice. Season to taste with salt and pepper. Fill tomatoes.

Vegetable Stuffing
Simmer tomato centers, and combine with a cooked vegetable: Lima beans, chopped broccoli or spinach, peas, or green beans. Season to taste with salt, pepper, and onion salt. Fill tomatoes.

SCALLOPED TOMATOES
- 4 cups stewed fresh or canned tomatoes
- Salt, pepper, and sugar
- ¼ teaspoon onion juice
- 1½ cups soft bread crumbs
- ¼ cup butter or margarine, melted

Season tomatoes with salt, pepper, and sugar to taste. Add onion juice. Mix crumbs and butter. Alternate layers of tomatoes and crumbs in shallow 1½-quart baking dish, ending with a thick layer of crumbs. Bake in preheated hot oven (400°F.) for about 20 minutes. Makes 4 to 6 servings.

GREEN BEANS AND GLAZED TOMATOES
- 1 pound whole green beans
- 2 tablespoons butter
- ½ cup sugar
- Dash of salt
- 4 cups chopped peeled tomatoes

Cook whole beans, covered, in small amount of boiling salted water until tender. Meanwhile, melt butter in skillet; stir in sugar and salt and add tomatoes. Cook over low heat until liquid has boiled down, turning tomatoes frequently to glaze on all sides. Drain beans and top with tomatoes. Makes 4 servings.

SALADS

LAYERED TOMATO-AND-COTTAGE-CHEESE SALAD
- 2 cups cottage cheese
- ⅓ cup mayonnaise
- 1 green onion, chopped
- 6 stuffed olives, chopped
- Salt and pepper to taste
- 6 large tomatoes
- Lettuce

Mix cottage cheese, mayonnaise, green onion, and olives. Season with salt and pepper. Cut a thin slice from stem ends of tomatoes; remove cores; cut each tomato into 3 slices. Put slices together with cheese mixture to make 6 servings. Serve on lettuce, romaine, escarole, or other salad greens, and top with remaining cheese mixture. Makes 6 servings.

TOMATOES WITH HERBS
Use one of the small varieties: Red Cherry, Yellow Pear, or Yellow Plum. Chill well and serve whole, in salad or as appetizers, sprinkled generously with salt and minced fresh sweet basil, marjoram, thyme, rosemary, or dill. Add French dressing, mayonnaise, or oil and vinegar.

COLD STUFFED TOMATOES
Cut out stem-end core of unpeeled tomatoes. Starting at center of other end, cut into quarters or eighths ¾ of way down. Pull gently apart. Fill with shrimp salad and whole shrimps, or creamy potato salad, tuna salad, cole-slaw, chicken salad, cottage cheese, vegetable salad, or diced avocado and lemon juice. Serve in lettuce cups, and garnish with dairy sour cream, mayonnaise, parsley, mint, olives, radishes, small pickles, or slices of green pepper.

ITALIAN TOMATO SALAD
Peel and slice 4 large ripe tomatoes and arrange in a serving dish. Sprinkle with salt and pepper. Pour over them a vinaigrette sauce made with 6 tablespoons olive oil, 2 tablespoons wine vinegar, 1 teaspoon salt, and some pepper. Add to this ½ to ⅔ cup coarsely crumbled tuna fish. Spoon over the tomatoes. Makes 4 servings.

SAUCES

TOMATO SAUCE
- 2 tablespoons olive oil
- 3 parsley sprigs, minced
- ½ cup chopped celery
- 1 garlic clove, minced
- 2½ pounds tomatoes, peeled and chopped
- 1 can (10½ ounces) tomato purée
- 1 teaspoon salt
- ½ teaspoon pepper
- 1 bay leaf, crumbled
- ½ teaspoon each of crumbled dried basil and oregano

Heat oil, add parsley and celery, and cook until lightly browned. Add garlic, tomatoes, purée, salt, and pepper. Simmer for about 45 minutes. Add remaining ingredients and cook for 10 minutes longer. Makes about 5 cups.

Note: Leftover sauce can be stored in a covered jar in refrigerator and used on vegetables or spaghetti.

TOMATO PURÉE
Wash, core, and quarter tomatoes. Put in large kettle and crush slightly. Cover, bring to boil, and simmer until soft, about 10 minutes. Strain off clear juice and boil it down to less than ⅓ of its original volume. Force remaining tomatoes through strainer to make purée. Add to concentrated juice; bring to boil. Pour into hot sterilized pint jars and add 1 teaspoon salt to each pint. Seal, and process in boiling water for 15 minutes.

■ **To Process**—Heat water while preparing purée. The kettle should be deep enough to cover jars with at least 1 inch of water. There must be a rack on the bottom of the kettle. Prepare only enough jars of purée at one time to fill canner. Place the jars on the rack in the canner far enough apart to allow free circulation of water around them. Start counting processing time as soon as the water boils. Keep the water boiling during entire processing time. Remove jars. Then cool on a rack away from drafts.

WOMAN'S DAY

PICKLES, RELISHES, AND PRESERVES

SWEET SPICY TOMATO RELISH

- 7 pounds ripe tomatoes
- 3 cups cider vinegar
- 4 pounds (8 cups) sugar
- 1 tablespoon salt
- ¼ cup whole cloves

Peel and chop tomatoes. Cover with vinegar and allow to soak overnight. Drain. Put tomatoes, sugar, and salt in kettle; add cloves tied in a piece of cheesecloth. Cook to consistency of preserves. Let stand overnight. Heat to boiling; remove cloves. Pour into hot sterilized jars; seal. Makes 5 pints.

TOMATO, PEPPER, AND CELERY RELISH

- 3 medium tomatoes
- 1 green pepper, minced
- ⅓ cup diced celery
- 1 small onion, minced
- 1½ teaspoons salt
- 2 tablespoons each of vinegar and sugar
- ½ cup cold water
- ⅛ teaspoon pepper

Peel and dice tomatoes. Combine with remaining ingredients. Chill for several hours. Drain. Makes about 2 cups.

YELLOW TOMATO PRESERVES

- 5 pounds yellow pear tomatoes
- 1 lemon, sliced very thin
- 1 teaspoon ground ginger
- 5 pounds (10 cups) sugar
- ¼ teaspoon salt

Pour boiling water over tomatoes. Let stand for 3 minutes, drain, rinse in cold water, and drain again. Discard lemon seeds and cut slices into halves. Add ginger, sugar, and salt; let stand overnight. Drain. Cook syrup until very thick. Add tomatoes and simmer until thick. Pour into hot sterilized jars, and seal. Makes about four ½-pint jars.

TOMATO BUTTER

- 4 pounds (about 12) ripe tomatoes
- 2½ cups firmly packed light brown sugar
- 1¼ teaspoons each of ground cinnamon and cloves
- ¼ teaspoon ground allspice
- Dash of salt

Scald, peel, and quarter tomatoes. Cook, covered, until mushy, stirring occasionally. Measure; there should be 1½ quarts. Put back into kettle and add remaining ingredients. Bring to boil and simmer, uncovered, stirring frequently, for 45 minutes, or until thick. Fill hot sterilized jars; seal. Makes 2 pints.

ENCYCLOPEDIA OF COOKERY

Tomato, Pepper, and Celery Relish

Tomato-and-Herb Soup on the Rocks

TONGUE

Savory Tomatoes, Beans, and Squash

TOMATO JAM
- 3 pounds (6 large) fully ripe tomatoes
- 1 lemon, thinly sliced
- 1 box (2½ ounces) powdered fruit pectin
- 5 cups sugar

Scald, peel, and quarter tomatoes, removing all of stem and core. Remove seeds and drain off juice, reserving only the pulp. Put in kettle, bring to boil, and simmer, uncovered, for 8 to 10 minutes. Measure; there should be 3 cups. Put tomatoes, lemon, and pectin in kettle. Bring to a full rolling boil, stirring constantly. Add sugar and boil rapidly for 2 minutes. Cool for 5 minutes, stirring occasionally to prevent floating fruit. Fill hot sterilized jars, and seal. Makes four or five ½-pint jars.

GREEN-TOMATO JAM
- 11 cups (about 5 pounds) chopped green tomatoes
- Hot water
- 8 cups sugar
- 2 lemons, thinly sliced

Cover tomatoes with hot water and boil for 5 minutes. Drain, and add sugar. Let stand for 3 hours or longer. Drain syrup into a kettle; bring to boil and cook rapidly until it spins a thread. Add tomatoes and sliced lemons; cook for 10 minutes until thick and clear. Pack into hot sterilized jars, and seal. Makes 4 pints.

GREEN TOMATO MARMALADE
- 3 quarts sliced green tomatoes
- 6 cups sugar
- 1 teaspoon salt
- 6 lemons

Mix tomatoes, sugar, and salt in bowl. Peel lemons and slice peel very thin. Boil peel in 1 cup water for 8 minutes; drain, and discard water. Slice lemon pulp thin and remove seeds. Combine lemon rind, pulp, and tomato mixture in large kettle. Heat to boiling and cook rapidly, stirring constantly, for about 45 minutes, or until thickened. Pour into hot sterilized jars, and seal. Makes about six ½-pint glasses.

TONGUE—The tongue of beef, veal, lamb, or pork is eaten as meat. Tongue is a nourishing and appetizing food, good hot or cold. Tongue needs long slow cooking in liquid to make it tender.

Availability and Purchasing Guide—Tongue is available all year round. It is sold fresh, smoked, corned, and pickled.

Beef tongue, weighing from 2 to 5 pounds, is available fresh, smoked, or corned. Cooked, it can be obtained in ready-to-serve packages, cans, and jars.

Veal tongue, weighing from ½ to 2 pounds, is sold fresh.

WOMAN'S DAY

Lamb tongue, weighing from 3 to 4 ounces, is sold fresh and pickled, or cooked in glass jars.

Pork tongue, weighing from ½ to 1¼ pounds, is sold cooked in cans or jars as "lunch tongue."

Storage—Fresh tongue should be refrigerated.
- Fresh, refrigerator shelf, uncooked: 1 day
- Fresh, cooked; and canned, opened, refrigerator shelf: 2 to 3 days
- Smoked, refrigerator shelf: 3 days
- Corned or pickled, refrigerator shelf: 7 days

Corned, pickled, or smoked tongue should not be frozen, since salt and fat interferes with proper freezing.

Nutritive Food Values—A good source of protein, high in fat content, with a good amount of iron, fair niacin and riboflavin.
- Beef, fresh, 3½ ounces, braised = 244 calories
- Veal, 3½ ounces, braised = 160 calories
- Pork, 3½ ounces, braised = 253 calories
- Lamb, 3½ ounces, braised = 267 calories
- Corned, 3½ ounces = 267 calories
- Smoked, 3½ ounces = 290 calories

Basic Preparation—Cover tongue with cold water, adding salt, pepper, and bay leaf to the water if the tongue is fresh. Use 1 teaspoon salt for each quart of water. Bring water to a boil. Reduce heat and simmer, covered, until easily pierced, 1 to 1¼ hours per pound; beef tongue, 2½ to 4 hours; veal tongue, 1½ to 3 hours. Remove tongue from water and cool slightly. Or, if the tongue is to be served cold, cool in liquid for added juiciness. Cut off bone and gristle at thick end of tongue. Slit skin on underside of tongue. Peel off skin. Cut tongue into ¼-inch-thick slices. Slice narrow part of tongue on a diagonal, gradually turning knife until the thickest part is cut into crosswise slices.

Tongue Twisters
By IRIS BROOKS

No, nothing to do with P. Piper and his produce, but new twists on that old favorite, tongue. Have it pickled or corned, smoked or fresh; canned or in jars, plain or in vinegar; beef, calf, pork, or lamb; but by all means, have it. Whether hot or cold, whole on the platter or in even pink slices, tongue is always a delight to the eye and a joy to the palate. And how nice to be able to eat every ounce you pay for! There's very little waste on tongue; just good meat, good protein, and good eating.

But if tongue automatically calls to mind the usual spinach-and-boiled potato accompaniment, why not change your way of thinking and try the four dinners we suggest? They're all planned for six.

MENU
CHILLED BROCCOLI BISQUE
TONGUE INDIENNE OR POLONAISE
ALMOND-SWEET-POTATO PUDDING
LETTUCE AND TOMATO AVOCADAISE
COFFEE SPONGE

While a saucy tongue may not be charming in a woman, it's a definite and delicious asset to this dinner: so much so that we give you a choice of sauce to serve with ready-to-eat canned tongue. Both soup and dessert can be made early in the day, and the unusual sweet potato pudding could also be prepared in advance and popped into the oven to warm while you make the salad and dressing.

CHILLED BROCCOLI BISQUE
Chop 6 scallions, green tops included; 1 young carrot, and 1 stalk celery. Simmer until tender in ¾ cup water. Chop 1 large bunch, or 2 packages frozen, broccoli and cook for about 6 minutes in a minimum of water. Purée all vegetables in the blender or put through a fine sieve. Add 3 cups rich chicken broth. Bring to a boil, then simmer just long enough to blend flavors, about 3 minutes. Chill. Before serving, stir in 1½ cups light cream and check seasoning. Add salt and pepper to taste.

Pick one of these spirited sauces; prepare it in a skillet, then add tongue slices, and simmer just enough to heat through.

SAUCE INDIENNE
Break up ½ cup mango chutney with a fork. Add 1 can beef gravy, 1 tablespoon fresh lemon juice, ½ tablespoon sugar, ½ teaspoon curry powder, and 1 teaspoon Worcestershire or beefsteak sauce. Taste, and season as you like, adding more sugar if the chutney is a hot one. The sauce should be spicy, not fiery. Mix well, bring to a boil, then simmer for a few minutes to blend the flavors. Makes about 1 cup.

SAUCE POLONAISE
Blanch and sliver enough almonds to make ¼ cup. Toast until golden 2 tablespoons all-purpose flour; and blend with 2 tablespoons butter, then add 2¼ cups beef bouillon or consommé. Cook until smooth and thickened; add the almonds, ¼ cup raisins, 2 teaspoons bottled sauce for gravy, juice of 1 small lemon, 1 tablespoon sugar, ½ cup red wine, and salt and pepper to taste. Simmer for 10 minutes, stirring frequently; then add tongue to heat through. Makes about 2½ cups.

ALMOND-SWEET-POTATO PUDDING
Beat 2 eggs well and combine with 3 cups hot mashed sweet potatoes. Add ¼ cup milk, 3 tablespoons butter, salt to taste, and a little grated nutmeg. Beat thoroughly. Put in baking dish, sprinkle with brown sugar and slivered almonds, and dot with butter. Bake in moderate oven (375°F.) for about 20 minutes.

LETTUCE AND TOMATO AVOCADAISE
Serve lettuce and tomato wedges with a dressing made by combining equal quantities of mayonnaise and avocado purée, thinned to taste with fresh lime or lemon juice, and spiced with hot pepper sauce.

COFFEE SPONGE
Beat 3 egg yolks well with ¼ cup sugar. Soften 1 envelope unflavored gelatin by sprinkling it over ¼ cup water, and dissolve in 1½ cups double-strength hot coffee. Add ¼ to ½ cup sugar, according to taste. Combine in top part of a double boiler with ½ cup milk. Cook over hot water, stirring, and be careful not to let mixture come to a boil. Pour a bit of the hot mixture over the egg yolks, combine, and cook, without boiling, just long enough to make a thin custard. Remove from heat and add 1 tablespoon brandy or rum. Chill until thickened. Beat egg whites stiff, adding a pinch of salt. Whisk chilled custard well, then fold in whites. Refrigerate for at least 3 hours before serving with cream, plain or whipped.

MENU
MINTED MELON BALLS
BRAISED TONGUE WITH POTATOES
BRUSSELS SPROUTS AND ONIONS
AU GRATIN
CARROT CURLS AND RIPE OLIVES
TANGELEMON ICE CREAM

BRAISED BEEF TONGUE
Here's a tongue that develops a mellow flavor as it cooks in the oven.

Cover a fresh beef tongue with boiling water and simmer for about 1 hour. Re-

TONGUE

move from water, trim off bone and gristle at thick end; then skin. Put on rack in roasting pan. Add 4 cups of the liquid in which tongue was boiled, 1 onion, 1 carrot; sprinkle with salt and pepper. Cover and bake in preheated slow oven (325°F.) for 1 hour; add 6 to 8 medium potatoes and bake for 1 hour longer, until meat and potatoes are tender. Remove tongue and strain liquid. Thicken with flour-and-water paste. Add a little gravy coloring if desired.

BRUSSELS SPROUTS AND ONIONS AU GRATIN

Drain 1 can (16 ounces) white onions. Cook 2 packages frozen Brussels sprouts according to directions. Make a sauce using ¼ cup butter, 3 tablespoons cornstarch, 2 cups undiluted evaporated milk, 1 cup water, a pinch of ground saffron, and salt and white pepper to taste. Combine with the drained vegetables and pour into casserole. Cover generously with grated Parmesan cheese, top with fine dry bread crumbs, dot with butter, and bake in preheated moderate oven (375°F.) for about 20 minutes, or until golden and bubbly. For a change, try this with broccoli instead of the sprouts.

TANGELEMON ICE CREAM

Blend ½ cup sugar with ½ cup fresh lemon juice and 1 can undiluted frozen tangerine-juice concentrate. Add about 2 drops of yellow and 1 drop of red food coloring to 4 cups chilled light cream. Stir into juice mixture gradually. Pour into 2 ice-cube trays and freeze until firm.

MENU

QUICK BORSCH
POTTED LAMB TONGUES
KASHA
MUSHROOMS À LA RUSSE
CUCUMBERS AND CRESS IN HORSERADISH DRESSING
JAM TARTS

This tongue speaks with a Russian accent. Delicate in texture and flavor, these little lamb tongues are slowly and simply simmered in an onion gravy. Plan on two, at least, for each serving. Of course, we begin with borsch, made in no time at all, thanks to canned beets and consommé. Add buckwheat groats and creamy mushrooms as perfect accompaniments, a hint of horseradish in the salad, and finish with a traditional Russian sweet.

QUICK BORSCH

Drain liquid from 1 can (16 ounces) whole baby beets and add to it 1 can condensed beef consommé diluted in ½ soup-canful water, 1 tablespoon sugar, and 1 large bay leaf. Bring to boil, then let simmer while you halve and slice one-third of the beets and shred the rest on a hand grater. Add beets to soup and simmer for 5 minutes. Squeeze 1 lemon and start adding juice to soup, tasting as you do. There's no way to measure how much more juice or sugar you may need. Keep sampling until soup is pleasantly sweet-and-sour.

Check for salt and pepper, and remove bay leaf. Beat 2 eggs with 2 tablespoons water. Bring soup to rolling boil and pour eggs in gradually, stirring constantly, so that eggs form a curd. If you like, you can pour the hot soup over a whole boiled potato in each bowl or, to serve it ice cold, omit the eggs, and put about 4 tablespoons dairy sour cream into each plate before adding soup.

POTTED LAMB TONGUES

In a Dutch oven over high heat, in 4 tablespoons butter, cook 2 cups chopped onion and 2 garlic cloves, minced. Let the onion get quite brown, and don't worry if some gets burnt; that's the idea. Pour in 1 cup water and add 2 teaspoons salt, 1 teaspoon sweet paprika, and ½ teaspoon pepper. Let cook dry. Then with spoon loosen all that good brown crust on the pan; add whole fresh lamb tongues and enough water just to cover them. Bring to boil, then cover and simmer for about 1¼ hours. Serve unsliced, garnished with parsley, and pass the gravy to go with:

KASHA

In a heavy skillet, toast 2 cups buckwheat groats over moderate heat for about 5 minutes, stirring to prevent sticking. Stir in 2 eggs, mixing well so that all groats are coated. Gradually add 4 cups boiling water, stirring constantly. Season with 1½ teaspoons salt. Turn heat low, cover, and let cook for 15 minutes or until double in bulk. Remove cover, place skillet on asbestos pad over low heat, and let moisture evaporate completely, leaving kasha dry and fluffy. Or dry in a slow oven.

MUSHROOMS À LA RUSSE

Slice 1½ pounds fresh mushrooms and sauté in 3 tablespoons butter for about 3 minutes. Add ¾ cup water and simmer, uncovered, until tender. Blend 2 tablespoons all-purpose flour and 1 teaspoon sweet paprika with ⅔ cup dairy sour cream. Add ½ small onion, grated, and ¾ cup light cream. Cook sauce, stirring, until thick. Add mushrooms and liquid with salt and pepper to taste and simmer for 5 minutes more. Makes 8 servings.

CUCUMBERS AND CRESS IN HORSERADISH DRESSING

Peel and slice cucumbers; cut into julienne strips. Chop watercress leaves and stems. Toss with mayonnaise blended with prepared horseradish, cider vinegar, and sugar to taste.

JAM TARTS

We've never overcome a childish passion for these jam tarts and, come to think of it, why should we? The cheese pastry is a snap to make, keeps well in the refrigerator, and can be used for all sorts of cookies, as piecrust, or as a cocktail-appetizer base.

Russian Cheese Pastry

Cut ½ cup butter into 1 cup sifted all-purpose flour. Cut in ¼ pound cream cheese. Blend with fingers to a smooth dough. Wrap in wax paper and chill for at least 2 hours before using.

Tarts

Roll out Russian Cheese Pastry about ¼ inch thick and cut into twenty-four 3-inch circles. With a 2-inch cutter, take the centers out of all but 8 of the circles, making 16 rings. Moisten the edge of each circle, top with a ring, moisten ring, and top with a second ring. Score edges of each tart with a sharp-tined fork. Place on cookie sheet and bake in preheated very hot oven (475°F.) for 15 minutes. Cool and fill with preserves: cherry, berry, apricot, or prune. Makes 8.

MENU

DUTCH BEAN SOUP
TONGUE IN WHITE-WINE ASPIC
CAPERED EGGS
TOMATOES, FINES HERBES
QUICK GINGER PUDDING WITH VANILLA SAUCE

When you boil tongue, there's a bonus: the good broth in which it was cooked is a tasty broth for soups such as this bean soup from Holland. With such a start, why not a soup-and-salad supper like this one? First let's boil the tongue.

BOILED TONGUE

(If tongue, corned or smoked, is highly seasoned, you may wish to soak it overnight in water.) Pour over tongue just enough fresh water to cover. Add 1 onion stuck with 3 cloves, 2 large bay leaves, 3 celery stalks with leaves, 1 large carrot, split; 1 slice parsnip, a few sprigs of parsley, and about 10 peppercorns. Bring to a boil, then simmer until tongue is tender. You can calculate about 45 minutes to 1 hour per pound: smoked tongue generally takes longer to cook than the corned variety. Let tongue cool in broth, then skin and remove root. (Trim off bone and gristle at thick end. To remove skin, slit skin from thick to thin end and pull off.) Skim and strain broth and reserve it for the Dutch Bean Soup.

TONGUE

Chilled Broccoli Bisque

Almond - Sweet Potato Pudding

Lettuce and Tomato Avocadaise

Tongue Indienne or Polonaise

DUTCH BEAN SOUP
Overnight, soak 1 cup navy beans in water to cover. Drain beans and cover with 12 cups reserved tongue broth, adding water if there is not enough. Boil until soup is reduced by half and has consistency of heavy cream. Check for seasoning, and add 1 grated onion and its juice. Cook for 10 minutes more, then add 1½ cups dairy sour cream. Heat to just under boiling; serve with croutons.

TONGUE IN WHITE-WINE ASPIC
For this festive mold, you'll need about 2 pounds boiled tongue, in thin slices.

Soak 2 envelopes unflavored gelatin in ½ cup water. Dissolve 3 chicken bouillon cubes in 3 cups hot water. Add gelatin; stir until dissolved. Add 1 cup white wine and 2 teaspoons Worcestershire. Lightly oil a large rectangular mold: a loaf pan will do fine. Pour in just enough aspic to make a thin layer on the bottom and let set in refrigerator. Chill remaining aspic. Overlap tongue slices across the width of the mold, layering them if necessary, and alternate "stripes" down the length of the mold with large pimiento-stuffed olives, cut into halves, and arranged cut side down. Fill mold with aspic, then chill until firm, about 4 hours. Unmold onto large platter and surround with Capered Eggs and Tomatoes, Fines Herbes, in lettuce cups.

CAPERED EGGS
Hard-cook and chill 6 eggs. Cut into halves lengthwise and remove yolks. Mash yolks smooth and combine with mayonnaise, about 1½ tablespoons capers, and enough of the caper liquid to bring them to a creamy consistency. Swirl into whites, dust very lightly with cayenne pepper, and decorate with a leaf or two of watercress.

TOMATOES, FINES HERBES
Slice firm, ripe plum tomatoes as the French do: very thin, and from the blossom end down. Layer in a large bowl, sprinkling each layer with minced parsley, finely chopped shallots or the white part of scallions, a bit of basil or oregano, salt, cracked black pepper, tarragon vinegar, and olive oil to taste. Let stand for about 2 hours, then drain and heap in crisp lettuce cups.

QUICK GINGER PUDDING
Chop enough preserved or crystallized ginger to make ¾ cup. Prepare 2 packages vanilla pudding according to directions. Stir in ginger after pudding has come to a boil. Pour into dessert glasses and serve warm or chilled with Vanilla Sauce.

Vanilla Sauce
In a saucepan, mix ½ cup sugar with 1 tablespoon cornstarch. Stirring constantly, add 1 cup hot water. Bring to a boil and keep boiling for 5 minutes. Stir in 1 teaspoon vanilla extract and about 2 tablespoons butter. Serve warm.

ENCYCLOPEDIA OF COOKERY

Menus

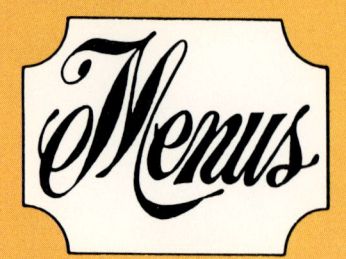

100 Menus to help you plan more varied meals for your family with the recipes in this volume

*All starred recipes found in this volume.

BREAKFASTS

Orange and Grapefruit Sections
Mississippi "Shushed" Eggs*
Crisp Bacon   Waffles
Apple Butter

Juice-into-Soup*
German Pancakes with Spinach*
Café au Lait

Broiled Grapefruit Halves
Creamed Eggs Supreme*
Toasted English Muffins

Es Advokat
(Iced Avocado Drink)*
Stekt Sill Eller Strömming (Fried Herring or Smelt Fillets)*
Rye Rolls   Butter

Cold Plum Soup*
Berner Leberli
(Sautéed Liver Bernese)*
Sweet-Potato Biscuits*

Vegetable Juice
Oeufs à la Crème
(Eggs with Cream Sauce)*
Soy-Wheat Muffins*

Lean Salt Pork with Cream Gravy
Louisiana Pancakes*
Sugar Cane Syrup
Tangerines and Apples

Southern Fried Chicken*
Sweet-Potato Waffles*
Syrup
Mixed Fruit

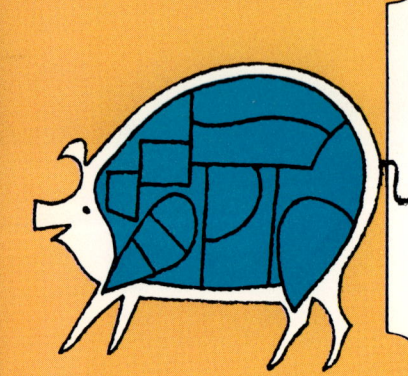

LUNCH or SUPPER

Orange Juice
Crab Cakes*
Corn Muffins
Whipped Butter
Squash and Apple Jam*

Apple Juice
Sausage Cakes
Spoon Bread*
Apricot Jam

Huckleberries and Cream
Fried Scrapple
Egg-and-Tomato Scramble*
Toast
Peach Preserves

Bananas and Pineapple
Tongue and Egg Tart*
Chilled Creamy Tomato Soup*

Sausage-Apple Bake*
Chinese Cabbage and Radish Slaw
Jelly Sponge Roll*

Fylld Blomkål
(Stuffed Cauliflower)*
Mushroom Sauce
Fried Tomatoes, Country Style*
Gingersnaps

Sweet-Potato and Roast-Beef Hash*
Cranberry Mold*
Hot Slaw
Coconut Macaroons

Dried Beef in Sour-Cream Sauce*
Popovers
Wilted Raw Spinach*
Sweet-Potato Apple Crisp*

Hot Tuna Tarts*
Canadian Parsley Soup*
Raw-Carrot Sticks
Tangerine Compote*

Tomato-and-Herb Soup on the Rocks*
Candied Sweet Potatoes and Ham Balls*
Cheese Toast Special*
Chocolate-Covered Raisins

Gazpacho
(Cold Salad-Soup)*
Lobster-Muffin Sandwiches*
Breast of Chicken on Toast
Bonbons or Petits Fours

Deviled Minute Steaks*
Sauce Diable*
Savory Tomatoes, Beans, and Squash*
Fresh Plums

Biff à la Lindström
(Beef Lindström)*
Fried Eggs
Fresh Tangerine and Apple Salad

Corn-Frankfurter Soup*
Empanadas de Queso
(Cheese Turnovers)*
Poached Pears and Mandarin Oranges

DINNERS

Pimiento Two-Cheese
Fusilli*
Mixed Salad Greens
French Dressing
Strawberry Whip*
Custard Sauce

Veal-Vegetable Soup*
Meat Pastries*
Fruit Salad
Sour-Cream Raisin
Nut Cookies*

Apple and Onion Soup*
Appetizer Beef Tartlets*
Coffee Sponge*

Chilled Sour-Cream
Tomato Soup*
Hamburger Sandwiches*
Wild Blackberry Cobbler*

Seafood-Vegetable Chowder*
Beaten Biscuits with
Ham Filling*
Tangerine, Grapefruit,
and Pear Fruit Cup

Bacon, Bean, and Onion
Chowder*
Herbed Toast*
Peaches
Spritz Cookies*

Baked Stuffed Ham Steaks with
Sweet Potato-Sausage
Stuffing*
Southern Style Green Beans*
Radishes   Celery Sticks
Tennessee Boiled Custard*

Southern Fried Chicken*
(Variations)
Rice   Cream Gravy
Stewed Corn*
Tomato Wedges
Beaten Biscuits*
Huckleberry Cobbler*

Rolled Fish Fillets
with Shrimp Sauce*
Brandied Sweet Potatoes*
Virginia Fried Apples*
Fried Fruit Pies*

Tomato Beef Loaf*
Mustard Greens with
Irish Potatoes*
Fried Okra*
Angel Parfait*

Spinach-Stuffed Fish
Fillets*
Stewed Green Tomatoes
and Peppers*
Scalloped Sweet Potatoes
and Chestnuts*
Lemon-Cheese Cake*

Gschnetzeltes (Minced Veal)*
Parsleyed Noodles
Asparagus Tips
Pickled Beets
Apfeltorte (Apple Tart)*

Mixed Grill*
Rösti (Home-Fried Potatoes)*
Watercress Salad
Beignets Soufflés
(Fritters)*

Stufato (Braised Beef)*
Sautéed Mushrooms
Boiled Potatoes
Orange and Onion Salad
Ramequins au Fromage
(Cheese Tartlets)*

Poisson en Papillote
(Fish Baked in Foil)*
Croquettes au Fromage
(Cheese Croquettes
with Green Noodles)*
Crisp Raw Relishes
Rosy Baked Apples

Basler Lachs
(Sautéed Salmon)*
Gnocchi (Dumplings)*
Mixed Green Salad
Rehruecken
(Chocolate Almond Torte)*

Brunkålssoppa
(Brown Cabbage Soup)*
Fiskgryta (Fish with
Onions and Tomatoes)*
Riced Potatoes
Rågkakor (Rye Rings)*
Raspberry Compote

Ärter och Fläsk
(Yellow Pea Soup)*
Plättar (Tiny Pancakes)*
Lingonberry Preserves

Kokt Lamm med Dillsås
(Boiled Lamb with
Dill Sauce)*
Boiled Potatoes
Green Peas
Äppelsoppa (Apple Soup)*
with Rusks

Spicy Barbecued
Spareribs*
Squash Fritters*
Cucumbers
Texas-Style Onion Toast*
Italian Strawberry Ice*

Basque Barbecue*
Roasted Onions
Stuffed Tomatoes,
Las Vegas*
Biscuits
Apple-Raisin-Nut Tarts*

Trucha Frita
(Southwestern Fried
Trout)*
Frijoles Refritos*
Sweet Potatoes, New
Indian Style*
Iced Pineapple*

Chili con Carne Verde*
Fruit Salad
(Casaba and Grapefruit)*
Burritos from Taos*
Caramela

Steak with Onions*
Quelites (Lamb's-Quarters)*
Stuffed Tomatoes*
Arizona's Biscuits*
Melon Cup   Aniseed Cookies*

Avocado Soup*
Gallina Rellena
(Stuffed Turkey,
Southwestern Style)*
Grapefruit and Melon
Salad*
Sopaipillas*
Southwestern Mocha*

Steak Fry*
Frijolitos (Mashed Beans)*
Sweet Spicy
Tomato Relish*
Chuck Wagon Pecan Bread*
"Piebox" Special
Vinegar Pie*

Fågelbon (Birds' Nests)*
Gravad Lax med Senapssås
(Marinated Salmon)*
Små Köttbullar (Small
Meatballs)*
Sill och Skinksallad
(Herring and Ham Salad)*
Rågbröd (Rye Bread)*
Butter

Kalvkotlett à la Oscar
(Veal Cutlet à la Oscar)*
Oven-Browned Potatoes
Tossed Green Salad
Mazarintårta
(Mazarin Torte)*

ENCYCLOPEDIA OF COOKERY

DINNERS

Menus

Kerie Kambing
(Indonesian Lamb Curry)*
Pazunkok Ngapi Gyaw
(Fresh Tomato Balachong)*
Rice   Braised Celery
Spiku
(Malay Layer Cake)*

Phra Ram Long Song
(Rama Bathing)*
Goreng Bajem
(Fried Spinach Leaves)*
Khanom Mo Kaeng
(Taro-Coconut-Egg Custard)*

Carne Adobada
(New Mexican Cured Pork)*
Baked Summer Squash*
Spinach and Cabbage Salad*
Fruit Salad
(Three-Color Grapefruits)*

Athae Chin Gyaw
(Deviled Liver)*
Gado Gado
(Vegetables with Peanut Sauce)*
Sweet Sticky Rice*

Pollo a la Costa Brava
(Costa Brava Chicken)*
Frituras de Garbanzos
(Chick-Pea Fritters)*
Buttered String Beans
Rosquillas (Fried Cakes)*

Steak with
Walnut-Anchovy Sauce*
Baked Eggplant
Artichoke Hearts
Mela's Ladyfinger Dessert*

Babi Ketjap (Braised Pork in Soy Sauce)*
Rempejek Katjang
(Crisp Peanut Fritters)*
Radishes   Chinese Cabbage
Trai Cay
(Cambodian Mixed Fruits)*

Hingha
(Shrimp and Squash Soup)*
Yam of Roses*
Raw-Spinach and
Pimiento Salad
Foi Tong (Shreds of Gold)*

Merluza Asado al Horno
(Baked Fish)*
Judías Verdes a la Vasca
(Basque Green Beans)*
Squash with Mexican-
Corn Stuffing*
Caramel Custard

Cocido (Spanish Boiled Beef)*
Verduras (Vegetable
Side Dish for Cocido)*
Tortillas
Sugar-Poached Oranges

Zarzuela de Mariscos
(Musical Comedy of Shellfish)*
Ensalada a la Andaluza
(Andalusian Vinaigrette Salad)*
Seeded Bread
Cinnamon Ice Cream*

Sopa de Almendras
(Almond Soup)*
Huevos a la Flamenca
(Eggs Flamenco)*
Crisp Greens
Grapes and Cheese

Puerco Asado
(Roast Leg of Pork)*
Peanut Sweet Potatoes*
Cucumber Relish
Ensalada de Aguacate
(Avocado Salad)*
Arroz con Coco y Pasas
(Rice with Coconut and Raisins)*

Hallacas (Meat Pies)*
Torrejas de Coliflor
(Cauliflower Fritters)*
Macedoine de Frutas
Exoticas (Tropical Fruits in Liqueur)*

Swordfish Amandine*
Duchesse Potatoes with
Yellow Turnips*
Cucumbers with Mint*
Tomato Jam*
Strawberry Ice Cream*

Veal Chops Supreme*
Baked Potato
Green Beans and
Glazed Tomatoes*
Artichoke-Heart Salad
Strawberry-Macaroon Cream*

Lamb Stew*
Garlic Toast, Italian Style*
Spiced Prunes in
Lemon Gelatin Salad*

Spicy Tomato Bouillon*
London Broil*
Asparagus*
Apple-Stuffed
Acorn Squash*
Strawberry Macaroon Torte*

Paella de la Costa Brava*
Pulled Toast*
Olive Butter*
Assorted Crisp Relishes
Cherry Strudel*

Baked Chicken and
Sweet Potatoes*
Broccoli with
Parmesan Butter
German Spinach Salad*
Toasted Spice Cake*

Fabada a la Asturiana
(Asturian Bean Casserole)*
Ensalada de Arroz a la
Valenciana (Rice Salad)*
Guava Shells with Cream
Cheese and Ginger

Sopa de Calabaza Maracay
(Pumpkin Soup Maracay)*
Bife Sauté a la Minuta
con Arroz (Fried Beef
with Rice)*
Buñuelos de Espinaca
(Spinach Fritters)*
Bananada com Queijo
(Banana Paste with Cheese)*

Braised Beef Tongue*
Whole Cranberry Sauce*
Corn with Pimiento and
Hot Pepper Sauce
South Carolina Benne-
Seed Biscuits*
Strawberry Snowbank Pie*

Spaghetti with Meatballs*
Tossed Salad
Herbed French Dressing
Deviled Toast*
Spumoni*

1842   WOMAN'S DAY

1843

Pork Shoulder Steak
Teriyaki*
French-Fried Squash
Slices*
Sag Paneer*
Hard Rolls   Herb Butter
Apple Strudel*

Liver in Mustard Sour-
Cream Sauce*
Skillet Squash and
Onions*
French-Fried Potatoes
Rolls   Tomato Butter*
Peaches   Spongecake*

Pastel de Papas o Choclos
(Potato or Sweet-Corn
Pie)*
Fried Tomatoes
Tortillas
Watermelon
Pickle
Bavaroise Frutillas
(Strawberry Snow)*

Albóndigas (Meatballs)*
Green Noodles
Kiveve (Creamed Squash)*
Sliced Tomato and
Lettuce Salad
Maduros en Gloria
(Heavenly Bananas)*

Beef in Sour Cream*
Poppy-Seed Noodles
Braised Red and
White Radishes*
Lettuce and Tomato
Avocadaise*
Apricot Jam Tart*

Crabmeat-Rice Soup*
Mayonnaise Swordfish*
Cheese Toast Roll-Ups*
Lattice Strawberry Tarts*

Creamed Crabs and Shrimps
in Timbale Cases*
Cold Stuffed Tomatoes*
(Coleslaw with
Mayonnaise and
Green Pepper)
Chocolate Spongecake*

Marinated Veal Steak*
Baked Zucchini*
Tomatoes, Fines Herbes*
Sesame Toast*
Glazed Cherry Tarts*

Herbed Chicken Casserole*
Hot Curried Fruit*
Salt Sticks*
Cheese Strudel*

Bratwurst (Cooked Sausage)*
Cheese Timbales*
Spinach-and-Potato Pie*
Strawberry Betty*

Sour-Cream Cabbage Rolls*
Dilled Noodles
Grapefruit-and-Tangerine
Stuffed Squash*
Applesauce Spongecake*

Chicken Normandy*
Polish Beets*
Wilted Lettuce Salad
Cinnamon-Layered
Quick Coffeecake*

Chicken Tetrazzini*
Asparagus with
Lemon Butter*
Cranberry Jelly*
Sweet Potato-Pecan
Pie*

Spiced Spareribs*
Succotash*
Fried Tomatoes with
Creamy Gravy*
Melba Toast*
Garlic Butter*
Mohn (Poppy-Seed)
Strudel*

Marinated Rump Steak*
Roast Corn   Herb Butter
Cherry Tomatoes
Cucumber Sticks
Poached Fresh-Fruit
Compote
Chocolate Spritz Cookies*

Chicken in Paprika Sour-
Cream Sauce*
Pilaf
Herb-Buttered Mushrooms
Tomato, Pepper, and
Celery Relish*
French Apple Tart*

Javanese Lamb*
Fluffy White Rice
Scalloped Tomatoes*
Cucumbers, Radishes,
and Onions in
Sour Cream*
Liqueur Soufflé*

Steak au Poivre
(French Pepper
Steak)*
Tarragon New Potatoes
Brussels Sprouts and
Onions au Gratin*
Tangelemon Ice Cream*

Tournedos Rossini*
Bordelaise Sauce*
Minted Green Peas*
Browned Baby Potatoes
Bibb Lettuce   Oil-and-
Vinegar Dressing
Peach Cream Tarts*

Roast Lamb with
Hot Curried Fruit*
Pan-Browned Potatoes
Layered Tomato-and-Cottage-
Cheese Salad*
Burnt-Almond Soufflé*

Ground Beef* Patties
Sauce Diable*
Tomato Soufflés*
Green-Bean-and-Onion
Salad
Rye Rolls   Butter
Strudel Filled with
Preserves*

Soy Pot Roast*
Mashed Potatoes
Herbed Wax Beans
Italian Tomato Salad*
Peach Cream Cake*

Roast Stuffed Squabs*
Scalloped Sweets and
Cranberries*
Creamed Spinach*
Dinner Rolls
Yellow Tomato Preserves*
Strawberry Shortcake*

Deviled Ham Steak*
Brown-Sugar Candied
Sweet Potatoes*
Coleslaw
Cornbread   Chive Butter*
Chocolate Soufflé*

Roast Lamb with
Sour-Cream Sauce*
Hash Browned Potatoes
Broccoli
Waffled Cooked Carrots
Spiced Oranges*
Chocolate Cake with
Sour-Cream Frosting*

Chateaubriand Steak*
Broiled Mushroom Caps
French-Fried Onion Rings
Baked Stuffed Tomatoes
(Savory Crumb Stuffing)*
Devonshire Berry Tarts*

ENCYCLOPEDIA OF COOKERY

GENERAL INFORMATION

The Ingredients and Measurements Used in Recipes

All recipes in this book have been tested in the Woman's Day Kitchens with standard American measuring cups (8 ounces = 16 tablespoons), measuring spoons (1 tablespoon = 3 teaspoons), and other standard kitchen equipment. All measurements are level. Liquids are measured in standard 8-ounce glass measuring cups, at eye level.

All sugar is granulated white sugar unless otherwise specified.

All flours, cake and all-purpose, are sifted before measuring unless otherwise specified. No self-rising flour is used.

All baking powder is double-acting baking powder.

All brown sugar is firmly packed when measured.

All confectioners' sugar is sifted before measuring.

All pepper is ground black pepper unless otherwise specified.

Fats and shortening are measured at room temperature, packed firmly into measuring cup and leveled with a straight knife. They are scraped out with a rubber spatula.

Salted butter or margarine, packed in ¼-pound sticks, is used unless otherwise specified. 1 stick = ½ cup = 8 tablespoons = ¼ pound.

1 tall can evaporated milk (14½ ounces) contains 1⅔ cups undiluted evaporated milk. Sweetened condensed milk is an entirely different product, and cannot be used interchangeably with evaporated milk.

⅓ to ½ teaspoon dried herbs can be substituted for each tablespoon fresh herbs. Crumble herbs before using to release flavor.

Before starting to cook or to bake, read the recipes carefully. Assemble all ingredients and equipment. Follow recipe exactly. Do not increase or decrease recipe unless you are a skilled enough cook to recognize what adjustments must be made as to ingredients, pan sizes, and/or cooking time.

Cooking Temperatures and Times

Cooking temperatures and times are approximate for meat. They depend not only on the weight and kind of meat, but also on its shape, temperature, and its bone and fat contents. A meat thermometer was used in testing.

Cooking times for meats are as recommended by the National Live Stock and Meat Board, 36 Wabash Avenue, Chicago, Illinois 60603.

Oven Temperatures

TEMPERATURES (Degree F.)	TERM
250 to 275	VERY SLOW
300 to 325	SLOW
350 to 375	MODERATE
400 to 425	HOT
450 to 475	VERY HOT
500 to 525	EXTREMELY HOT

Important—Preheat oven for 10 to 15 minutes before placing food in it. Many a cake has been spoiled by being placed in a barely heated oven. Baking times are based on the assumption that the oven is already at the stated temperature.

Check the oven temperature control frequently, especially if baking times vary from those given in recipes. (This can be done with a portable oven thermometer.) If a control is consistently off, call your public utility. They should be able to reset the oven temperature control.

Caloric Values

The caloric values, where mentioned, for each food are based on 100 grams, about 3½ ounces edible portion, as mentioned in Composition of Foods, Agriculture Handbook No. 8, Agricultural Service of the United States Department of Agriculture, Washington, D. C., revised December 1963.

COMPLETE RECIPE INDEX—Volume 11—770 Recipes

APPETIZERS

Alcachofas Rellenos con Sardinas . 1741
Almonds, Soyed 1734
Anchoas a la Vinagreta 1741
Apple-Tomato Appetizer, Hot . . .1832
Beef Tartlets, Appetizer 1811
Biscuits with Ham Filling, Beaten .1724
Cheese Straws 1822
Chicken Tartlets, Curried 1811
Cucumber Tomato Cocktail 1832
Dip, Bacon 1697
Dip, Sour-Cream Ham 1697
Egg and Anchovy Tartlets 1811
Egg Tart 1811
Fågelbon (Bird's Nests) 1786
Frankfurter Custard Tarts 1811
Gravad Lax med Senapssås 1786
Ikan Goreng Atjar (Fish) 1714
Meat Pastries 1696
Meat Tarts, Two-Cheese 1811
Mushrooms, Stuffed 1782
Onion Cheese Tarts 1811
Pescado a la Vinagreta (Fish) 1741
Salmonetes Levantinos 1741
Sardinas con Salsa de Tomates . . .1741
Seviche (Pickled Fish) 1704
Sill och Skinksallad 1787
Små Köttbullar (Small Meatballs) .1786
Sturgeon Deviled Eggs, Smoked- . .1782
Tomato Cocktail, Spiced 1832
Tongue and Egg Tarts 1811
Tuna Tarts, Hot 1811

BEVERAGES

Cider, Spiced 1754
Es Advokat (Iced Avocado) 1714
Glögg 1794
Ice-Cream Soda, Strawberry 1779
Ponche de Piña (Hot Pineapple) . .1709
Syllabub, Old English 1807
Tea, Hot Spiced 1815
Tea, Lemon Iced 1816
Tea, Minted Iced 1816

BREADS, PANCAKES, DUMPLINGS

Biscuits, Arizona's 1732
Biscuits, Beaten 1724
Biscuits, South Carolina Benne-Seed 1724
Biscuits, Sweet-Potato 1797
Burritos from Taos 1732
Butters for Sweet Toast 1829
Butters, Nonsweet Toast 1829
Coffeecake, Cinnamon-Layered Quick 1754
Doughnuts, Sweet-Potato 1798
Dumpling Floats 1697
Dumplings, Italian Bread 1696
Ginger Cakes 1818
Muffins, Soy-Wheat 1734
Oatcakes, Hot 1818
Pancakes, Louisiana 1797
Pecan Bread, Chuck Wagon 1732
Plättar (Pancakes) 1792
Pompushkes 1700
Potatisbullar (Potato Dumplings) .1791
Rosquillas (Fried Cakes) 1747
Scones, Potato 1818
Sopaipillas 1731
Spoon Bread 1724
Toast, Non-Sweet
  Bacon-Cheese Toast 1825
  Beef Toast, Chopped 1825
  Callie-Toast 1825
  Celery-Seasoned Toast 1697
  Cheese Toast Roll-Ups 1825
  Cheese Toast Special 1825
  Croutons 1826
  Croutons, Cheese 1697
  Danish Toast 1826
  Deviled Toast 1826
  Egg and Cheese Toast 1826
  French Toast 1826
  Fried Toast with Anchovies 1826
  Garlic Toast, Italian Style 1826
  Goldenrod Toast 1826
  Herbed Toast 1826
  Lemon Toast 1826
  Melba Toast 1826
  Milk Toast 1828
  Onion Toast, Texas-Style 1828
  Pulled Toast 1828
  Puffed Toast Squares 1828
  Raisin Scramble Toast 1828
  Salt Sticks 1828
  Sesame Toast 1828
  Shrimp Toast 1828
  Toast Boxes 1828
  Toast Cups 1828
  Toasted Rounds and Sticks 1829
  Toast Luncheonettes 1829
  Toast with Bacon, Island 1826
  Tomato-Soup Toast 1829
  Town Toast 1829
  Twist Toast 1697
Toast, Sweet
  Apricot-Honey Toast 1825
  Banana Toast 1825
  Brandy Toast, Fluffed 1826
  Caramel-Cardamom Toast 1825
  Cinnamon Toast de Luxe 1825
  Honey Pecan Tea Toast 1826
  Jam Toast, Rolled 1826
  Marmalade Toast, Spiced 1828
  Peach Pudding Toast 1828
  Pineapple Finger Toast 1828
  Praline Toast 1828
  Raspberry Toast, Dutch 1826
  Rum-Cinnamon Toast Sticks . . .1828
  Sour-Cream Date Toast 1828
  Waffle Toast with Cinnamon-Nut Topping 1829
Waffles, Sweet-Potato 1798
Yeast Breads
  Crumpets 1818
  Currant Bread 1818
  Rågbröd (Rye Bread) 1791
  Semlor (Shrove Tuesday Buns) . .1791
  Stollen .1775

CAKES

Chocolate Cake with Sour-Cream Frosting 1701
Gingerbread, Sour-Cream 1701
Jelly Sponge Roll 1751
Lemon-Cheese Cake 1725
Peach Cream Cake 1701
Seedcake .1819
Spice Cake, Toasted 1754
Spiku (Malay Layer Cake) 1715
Spongecake 1756
Spongecake, Applesauce 1756
Spongecake, Chocolate 1756
Spongecake, Hot-Water 1756
White Mountain Cake 1819

CASSEROLES

Bacalao a la Vizcaína (Salt-Cod) .1743
Beef Casserole, Chinese 1734
Cabbage Rolls, Sour-Cream 1698
Chicken, Baked Soy 1734
Chicken Casserole, Herbed 1824
Chicken, Sweet Potatoes, Baked . .1796
Chicken Tetrazzini 1736
Chili Pie, Cowpuncher 1728
Company Casserole 1734
Fbada a la Asturiana (Bean) 1744
Ham-Cheese-Tomato Parlay 1747
Ham Steaks with Sweet Potato-Sausage Stuffing, Baked Stuffed . .1722
Ham Tetrazzini 1736
Hubbard Squash, Scalloped 1762
Pastel de Carne (Meat Pie) 1705
Sausage-Apple Bake 1796
Slavic Casserole 1698
Squash Casserole 1762
Sweet Potatoes and Ham Balls, Candied 1796
Tamale Pie, Hot 1728
Turkey and Sweet-Potato 1796
Turkey Tetrazzini 1736
Veal Chops Supreme 1698

CEREALS AND PASTA

Arroz con Coco y Pasas (Rice) . . .1709
Farofa 1709
Kasha 1838
Mi Krob (Fried Noodles) 1715
Nasi Goreng (Fried Rice) 1714
Rempejek Katjang 1714
Spaghetti Amatriciana 1736
Spaghetti, Caruso 1736
Spaghetti, Clam 1736
Spaghetti, Garlic Lover's 1736
Spaghetti, Home-Fried 1737
Spaghetti, Sicilian 1737
Spaghetti with Meatballs 1736
Spaghetti with Tuna Sauce 1736
Spaghetti with Zucchini Sauce . . .1737

CHEESE

Cheese Timbales 1824
Croquettes au Fromage 1803
Empanadas de Queso 1708
Fondue Bourguignonne 1803
Fondue (Melted Cheese Dish) 1803
Gnocchi (Dumplings) 1804
Käsesalat (Cheese Salad) 1804
Steak de Fromage 1803
Two-Cheese Fusilli 1737
Two-Cheese Fusilli, Olive 1737
Two-Cheese Fusilli, Pimiento 1737
Two-Cheese Fusilli, Poppy-Seed . .1737

COOKIES AND CANDY

Aniseed Cookies 1732
Candied Spearmint Leaves 1749
Ginger Cookies 1754
Kanelkakor (Swedish Cinnamon) .1794
Molasses Drop Cookies 1798
Molasses Squares, Sour-Cream . . .1701
Mormor's Syltkakor (Jelly) 1793
Punschkakor (Punch Rings) 1793
Rågkakor (Rye Rings) 1793
Raisin Nut Cookies, Sour-Cream . .1701
Shortbread 1819
Spritz Cookies 1757
Spritz Cookies, Almond 1758
Spritz Cookies, Chocolate 1757
Taffy, Chocolate 1808
Taffy, Molasses 1808
Toffee 1829

DESSERTS

Beignets Soufflés (Fritters) 1804
Charlotte Russe, Southern 1725
Cheesecake, Golden 1798
Coffee Sponge 1837

ENCYCLOPEDIA OF COOKERY

Frozen
  Angel Parfait 1724
  Caramela 1732
  Ice Cream, Strawberry 1779
  Ice Cream, Tangelemon 1838
  Ice, Italian Strawberry 1779
  Mousse, Strawberry 1778
  Sherbet, Tropical 1701
  Spumoni 1758
  Strawberry-Almond Roll 1778
  Strawberry Cake Roll 1779
  Strawberry-Macaroon Cream ..1778
Fruit
  Aguacates Batidos (Avocado) ...1709
  Ambrosia in Frozen Orange
    Shells 1824
  Apple Cobbler 1725
  Bananda com Queijo 1709
  Bavaroise Frutillas (Strawberry).1709
  Blackberry Cobbler, Wild 1725
  Huckleberry Cobbler 1725
  Macedoine de Frutas Exoticas ..1709
  Maduros en Gloria (Bananas) ..1709
  Peach Cobbler 1725
  Pears, Devonshire 1701
  Pineapple, Iced 1732
  Strawberries, Fondant-Dipped ..1779
  Strawberry Angel-Food Dessert.1778
  Strawberry Betty 1776
  Strawberry Cobbler 1776
  Strawberry Shortcake 1779
  Strawberry Whip 1778
  Sweet-Potato Apple Crisp.....1798
  Tangerine Compote 1808
  Trai Cay (Mixed Fruits) 1717
Mela's Ladyfinger Dessert 1747
Mocha, Southwestern 1732
Puddings
  Boiled Custard, Tennessee 1725
  Ginger Pudding, Quick 1839
  Rice Pudding, Strawberry 1778
  Rice, Sweet Sticky 1717
  Suet Pudding 1783
  Sweet-Potato Pudding, Almond.1837
  Sweet-Potato Pudding, Lemon..1724
  Sweet-Potato Pudding, Spicy ...1798
  Tapioca Cream, Butterscotch ...1810
  Tapioca Cream Pudding 1810
Soufflé, Burnt Almond 1688
Soufflé, Chocolate 1688
Soufflé, Liqueur 1688
Soufflé, Orange 1688
Soufflé Rothschild 1688
Soufflé, Vanilla 1688
Torrijas (Ladyfingers in Syrup) ...1709
Tortes
  Marängsuisse (Cream Meringue).1792
  Mazarintårta (Mazarin Torte) ..1793
  Rehruecken (Chocolate Almond).1804
  Strawberry Macaroon Torte 1779
  Tusenbladstårta 1792

DESSERT SAUCES
Chocolate Syrup 1807
Cocoa Syrup 1807
Hard Sauce, Strawberry 1776
Lemon Cream Sauce 1757
Orange Syrup 1807
Spiced Syrup, Hot 1807
Strawberry Velvet Sauce 1776
Vanilla Sauce 1839

DRESSINGS
French Cream Dressing 1700
Honey-Cream Dressing 1776
Mint Dressing, Fresh- 1700
Olive Dressing 1700
Stuffings
  Apple Stuffing, Savory 1749
  Brazil-Nut Stuffing, Creamy 1781
  Bread Stuffing 1781
  Bread Stuffing, Chestnut 1781
  Bread Stuffing, Oyster 1781
  Celery-Almond Stuffing 1781
  Cheese Stuffing 1780
  Cheese Stuffing, Italian 1782
  Chestnut and Sausage Stuffing ..1781
  Corn-Bread Stuffing, New
    England 1780
  Corn Stuffing, Mexican- 1782
  Cucumber Stuffing 1781
  Meat-and-Rice Stuffing Turkish.1782
  Mint Stuffing 1781
  Mushroom and Wild Rice 1781
  Olive Stuffing 1782
  Pickle Stuffing 1781
  Piedmont Stuffing 1782
  Piquant Stuffing 1780
  Raisin-Rice Stuffing 1781
  Rice Stuffing 1781
  Sage and Onion Stuffing 1781
  Sauerkraut Stuffing 1781
  Savory Stuffing 1823
  Savory Stuffing, Sweet-Potato ..1798
  Syrian Stuffing 1782
  Veal-and-Vegetable Stuffing ...1781
  Vegetable Stuffing 1780
Walnut-Ginger Dressing 1700

EGGS
Capered Eggs 1839
Cassolettes 1688
Cha Tom (Vietnamese Omelet) ..1717
Creamed Eggs Supreme 1755
Egg-and-Tomato Scramble 1833
Egg Timbales with Curry Sauce ..1824
Foi Tong (Shreds of Gold) 1716
Huevos a la Flamenca 1744
Huevos con Salsa de Chiles 1708
Italian Eggs Florentine 1755
Khanom Mo Kaeng (Custard) ...1716
Mississippi "Shushed" Eggs 1723
Oeufs à la Crème 1804
Oeufs au Four (Baked Eggs) 1804
Soufflé, Basic Savory 1685
Soufflé Laurette 1688
Telur Masak Bali (Balinese Spiced).1714
Thousand Island Eggs 1698

FISH
Basler Lachs (Sautéed Salmon)...1800
Fish Fillets, Spinach-Stuffed 1755
Fish Fillets with Shrimp Sauce,
  Rolled 1753
Fish in Sweet-Sour Sauce 1734
Fiskgryta 1788
Fried Fish with Tamarind Sauce ..1809
Hmoh Nga Baung (Soufflé) 1716
Kaeng Phed (Fish Stew) 1717
Kokt Lutfisk (Boiled Lutfisk) 1787
Marmitako (Fresh-Tuna Stew) ..1743
Merluza Asado al Horno (Baked) .1744
Pescado al Horno (Baked Fish) ...1705
Poisson en Papillote 1800
Steaks, Fish 1771
Stekt Sill Eller Strömming 1787
Sturgeon in Ramekins, Sherry
  Smoked 1782
Sunfish with Dill Sauce, Panfried .1784
Swordfish Amandine 1806
Swordfish, Deep-Fried 1806
Swordfish, Mayonnaise 1806
Swordfish with Tomato Sauce 1806
Trucha Frita (Fried Trout) 1727
Vatapá (Fish Stew) 1703

FROSTINGS, ICINGS, AND FILLINGS
Applesauce Filling 1792
Chocolate Filling 1812
Chocolate Frosting, Sour-Cream .1701
Chocolate Glaze 1756
Custard Cream Filling 1792
Lemon-Cheese Filling 1725
Lemon Filling, Fancy 1792
Lemon Icing 1793
Orange Filling 1792
Sour-Cream Frosting 1701
Strawberry Cream Filling 1779
Vanilla Cream Filling 1812
Whipped Cream Topping 1792

JAMS, JELLIES, AND PRESERVES
Green-Tomato Jam 1836
Green-Tomato Marmalade 1836
Squash and Apple Jam 1762
Tomato Butter 1835
Tomato Jam 1836
Tomato Purée 1834
Yellow Tomato Preserves 1835

MEATS
Beef
  Albóndigas (Meatballs) 1705
  Barbecued Beef 1722
  Beef in Sour Cream 1700
  Bife Sauté a la Minuta con Arroz
    (Fried Beef with Rice) 1705
  Biff à la Lindström 1788
  Carne Asada (Broiled Beef) 1705
  Chateaubriand Steak 1766
  Chile con Carne Verde 1728
  Cocido (Spanish Boiled Beef) ...1842
  Dried Beef in Sour-Cream Sauce.1700
  Entrecôte Bercy 1767
  Filet de Boeuf à la Suisse
    (Roast Beef) 1802
  Hallacas (Meat Pies) 1706
  Loin-Strip Steak 1766
  London Broil 1768
  Minute Steaks, Deviled 1768
  Phra Ram Long Song (Rama
    Bathing) 1715
  Pot Roast, Soy 1734
  Rib Steak Bordelaise 1767
  Rump Steak, Marinated 1767
  Sirloin for a Large Party,
    Whole Thick 1766
  Skirt Steak, Deviled 1768
  Skirt Steak, Marinated 1768
  Slottsstek (Royal Pot Roast) 1788
  Spencer Steak 1767
  Steak au Poivre (French Pepper) .1767
  Steak Fry 1728
  Steak Tartare en Croûte 1770
  Steak with Onions 1767
  Steak with Walnut-Anchovy
    Sauce 1746
  Stufato (Braised Beef) 1802
  Sweet-Potato and Roast-Beef
    Hash 1796
  Teriyaki 1768
  Tomato Beef Loaf 1810
  Top Sirloin Steak 1767
  Tournedos Béarnaise 1766
  Tournedos Rossini 1766
  Bernerplatte (from Bern) 1803
  Bratwurst (Cooked Sausage) 1802
  Fylld Blomkål (Stuffed
    Cauliflower) 1790

Lamb
  Basque Barbecue 1728
  Garlic Lamb Steaks 1770
  Javanese Lamb 1753
  Kerie Kambing (Lamb Curry) ..1714
  Kokt Lamm med Dillsås (Boiled
    Lamb with Dill) 1788
  Pueblo Lamb Chili 1728
  Roast Lamb with Hot Curried
    Fruit 1753
  Roast Lamb with Sour-Cream
    Sauce 1698
Mixed Grill 1803
Pork
  Babi Ketjap (Braised Pork) 1714
  Carimañolas (Fritters) 1706
  Carne Adobada (Cured Pork)...1728
  Côtelettes de Porc au Fromage
    (Pork Chops with Cheese) 1802
  Ham, North-Carolina Style,
    Baked Country 1722
  Ham Steak, Deviled 1770
  Ham Steak, Fresh 1770
  Ham Steaks 1770
  Julskinka (Christmas Ham) 1788
  Pork-Chop and Sweet-Potato
    Skillet 1796
  Pork Shoulder Steak Teriyaki ..1770
  Puerco Asado (Roast Leg of) ...1706
  Relleno (Pork Roll for Cocido) .1743
  Spareribs, Apple-Stuffed 1749
  Spareribs, Chinese Sweet-and-
    Sour 1749
  Spareribs, Spiced 1748
  Spareribs, Spicy Barbecued 1749
  Spareribs, Stuffed 1781
  Pytt i Panna (Swedish Hash) 1790
  Squirrel, Fricasseed 1763
Variety
  Athae Chin Gyaw (Liver) 1717
  Berner Leberli (Sautéed Liver) ..1802
  Liver in Mustard Sour-Cream
    Sauce 1698
  Liver Steaks 1771
  Rognons Bolo (Kidneys) 1802
  Sweetbreads, Creamed 1794
  Sweetbreads, Normandy Style ..1794
  Tongue, Boiled 1838
  Tongue, Braised Beef 1837
  Tongue in White-Wine Aspic ...1839
  Tongues, Potted Lamb 1838
Veal
  Gschnetzeltes (Minced Veal) ...1802
  Kalvkotlett à la Oscar (Cutlet) ..1788
  Marinated Veal Steak 1770
  Sour-Cream Veal Loaf 1698
  Veal with Sweet Potatoes in
    Sour-Cream Sauce 1796
Verduras (Vegetable Side Dish for
  Cocido) 1743

PICKLES, RELISHES, GARNISHES
Cranberry Mold 1823
Cranberry Sauce, Whole 1823
Cucumbers with Mint 1749
Curried Fruit, Hot 1753
Oranges, Spiced 1754
Pazundok Ngapi Gyaw (Fresh
  Tomato Balachong) 1716
Tomato, Pepper, Celery Relish ...1835
Tomato Relish, Sweet Spicy 1835

PIES, TARTS, AND PASTRIES
Anise Squash Pie 1762
Apfeltorte (Apple Tart) 1806
Apple-Raisin-Nut Tarts 1812
Apple Strudel 1780

Apple Tart, French 1812
Apricot-Jam Tart 1812
Banana Christmas Tarts 1812
Berry Tarts, Devonshire 1812
Cheese Strudel 1780
Cherry Strudel 1780
Cherry Tarts, Glazed 1812
Fruit Pies, Fried 1725
Fruit Tarts, Glazed 1812
Jam Tarts 1838
Kuchenteig (Tart Pastry) 1804
Lemon-Cheese Tarts 1725
Mince Tarts 1824
Mohn (Poppy-Seed) Strudel 1780
Pastry, Standard 1814
Pastry, Sweet 1814
Peach Cream Tarts 1812
Pumpkin Pie with Ginger
  Rosettes 1823
Ramequins au Fromage (Cheese) .1804
Strawberry Chiffon Tarts.......1812
Strawberry Glacé Pie 1778
Strawberry Snowbank Pie 1778
Strawberry Tarts, Lattice 1778
Strudel Dough 1779
Strudel Filled with Preserves 1780
Sweet Potato-Pecan Pie 1798
Tart Shells 1814
Vinegar Pie, "Piebox" Special 1732

POULTRY
Chicken
  Chicken Normandy 1736
  Chicken in Paprika Sour-Cream
    Sauce 1698
  Enchiladas de Gallina 1706
  Paella de la Costa Brava 1746
  Pollo a la Costa Brava 1746
  Pollo con Salsa (in Sauce) 1706
  Sate Ajam (on Skewers) 1714
  Southern Fried Chicken 1723
  Southern Fried Chicken,
    Variations in Preparing 1723
  Gallina Rellena (Stuffed Turkey)..1730
  Panggang Golek (Roast Duck) ..1715
  Pavo a la Nicaragüense (Turkey) .1706
  Squabs, Roast Stuffed 1758
  Turkey, Roast 1822
  Turkey Steaks 1771

SALADS
Avocado Ring with Strawberries..1776
Bean Salads 1727
Cheese and Strawberry Salad,
  Jellied 1776
Cucumbers and Cress in
  Horseradish Dressing 1838
Cucumbers, Hapsburg 1700
Cucumbers, Radishes, and Onions
  in Sour Cream 1700
Ensalada a la Andaluza 1741
Ensalada de Aguacate (Avocado) .1709
Ensalada de Arroz a la Valenciana .1742
Fruit Salads 1727
Kålsallad med Lingon (Cabbage
  Salad with Lingonberries) 1791
Lettuce and Tomato Avocadaise..1837
Nham (Salad) 1717
Prunes in Lemon Gelatin Salad,
  Spiced 1754
Rödbetssallad med Äpplen (Beet
  Salad with Apples) 1790
Spinach and Cabbage Salad 1756
Spinach Ring with Eggs, Baked ..1755
Spinach Salad, German 1756
Spinach Salad, Sour-Cream 1700

Spinach, Wilted Raw 1756
Sweetbread and Cucumber Salad.1794
Tangerine and Apple Salad, Fresh.1808
Thon en Salade (Tuna Salad) 1802
Tomato-and-Cottage-Cheese
  Salad, Layered 1834
Tomatoes, Cold Stuffed 1834
Tomatoes with Herbs 1834
Tomato Salad, Italian 1834
Yam of Roses 1716

SANDWICHES
Biftecks Tartare (Tartar
  Sandwiches) 1802
Gefülltes Brot (Stuffed Bread) 1803
Hamburger Sandwiches 1770
Lobster-Muffin Sandwiches 1722
Open-Faced Sandwiches, Swiss ...1800
Tamales de Maiz con Pollo
  (Tamales with Chicken Filling)..1808
Taos Tacos 1731
Tostadas Indio 1731

SAUCES, GLAZES, AND GRAVIES
Anchovy Sauce 1738
Béarnaise Sauce 1766
Bolognese Meat Sauce 1738
Bordelaise Sauce 1766
Chateaubriand Sauce 1766
Chili Sauce, Green 1731
Chili Sauce, Red 1731
Chili Sauce, Southwestern 1731
Cucumber Sauce 1700
Curry Sauce 1824
Dill Sauce 1784, 1788
Garbanzo Sauce 1737
Gravy, Cream 1723
Gravy, Giblet 1823
Hollandaise, Sour-Cream 1700
Kaprissås (Caper Sauce) 1791
Madeira Sauce 1766
Marinara Sauce 1737
Mushroom-Olive Sauce 1737
Mustard Sauce, Creamy 1700
Parmesan Parsley Sauce 1738
Parsley-Olive Sauce 1738
Pepper Sauce, Roasted 1738
Rhubarb Sauce For Meats 1753
Sauce Diable 1768
Sauce Indienne 1837
Sauce Polonaise 1837
Senapssås (Mustard Sauce) 1786
Skarpsås (Sharp Dill Sauce) ...1791
Soppin' Sauce 1731
Stracotto Sauce 1738
Tomato-Meat Spaghetti Sauce ...1737
Tomato Purée Sauce 1738
Tomato Sauce 1834
Tomato Spaghetti Sauce 1737
Trevisano Sauce 1738
White Clam Sauce, Quick 1738
White Sauce 1722
White Tuna Sauce 1738
Wine-Shallot Sauce 1767

SHELLFISH
Camarões a Bahia (Shrimps) 1704
Crab Cakes 1721
Crabs and Shrimps, Creamed, in
  Timbale Cases 1824
Escabeche de Mariscos........1704
La Tieng (Shrimp Nets) 1716
Oysters, Escalloped 1823
Seafood in Chili 1727
Shrimps de Jonghe 1722
Squid, Italian Style 1763

Squids in the Portuguese Manner,
   Stewed 1763
Squids, Sautéed Stuffed 1763
Zarzuela de Mariscos 1743

SOUPS AND STEWS

Apple and Onion Soup..........1694
Äpplesoppa (Apple Soup) 1787
Avocado-Chicken Soup 1690
Avocado Soup 1727
Bombay Refresher 1692
Buttermilk Soup, Belgian 1690
Callalu 1704
Egg-Petal Soup with Cucumbers..1691
Egg Soup, Portuguese 1691
Fruit Soup, Chilled Scandinavian.1694
Garlic Soup, Vera Cruz 1691
Meat
   Beef and Vegetable Soup 1694
   Beef-Okra Soup 1721
   Beef Soup à la Paysanne 1695
   Beef Stew 1773
   Brown Stock (Bouillon or Beef).1774
   Brunswick Stew for a Crowd ...1722
   Chicken and Sweet-Potato Soup.1795
   Chicken Soup or Stew, Friar's..1721
   Chicken Soup, Ujhazy 1695
   Chicken Stew 1774
   Chicken Stock 1775
   Chowder, Italian 1695
   Frankfurter Soup, Corn- 1695
   Hunter's Reward 1730
   Lamb and Barley Soup 1695
   Lamb Stew 1773
   Lamb Stew, Brown 1773
   Masak Nadi (Spiced Meat Stew) 1715
   Moeun Sngo (Chicken Soup) ...1717
   Mulligatawny Shorba 1691
   Pepper Pot Soup, Philadelphia..1694
   Pho (Ginger Beef Soup) 1717
   Sopa de Mondongo (Tripe Soup).1704
   Turkey Soup, Parmentier 1695
   Veal Stew with Mushrooms,
     Creamy 1774
   Veal Stock, White or 1774
   Zoo-Tosopy (Ground-Meat) 1704
Plum Soup, Cold 1698
Puchero (Meat and Vegetable) ...1706
Seafood
   Bisque, Chilled Clam 1692
   Bisque, Sherried Tomato-
     Shrimp 1832
   Chowder, Bonito 1696
   Chowder, Oven Fish 1694
   Chowder, Seafood-Vegetable ...1696
   Crabmeat-Rice Soup 1696
   Fish Stock 1775
   Hingha (Shrimp and Squash) ...1716
   Scallop Cream Soup 1695
   Sopa a la Limeña (Lima Style).1703
   Sopa de Pescado a la Vasca ...1743
   Terrapin Stew, Maryland
     Diamondback 1819
   Tuna Soup, Tapioca 1810
Sopa de Ajos (Garlic Soup) 1742
Sopa de Almendras (Almond) ...1742
Sopa de Queso (Cheese Soup) ...1747
Sunset Soup 1694
Tarragon Soup, French 1692
Vegetable
   Ärter Och Fläsk (Yellow Pea)..1787
   Bean, and Onion Chowder,
     Bacon 1691
   Bean Chiller, Black- 1692
   Bean Soup, Dutch 1839
   Bean Soup, Near-East White-...1690
   Bean Soup, Savory Black 1691
   Borsch, Quick 1838
   Broccoli Bisque, Chilled 1837
   Brunkålssoppa (Brown Cabbage).1787
   Cabbage Soup, Danish Browned.1690
   Chive and Cress Soup 1690
   Crème Mongole 1692
   Estofado I, II 1705
   Feijoada (Black Bean Stew) ...1704
   Gazpacho (Cold Salad-Soup) ...1742
   Juice-into-Soup 1691
   Lentil Soup, Syrian Style,
     Chilled 1692
   Minestrone 1691
   Mushroom Consommé 1822
   Onion Soup, Italian 1690
   Parsley Soup, Canadian 1690
   Pea Soup, Basic Recipe 1696
   Pea Soup Variations 1696
   Potato, and Mushroom
     Chowder, Sour-Cream 1697
   Potato-Cheese Soup, Savory ...1690
   Potato Soup, Quick French 1690
   Pumpkin Soup, Chili 1727
   Sopa de Calabaza Maracay 1704
   Sweet-Potato Gumbo 1795
   Sweet-Potato Soup, Cream of ..1796
   Tomato-and-Herb Soup on the
     Rocks 1832
   Tomato Bouillon, Spicy 1832
   Tomato Quickie 1694
   Tomato Soup, Chilled Creamy..1832
   Tomato Soup, Chilled Sour-
     Cream 1697
   Tomato Soup, Cream-of-Fresh..1832
   Tomato Soup, Pale-Pink 1690
   Vegetable Soup, Veal- 1694
   Vegetable Stock 1775

VEGETABLES

Apples, Virginia Fried 1724
Beans
   Frijoles, Frijolitos, y Frijoles ...1731
     Refritos
   Frijoles Negros Batidos 1708
   Judías Blancas a la Leridana ...1744
   Green Beans, Glazed Tomatoes.1834
   Green Beans, Southern Style ..1723
   Judías Verdes a la Vasca 1744
   Whole Green Beans 1823
Beets, Buttered Spiced 1754
Beets, Polish 1700
Broccoli, Buttered 1823
Brussels Sprouts and Onions au
   Gratin 1838
Corn, Stewed 1723
Empanadas de Plátanos (Banana).1708
Frituras de Garbanzos(Chick-Pea).1747
Gado Gado (Vegetables with) ...1715
Hoppin John 1723
Mushrooms à la Russe 1838
Mustard Greens, Irish Potatoes..1723
Okra, Fried 1723
Onions and Celery in Cream 1823
Peas, Minted Green 1749
Peas, Mushrooms, and Pimiento..1823
Potatoes
   Duchesse Potatoes with Yellow
     Turnips 1823
   Llapingachos 1708
   Papas con Salsa Huancaina Fría.1708
   Pastel de Papas o Choclos 1705
   Potatis och Svamp 1790
   Rösti (Home-Fried Potatoes) ..1804
   Skånsk Potatis (Creamed) 1790
Quelites (Lamb's-Quarters) 1730
Soybean Shepherd's Pie 1734
Soybean Stew 1734
Spinach
   Buñuelos de Espinca (Fritters)..1708
   Creamed Spinach 1756
   German Pancakes with Spinach.1755
   Goreng Bajem (Fried)........1715
   Kiveve (Creamed Squash) 1708
   Pie, Greek Spinach 1755
   Pie, Spinach-and-Potato 1755
   Sag Paneer 1755
   Spinach with Almonds 1756
Squash
   Acorn Squash, Apple-Stuffed ..1762
   Acorn Squash with Whipped
     Potato Rosettes, Baked 1762
   Cymlings, Baked 1761
   French-Fried Squash Slices 1762
   Fritters, Squash 1761
   Skillet Squash and Onions 1761
   Squash Mandarin 1759
   Stuffed Squash, Cheese- 1762
   Stuffed Squash, Grapefruit-and-
     Tangerine 1762
   Summer Squash, Baked 1761
   Zucchini, Baked 1762
Succotash 1783
Sweet Potatoes
   Brandied Sweet Potatoes 1724
   Brown-Sugar Candied Sweet
     Potatoes 1796
   Creamed Sweet Potatoes 1797
   Flambéed Sweet Potatoes 1796
   Fried Sweet Potatoes, Home-...1797
   Maple-Candied Sweet Potatoes..1796
   Mashed Sweet Potatoes and
     Yellow Turnips 1797
   Orange Sweet Potatoes 1797
   Peanut Sweet Potatoes 1797
   Porcupines, Almond 1797
   Porcupines, Brazil-Nut 1797
   Scalloped Sweet Potatoes, Apples 1797
   Scalloped Sweet Potatoes and
     Chestnuts 1797
   Scalloped Sweets, Cranberries ..1797
   Sherried Sweet Potatoes 1724
   Soufflé, Sweet-Potato 1796
   Sweet Potatoes, New Indian
     Style 1730
   Sweet Potatoes with Mincemeat.1797
   Sweet Potatoes with Tomatoes..1797
   Sweet-Potato Marshmallow
     Balls 1797
   Sweet-Potato Tournedos 1796
   Sweets à la Rector 1797
Tomatoes
   Fried Green-Tomato and
     Cucumber Slices 1833
   Fried Tomatoes, Country Style..1700
   Fried Tomatoes with Creamy
     Gravy 1833
   Savory Tomatoes, Beans, and
     Squash 1832
   Scalloped Tomatoes 1834
   Stewed Green Tomatoes and
     Peppers 1832
   Stuffed Tomatoes, Baked 1834
   Stuffed Tomatoes, Las Vegas ...1730
   Tomatoes, Corn, and Okra ...1832
   Tomatoes, Fines Herbes 1839
   Tomato Soufflés 1688
Torrejas de Coliflor 1708
Yams, Candied 1823